Reinventing Management through Sustainability, Innovation and Analytics

Reinventing Management through Sustainability, Innovation and Analytics

Patron

Prof. (Dr) Atmanand

Director, MDI Murshidabad

Editors

Dr Biranchi Narayan Swar

Dr Neeraj Singhal

BLOOMSBURY

NEW DELHI • LONDON • OXFORD • NEW YORK • SYDNEY

BLOOMSBURY INDIA
Bloomsbury Publishing India Pvt. Ltd
Second Floor, LSC Building No. 4, DDA Complex,
Pocket C – 6 & 7, Vasant Kunj,
New Delhi 110070

BLOOMSBURY, BLOOMSBURY PRIME and the Diana logo are
trademarks of Bloomsbury Publishing Plc

First published in India 2023
This edition published 2023

ISBN: 978-93-56403-45-1
2 4 6 8 10 9 7 5 3 1

Typeset by Fortune Graphics, Naraina, New Delhi
Printed and bound in India by Replika Press Pvt. Ltd

Contents

Section III: *Reinventing Management through Sustainability, Innovation and Analytics: SCM & ITM*

Section IV: *Reinventing Management through Sustainability, Innovation and Analytics: Business Policy, Strategy and Entrepreneurship*

Foreword

It gives me immense pleasure to introduce you to the edited volume brought out by MDI Murshidabad, titled *Reinventing Management through Sustainability, Innovation and Analytics.*This book fosters the multidisciplinary discussion about emerging theories, concepts and models in general, practical challenges encountered and solutions adopted in particular in the field of innovations in management practices. The book will create a strong landscape for academicians, managers and practitioners to focus on *Reinventing Management through Sustainability, Innovation and Analytics*. The four sections of the book cover the various business domains such as Marketing, Finance, Human Resources, Operations and Supply Chain Management, ITM, Business Policy, Strategy and Entrepreneurship.

MDI is a leading business school of India; it launched its Murshidabad campus in the year 2014. MDI Murshidabad is fostering the culture of research among faculty members, researchers, corporate and students. This book is an effort in that direction.

Prof. (Dr) Biranchi Narayan Swar and Dr Neeraj Singhal have done a great job in editing this book. They both have a rich experience in teaching, research, and writing books. I am sure that this book will create interest among the readers, and will have a great impact on the society at large.

I wish them great success.

Prof. (Dr) Atmanand
Director, MDI Murshidabad

Preface

MDI Murshidabad organised the International conference on Changing Business Paradigm (ICCBP–2023). It was organised with the aim of capturing the role of innovations in management practices. The basic theme of the conference was *Reinventing Management through Sustainability, Innovation and Analytics.*

Apart from this, one of the added advantages of ICCBP–2023 was to promote research and related activities in the area of Marketing, Finance and Accounting, OB and HRM, Operations and SCM, IT, Strategy, Entrepreneurship and case studies with respect to various functional activities. The conference provided a platform to practitioners, researchers, consultants and students to exchange their thoughts and contribute or share their views and expertise in formulation and implementation of various strategies during these uncertain times. We hope this book will find some space in the minds of the stakeholders and provide some important strategies for the future.

Biranchi Narayan Swar
Neeraj Singhal

Acknowledgements

We would like to thank Prof. (Dr) Atmanand, Director, MDI Murshidabad, West Bengal, India, for his continuous support and encouragement in organising this International Conference on Changing Business Paradigm–2023 (ICCBP–2023). This book, published with Bloomusbury India, is an outcome of this conference. We would also like to thank all the faculty members, non-teaching staff and students of MDI Murshidabad for extending their unwavering support at all times.

Our thanks to the international conference advisory committee for their continuous support and encouragement in organising this event. We take this opportunity to thank all keynote speakers, the session chairs for sharing their valuable insights during the conference. A sizable number of acclaimed authors from academia and seasoned managers from the industry showed intense interest in contributing their research papers and cases for this conference. As a result of their contributions, we were able to come up with this book. We would like to thank our editorial team for their continued guidance, inputs and review comments which helped immensely in enhancing the quality of the papers. We also thank Bloomsbury India, their editors, production experts and the entire team for their cooperation in bringing out this book in time.

We value the feedback and suggestions given by you to improve the quality of this book. We look forward to your comments on email iccbp@mdim.ac.in in order to bring out a better book in the future.

Biranchi Narayan Swar
Neeraj Singhal

SECTION I

Reinventing Management through Sustainability, Innovation and Analytics: Marketing

Measuring In-store Consumer Acceptance for IoT Beacon Technology

Dr Syed Md. Faisal Ali Khan[1], Dr Riyaz Sheikh[2], Dr Nasser Khalufi[3] and Hasan Alsalem[1]

[1]*Lecturer – Department of MIS, CBA, Jazan University, Ministry of Education, Saudi Arabia*
[2]*Associate Professor – Department of MIS, CBA, Jazan University, Ministry of Education, Saudi Arabia*
[3]*Lecturer – Department of Marketing & E-commerce, CBA, Jazan University, Saudi Arabia*

Abstract

This study was designed to ascertain whether or not beacon technology is acceptable to consumers by investigating the effects of knowledge, privacy and security, cost, convenience, social influence, and behaviour on IoT adoption. Two hundred and thirty-one actual local consumers were chosen as the study's sample. The 'Confirmatory Factor Analysis (CFA)' is used to assess the questionnaire's reliability, validity and applicability for the research. In addition, the 'Structural Equation Modelling (SEM)' is utilised to assess the study's hypotheses, both CFA model fit and SEM model indices are determined to be good relative to recommended values. The findings show attitude, perception, self-efficacy and trust towards 'perceived usefulness' do not influence towards adoption of beacon technology whereas 'perceived ease of use', 'perceived usefulness', 'self-efficacy' influence adoption of beacon technology. As such, this research aims to assist policymakers and retailers in understanding the changing preferences of customers regarding their purchasing behaviour and the impact of proximity technology as a factor influencing purchasing decisions. Additionally, it can aid manufacturers of beacon devices in embedding customer-preferred services.

Keywords: *Beacon Technology, Proximity Marketing, Proximity Sensors, Technology Adoption Model, IoT, Consumer Behaviour, Buying Pattern*

Introduction

As human wants are insatiable in the twenty-first century, buying has become an unavoidable component of one's life, and it can be accomplished either through traditional/ retail shopping or internet shopping (Demir & Ventura, 2021; Ofori & Appiah-Nimo, 2019) or beacon based proximity marketing. Beacons came into existence in 2013 when Apple Inc. announced new iBeacon technology (Apple.inc, n.d.; Bhattacharya et al., 2017) to enable smart devices to perform functions when the devices are kept into proximity to an iBeacon (Bfonics - Crunchbase Company Profile & Funding, n.d.; Lim et al., 2016). Beacon technology start to change the consumers' attitude towards the brands, taking devices more powerful and revolutionising the retailers offline impact of online advertisement (Lau et al., 2018; Levesque et al., 2015) leading marketers with an opportunity for location-based marketing (Bauer & Strauss,

2016; Moody, 2015). The new technology has an ability to change the consumer behaviour rapidly (Rangaswamy et al., 2022) using mobile (Chung, 2019; Tran Le Na & Hien, 2021). Beacon is now offering more potential reshape to consumer mobile interactions and empower them for more localised as well as personalised engagement (Saranya et al., 2019; Thamm et al., 2016) giving rise to a new concept of proximity marketing. The iBeacon technology is used as an application for indoor positioning system '(Beacon Technology: The Where, What, Who, How and Why, 2015; What Is Apple's IBeacon? | Apple | The Guardian, 2014)' and mobile marketing '(The State Of Mobile Marketing: It's The Best Of Times And The Worst Of Times, n.d.)' leading to the development of Internet of things (IoT) (Ashton, 2009; Atzori et.al., 2010). Beacon technology start to offer a low-cost and widely accepted method for interacting smartphones utilising low energy consumption mechanism like Bluetooth within the physical store (Sazonov & Sazonova, 2021) enabling customers to provide information rich notifications based on the location they are standing (Wibisurya, 2018). Beacons Technology provides seamless ability to the retailers to connect with customers in a totally new way that not only improves and personalise the customer experience, but also enhances marketing capabilities, customer intelligence, and increases sales through IoT (Valmohammadi, 2016). Proximity marketing increased due to the wide usage of smartphones and mobile app (Saranya et al., 2019). At one-point beacon technology provides strategic communication whereas the same technology as numerous constraints and challenges to face, one such challenges include; customers might not be comfortable using push notifications or he is too busy to use mobile shop while shopping in the retail store. The study will explore beacon technology and its adoption mechanism in context to consumer's perspective.

Literature Review

Burke (2002) mentioned that retailers should support customers to take advantage of channels through seamless integration. In recent years, RFID's potential applications in logistics and supply chain management have received extensive coverage (Chanchaichujit et al., 2020). The study emphasised on in-store features and technologies including digital signage, handheld scanners, info kiosks, store navigation, sales assistance, product information, offers and pricing, availability, and electronic checkouts. Whereas location based services only suggests store navigation to customers who are mostly responsive to the SMS that relates the work and their immediate requirement (Yun et al., 2013). Burke (2002) and Lazaris et al. (2015) confirmed the role technologies and in-store practices, fast electronic checkouts, electronic availability of products, online prices/coupons/offers, free in-store wi-fi, in-store shopping assistance, product presentations and customer reviews, electronic recommendation systems, product/service posts purchase opinion on social networks and location-based services which include navigation, location-based offers or promotions, electronic check-ins in promoting in-store sales promotion. Later (Lazaris et al., 2015) advocated mobile app and mobile web application to access location based services in retail stores are equally important to the shoppers. GPS is generally being used as outdoor navigation support service, in 1998 an alternative service came in existence popularly known as Bluetooth services for establishing personal area network for providing short range communication service.

Later the services were integrated with audio, wireless control, data transmission, early reference regarding location based services was cited by (Lazaris et al., 2018) following Social-Local-Mobile principles. The aim of this study is to explore consumer acceptance of such services and related omnichannel touchpoints that could provide them, as well as to examine implications for the store atmosphere. A brief literature review of proximity services in retailing is presented, concentrating mainly on Bluetooth Technology. The findings of a consumer survey indicate that apart from promotions, product information, stock availability, electronic checkouts and social media in the form of user ratings were perceived as equally useful to each other. Furthermore, both mobile apps and mobile web approaches were perceived as easy to use, providing satisfactory web atmospherics representation (m-atmospherics formulation proposing location system to utilise navigation featuring for proximity marketing (Nicholas & Shapiro, 2021) using beacon device. Beacons are small electronic devices that transmit Bluetooth signals to compatible nearby devices to approximate distance based on the signal strength. Niu et al. (2018) advocated the potential impact beacon technology creating interactive services. Hence, Bluetooth beacons technology emerged as a potential indoor positioning device for communication (Wu & Tsai, 2018). In 2005 proximity services where associated with beacons technology using smartphones (Quigley & West, 2005). In addition, beacons introduced computing devices that aim to combine the physical world with the web, which was investigated in a study that speculated that beacons would be the killer apps of future smartphones (Debaty et al., 2005).

Trust

Privacy concerns was developed by (Cole & Smith, 1996) in IoT. A study by (Liu et al., 2005) illustrated trust in provided services is negatively impacted by privacy worries, which in turn affects a person's propensity to adopt new technologies..

Social Norm

Introduction of Internet of Things and its development has brought drastic changes in the lifestyle, social norms, work style and completing tasks (Thierer, 2014) and encourages policymakers to allow these technologies to develop in a relatively unabated fashion. As with other new and highly disruptive digital technologies, however, the Internet of Things and wearable tech will challenge existing social, economic, and legal norms. In particular, these technologies raise a variety of privacy and safety concerns. Other technical barriers exist that could hold back IoT and wearable tech—including disputes over technical standards, system interoperability, and access to adequate spectrum to facilitate wireless networking—but those issues are not dealt with here. The better alternative to top-down regulation is to deal with these concerns creatively as they develop using a combination of educational efforts, technological empowerment tools, social norms, public and watchdog pressure, industry best practices and self-regulation, transparency, and targeted enforcement of existing legal standards (especially torts. Consumers in different culture pay varying amounts of attention to a similar goods and have varied emotional tendencies toward the same product attribute (Zhong et al., 2019).

TAM

In the IT, different types of models were proposed to explain innovation usage (McCord, 2006). According to the TAM, by (Davis, 1989) is one among the most popular to be used(Cheong & Mohammed-Baksh, 2019; Gao & Bai, 2014; Svendsen et al., 2013)internet of things (IoT. According to the Technology Adoption Model (TAM), the likelihood that a user would accept a new technology is heavily influenced by their impressions of how simple and helpful they will find it to be. For any given piece of technology, its 'perceived utility' is someone's level of intellectual engagement and it will boost his performance (Davis et al., 1989) but the degree to which technology is effortless depends on how easy it is seen to be to use. According to TAM, the perceived utility can be illustrated by the perceived ease of use. TAM is being used over wide range of tech products like retail IoT adoption and other examples (Haddud et al., 2017), mobile marketing technology (Zhang & Mao, 2008)an increasingly popular mobile marketing practice, among young Chinese consumers. A modified technology acceptance model (TAM, additional features for mobile devices (Kuo & Yen, 2009), community involvement (Domingo, 2012), supply chain (Samaranayake et al., 2022), smart tourism (Novera et al., 2022)the articles have not yet been combined into a thorough literature review that can examine research streams and the scope of future research. The purpose of this study is to examine the literature on the impact of deploying the Internet of Things (IoT, media (Prasad, 2022), etc. Therefore, this model might be used to foretell how people will interact with IoT devices across a range of factors. TAM is very helpful tool in investigating consumer acceptance for IoT technology (Gao & Bai, 2014; Sharma & Sood, 2022)internet of things (IoT emphasising on beacon technology. TAM is believed to have more robust model to explain consumer acceptance which basically focuses on 'ease of use and usefulness' of the technology.

However, social influence, or the actions of other people, can play a role in shaping users' attitudes regarding the Internet of Things (V. Venkatesh et al., 2012). A study also highlighted that a user may not be able to use the technology even though having strong motivational intend due to lack of resources and skills which in other term defined as self-efficacy or 'perceived behavioural control' (PBC) (Ajzen, 2011). For this reason, several researchers have recommended expanding TAM to account for other factors that affect consumers' openness to embracing IoT (Gao & Bai, 2014; To & Trinh, 2021). (Schierz et al., 2010) mentioned that TAM need expansion by the factors in regard to the relevant technology being used for consideration. Consumers' willingness to adopt a new technology may be influenced by characteristics such as how much they enjoy using it, how influential their peers are, how trustworthy the company is, and how much they value the product's potential for (Broman Toft & Thøgersen, 2015; Childers et al., 2001; Koufaris, 2002; van der Heijden & Verhagen, 2004; Zhang & Mao, 2008). Further (van der Heijden & Verhagen, 2004) suggested that enjoyment and PBC has influence on how one feels about using the technology. (Childers et al., 2001; Koufaris, 2002) in their studies suggested to incorporate enjoyment in adopting technology in TAM. (Hsu & Lu, 2004) integrated social influence into TAM, demonstrating the technology's powerful impact on consumers' propensity to make a purchase (He et al., 2018). Further (Shih, 2004) proposed trust into TAM. (Svendsen et al., 2013) made suggestions for changes in TAM to improve its predictive capacity by amending more antecedent factors that integrated trust, perceived enjoyment, social influence, perceptions about one's own ability to influence their existing TAM, to explain consumer acceptance of IoT in a better way (Bhadauria & Chennamaneni, 2022; Pham et al., 2022). From the views of the technology, the social setting, and the personal characteristics of each user, to determine what makes people interested in adopting IoT technologies, an embedded TAM is analysed in a unified model. Hence, the TAM is used as a reference model to test and qualify the research hypothesis proposed in context to new product and services launched with Beacon Technology.

Beacons are simple devices, yet they pose complications. Consider these limits before using beacons for proximity marketing. Beacons can precisely locate a gadget, but the technique has flaws. Depending on nearby materials or the amount of beacons, the beacon's signal may be reflected or absorbed. It may lose sight of some parts of the stores store. Beacons may broadcast undesired data. Another concern is alert timeliness. Bluetooth signal strength, cell phone antenna maintenance, and delayed beacon signals might generate late messages and disrupt a seamless experience. Beacon-sent, personally relevant communications seem to inspire increased user loyalty, as shown by higher open rates. To send a message using a beacon, make sure the receiver is running your app and has Bluetooth enabled. Even with these precautions, some may find your warnings intrusive and disable them. Users may worry about the safety of their information while you balance being intriguing and imposing irrelevant material. Most people are willing to provide their data for a more intimate experience. Most people minimise Big Brother's impact and protect their privacy. Beacon technology can spook customers. Stores should track all customers, not just those who download their apps. As a result, retailers need beacon-tracking code development kits. Weather and news app developers can collaborate with these toolkit suppliers to incorporate their code. Organisations claim consumers can opt out of location services and are provided clear guidelines for giving informed consent. Informed consent isn't just about user privacy. When requesting consent to process personal information, incomplete and erroneous explanations are typical. People must be aware about beacons before giving approval. It's hard to tell if scanned gadgets belong to the corporation (Jeon et al., 2018) (Padiya & Gulhane, 2020).

Conceptual Framework and Research Hypotheses

Attitude Towards IoT Beacon Technology

(Ajzen, I., & Fishbein, 1980) define BI as a measure of the chance that a person would exhibit the particular behaviour. Attitude (AT) is the initial BI factor to consider, and it reflects whether an individual has a good or unfavorable opinion of relevant behaviour. The majority of modern social psychologists' approach attitude formation from a cognitive or information processing perspective. There is numerous research that show a favorable link between two constructs, Attitude and adoption (Aas et al., 2015; Almugari et al., 2020; Karahoca et al., 2018; Westaby, 2005; Yoon & Lim, 2020) mentioned that technology adoption is associated with reasons and attitude. As a result, the hypothesis that follows is proposed by extrapolating these findings to the scenario of IoT adoption.

- H_1: Attitude has a significant effect on adoption of IoT Beacon Technology.

'Perceived ease of use' and IoT Beacon Technology

'Perceived ease of use' is anticipation of work of UTAUT (Rondan-Cataluña et al., 2015) plus the complexities of IDT (Viswanath Venkatesh et al., 2003b). It focuses on how hard people think they have to work to make advantage of IoT tools and services. Users of IoT need to have a positive experience using IoT before they will adopt it. 'Perceived ease of use' is a major predictor of behavioural intentions toward technology, according to a large body of research. (Abdinoor & Mbamba, 2017; Davis, 1989; Karahoca et al., 2018; Yun et al., 2013). In accordance with TAM and UTAUT, The ease with which something is considered to be used also has a favorable impact on how beneficial it is thought to be (Firth et al., 2019; Kuo & Yen, 2009; V Venkatesh et al., 2012). Hence, we propose: The study conducted in Saudi Arabia by (Yildirim & Ali-Eldin, 2019) demonstrate that the 'Perceived usefulness' for wearable IoT device has stronger motive for an individual's towards the use at the workplace.

Perceived Usefulness

According to the model, an individual's perspective and motivation to adopt a technology are affected by their estimation of that technology's usefulness (Bastan et al., 2022). The 'Perceived usefulness' is impacted by the perceived ease of use, which in turn impacts attitude. One of the most popular technology models, TAM is useful for gauging whether or not employees would embrace new tools in the workplace (Lescevica et al., 2013; Viswanath Venkatesh et al., 2003a; Yildirim & Ali-Eldin, 2019). The TAM defines 'Perceived usefulness' as an individual's expectation that adopting a certain technology will lead to improved productivity in the workplace. The more the wearable device's perceived utility, the greater the likelihood of its adoption (C.-H. Chen, 1992; Y. Chen & Barnes, 2007; Indiani & Febriandari, 2021). Ahmad & Zulkifli (2022) pleasant attitude is created when people's expectations of how simple and helpful something will be are met.

As the survey respondents cannot try on the wearable gadgets for 'Perceived usefulness' and ease of use, we will only be looking at how useful they are assumed to be based on their descriptions.

- H_2: Perceive ease of use (PEOU) significantly affect adoption of IoT Beacon Technology.
- H_3: Perceive ease of use (PEOU) significantly affect attitude towards adoption of IoT Beacon Technology.
- H_4: PEOU significantly affect 'Perceived usefulness' towards adoption of IoT Beacon Technology.
- H_5: 'Perceived usefulness' significantly affect adoption of IoT Beacon Technology.
- H_6: 'Perceived usefulness' significantly affect attitude towards adoption of IoT Beacon Technology.

Perception Towards IoT Beacon Technology

The term 'consumer acceptance' refers to a person's mental and emotional reaction to a good or service. A study was conducted by (Mathieson, 1991; McCord, 2006; Viswanath Venkatesh & Davis, 2000) about intention to use and adoption of technology by consumer. A study by (Park et al., 2017; Sheppard et al., 1988) mentioned intention to use is a major predictor factor towards using product (Shetty et al., 2020; Vera-Martínez, 2021)which can reduce emissions leading to the greenhouse effect and dependence on fossil fuels that are correlated with conventional vehiclesconventional vehicles (CVs. In order to simplify the model, the original TAM's attitude component has been removed (Heinssen et al., 1987). Several studies have demonstrated the existence of a strong and significant correlation between user beliefs and technological activity intentions (Gao & Bai, 2014; Zhang & Mao, 2008)internet of things (IoT. Theoretically, it is therefore justifiable to analyse the adoption of an IoT Beacon device using a relationship between one dependent variable measuring behavioural intention. A study conducted previously mentioned 'perceived ease of use, perceived usefulness, social influence, trust, perceived enjoyment, and PBC' has positive behavioural intention toward using IoT enabled technologies. Similarly trust and 'Perceived ease of use' has positive relation towards perceived usefulness. The study further extends the TAM by boosting users' positive feelings about IoT-enabled devices, which can then serve as a driving factor in getting people to embrace them (Bruner & Kumar, 2005). Researchers use the term 'enjoyment of adoption' to refer to how much people look forward to embracing IoT technology even if they don't expect any immediate benefits to their performance (Deci, 1971). Users will be more eager to adopt Internet of Things technologies if doing so may be enjoyable. Previous studies have shown that consumers' interest in making a purchase is largely affected by their intention to participate in a pleasurable activity (Doolin et al., 2005; Gonçalves et al., 2019; Lu & Su, 2009). The significance of enjoyment on users' intentions and actions has also been shown through studies on mobile commerce's involvement in pleasure (Aggrawal et al., 2020; Gao & Bai, 2014)internet of things (IoT.

(G.S. Kim et al., 2008) perceived monetary value (PMV found that the likelihood of using a SMS service was highly influenced by how much fun they thought they'd have using.

In order to apply these findings to the field of Internet of Things adoption, we hypothesise that:

- H_7: Perception significantly affect adoption of IoT Beacon Technology.
- H_8: Perception significantly affect PEOU towards adoption to IoT Beacon Technology.
- H_9: Perception significantly affect PU towards adoption of IoT Beacon Technology.

Self-Efficacy

Ajzen (2011) & Bandura et al. (1999) mentioned ICT self-efficacy is an important determinant for IOT adoption (Hossain et al., 2021). Information and communication technology user self-efficacy was identified by (Bandura et al., 1999; Boon et al., 2020) as a crucial factor in the final purchase decision. A person with high self-efficacy seems to be more likely to embrace a novel technology because they are willing to persevere through obstacles and unfamiliar settings. Individuals' confidence in their own abilities to complete technological tasks is quantified by a concept called 'ICT self-efficacy' (Viswanath Venkatesh & Bala, 2008). Studies in the past have shown a favorable correlation between self-efficacy and the purpose to use ICT (Boon et al., 2020; Salimon et al., 2018). Others, though, saw a negative correlation (Ozturk et al., 2016). It is clear from these findings that further research is required, and not just generally, but specifically in the Malaysian context. Perceived utility, facilitating conditions of use, social conditioning, user satisfaction, and behavioural control all received solid support from the data. When it came to forecasting actual behaviour, however, trust played just a little role (Gao & Bai, 2014).

- H_{10}: Self-efficacy significantly affects towards adoption of IoT Beacon Technology.
- H_{11}: Self-efficacy significantly affects perceived ease of use.
- H_{12}: Self-efficacy significantly affects perceived ease of use.

Perceived Trust

The study conducted in USA by (Jayashankar et al., 2018) indicated trust correlates positively with perceived worth and negatively with perceived danger. The adoption of IoT was influenced positively by the perception of value and negatively by the perception of risk (Yu et al., 2022). The cognitive trust that people have in a technology has an effect on their emotional trust, which in turn influences their intention to adopt. Evidence from studies of consumers' use of online shopping comparison tools substantiated their usefulness. According to the findings, trust correlates positively with assessments of value and negatively with assessments of danger. Value perception was positively related to Internet of Things adoption, while risk perception was negatively related to IoT uptake (Jayashankar et al., 2018; LY, 2020; Suhluli & Ali Khan, 2022).

H_{13}: Trust significantly affects adoption of IoT Beacon Technology.

H_{14}: Trust significantly affects PEOU to adopt IoT Beacon Technology.
H_{15}: Trust significantly affects the PU to adopt IoT Beacon Technology.

Objective of the Study

To understand Beacon Technology in context to Proximity Marketing. To understand and evaluate adoption of Beacon Technology among consumers of Saudi Arabia. To understand barriers to beacon technology in penetrating the market.

Research Methodology

Qualitative and quantitative research methods was used for this study. According to (Saunders et al., 2009), qualitative methodology consisting of data gathering and analysis of non-numerical data to get an in-depth understanding of a given research phenomenon. To complete this qualitative research, descriptive research design was employed. J.F. Hair & Brunsveld (2019) indicated that descriptive design allows research participants to develop a detailed explanation concerning their experiences, attitudes and understanding of a given research phenomenon. On contrary quantitative research process involves collecting as well as analysing the numerical data. This study uses quantitative research to uncover patterns and cause-and-effect linkages between variables. In the context of this research, descriptive research design will enable to collect descriptive data that will help to understand the experiences of shoppers to access perception, values, challenges, and behaviour involved in. Print copies of questionnaires were given to the shoppers in person for their response. Researchers will pick individuals at random using a systematic sampling method. 'Research Methods for Business: A Skill-Building Approach', 2013 indicates that the random sampling technique is one where members of the target population are given an equal chance of being selected to take part in the gathering of information. The use of random sampling technique is vital in this research project, as it helps to avoid selection bias, which can impact negatively on the overall quality of the data collected (Taylor et al., 2010). This study will make use of both secondary as well as primary sources of data. The primary sources of data will be obtained by collecting data from the field using interviews. The secondary data will be obtained by reviewing the existing literature connected to this research topic.

The study will make use of interviews as the major data collection technique. The interview approach involves a research asking questions to the participants related to the study problem and the participants responding to the questions. Although this approach is time-consuming and expensive to implement (Adeleke, 2020), the main reason for selecting this data collection technique is that it encourages flexibility during the data collection process. Here the researcher asked further questions to the participants to better understand their responses and get their perspectives, opinions, etc., concerning various issues towards beacon technology. Once the data was collected the next step is to analyses. The researcher made use of thematic coding as a technique for analysing the data collected from a range of sources. Data triangulation serves to avoid subjective bias during the analysis of data (Zikmund et al., 2013).

Research Design

Studies are cross-sectional, descriptive, non-experimental quantitative, and one-time, with a sample size of 231. (panoramic snapshots).

Sampling Plan

The simple random sampling method is being used for selecting the representative sample by including only those who voluntarily participated in research (Saunders et al., 2009). The strategy of data collecting is determined with respect to the theoretical underpinnings. So, for this study, the information is gathered via a structured questionnaire survey from shoppers who were observed shopping in the malls. The purposing sampling aims to get a heterogeneous response from some different regions of Saudi Arabia including Saudi citizens and residents from foreign origin. The analysis is done on R 4.02 using the library (plspm).

Data Collection and Data Cleaning

Before entering into statistical studies, it's important to make sure the data is useable, reliable, and valid. The information was collected using a Google Doc survey with a structured questionnaire and the results have been imported into MS-EXCEL. The 231 samples chosen for further analysis all contain only completed forms (respondents).

Statistical Perspective of PLS-SEM

The purpose of the second-generation statistical method known as structural equation modeling is to investigate potential causal links between latent variables. There are two approaches to SEM (Hair et al., 2014); both the more rigorous 'Covariance-Based SEM' and the more flexible PLS-SEM (Wold, 1982) or Variance-Based approach to modeling. PLS-SEM was selected as the modelling method of choice since it does not necessitate multivariate normality, the data are reflecting, and the sample size is small enough to allow for modelling.

Data Analysis and Data Interpretation

Due to its suitability for analysing small sample numbers, SmartPLS 3 was utilised to do data analysis in the present investigation, allowing for the achievement of the study's aims. (Chin et al., 2003) Measurements and structural model assessment is performed in two stages.

Handling Common Method Bias

Podsakoff et al. (2003), illustrated that, 'common method bias (CMB) is the bias that is attributable to the measurement method rather than to the constructs the measures represents'. Construct-spanning items were collapsed into a unifying factor, explaining a total of 47.73 per cent of the sample's variance (a value that is less than 50 per cent). As a result, the data set did not show any substantial bias due to the most often used research technique (Podsakoff et al., 2003).

Measurement Model Evaluation

'Internal consistency, convergent validity, and indiscriminant' validity was examined to determine the reliability of the measurement model. To what extent do various measures all point towards the same conceptual construct? that's what convergent validity reveals (Dinev et al., 2006; D.-H. Kim et al., 2015)intensions, and behaviors of Millennials. Study 1 considers broadly how prevalent the privacy paradox is among Millennials (assessing whether there is an incongruity between Millennials' privacy attitudes and their personal information disclosure behavior.

Table 1: Reliability Test for Constructs

Construct	*No. of Items*	*Cronbach's Alpha*	*Composite Reliability*	*Average Variance Extracted*
Trust	3	0.817	0.858	0.788
Self-efficacy	4	0.918	0.877	0.797
Perception	6	0.726	0.892	0.792
Perceived usefulness	9	0.867	0.943	0.798
Perceived ease of use	5	0.906	0.921	0.734
Attitude	3	0.804	0.884	0.718
Adoption of Beacon technology	1	0.716	0.775	0.741

Source: Author Compilation

In Table 1, it is observed that both the 'composite reliability' and the 'average variance extracted' were more than 0.7 (J. Hair et al., 2010). The internal consistency was confirmed by a Cronbach's alpha value over 0.7 (Adam et al., 2021; Fornell & Larcker, 1981b; Hilkenmeier et al., 2020). Consequently, convergent validity of the constructs was attained. The (Fornell & Larcker, 1981a) criteria were used to analyse the 'discriminant validity'. The (Fornell & Larcker, 1981a) criterion was met when the 'square root of AVE' of average variance derived from the constructs were greater than

Table 2: Discriminant Validity–Fornell–Larcker Criterion

	Adoption of Beccon Tel.	*Attitude*	*Perceived Ease of Yse*	*Perceived Usefulness*	*Perception*	*Self-efficacy*	*Trust*
Adoption of Beccon Tel.	1.000						
Attitude	0.595	0.847					
Perceived ease of use	0.810	0.841	0.957				
Perceived usefulness	0.694	0.847	0.932	0.893			
Perception	0.238	0.444	0.773	0.649	0.626		
Self-efficacy	0.645	0.796	0.856	0.777	0.450	0.893	
Trust	0.261	0.663	0.566	0.540	0.735	0.790	0.699

Source: Author Compilation

the correlation coefficients between the individual constructs and all the others (as shown in the table). Thus, the Fornell-Larcker requirement for discriminant validity was met.

Model Fit Estimates

The 'structural equation model' is used to examine four hypotheses in this investigation. With a value of '$\chi^2 = 142.17$, $p < 0.00$; GFI = 0.95; CFI = 0.97; and RMSEA = 0.078', it was determined that this model adequately fit the data. Path diagram of variables in this study, with associated path coefficients and p-values shown in figure.

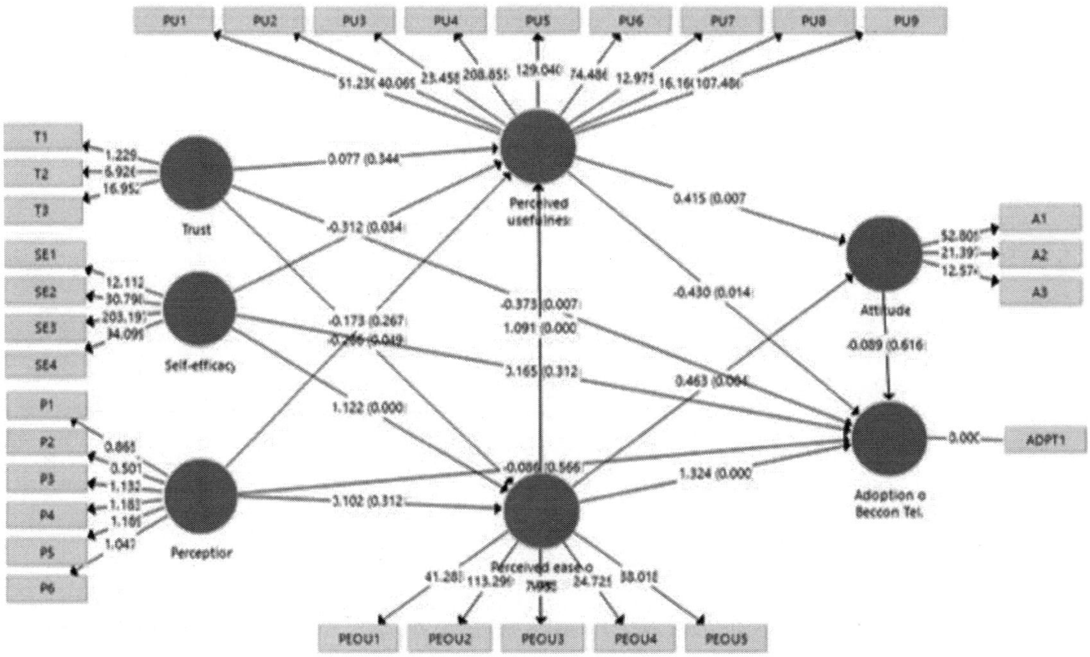

Fig. 1: Coefficient Path Model and Relationship among Variables

Source: Author Compilation

Hypotheses Testing

This study used a bootstrapping technique to determine the theoretical model's path coefficient, which allowed the researchers to test the hypothesis' significance. Research sample standardised coefficients from visual representations of the structural model in the figure.

The relevance of each construct's standardised route coefficient is displayed in Table 3. The standardised path coefficients were found to be insignificant and positive at $p < 0.01$ and $p < 0.05$, that pointed to substantial backing for rejection of the hypotheses 'H_1, H_7, H_8, H_9, H_{10} and H_{15}' except 'H_2, H_3, H_4, H_5, H_6, H_{11}, H_{12}, H_{13}, and H_{14}'.

Table 3: Hypothesis Testing and SEM Results

Hypothesis	*Path*	*Path Coefficient*	*Standard Error*	*t-static*	*P*	*Hypothesis*
H_1	Attitude → Adoption of Beccon Tel.	-0.089	0.178	0.502	0.616	Not Supported
H_2	'Perceived ease of use' → Adoption of Beccon Tel.	1.324	0.235	5.644	0.000	Supported
H_3	'Perceived ease of use' → Attitude	0.463	0.159	2.919	0.004	Supported
H_4	'Perceived ease of use' → Perceived usefulness	1.091	0.092	11.908	0.000	Supported
H_5	'Perceived usefulness' → Adoption of Beccon Tel.	-0.430	0.173	2.477	0.014	Supported
H_6	'Perceived usefulness' → Attitude	0.415	0.153	2.708	0.007	Supported
H_7	Perception → Adoption of Beccon Tel.	-0.086	0.150	0.574	0.566	Not Supported
H_8	Perception → Perceived ease of use	0.102	0.101	1.012	0.312	Not Supported
H_9	Perception → Perceived usefulness	-0.173	0.155	1.112	0.267	Not Supported
H_{10}	Self-efficacy → Adoption of Beccon Tel.	0.165	0.163	1.011	0.312	Not Supported
H_{11}	Self-efficacy → 'Perceived ease of use'	1.122	0.113	9.918	0.000	Supported
H_{12}	Self-efficacy → 'Perceived usefulness'	-0.312	0.147	2.126	0.034	Supported
H_{13}	Trust → Adoption of Beccon Tel.	-0.373	0.137	2.720	0.007	Supported
H_{14}	Trust → 'Perceived ease of use'	-0.266	0.135	1.970	0.049	Supported
H_{15}	Trust → 'Perceived usefulness'	0.077	0.081	0.947	0.344	Not Supported

Source: Author Compilation

Conclusion

The literature reviews revealed that modern consumers seek advanced IT enabled technology to interact with retailers (Mangold & Faulds, 2009). Research aims to understand Beacon Technology in context to Proximity Marketing in evaluating adoption of Beacon Technology among consumers of Saudi Arabia. Technology has allowed situational awareness in changing environment (Mayfield, 2008) resulting increasingly important role in marketing (Haziri et al., 2019). It is concluded that technology marketing marketers with most cost effective form of marketing that could be beneficial for the retailers and presents consumers. The literature review in the present study outlined the importance proximity marketing in promoting in store sales specifically in communicating and establishing customer relationships. In order to have a successful communication with consumers and constructing long term long term relationships it is vital to ensure that retailers communicates consumers the about the products and services offered during all stages of purchase decision (Amodu et al., 2019; McKinsey & Company, 2016). By establishing an online connection, beacon technology may save traditional brick-and-mortar businesses. With the use of beacons, that can analyse customer information and provide them personalised services both in-store and on the web, such discounts and other loyalty rewards. Beacons additionally demonstrate the connection between online and offline purchases. There are imperfections and security risks associated with beacons. Avoiding this can be accomplished if stores personalise without being intrusive or overbearing. It is planned to keep using beacons. To the extent that they can make people's lives simpler and more convenient, they will grow. Maintaining relationships with customers both online and in-store requires retailers to be beacon experts.

The main concern about the present is to address Saudi consumer's attitudes towards acceptance of beacon technology emphasising on the impact of proximity marketing as a research tool during the buying intention. The acceptance level is addressed through the proposed hypothesis which was tasted for its significance. Using the SEM to provide an adequate fit to the data. Hence in the present study Attitude, Perception, self-efficacy and trust towards 'Perceived usefulness' do not significantly impact towards adoption of beacon technology on contrary Perceived ease of use, perceived usefulness, Self-efficacy towards perceived ease of use, self-efficacy towards usefulness has a significant impact towards acceptance of beacon technology. Trust plays a vital role towards acceptance of beacon technology as it has a significant positive relation with 'Perceived ease of use' resulting developing attitude towards acceptance of beacon technology. This study also provides an opportunity to real time engagement with the customers, improving service delivery and alignment of brand strategies ensuring further change in buying pattern among the consumer and opening future research avenues for the researcher.

References

[1] Aas, T. H., Pedersen, P. E., Abramovici, M., Bancel-Charensol, L., Agarwal, R., Selen, W., Akamavi, R. K., Alam, I. (Ian) I., Perry, C., Amara, N., Landry, R., Doloreux, D., Andreassen, T. W., Streukens, S., Atuahene-Gima, K., Avlonitis, G. J., Papastathopoulou, P. G., Gounaris, S. P., Bae, D. J., … Soriano, D. R. (2015). From the Editor. *Service Industries Journal, 29*(1).

[2] Abdinoor, A., & Mbamba, U. O. L. (2017). Factors influencing consumers' adoption of mobile financial services in Tanzania. *Cogent Business and Management*, *4*(1). https://doi.org/10.1080/23311975.2017.1392273

[3] Adam, E., Panjaitan, R., Sumarlin, T., & Adriana, M. (2021). Financial Well-Being Resilience: Financial Literacy and Financial Inclusion Toward Financial Attitude. *Majalah Ilmiah Bijak*, *18*(1).

[4] Adeleke, A. (2020). A Case Study of the Marketing Tools Coffee Shop Owners Use to Sustain Businesses. *Open Journal of Business and Management*, *08*(02). https://doi.org/10.4236/ojbm.2020.82044

[5] Aggrawal, N., Arora, A., Anand, A., & Dwivedi, Y. (2020). Early viewers or followers: a mathematical model for YouTube viewers' categorization. *Kybernetes*, *50*(6). https://doi.org/10.1108/K-03-2020-0128

[6] Ahmad, N., & Zulkifli, A.M. (2022). Internet of Things (IoT) and the road to happiness. *Digital Transformation and Society*, *1*(1), 66–94. https://doi.org/10.1108/DTS-05-2022-0009

[7] Ajzen, I., & Fishbein, M. (1980). Understanding attitudes and predicting social behaviour. New Jersey: Prentice-Hall. *Englewood Cliffs*, *50*.

[8] Ajzen, I. (2011). The theory of planned behaviour: Reactions and reflections. *Psychology & Health*, *26*(9), 1113–1127. https://doi.org/10.1080/08870446.2011.613995

[9] Almugari, F., Bajaj, P., Tabash, M. I., Khan, A., & Ali, M. A. (2020). An examination of consumers' adoption of internet of things (IoT) in Indian banks. *Cogent Business and Management*, *7*(1). https://doi.org/10.1080/23311975.2020.1809071

[10] Amodu, L., Omojola, O., Okorie, N., Adeyeye, B., & Adesina, E. (2019). Potentials of Internet of Things for effective public relations activities: Are professionals ready? *Cogent Business and Management*, *6*(1). https://doi.org/10.1080/23311975.2019.1683951

[11] Apple.inc. (n.d.). *Apple iBeacons Explained – Smart Home Occupancy Sensing Solved? – Automated Home*. 2015. Retrieved October 5, 2021, from https://www.automatedhome.co.uk/apple/apple-ibeacons-explained-smart-home-occupancy-sensing-solved.html

[12] Bandura, A., Freeman, W.H., & Lightsey, R. (1999). Self-Efficacy: The Exercise of Control. *Journal of Cognitive Psychotherapy*, *13*(2). https://doi.org/10.1891/0889-8391.13.2.158

[13] Bastan, M., Zarei, M., Tavakkoli-Moghaddam, R., & G, H. S. (2022). A new technology acceptance model: a mixed-method of grounded theory and system dynamics. *Kybernetes*, *51*(1). https://doi.org/10.1108/K-03-2020-0127

[14] Bauer, C., & Strauss, C. (2016). Location-based advertising on mobile devices: A literature review and analysis. *Management Review Quarterly*, *66*(3). https://doi.org/10.1007/s11301-015-0118-z

[15] *Beacon Technology: The Where, What, Who, How and Why*. (2015). Forbes. https://www.forbes.com/sites/homaycotte/2015/09/01/beacon-technology-the-what-who-how-why-and-where/?sh=3f4d7cd71aaf

[16] *bfonics – Crunchbase Company Profile & Funding*. (n.d.). Retrieved September 23, 2022, from https://www.crunchbase.com/organization/bfonics-inc-

[17] Bhadauria, V. S., & Chennamaneni, A. (2022). Do desire, anxiety and personal innovativeness impact the adoption of IoT devices? *Information & Computer Security*, *ahead-of-p*(ahead-of-print). https://doi.org/10.1108/ICS-07-2021-0096

[18] Bhattacharya, D., Canul, M., & Knight, S. (2017). Case study: Impact of the physical web and BLE beacons. *Proceedings of the Annual Hawaii International Conference on System Sciences*, *2017-January*. https://doi.org/10.24251/hicss.2017.516

[19] Boon, N. S., Noor, M. N. M., & Kebaili, B. (2020). *A Proposed Conceptual Framework on the Adoption of Internet of Things (IoT)*. https://doi.org/10.15405/epsbs.2020.10.31

[20] Broman Toft, M., & Thøgersen, J. (2015). Exploring private consumers' willingness to adopt Smart Grid technology. *International Journal of Consumer Studies*, *39*(6). https://doi.org/10.1111/ijcs.12201

[21] Bruner, G., & Kumar, A. (2005). Explaining consumer acceptance of handheld Internet devices. *Journal of Business Research*, *58*(5), 553–58. https://econpapers.repec.org/RePEc:eee:jbrese:v:58:y:2005:i:5:p:553-58

[22] Burke, R. R. (2002). Technology and the customer interface: What consumers want in the physical and virtual store. In *Journal of the Academy of Marketing Science* (Vol. 30, Issue 4). https://doi.org/10.1177/009207002236914

[23] Chanchaichujit, J., Balasubramanian, S., & Charmaine, N. S. M. (2020). A systematic literature review on the benefit-drivers of RFID implementation in supply chains and its impact on organizational competitive advantage. In *Cogent Business and Management* (Vol. 7, Issue 1). https://doi.org/10.1080/23311975.2020.1818408

[24] Chen, C.-H. (1992). Modernization in Mainland China: *American Journal of Economics and Sociology*, *51*(1), 57–68. https://doi.org/https://doi.org/10.1111/j.1536-7150.1992.tb02507.x

[25] Chen, Y., & Barnes, S. (2007). Initial trust and online buyer behaviour. *Industrial Management & Data Systems*, *107*(1), 21–36. https://doi.org/10.1108/02635570710719034

[26] Cheong, H. J., & Mohammed-Baksh, S. (2019). U.S. consumer m-commerce involvement: Using in-depth interviews to propose an acceptance model of shopping apps-based m-commerce. *Cogent Business and Management*, *6*(1). https://doi.org/10.1080/23311975.2019.1674077

[27] Childers, T. L., Carr, C. L., Peck, J., & Carson, S. (2001). Hedonic and utilitarian motivations for online retail shopping behaviour. *Journal of Retailing*, *77*(4), 511–535. https://doi.org/https://doi.org/10.1016/S0022-4359(01)00056-2

[28] Chin, W. W., Marcelin, B. L., & Newsted, P. R. (2003). A partial least squares latent variable modeling approach for measuring interaction effects: Results from a Monte Carlo simulation study and an electronic-mail emotion/adoption study. *Information Systems Research*, *14*(2). https://doi.org/10.1287/isre.14.2.189.16018

[29] Chung, K. C. (2019). Mobile (shopping) commerce intention in central Asia. *Asia-Pacific Journal of Business Administration*, *11*(3), 251–66. https://doi.org/10.1108/APJBA-11-2018-0215

[30] Cole, B. C., & Smith, D. L. (1996). Perceptions of business ethics: Students vs. business people. *Journal of Business Ethics*, *15*(8), 889–96. https://doi.org/10.1007/BF00381856

[31] Davis, F. D. (1989). Perceived Usefulness, Perceived Ease of Use, and User Acceptance of Information Technology. *MIS Q.*, *13*, 319–40.

[32] Debaty, P., Goddi, P., & Vorbau, A. (2005). Integrating the physical world with the web to enable context-enhanced mobile services. *Mobile Networks and Applications*, *10*(4). https://doi.org/10.1007/s11036-005-1552-2

[33] Deci, E. L. (1971). Effects of externally mediated rewards on intrinsic motivation. *Journal of Personality and Social Psychology*, *18*(1), 105–15. https://doi.org/10.1037/h0030644

[34] Demir, B., & Ventura, K. (2021). Exploring the Internet of Things Within the New Generation Smart Home Systems: A Qualitative Study. In E. Özen, S. Grima, & R.D. Gonzi (Eds.), *New Challenges for Future Sustainability and Wellbeing* (pp. 363–376). Emerald Publishing Limited. https://doi.org/10.1108/978-1-80043-968-920211019

[35] Dinev, T., Bellotto, M., Hart, P., Russo, V., Serra, I., & Colautti, C. (2006). Privacy calculus model in e-commerce - A study of Italy and the United States. *European Journal of Information Systems*, *15*(4). https://doi.org/10.1057/palgrave.ejis.3000590

[36] Domingo, M. C. (2012). An overview of the Internet of Things for people with disabilities. *Journal of Network and Computer Applications, 35*(2), 584–596. https://doi.org/https://doi.org/10.1016/j.jnca.2011.10.015

[37] Doolin, B., Dillon, S., Thompson, F., & Corner, J. L. (2005). Perceived Risk, the Internet Shopping Experience and Online Purchasing Behaviour: A New Zealand Perspective. *J. Glob. Inf. Manag., 13*, 66–88.

[38] Firth, J., Torous, J., Stubbs, B., Firth, J. A., Steiner, G. Z., Smith, L., Alvarez-Jimenez, M., Gleeson, J., Vancampfort, D., Armitage, C. J., & Sarris, J. (2019). The 'online brain': how the Internet may be changing our cognition. *World Psychiatry, 18*(2). https://doi.org/10.1002/wps.20617

[39] Fornell, C., & Larcker, D. F. (1981a). Evaluating Structural Equation Models with Unobservable Variables and Measurement Error. *Journal of Marketing Research, 18*(1). https://doi.org/10.2307/3151312

[40] Fornell, C., & Larcker, D. F. (1981b). Fornell, C. and Larcker, D.F. (1981), 'Evaluating structural equation models with unobservable variables and.pdf. *Journal of Marketing Research, XVIII* (February).

[41] Gao, L., & Bai, X. (2014). A unified perspective on the factors influencing consumer acceptance of internet of things technology. *Asia Pacific Journal of Marketing and Logistics, 26*(2), 211–31. https://doi.org/10.1108/APJML-06-2013-0061

[42] Gonçalves, S.C., Barbosa, B., & Rocha, A. (2019). Perceptions and Intentions of Adopting the Internet of Things by Generation Z. *CBU International Conference Proceedings, 7*. https://doi.org/10.12955/cbup.v7.1346

[43] Haddud, A., DeSouza, A., Khare, A., & Lee, H. (2017). Examining potential benefits and challenges associated with the Internet of Things integration in supply chains. *Journal of Manufacturing Technology Management, 28*(8), 1055–085. https://doi.org/10.1108/JMTM-05-2017-0094

[44] Hair, J., Black, W., Babin, B., & Anderson, R. (2010). Multivariate Data Analysis: A Global Perspective. In *Multivariate Data Analysis: A Global Perspective* (Vol. 7th).

[45] Hair, J. F., & Brunsveld, N. (2019). Essentials of business research methods. In *Essentials of Business Research Methods*. https://doi.org/10.4324/9780429203374

[46] Haziri, F., Pagria, I., & Chovancova, M. (2019). Game Dynamics and the War between Social Platforms. In *Economic and Social Development (ESD): 39th International Scientific Conference on Economic and Social Development – Sustainability from an Economic and Social Perspective* (Issues 39th International Scientific Conference on Economic and Social Development-Sustainability from an Economic and Social Perspective).

[47] He, Y., Chen, Q., & Kitkuakul, S. (2018). Regulatory focus and technology acceptance: Perceived ease of use and usefulness as efficacy. *Cogent Business and Management, 5*(1). https://doi.org/10.1080/23311975.2018.1459006

[48] Heinssen, R. K., Glass, C. R., & Knight, L. A. (1987). Assessing computer anxiety: Development and validation of the Computer Anxiety Rating Scale. *Computers in Human Behaviour, 3*(1). https://doi.org/10.1016/0747-5632(87)90010-0

[49] Hilkenmeier, F., Bohndick, C., Bohndick, T., & Hilkenmeier, J. (2020). Assessing Distinctiveness in Multidimensional Instruments Without Access to Raw Data – A Manifest Fornell-Larcker Criterion. *Frontiers in Psychology, 11*. https://doi.org/10.3389/fpsyg.2020.00223

[50] Hossain, M. I., Yusof, A. F., Hussin, A. R. C., lahad, N. A., & Sadiq, A. S. (2021). Factors influencing adoption model of continuous glucose monitoring devices for internet of things healthcare. *Internet of Things (Netherlands), 15*. https://doi.org/10.1016/j.iot.2020.100353

[51] Hsu, C.-L., & Lu, H.-P. (2004). Why do people play on-line games? An extended TAM with social influences and flow experience. *Information & Management*, *41*(7), 853–868. https://doi.org/https://doi.org/10.1016/j.im.2003.08.014

[52] Indiani, N. L. P., & Febriandari, S. N. S. (2021). Key antecedents of consumer purchasing behaviour in emerging online retail market. *Cogent Business and Management*, *8*(1). https://doi.org/10.1080/23311975.2021.1978370

[53] Jayashankar, P., Nilakanta, S., Johnston, W. J., Gill, P., & Burres, R. (2018). IoT adoption in agriculture: the role of trust, perceived value and risk. *Journal of Business and Industrial Marketing*, *33*(6). https://doi.org/10.1108/JBIM-01-2018-0023

[54] Jeon, K. E., She, J., Soonsawad, P., & Ng, P. C. (2018). BLE Beacons for Internet of Things Applications: Survey, Challenges, and Opportunities. In *IEEE Internet of Things Journal* (Vol. 5, Issue 2). https://doi.org/10.1109/JIOT.2017.2788449

[55] Karahoca, A., Karahoca, D., & Aksöz, M. (2018). Examining intention to adopt to internet of things in healthcare technology products. *Kybernetes*, *47*(4). https://doi.org/10.1108/K-02-2017-0045

[56] Kim, D.-H., Hettche, M., & Clayton, M. J. (2015). The Privacy Paradox and Calculus Among Millennials: An Empirical Study of Privacy Attitude-Behaviour Congruence. *AMA Marketing & Public Policy Academic Conference Proceedings, 25.*

[57] Kim, G. S., Park, S.-B., & Oh, J. (2008). An examination of factors influencing consumer adoption of short message service (SMS). *Psychology & Marketing*, *25*(8), 769–786. https://doi.org/https://doi.org/10.1002/mar.20238

[58] Koufaris, M. (2002). Applying the Technology Acceptance Model and Flow Theory to Online Consumer Behaviour. *Information Systems Research*, *13*(2), 205–23. https://doi.org/10.1287/isre.13.2.205.83

[59] Kuo, Y.-F., & Yen, S.-N. (2009). Towards an understanding of the behavioural intention to use 3G mobile value-added services. *Computers in Human Behaviour*, *25*(1), 103–10. https://doi.org/https://doi.org/10.1016/j.chb.2008.07.007

[60] Lau, H., Mok, Y., Daut, N., Tahir, A., Chung, S., & Chua, B. (2018). Beacon-Integrated Attendance App. *Advanced Science Letters*, *24*(2). https://doi.org/10.1166/asl.2018.10698

[61] Lazaris, C., Vrechopoulos, A., & Doukidis, G. (2018). Consumer Acceptance of Proximity-Based Location Services in Omnichannel Retailing: Exploring Implications for Mobile Channels & Store Atmosphere. *6th International Conference on Contemporary Marketing Issues, (ICCMI), 27-29 June.*

[62] Lazaris, C., Vrechopoulos, A., Doukidis, G., & Fraidaki, K. (2015). The interplay of omniretailing & store atmosphere on consumer's purchase intention towards the physical retail store. *Proceedings of the 12th European, Mediterranean and Middle Eastern Conference on Information Systems, EMCIS 2015.*

[63] Lescevica, M., Ginters, E., & Mazza, R. (2013). Unified Theory of Acceptance and Use of Technology (UTAUT) for Market Analysis of FP7 CHOReOS Products. *Procedia Computer Science*, *26*, 51–68. https://doi.org/https://doi.org/10.1016/j.procs.2013.12.007

[64] Levesque, N., Durif, F., Boeck, H., & Bilolo, A. (2015). The impact of Proximity Marketing

on consumer reaction and firm performance: A conceptual and integrative model. *2015 Americas Conference on Information Systems, AMCIS 2015.*

[65] Lim, J. M. Y., Chang, Y. C., Alias, M. Y., & Loo, J. (2016). Cognitive radio network in vehicular ad hoc network (VANET): A survey. In *Cogent Engineering* (Vol. 3, Issue 1). https://doi.org/10.1080/23311916.2016.1191114

[66] Liu, C., Marchewka, J.T., Lu, J., & Yu, C.S. (2005). Beyond concern-a privacy-trust-behavioural intention model of electronic commerce. *Information and Management, 42*(2). https://doi.org/10.1016/j.im.2004.01.003

[67] Lu, H.-P., & Su, P. Y.-J. (2009). Factors affecting purchase intention on mobile shopping web sites. *Internet Res., 19*, 442–58.

[68] LY, B. (2020). Challenge and perspective for Digital Silk Road. *Cogent Business and Management, 7*(1). https://doi.org/10.1080/23311975.2020.1804180

[69] Mangold, W. G., & Faulds, D. J. (2009). Social media: The new hybrid element of the promotion mix. *Business Horizons, 52*(4). https://doi.org/10.1016/j.bushor.2009.03.002

[70] Mathieson, K. (1991). Predicting User Intentions: Comparing the Technology Acceptance Model with the Theory of Planned Behaviour. *Information Systems Research, 2*(3), 173–191. https://doi.org/10.1287/isre.2.3.173

[71] Mayfield, A. (2008). What is Social Media? An eBook from iCrossing. *What Is Social Media ? An EBook from ICrossing.*

[72] McCord, M. (2006). Technology acceptance model. In *Handbook of Research on Electronic Surveys and Measurements* (pp. 306–08). https://doi.org/10.4018/978-1-59140-792-8.ch038

[73] McKinsey & Company. (2016). Customer Experience: Creating Value Trough Transforming Customer Journeys. *McKinsey & Company Publications, 1.*

[74] Moody, M. (2015). Analysis of Promising Beacon Technology for Consumers. *The Elon Journal of Undergraduate Research in Communications, 6*(1).

[75] Nicholas, G., & Shapiro, A. (2021). Failed hybrids: The death and life of Bluetooth proximity marketing. *Mobile Media and Communication, 9*(3). https://doi.org/10.1177/2050157920975836

[76] Niu, R., Vempaty, A., & Varshney, P. K. (2018). Received-Signal-Strength-Based Localization in Wireless Sensor Networks. *Proceedings of the IEEE, 106*(7). https://doi.org/10.1109/JPROC.2018.2828858

[77] Novera, C. N., Ahmed, Z., Kushol, R., Wanke, P., & Azad, M. A. K. (2022). Internet of Things (IoT) in smart tourism: a literature review. *Spanish Journal of Marketing - ESIC, ahead-of-p*(ahead-of-print). https://doi.org/10.1108/SJME-03-2022-0035

[78] Ofori, D., & Appiah-Nimo, C. (2019). Determinants of online shopping among tertiary students in Ghana: An extended technology acceptance model. *Cogent Business and Management, 6*(1). https://doi.org/10.1080/23311975.2019.1644715

[79] Ozturk, A. B., Bilgihan, A., Nusair, K., & Okumus, F. (2016). What keeps the mobile hotel booking users loyal? Investigating the roles of self-efficacy, compatibility, perceived ease of use, and perceived convenience. *International Journal of Information Management, 36*(6). https://doi.org/10.1016/j.ijinfomgt.2016.04.005

[80] Padiya, S. D., & Gulhane, V. S. (2020). IoT and BLE Beacons: Demand, challenges, requirements, and research opportunities- planning-strategy. *Proceedings – 2020 IEEE 9th International Conference on Communication Systems and Network Technologies, CSNT 2020.* https://doi.org/10.1109/CSNT48778.2020.9115765

[81] Park, A., Chang, H., & Lee, K. J. (2017). Action Research on Development and Application of Internet of Things Services in Hospital. *Hir*, *23*(1), 25–34. https://doi.org/10.4258/hir.2017.23.1.25

[82] Pham, T.B.C., Nguyen, H.L., Vu, T.M.T., & Truong, V.T. (2022). Corporate governance and earnings management struggles: responses to adapt a modern capital mobilisation in the transitional economy. *Cogent Business & Management*, *9*(1), 2108216. https://doi.org/10.1080/23311975.2022.2108216

[83] Podsakoff, P. M., MacKenzie, S. B., Lee, J.-Y., & Podsakoff, N. P. (2003). Common method biases in behavioural research: A critical review of the literature and recommended remedies. In *Journal of Applied Psychology* (Vol. 88, Issue 5, pp. 879–903). American Psychological Association. https://doi.org/10.1037/0021-9010.88.5.879

[84] Prasad, S. S. (2022). Impact of OTT media on the society: insights from path analysis. *Asia-Pacific Journal of Business Administration*, *14*(2), 185–98. https://doi.org/10.1108/APJBA-06-2021-0261

[85] Quigley, A., & West, D. (2005). *Proximation: Location-Awareness Though Sensed Proximity and GSM Estimation BT - Location- and Context-Awareness* (T. Strang & C. Linnhoff-Popien (Eds.); pp. 363–376). Springer Berlin Heidelberg.

[86] Rangaswamy, E., Nawaz, N., & Changzhuang, Z. (2022). The impact of digital technology on changing consumer behaviours with special reference to the home furnishing sector in Singapore. *Humanities and Social Sciences Communications*, *9*(1). https://doi.org/10.1057/s41599-022-01102-x

[87] Research Methods for Business: A Skill-Building Approach. (2013). *Leadership & Organization Development Journal*, *34*(7). https://doi.org/10.1108/lodj-06-2013-0079

[88] Rondan-Cataluña, F. J., Arenas-Gaitán, J., & Ramírez-Correa, P. E. (2015). A comparison of the different versions of popular technology acceptance models a non-linear perspective. *Kybernetes*, *44*(5). https://doi.org/10.1108/K-09-2014-0184

[89] Salimon, M. G., Gorondutse, A. H., & Abdullah, H. H. (2018). User adoption of Smart Homes Technology in Malaysia: Integration TAM 3,TPB, UTAUT 2 and extension of their constructs for a better prediction. *Journal of Business and Management*, *20*(4).

[90] Samaranayake, P., Laosirihongthong, T., Adebanjo, D., & Boon-itt, S. (2022). Prioritising enabling factors of Internet of things (IoT) adoption in digital supply chain. *International Journal of Productivity and Performance Management*, *ahead-of-p*(ahead-of-print). https://doi.org/10.1108/IJPPM-12-2021-0698

[91] Saranya, K., Syed Ali Fathima, S. J., & Azri Ismail, M. N. (2019). Enhancing customer engagement using beacons. *International Journal of Recent Technology and Engineering*, *7*(4).

[92] Saunders, M., Lewis, P., & Thornhill, a. (2009). Research Methods for Business Students. In *Business* (Vol. 5th).

[93] Sazonov, A. A., & Sazonova, M. V. (2021). Omnichannel marketing and beacon technologies: experience and prospects in Europe. *Upravlenie*, *9*(1). https://doi.org/10.26425/2309-3633-2021-9-1-112-126

[94] Schierz, P. G., Schilke, O., & Wirtz, B. W. (2010). Understanding consumer acceptance of mobile payment services: An empirical analysis. *Electronic Commerce Research and Applications*, *9*(3), 209–16. https://doi.org/https://doi.org/10.1016/j.elerap.2009.07.005

[95] Sharma, V., & Sood, D. (2022). Adoption of Internet of Things and Services in the Indian Insurance Industry. In K. Sood, R. K. Dhanaraj, B. Balusamy, S. Grima, & R. Uma

Maheshwari (Eds.), *Big Data: A Game Changer for Insurance Industry* (pp. 35–42). Emerald Publishing Limited. https://doi.org/10.1108/978-1-80262-605-620221003

[96] Sheppard, B. H., Hartwick, J. M., & Warshaw, P. R. (1988). The Theory of Reasoned Action: A Meta-Analysis of Past Research with Recommendations for Modifications and Future Research. *Journal of Consumer Research, 15*, 325–43.

[97] Shetty, D. K., Shetty, S., Raj Rodrigues, L., Naik, N., Maddodi, C. B., Malarout, N., & Sooriyaperakasam, N. (2020). Barriers to widespread adoption of plug-in electric vehicles in emerging Asian markets: An analysis of consumer behavioural attitudes and perceptions. *Cogent Engineering, 7*(1). https://doi.org/10.1080/23311916.2020.1796198

[98] Shih, H.-P. (2004). An empirical study on predicting user acceptance of e-shopping on the Web. *Information & Management, 41*(3), 351–68. https://doi.org/https://doi.org/10.1016/S0378-7206(03)00079-X

[99] Suhluli, S. A., & Ali Khan, S. M. F. (2022). Determinants of user acceptance of wearable IoT devices. *Cogent Engineering, 9*(1), 2087456. https://doi.org/10.1080/23311916.2022.2087456

[100] Svendsen, G. B., Johnsen, J.-A. K., Almås-Sørensen, L., & Vittersø, J. (2013). Personality and technology acceptance: the influence of personality factors on the core constructs of the Technology Acceptance Model. *Behaviour & Information Technology, 32*(4), 323–334. https://doi.org/10.1080/0144929X.2011.553740

[101] Taylor, K., Nettleton, S., Harding, G., & Bartholomew's, S. (2010). Social Research Methods. In *Sociology for Pharmacists*. https://doi.org/10.4324/9780203381175_chapter_9

[102] Thamm, A., Anke, J., Haugk, S., & Radic, D. (2016). Towards the omni-channel: Beacon-based services in retail. *Lecture Notes in Business Information Processing, 255*. https://doi.org/10.1007/978-3-319-39426-8_15

[103] *The State Of Mobile Marketing: It's the Best of Times and the Worst of Times* (n.d.). Retrieved September 23, 2022, from https://www.forbes.com/sites/steveolenski/2014/02/28/the-state-of-mobile-marketing-its-the-best-of-times-and-the-worst-of-times/?sh=1a73c4303114

[104] Thierer, A. D. (2014). The Internet of Things & Wearable Technology: Addressing Privacy & Security Concerns Without Derailing Innovation. *SSRN Electronic Journal*. https://doi.org/10.2139/ssrn.2494382

[105] To, A. T., & Trinh, T. H. M. (2021). Understanding behavioural intention to use mobile wallets in vietnam: Extending the tam model with trust and enjoyment. *Cogent Business and Management, 8*(1). https://doi.org/10.1080/23311975.2021.1891661

[106] Tran Le Na, N., & Hien, N. N. (2021). A study of user's m-wallet usage behaviour: The role of long-term orientation and perceived value. *Cogent Business and Management, 8*(1). https://doi.org/10.1080/23311975.2021.1899468

[107] Valmohammadi, C. (2016). Examining the perception of Iranian organizations on Internet of Things solutions and applications. *Industrial and Commercial Training, 48*(2), 104–108. https://doi.org/10.1108/ICT-07-2015-0045

[108] van der Heijden, H., & Verhagen, T. (2004). Online store image: conceptual foundations and empirical measurement. *Information & Management, 41*(5), 609–617. https://doi.org/https://doi.org/10.1016/j.im.2003.07.001

[109] Venkatesh, V, Thong, J. Y. L., & Xu, X. (2012). Consumer Acceptance and Use of Information Technology: Extending the Unified Theory of Acceptance and Use of Technology. *Behavioural Marketing EJournal*.

[110] Venkatesh, Viswanath, & Bala, H. (2008). Technology acceptance model 3 and a research agenda on interventions. *Decision Sciences, 39*(2). https://doi.org/10.1111/j.1540-5915.2008.00192.x

[111] Venkatesh, Viswanath, & Davis, F. D. (2000). A Theoretical Extension of the Technology Acceptance Model: Four Longitudinal Field Studies. *Management Science, 46*(2), 186–204. https://doi.org/10.1287/mnsc.46.2.186.11926

[112] Venkatesh, Viswanath, Morris, M. G., Davis, G. B., & Davis, F. D. (2003a). User acceptance of information technology: Toward a unified view. *MIS Quarterly: Management Information Systems, 27*(3). https://doi.org/10.2307/30036540

[113] Venkatesh, Viswanath, Morris, M. G., Davis, G. B., & Davis, F. D. (2003b). Venkatesh et al (2003) User acceptance of information technology (1). *MIS Quarterly, 27*(3).

[114] Vera-Martínez, J. (2021). Consumer technology brands and the source of their performance. *Cogent Business and Management, 8*(1). https://doi.org/10.1080/23311975.2021.1969632

[115] Westaby, J. D. (2005). Comparing attribute importance and reason methods for understanding behaviour: An application to internet job searching. *Applied Psychology, 54*(4). https://doi.org/10.1111/j.1464-0597.2005.00231.x

[116] *What is Apple's iBeacon? | Apple | The Guardian*. (2014). https://www.theguardian.com/technology/2014/jan/13/what-is-apple-ibeacon-retail-tracking

[117] Wibisurya, I. (2018). The Effect of Digital Marketing Implementation through Location Based Advertising on Customer's Purchase Intention. *Binus Business Review, 9*(2). https://doi.org/10.21512/bbr.v9i2.4618

[118] Wu, H. Te, & Tsai, C. W. (2018). A home security system for seniors based on the beacon technology. *Concurrency and Computation: Practice and Experience, 30*(15). https://doi.org/10.1002/cpe.4496

[119] Yildirim, H., & Ali-Eldin, A. M. T. (2019). A model for predicting user intention to use wearable IoT devices at the workplace. *Journal of King Saud University - Computer and Information Sciences, 31*(4), 497–505. https://doi.org/https://doi.org/10.1016/j.jksuci.2018.03.001

[120] Yoon, C., & Lim, D. (2020). An empirical study on factors affecting customers' acceptance of internet-only banks in Korea. *Cogent Business and Management, 7*(1). https://doi.org/10.1080/23311975.2020.1792259

[121] Yu, Z., Song, L., Jiang, L., & Khold Sharafi, O. (2022). Systematic literature review on the security challenges of blockchain in IoT-based smart cities. In *Kybernetes* (Vol. 51, Issue 1). https://doi.org/10.1108/K-07-2020-0449

[122] Yun, H., Han, D., & Lee, C. C. (2013). Understanding the use of location-based service applications: Do privacy concerns matter? *Journal of Electronic Commerce Research, 14*(3).

[123] Zhang, J., & Mao, E. (2008). Understanding the acceptance of mobile SMS advertising among young Chinese consumers. *Psychology & Marketing, 25*(8), 787–805. https://doi.org/https://doi.org/10.1002/mar.20239

[124] Zhong, Q., Liang, S., Cui, L., Chan, H. K., & Qiu, Y. (2019). Using online reviews to explore consumer purchasing behaviour in different cultural settings. *Kybernetes, 48*(6). https://doi.org/10.1108/K-03-2018-0117

[125] Zikmund, W. G., Babin, B. J., Carr, J. C., & Griffin, M. (2013). Business research methods. Cengage Learning. In *Business Research Methods* (Vol. 3, Issue 1).

Interdisciplinary Approaches of Marketing to Sustain in the Imminent Market of Solar Renewable Green Energy

Shalaka Patil[1] and Dr Shabana Memon[2]

[1]*Research Scholar, Bharati Vidyapeeth, Institute of Management, Kolhapur, Maharashtra, India*

[2]*Professor, Bharati Vidyapeeth, Institute of management, Kolhapur, Maharashtra, India*

E-mail: shalakapatil87@gmail.com; shabana.memon@bharatividyapeeth.edu

Abstract

Conventional energy sources are reducing day by day. Since this is causing environmental and health issues, the use of natural resources is growing rapidly since the past few years. This shift towards sustainable natural sources is important. Natural sources like solar energy, wind and biomass can be used to generate energy. Small and medium-sized enterprises are taking up this business but some of them fail in the long run. In this research, we concentrate on solar energy, its current status, and marketing and business practices to sustain in renewable market.

Keywords: *Renewable Energy, Barriers, Sustainable Business Practices, ICT, Marketing Strategies*

Introduction

Renewable sources are easily available and can be used to produce energy. The use of sustainable products is good for environment, good for health, cheaper to run, alternative to exhaustive sources of energy and provide more control to own energy. This report will focus on detailed literature review to find out the available energy sources, status of solar renewable energy, barriers to solar sector, and marketing strategies for a long life of business in renewable market.

The oil crisis of the year 1970 forced the world to find a replacement for conventional energy sources and started focusing on renewable energy sources. In the Indian economy, renewable energy sector growth boost up in the year 1991[38].

Solar energy depends upon the sun. In India, the use of solar energy is increasing since the past few years. India had installed 101.53 GW solar capacity as on September 2021, which contributes to ~38 per cent of total capacity. India has an upcoming future plan and we are looking forward to about 450 GW of renewable energy in which solar energy is expected to contribute 280 GW—over 60 per cent of total energy by 2030[15].

Review of Literature and Research Methodology

To understand the status and marketing strategies in solar renewable field, primary and secondary data collection methods were used. The following steps were used in the research:

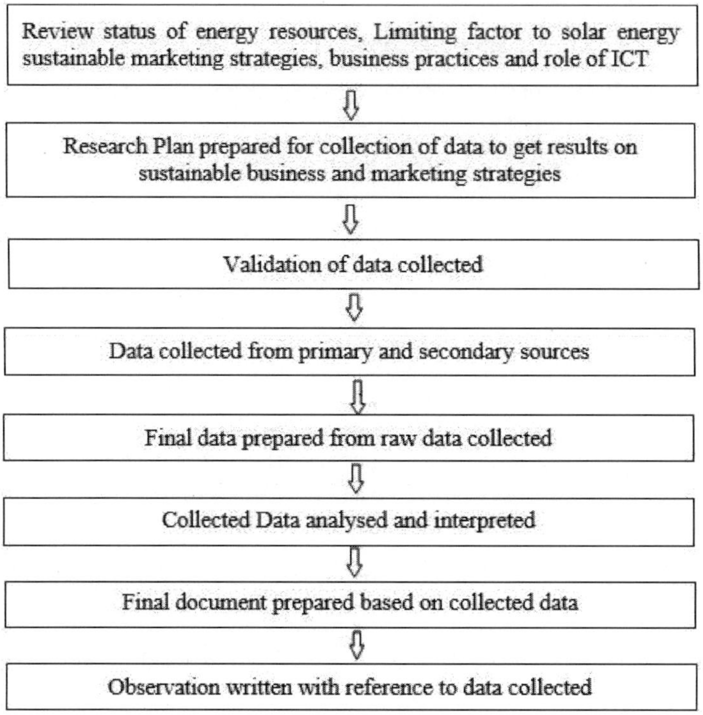

Fig. 1: Step by Step Research Flow Chart
Source: Author's Creation

In primary data collection method, questionaries on solar renewable field focusing on customer, government policy, financial aspects and installer are prepared. Feedback from various solar installer for sustainable business in market contribute to research as shown in Fig. 2.

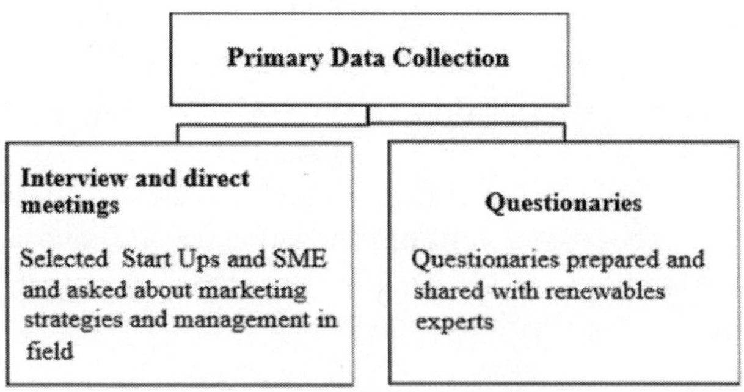

Fig. 2: Primary Data Collection Methods
Source: Author's Creation

Secondary data considered as published data on government websites, reports, related research studies in various journals and opinion of renewable field expert as shown in Fig. 3.

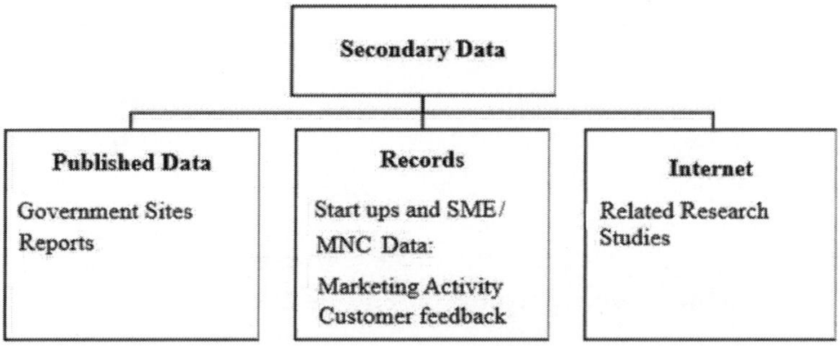

Fig. 3: Secondary Data Collection Methods
Source: Author's Creation

Result and Discussion

Types of Energy Sources

Available energy sources can be classified into commercial and non-commercial energy sources. Non-commercial energy sources usually are not sold in the market which include fuel as logs, cattle dung, woods, agriculture residues.

Commercial energy sources are sold in the market and used to produced energy in mass. Commercial sources include coal, natural gas and electricity. Fig.4 shows the available energy source.

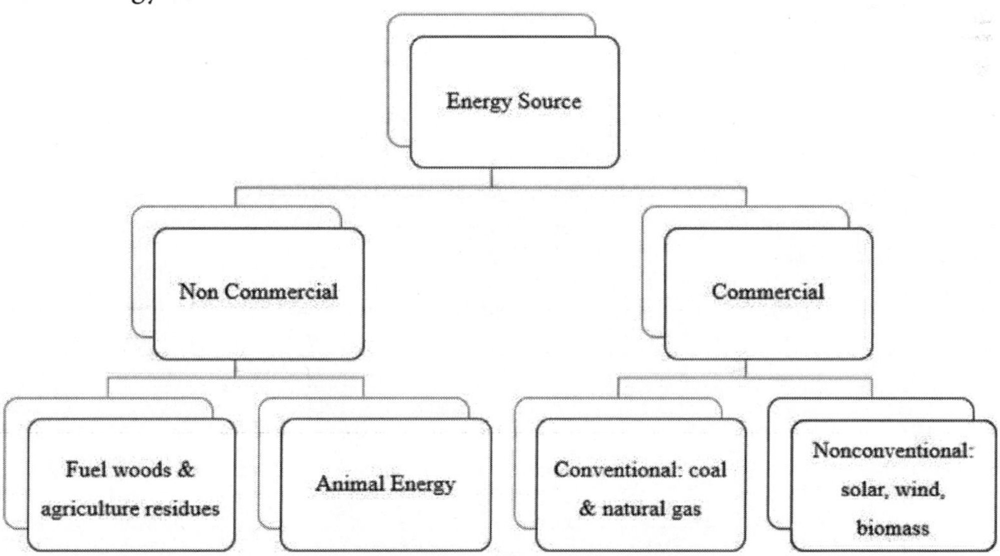

Fig. 4: Energy Sources [55]
Source: The energy source is an important parameter for discussion about methanol production from renewable sources, https://www.sciencedirect.com/topics/engineering/energy-source

Coal, oil and natural gas can be sustained for a few years. Using wood and agriculture residue as energy source will affect the environment, so it is important to move towards sustainable sources of energy.

Non-renewable sources are not only creating harm for the environment but are also affecting the health of human beings. Major negative impact to environment include rise in temperature and acid rain. Air pollutants cause asthma, allergies and lung disease.

Non-conventional energy sources are easily available in nature and they are found in abundance. These include solar, wind and hydro energy. Renewable energy sources do not cause harm to environment or humans, and contribute to minimise greenhouse gases. Renewable energy sources are environment friendly whereas conventional energy sources cause harm to both the environment and humans.

Overview of Energy Consumption in India

India is focusing on the renewable energy expansion programme. Table 1 represents the energy produce from various sources like thermal, nuclear and hydropower. We can see shares of renewable energy have increased tremendously from the year 2002. There is an expectation of 35 per cent share in upcoming years[21, 22]. As the share of renewable energy has grown exponentially, renewable energy sources have a bright future in the coming years.

Table 1: Shares of Renewable Sources [38]

Sources (GW)	*2002*	*2007*	*2012*	*2017*	*2022*	*2027*	*2032*
Thermal	74.4	86.0	131.6	218.3	296.1	389.3	552.4
Renewable	3.4	10.2	24.9	57.3	175.0	250.4	350.4
Nuclear	2.7	3.9	4.7	6.78	11.84	19.10	23.30
Large Hydropower	26.20	34.60	38.90	44.48	60.90	67.10	74.60
Total	106.7	134.7	200.1	326.86	543.84	725.9	100.7
% of renewable energy shares in the total installed capacity	3%	8%	12%	18%	32%	34%	35%

Source: Renewable energy, Indian brand equity foundation (2018). Available at https://www.ibef.org/download/renewable-energy-dec-2018.pdf. Accessed 05 Jan 2019.

Table 2: Shares of Solar and Non-Solar Sources [38]

FY-April-March	*Solar*	*Non-Solar*	*Total*
FY 2016-17	2.75%	8.75%	11.50%
FY 2017-18	9.50%	4.75%	14.25%
FY 2018-19	10.25%	6.75%	17.00%
FY 2019-20	10.25%	7.25%	17.50%
FY 2020-21	10.25%	8.75%	19.00%
FY 2021-22	10.50%	10.50%	21.00%

Source: Renewable energy, Indian brand equity foundation (2018). Available at https://www.ibef.org/download/renewable-energy-dec-2018.pdf. Accessed 05 Jan 2019.

Table 2 shows the share of solar and non-solar energy. If we look from the year 2016 onwards, the percentage of solar energy has increased from 2.75 per cent to 10.50 per cent. Dependence on solar energy is increasing year by year.

So, we can say there is huge scope in the renewable field in terms of opportunities, innovation, economic growth and employment.

A. Limiting Factor to Solar Residential Sector

Based on the analysis of selected publications and study of various published paper, some of the barriers to solar renewable field are listed in Fig. 5.

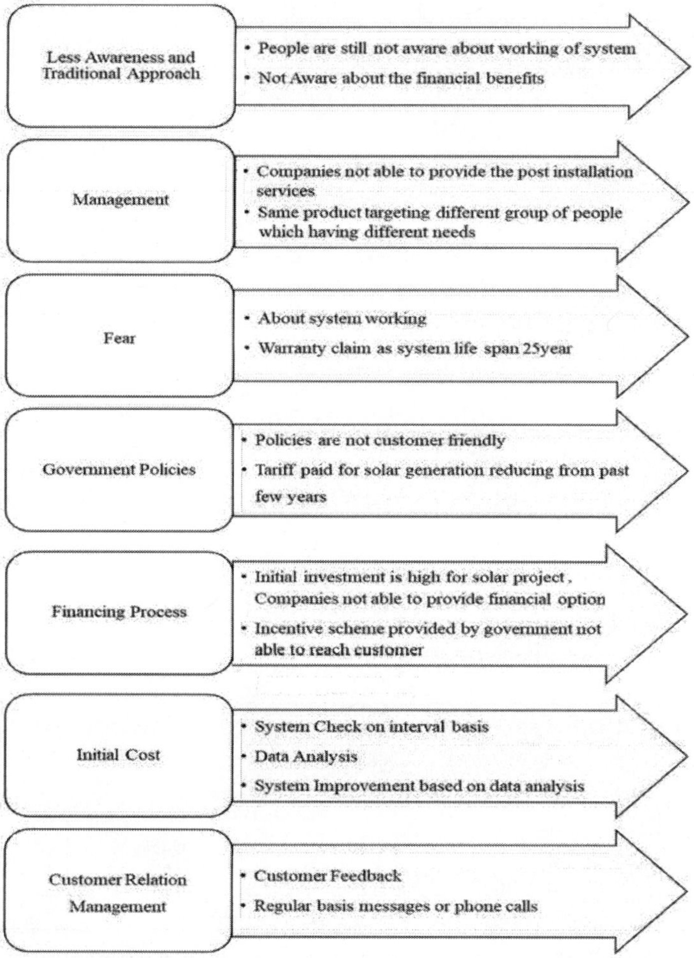

Fig. 5: Limiting Factors to Adoption of Solar Energy

Source: Author's Creation based on The Concept of Multiple Impacts of Renewable Energy Sources: A Critical Review. Article Published: 29 May 2021, MDPI, *Factors Influencing Households' Intention to Adopt Solar PV: A Systematic Review*, J.I. Kantola et al. (Eds.): AHFE 2020, AISC 1209, pp. 282–289, 2020 and an assessment of public awareness Article in *International Journal of Ambient Energy*, July 2010. DOI: 10.1080/01430750.2010.9675112

B. Ways to Improve Perspective towards Solar Green Energy

Creating Awareness

Many people are still not aware about the advantages of solar energy, and it is important to make them aware about it over use of conventional sources in order to change the perspective of people towards going green. Advertisements through multimedia like radio and TV, pamphlets, seminars, meetings with stakeholders etc. will play a key role in this [26],[40].

Different Plan and Product

Different strategies are required to be used while targeting rural and urban customers. These require wide range of solutions with best quality while targeting the different economic groups [27].

Government Policies

Government customer-centric policies are important for the bright future of solar renewable energy [40]. Most of the times, policies and subsidies are not able to reach the customer, so government should encourage people for going green using the easiest way. Online facilities where the customers can see the status of their applications is a simple way to do so.

Providing various Financial Options of Payment

Companies should provide the part payment option or can tie up with banks to provide low interest loan to their customer [41]. In cases of new construction, banks should give concession on interest for those who use renewable energy sources.

Sustainable Business and Marketing Practices in Solar Renewable Energy

The questionnaires on the business and strategies prepared and shared among the EPC installer feedback received from 60 people is seen below. For question number 11, more than 97 per cent installers responded that solar energy will increase in the next 10 years.

Table 3

	Question	*Feedback Received in %*				
1	Which of the following strategy will increase the solar business?	Creating Awareness	Government Policy	Marketing	All	Not Sure
		18.4%	10.5%	5.3%	65.8%	0.0%
2	How will you rate the inventory and supply chain management as the key factor in sustainable business practices?	Very Important	Important	Fairly Important	Slightly Important	Not Important
		63.90%	25%	8.30%	0%	2.80%
3	On a scale of 1-5, how much are policies and incentives important to boost solar installations?	Very Important	Important	Fairly Important	Slightly Important	Not Important
		45.90%	43.20%	43.20%	0%	1.60%

	Question	*Feedback Received in %*				
4	On a scale of 1-5, how much would you rate the monitoring of installed system as sustainable business practice?	Very Important	Important	Fairly Important	Slightly Important	Not Important
		35.1%	51.4%	10.8%	0.0%	2.7%
5	On a scale of 1-5, how much would you rate the digital marketing and online purchase as sustainable business practice?	Very Important	Important	Fairly Important	Slightly Important	Not Important
		41.7%	38.9%	16.7%	2.7%	0.0%
6	On a scale of 1-5, how much would you rate diversification in solar business is important for the bright future of the company?	Very Important	Important	Fairly Important	Slightly Important	Not Important
		47.2%	41.7%	8.3%	0.0%	2.8%
7	What would be the return on investment of solar project?	1 to 3Year	4-6 Year	7-9 Year	10Year	>10 Year
		48.6%	32.4%	9.1%	7.8%	2.1%
8	Do you believe sustainable business strategies have a marketing advantage in renewable sector?	Yes	No	Other		
		83.8%	13.5%	2.7%		
9	What do you feel is the main barrier for not using renewable energy to meet some of their demands today?	Initial Cost	Time	Maintenance	Availability and Ease	Traditional Sources
		52.6%	8.3%	10.5%	23.7%	4.9%
10	Do you agree renewable market will expand over the next decade?	Yes	No			
		97.3%	2.7%			

Fig. 6: Sustainable Business Practices

Source: Author's creation based on Clean Energy Group and Smart Power August 2009 Smart Solar Marketing Strategies cleanegroup.org/wp-content/uploads/Smart-Solar-Marketing-Strategies and Article Web FX 5 Proven Strategies for Solar Marketing https://www.webfx.com/industries/home-repair/solar/

Based on questionnaires, feedback and the literature review of the selected paper, following are the sustainable business practices used in the solar energy market as shown in Fig. 6.

Marketing Strategies

Awareness of customer about residential and commercial projects creates the main barrier to renewable market growth, so it is important to understand their view to prepare the marketing plan to attract the customer [47].

While launching a new or existing solar service, it is useful to think about how all its elements will reinforce each other and can lead to success. The classic four Ps of marketing–product, place, price and promotion—should be used.

Digital Resources

As the use of digital marketing and social media is increasing, providing right information at the right time to the right customer helps to attract the customer towards green purchase. The internet helps companies interact with customers directly or indirectly regarding their product and services, and how they are unique and better than the available services.

Search Engine Optimisation (SEO)

There are searches on solar installation provider near me etc... to get notice it is required to optimize site for search engine [48].

Content Marketing

The content is important as it creates trust about the service or product in the customer's mind. [48][49].

Social Media Marketing

Social media can be used to reach large number of people at a time. It includes the sharing of product and service offering information on Facebook, Twitter, LinkedIn and WhatsApp. [48][50].

Online Sale

Sites such as Amazon, India Mart, etc., where companies can register and do online sales of solar energy equipment or the whole system are also useful.

Inventory and Supply Chain Management

Solar industry is innovative, disruptive industry and facing the unpredictable demand. Since price fluctuations are very common in the industry, inventory management is very important.

Major solar inventory includes solar panel, inverter, batteries, cables, connectors, solar panel mounting structure, tools, etc. Figure 7 shows the key factors needed for inventory management.

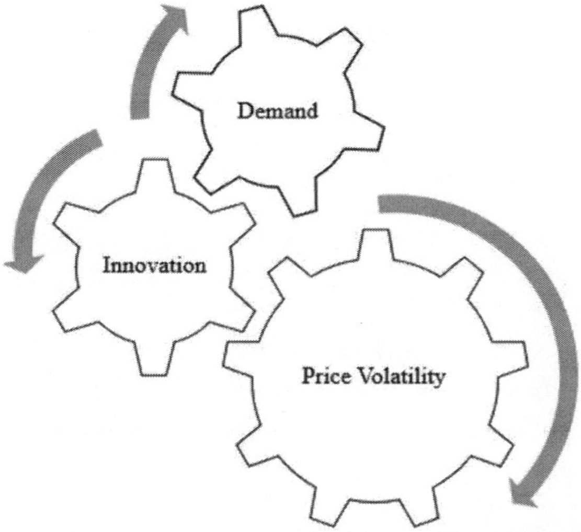

Fig. 7: Key Factors of the Inventory Management [51]
Source: Authors creation based on Article Solar Inventory, Oct 26, 21
https://amplifyxl.com/solar-inventory/

Demand

It's not easy to predict the demand in the competitive solar market. However, companies can use previous sales patterns to understand the inventory requirement.

Price Fluctuations

The cost of solar technology has been declining for the past few years. There is notable price change as well improvement in case of panel wattage and efficiency over the years. Keeping inventory for a long span is risk to business. In case there is a fall in price, it will lead to loss for the company. It is important to create inventory predicting future demands and price changes [51].

Innovation

Innovation improves the solar modules in terms of efficiency and panel wattage which helps to bring the prices down. In solar inverter technology, string inverter, micro-inverter and optimiser are available in the market. Innovation can also affect inventory storage [51].

Supply chain Management

Supply chain management is also a key feature in solar installation as it helps to complete the projects on time and save on the installation cost [53].

Figure 8 shows the typical supply chain of the solar power plant installation system.

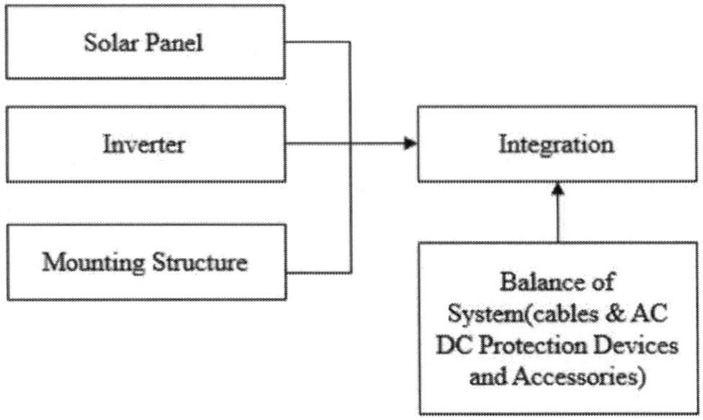

Fig. 8: Framework of Solar Energy Supply Chain
Source: Author's Creation

Diversification

Diversification is one of the key factors to sustain the business in the long run. Diversification includes entering a new market or starting business related to core business while doing the core business. Diversification also includes creating the new product line or service. Diversification helps business by providing another source of the revenue in case original market stops growing or is hit by heavy competition. Diversification helps to boost market share, increase customer loyalty, minimise risk, improve the visibility and credibility [54].

E.g. Polycab is one of the leading companies whose core business is cables. However, they have diversified their business to solar inverter and EPC of solar power plant. Like many small businesses whose core business is EPC of solar power plant, they have also diversified their business in trading of solar panel, solar inverter and other require bill of the material.

One Step Solution

When the customer reaches out to a company, they should be able to supply all the solutions to them which include quotations, procurement, installation, government interaction and after installation operation and maintenance of the solar power plant.

Monitoring, Analysing and Customer Relation Management

Monitoring of the projects during ongoing installation and upon completions is very important. It helps to understand the strength, weakness, threat and opportunity of the companies which are at work and can be improved in the future.

All energy industry businesses are operated on repetitive business service routines. As CRM builds the customer base, energy industry business revenues and profits experience unprecedented growth. It is important that all communication with customers and potential customers can be controlled to ensure quality of service. Messages and phone calls at regular intervals, checking the installed system, and regular updates of the products and service offering to the customer helps to maintain customer relations.

Information Technology in Marketing

Information technology helps to gather the daily power generation data of solar installation, which helps to analysis the system remotely. In case of non-working of one of the components or faults in the system, it can be detected easily which increases the efficiency of the system [44,45]. One can easily give on off command to the system with the help of ICT.

Generation data can be used as base data for other customers which will increase the customer liability and create trust in the customer's mind.

There are software available which help to calculate the solar plant capacity and estimate other major bill components require in the installation like cables, conduit, etc. Solar power plant generation can be predicted with the help of various software available.

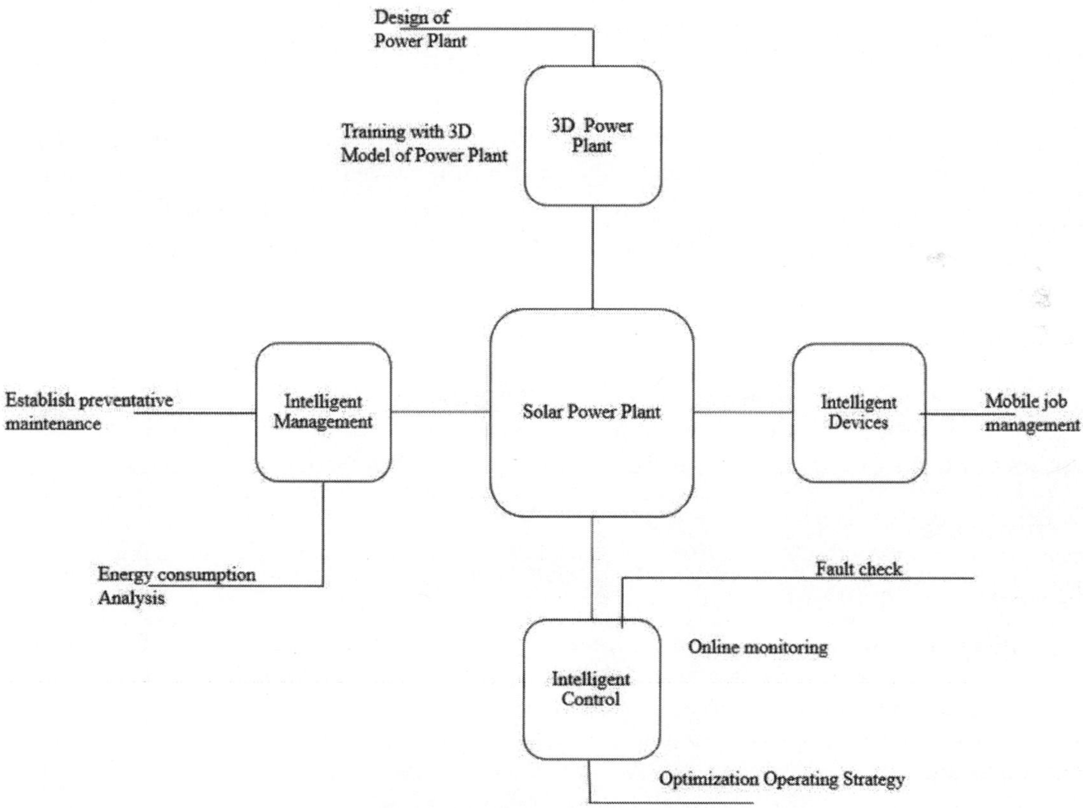

Fig. 9: Functions-ICT [46]

Source: Authors creation based on the Yongping Yang, Chengzhou Li, Zhiping Yang Progress and prospects of innovative coal-fired power plants within the energy internet page No 174.

Conclusions

There is not much awareness in society towards going green. Customer centric government policies and marketing strategies will help to change the perspective of people towards it.

For the long run, it is important that the companies adapt to sustainable marketing and business practices which focus on marketing strategies, inventory and supply chain management, business diversifications, use of the social media and maintaining customer relations.

Diversification strategy minimises the risk of business, as even if one of the businesses is not working to a satisfactory level, revenue can still be generated through other business branches. Inventory management improves the demand planning, cash flow, support distributed storage and helps with labour scheduling. Supply chain management helps to boost customer services, reduce operating costs and improves the financial position of the company. Social media like Facebook, WhatsApp, other networking sites help to reach the right customer at the right time. Word of mouth can either help or hurt the brand, depending upon the experience that each customer has had. Therefore, positive customer relations is very important to the business. Use of online sales, digital resources, social media marketing, and information seminars will help to reach the target customer.

Information technology helps in pre and post installation of power plants. It also helps in solar power plant capacity calculation as well as system design. System generation can be monitored remotely with the help of ICT; system faults can be removed on priority basis which reduce the maintenance time and increase the working efficiency of the system.

Acknowledgment

We are thankful to the Management Development Institute, Murshidabad, India, for giving us the opportunity to present this paper. We would like to appreciate other authors and the publishers for the publication of these knowledgeable papers.

References

[1] Heather P. Bedi. *Lead the district into the light: Solar energy infrastructure injustices in Kerala, India.*

[2] Raj Vikram Madurai Elavarasan, Leoponraj Selvamanohar, Kannadasan Raju, Raghavendra Rajan Vijayaraghavan, Ramkumar Subburaj, *Holistic Review of the Present and Future Drivers of the Renewable Energy Mix in Maharashtra, State of India.*

[3] Report by IREF Addressing Barriers to Scaling Up Renewable Energy Through Industry Involvement

[4] Suprava Chakraborty, Pradip Kumar Sadhu, Utpal Goswami. *Barriers in the Advancement of Solar Energy in Developing Countries like India* Problems of Sustainable Development 2016, vol. 11, no. 2, 75–80.

[5] Discussion by Infrastructure Development Finance Company Ltd. *Barriers to development of renewable energy in India & proposed recommendations.*

[6] Shreemat Pandey, Vijai Shanker Singh, Naresh Pal Gangwar, M.M. Vijayvergia, Chandra Prakash, Deep Narayan Pandey. Determinants of success for promoting solar energy in Rajasthan, India doi: 10.1016/j.rser.2012.03.012

[7] Hooman Peimani. *Financial Barriers to Development of Renewable and Green Energy Projects in Asia.*

[8] Elisa Asmelash and Gayathri Prakash. *Future of Solar Photovoltaic Deployment, investment, technology, grid integration and socio-economic aspects.*

[9] Shuaib Kamili, under the guidance of Ashish Kulkarni and Yuvaraj Dinesh Babu Nithyanandam. *Identifying barriers for rooftop solar uptake in MSMEs and development of a mitigating financial framework.*

[10] Report by *Esmap Report on Barriers for Solar Power Development in India 2010.* South Asia Energy Unit Sustainable Development Department the World.

[11] Batzelis, Efstratios, Zakir Hussain Rather, John Barton, Bonu Ramesh Naidu, Billy Wu, Firdous Ul Nazir, Onyema Sunday Nduka, et al. 2021. *Solar Integration in the UK and India: Technical Barriers and Future Directions.* Loughborough University. https://doi.org/10.17028/rd.lboro.14453133.v1

[12] Radhey Shyam Meena, Deepa Sharma, Ritam Rathore. *The Most Promising Solar Hot Spots in India Development and Policy: The Thar Desert of Rajasthan.*

[13] Rahul Choudhary, Pradip Kumar Sadhu, Suprava Chakraborty. *Eminent Economic Policies & Dominant Barriers of Solar Energy in India* IJERTV3IS031521

[14] Seetharaman, Krishna Moorthy, Nitin Patwa, Saravanan, Yash Gupta. *Breaking barriers in deployment of renewable energy.*

[15] *Indian Renewable Energy Industry Report.*

[16] Aashish Jaiswal, Garima Sikka. *Future Scope and Potential of Solar Energy in India* an Overview ISSN: 2319-6386, Vol.-4 Issue-10, April 2017.

[17] Ashok Upadhyay, Arnab Chowdhury. *Solar Energy Fundamentals and Challenges in Indian restructured power sector International Journal of Scientific and Research Publications,* Vol. 4, Issue 10, October 2014 1 ISSN 2250-3153

[18] *Different Financing Models for Solar Roof Top Projects Indigo Solar Article.*

[19] Yatish Joshi and Zillur Rahman. Factors Affecting *Green Purchase Behaviour and Future Research Directions* doi.org/10.1016/j.ism.2015.04.001 Volume 3, Issues 1–2, June–December 2015, pp. 128-143.

[20] Md. Masood Ahmad, Amit Kumar and Raushan Ranjan. *Current Trends in Renewable Energy: An Overview,* E-ISSN: 2454-6135, Volume 4, Issue 5 May 2018.

[21] How embracing renewable energy can help India achieve its target of becoming a $5 trillion economy by 2024-25 Sections Article the *Economic Times,* 30 Nov. 2021.

[22] Michaela Makešová and Michaela Valentová. *The Concept of Multiple Impacts of Renewable Energy Sources: A Critical Review* Article Published: 29 May 2021 MDPI.

[23] Kawaljeet Kaur Kapoor. *Sustainable Consumption from the Consumer's Perspective: Antecedents of Solar Innovation Adoption* com/science/article/pii/S0959378018301894

[24] Atul Sharma. *A comprehensive study of solar power in India and world* 1364-0321/$ – see front matter © 2011 Elsevier Ltd. All rights reserved. doi: 10.1016/j.rser.2010.12.017

[25] Shah Rukh Shakeel and Arto Rajala. *Factors Influencing Households' Intention to Adopt Solar PV: A Systematic Review* J. I. Kantola et al. (Eds.): AHFE 2020, AISC 1209, pp. 282–89, 2020.

[26] *Renewable energy: An assessment of public awareness Article* in *International Journal of Ambient Energy*. July 2010 DOI: 10.1080/01430750.2010.9675112

[27] Ramiar Sadegh-Vaziri. *Entrepreneurship and Innovation in Energy and Environmental Technologies; Barriers and Opportunities Master of Science* Thesis Stockholm, Sweden 2013.

[28] Klaus Topfer, Tim Wirth *Entrepreneurship and Innovation in Energy and Environment,* ISBN: 92-807-2163-I

[29] Ramana Nanda (HBS), Ken Younge (Purdue) and Lee Fleming. (UC Berkeley) *Innovation and Entrepreneurship in Renewable Energy.* This chapter was prepared for an NBER conference volume, The Changing Frontier: Rethinking Science and Innovation Policy.

[30] Sahar Cheraghi, Shahla Choobchain, Enayat Abbasi. *Investigation of Entrepreneurship Development Barriers in the Field of Renewable Energies Technologies in Developing Countries: A Case of Iran*, ISSN 2277–8616.

[31] Charles Rajesh Kumar. J and M.A. Majid. *Renewable energy for sustainable development in India: current status, future prospects, challenges, employment, and investment opportunities* doi.org/10.1186/s13705-019-0232-1

[32] Adam Sulich, Adam Grudziński. *The Analysis of Strategy Types of the Renewable Energy Sector Acta Universitatis Agriculture Et Silviculture Mendelianae Brunensis*, Vol. 67(146), No. 6, 2019. Accepted: 6. 9. 2019.

[33] Renewable Energy *Strategy to promote an enhanced investment climate for renewable energy technologies for submission to national and regional authorities in participating CIS countries* Article UNECE.

[34] Christian Schlenker, Senior Consultant, Tefen Germany. *Go-to-Market Strategies for Renewable Energy Market* Article on Tefen.

[35] Sumant Sinha. ReNew *Power A 5-point plan to maximize India's renewable energy potential.* Article on World Economic Forum.

[36] Indrajith P. *A Study on Customer's Satisfaction on Solar Energy Products with Special Reference to Coimbatore City*, ISSN: 2455–7838.

[37] Liping Ding, Yin Shi, Qiyao Dai, Zumeng Zhangjiajie Li, Ling Zhou. *Does Beneficiaries' Satisfaction Enhance Their Trust in State Grid for Solar PV Adoption? – An Evidence from PAPs in Rural China*, doi.org/10.21203/rs.3.rs-364467/v1, April 19th, 2021.

[38] Charles Rajesh Kumar J. and M.A. Majid. *Renewable energy for sustainable development in India: current status, future prospects, challenges, employment, and investment opportunities,* doi.org/10.1186/s13705-019-0232-1

[39] Emrah Karakaya, Pranpreya Sriwannawit. *Barriers to the adoption of photovoltaic systems: The state-of-the-art*, http://dx.doi.org/10.1016/j.rser.2015.04.0581364-0321/& 2015

[40] Olayinka S. Ohunakin, Muyiwa S. Adaramola, Olanrewaju. M. Oyewola, Richard O. Fagbenle *Solar energy applications and development in Nigeria: Drivers and barriers*

[41] Renewable energy for sustainable development in India: *current status, future prospects, challenges, employment, and investment.*

[42] *The Role of ICT In Energy Efficiency Management Household Sector* | 2018-World Energy Council.

[43] Faran Ahmed, Muhammad Naeem, Muhammad Iqbal. *ICT and renewable energy: a way forward to the next generation telecom base stations.*

[44] Isha M. Shirbhate, Sunita S. Barve. Solar panel monitoring and energy prediction for smart solar system Vol. 8, No. 2, June 2019, pp. 136~142 ISSN: 2252-8814, DOI: 10.11591/ijaas. v8. i2., pp. 136-14.

[45] Tanuja Ganu, Mayuri Ejgar, Bashirahamad Momin. *Intelligent Monitoring and Maintenance of Solar Plants using Real-time Data Analysis*

[46] Yongping Yang, Chengzhou Li, Zhiping Yang. *Progress and prospects of innovative coal-fired power plants within the energy internet*

[47] Clean Energy Group and Smart Power August 2009 *Smart Solar Marketing Strategies* cleanegroup.org/wp-content/uploads/Smart-Solar-Marketing-Strategies.pdf

[48] Article Web FX *5 Proven Strategies for Solar Marketing* https://www.webfx.com/industries/home-repair/solar/

[49] Kalpana Ambepitiya. Research Gate December 2015 Strategies to Promote Solar Power Energy: A Review of Literature https://www.researchgate.net/profile/Kalpana-Ambepitiya

[50] Vardhan V, P. Raja, Kabirdoss Devi. *International Journal of Innovative Technology and Exploring Engineering* (*IJITEE*), ISSN: 2278-3075, Volume-8, Issue-11S, September 2019 social media as the Next Trend in Social Business Marketing social media as the Next Trend in Solar Business Marketing https://www.ijitee.org/wp-content/uploads/papers/v8i11S/K113309811S19.pdf

[51] *Article Amplify XL October 2021 Solar Inventory* https://amplifyxl.com/solar-inventory/

[52] Article NREL February 2021 *Documenting a Decade of Cost Declines for PV Systems* https://www.nrel.gov/news/program/2021/documenting-a-decade-of-cost-declines-for-pv-systems.html

[53] FICCI Subgroup on Securing Solar Supply Chain FICCI Solar Energy Task Force Report on Securing the Supply Chain for Solar in India https://ficci.in/spdocument/20294/Supply-Chain-paper.pdf

[54] Article Fraser Sherman Updated April 19, 2022 Diversification and its importance https://smallbusiness.chron.com/diversification-its-importance-77562.html

[55] Ibrahim Dincer, Azzam Abu-Rayash. The energy source is an important parameter for discussion about methanol production from renewable sources Science Direct Topics 11/30/21,

[56] Charles Rajesh Kumar. J and M. A. Majid. Renewable energy for *sustainable development in India: current status, future prospects, challenges, employment, and investment opportunities* doi.org/10.1186/s13705-019-0232-1

What Determines the Purchase of Superfoods? An Empirical Assessment of Indian Consumers

Shahbaz Indu[1], Dr Rashi Taggar[2] and Sunanda Kumari[1]

[1]Research Scholar, [2]Assistant Professor
School of Business, SMVD University, Kakryal-Katra, UT of J&K, India
E-mail: shahbazindu01@gmail.com; rashi.taggar@smvdu.ac.in; sunandakumari4268@gmail.com

Abstract

Purpose: These days, most diet styles across the world are talking about the inclusion of superfoods in their plans. The purpose of this study is to accentuate the determinants that influence the purchasing behavior of an individual with reference to superfood consumption.

Design/methodology: A researcher-made questionnaire based on the past literature and surveyed through survey administration software (Google Forms) to collect the primary data from different states. Out of 430 collected responses, 365 responses (approx. 85 per cent) were found to be useful for the application of CFA using AMOS 25.0 and other statistical analyses.

Findings: The relative advantage of superfoods acts as a mediator in converting the value determinants to impulsive purchase intention. Buffering effect of the perceived cost and health consciousness of the consumers were also studied.

Implications: Marketing practitioners may devise their positioning strategies accordingly. The values of superfoods along with other stimulating facets may help the marketers and the sellers to push the superfoods and pull the consumers.

Originality: Despite being a hot topic across the globe, the essential drivers responsible for the superfood's impulsive purchase remains unexplored. This study furthers the understanding of the healthy dietary habits and lifestyles of modern consumers with special reference to superfoods.

Keywords: *Confirmatory Factor Analysis (CFA), Consumption Values, Health Consciousness, Perceived Cost, Relative Advantage*

Introduction

Many of us today are familiar with one old expression "An apple a day keeps the doctor away.". Though this expression was first coined in the year 1913 in a published article named "Rustic Speech and Folklore", it was originally based on a Pembroke shire proverb that was published in the Notes and Queries magazine in the year 1866. This saying had its roots in the popular belief that adding apples to your daily diet improves your health to a much greater extent (Link, 2020). Though apple has been there for a long time, recently fruits like apples which are rich in nutrients and offer maximum nutritional benefits have been taken under the term "Superfoods". Any person can add these superfoods to their daily healthy dietary habits whenever these foods are available (Ware, 2019). Fruits such as quinoa are generally considered "superfoods of the future" because of their popularity as a functional food and their high environmental adaptability.

According to data from google trends, superfood term has been searched 60 thousand times per month whereas the best superfood term has been searched 12 thousand times per month in recent months. The superfood category in the retail market was also one of the retail categories that saw a huge spike in sales during the COVID-19 outbreak period. The superfood market has emerged as one of the fastest-growing markets which is estimated to reach $5.61 billion by 2024 (Wright, 2020). However, in contrast to the increased interest of the consumer towards superfoods, there has been a dearth of studies that specifically explore the driver for superfood consumption among consumers (Muziri et al., 2020).

Inquiries such as what factors drive the consumer to evaluate the superfood when compared to other food categories have remained unexplored. Such inquiries are important as they can help market practitioners and policymakers in developing sales strategies. This research aims to unravel the fundamental motives behind consumers' superfood consumption and to present a clear vista that why consumers go for the impulsive purchase of products such as superfoods. Impulsive buying means making an unplanned purchase. Impulse buying can be termed as purchasing a product without any actual intention of doing so while in a hypermarket. Impulse purchases can be seen as not-so-consciously planned purchases. The present study takes impulse buying in the context of buying products at a lower price now to save money in the longer run. According to a survey done by Slickdeals, 52 per cent of the US respondents feel that they will take advantage of the lower price and deals than pay extra later. Sales promotions do tend to drive an impulse purchase decision (Keenan, 2021). Apart from being price-conscious, Consumers are becoming conscious of the health benefit of superfoods. Over the past two decades, the theory of consumption values (Sheth et al., 1991) has been widely in use in understanding consumer motivation for product choices across various food categories. In responding and answering to the various research questions proposed in the study, the present research draws upon and makes use of the theory of consumption value about superfood consumption. Further, it looks for the prominent of the various dimensions which motivate the consumer and shapes their perception of the relative advantage of the consumption of superfoods. The prime research gap in the present written literature in terms of the existing theory of food product consumption values was these values usually try to predict consumer purchase intention whereas consumers' other behavioral tendencies remain unexplored. In addition to the purchase intention of consumers, the study has tried to examine which of these earlier discovered consumption values influence impulsive buying behavior among consumers. Accentuating various pre-existing consumption values to predict the various behavioral tendencies among consumers disregards the concept of perceived cost in fashioning the behavior of the consumers, this study also attempts to explore the perceived cost's moderating role in the associated connection between consumers' impulse buying behavior and relative advantage.

Review of Literature

With the increase in awareness and interest in healthy habits, a new market under the food product category has emerged (Lucas et al., 2022). Formal traditional foods have become the food products of high-health luxury in the present age. With their innate quality of being rich in nutrients and healthy compounds, this newly emerged food category is popularising itself by being called 'Superfoods' (Wiedenroth & Otter, 2021). With the absence of any explicit or official criteria as to what should be called a superfood, any food with nutrient-rich quality can be called a superfood without much scientific support (Barsby et al., 2021). Considering the inconclusive scientific evidence about superfoods that they are superior to other alternatives, consumer perception of healthy eating habits has led to their escalated popularity (Oude Groeniger et al., 2017). Superfoods represent the category of those food products which are minimally processed and the production of such foods is expected to be carried with practices that emerged from primordial cultures (Loyer, 2016). While being similar to functional food that boosts immunity in the human body by providing required macro-level and micro-level nutrients, superfoods still differ in some aspects (Jagdale et al., 2021). Recently, with the profusion of various immedicable diseases such as obesity or cancer, the adoption of superfoods in relevant dietary habits has gained significant importance in defending the human body (PROESTOS, 2018).

Consumers' interest and concern towards the environment have risen exponentially during the last decade. There has been increasing demand for clean and healthy nutrient-rich food. This rise in concern by consumers has also been reflected in the food industry as well (Santeramo et al., 2018; Cummins et al., 2019). Marketing philosophy in the ongoing era is value-oriented, whereas the marketing theories unraveling those values from the customer's perspective are much less (Tanrikulu, 2021). Consumer value towards a particular product is derived from a person's interaction with that product as well as past experiences (Turel et al., 2010). Three decades ago, one of the most popular understandings of consumer's perceived value among consumer was suggested. Zeithaml (1988) described 'perceived value' as an overall assessment of the product's utility from the consumer's perspective based on what is given by the customer to obtain that product and what is received in its exchange. These values are crucial for consumers as they influence the consumers for making their preference towards the product and thus make judgments. Perceived values also refer to the differences that consumers evaluate while comparing all the benefits and costs related to that product (Kotler et al., 2020).

The theory of consumption values was developed to describe why consumers model their choice while choosing some particular product or brand over another. It provided an insight into the consumer's motivational cues that lead to consumer's consumption behavior on a large scale (Tanrikulu, 2021). Consumers' preference for any product is a function of multidimensional consumption values. Five dimensions were developed by Sheth et al. (1991) namely functional values, emotional values, social values, epistemic values, and situational values to explain the overall concept of consumption values.

Functional values are the perceived utilities that a consumer derives from any product's functional or physical attributes (Sheth et al., 1991). According to Long and Schiffman (2000), the dimension of functional value is mainly dependent on the internal and native value of any service or product in lieu of any extraneous value. The social value dimension is derived from any individual's association with a particular socioeconomic or ethnic or a specific demographic group (Sheth et al., 1991). While studying values that are expected to drive the behavioral response of consumers towards superfoods, de Regt et al. (2019) explained social values as a part of self-enhancement and presented the prestige of a healthy lifestyle among their social group. Dimension of emotional value can be termed as an aroused feeling or affective state from the use of a product or a service, such as comfort after consuming a healthy meal (Liu et al., 2021).

Regarding superfoods, there has been an increase in curiosity among various different segments of the population (MacGregor et al., 2018). The epistemic value dimension describes itself as the innate capacity of a product to arouse curiosity about the same as well as provide originality and newness. Superfoods have been found to elicit curiosity among consumers and motivate them to experience more while developing a taste for them. In the presence of social or certain physical contingencies, the social or functional value of a product increases or decreases (Tanrikulu, 2021). This gives rise to the conditional value dimension. It is the perceived utility acquired by a consumer in certain situations or conditions (Sheth et al., 1991). Dimension of emotional value has been a crucial factor while understating and designing strategies to improve health. While studying the effect of emotional eating on eating behavior tendencies, Pentikäinen et al. (2018) asserted that emotions can be precursors or even successors of eating.

Relative advantage has been a major determinant in the adoption of a new product and the degree to which the new product is finer and far more superior to the existing one (Relative Advantage, 2018). Relative advantage has been an important characteristic in promoting brand loyalty (Leckie et al., 2017). In many of the studies, relative advantage has been discussed as important and significantly related to the adoption behavior of consumers (Labay & Kinnear, 1981; Venkatraman, 1991).

Superfoods are often seen as natural products. Production techniques and practices followed by primordial communities for producing these superfoods are less impacting on the environment (Loyer & Knight, 2018). Ever-changing customer needs and demands and evolving lifestyles have provoked certain changes in the consumption of food products (Graeff-Hönninger & Khajehei, 2019). The superfood market is customer oriented. Belief in the innumerable health benefits of the consumption of superfood products and comprehension of the nutrient potential of the same has been an essential driver for superfood consumption (Lucas et al., 2021). The health consciousness of consumers influences their preference for organic food over conventional food. This influence is by and large due to the prevalent rate of lifestyle diseases like depression

(Rana & Paul, 2017; Pacho & Batra, 2021). The same is undiscovered for the influence of health consciousness over the preference of superfoods over other conventional food products.

The perceived cost has been an important moderator in several studies while measuring consumer purchases as well as consumption intention for organic food. According to research by (J. Wang et al., 2020), price sensitivity and perceived cost have been found to moderate the relationship between the quality of organic food and consumers' purchase intention. In similar research to study the effect of price and purchase intention of organic food, consumers need more confidence in the product while purchasing a higher priced organic food (Liang, 2016). In research conducted to study the price perception of consumers towards organic food and their continued purchase intention, it was found that consumers with higher incomes are more inclined towards purchasing organic food in the future (Jaidev, 2022). According to research by Hansen (2013), consumers who have prior knowledge about the product they are purchasing are negatively affected by price consciousness. When consumers have prior information about a product, then only price consciousness seems to affect them. Several studies have been conducted over the years studying the perception of consumers towards superfoods and their motivational driver responsible for repurchase or continuous purchase in the future, there has been a dearth of studies exploring the relative advantage of superfood products and the moderating effect of perceived cost of a product towards impulsive buying attitude of the customer.

In recent years, researchers have come up with a lot of factors that consumers take into consideration while making a buying decision. These decisions could be planned or unplanned. It has been further observed by the researchers that unplanned buying also known as impulse buying is in primacy today (Yeboah & Owusu-Prempeh, 2017). Sohn and Ko (2021) were of the view that though all purchases made impulsively can be considered unplanned purchases but all unplanned purchases cannot be considered impulsive purchases. The inability to think of consequences and urging irresistibly into buying the product in front are often the triggers faced by many impulse buyers. Even though being aware of the negative effects of purchases that they are making, their desire to satisfy the most immediate and pressing need never lets them stop (Meena, 2018). Consumers make impulse behavior that is stimulated by unexpected needs. Impulsive buying behavior is most commonly triggered by the emotional desire that leads to a decrease in the cognitive capacity of consumers to evaluate the advantages as well as disadvantages of a product (Burton et al., 2018; Gogoi, 2020).

Research Methodology

Objective

From past research, it is evident that there is a high degree of adaptability of the theory of consumption values about various food products in the practical world. This study thus extends an abducting viewpoint to accentuate the factors amidst various demographic profiles that influence the impulse purchasing behavior of the individual within the particular context of consumption of superfoods.

Conceptual Model and Hypothesis development

Several factors affect our cognitive process of making a selection between complex food choices. To promote the importance of healthy food choices among the general public, determinant factors that affect food choices could aid policymakers to a great extent.

Based on the theoretical background, our conceptual model and the relative hypothesis for the study is generalised.

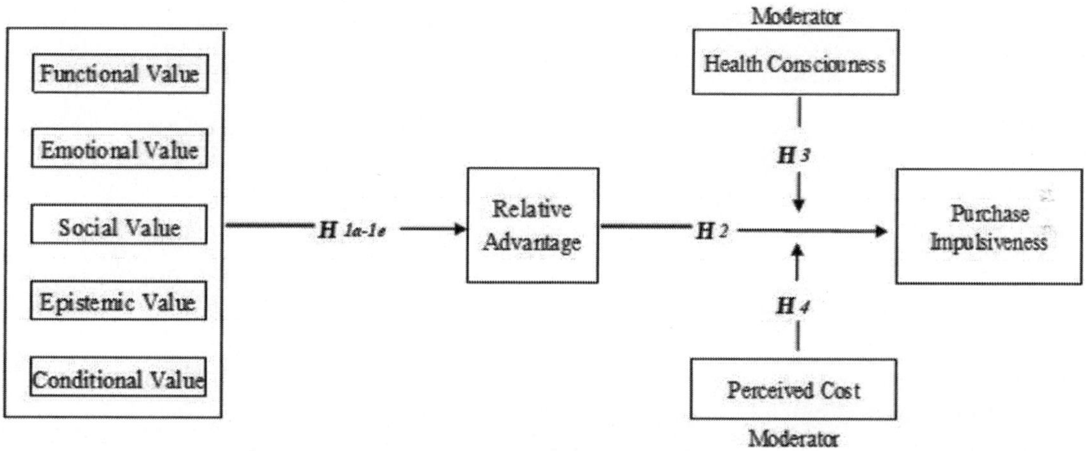

Fig. 1: Research Framework
Source: Author's Compilation

- **H_{1a-1e}**: (a) Functional Value, (b) Conditional Values, (c) Epistemic Value, (d) Social values, (e) Emotional Values positively relate to the relative advantage of superfood products.
- **H_2**: Relative Advantage positively relates to the consumer's impulsive buying behavior of superfood products.
- **H_3**: Perceived cost negatively moderate the influence of relative advantage on impulsive buying behavior of superfood products among consumers.
- **H_4**: Health consciousness positively moderates the influence of relative advantage on impulsive buying behavior of superfood products among consumers.

Sample and Procedures

A researcher-made questionnaire based on the past literature was used and surveyed through administration software such as google forms. The data was the study was collected from individuals who visit grocery stores or food marts or food markets. Snowball sampling technique was used to collect the data and the total sampling size collected for the study was 430. Out of 430 collected samples, 365 (85 per cent) useful samples were used for the study. Response coding was done on a 7-point Likert scale.

For this study, the particular 7-point Likert scale was chosen to increase the likelihood and fair certainty of meeting the objective reality of the empirical world (Joshi et al., 2015).

The demographic profile of the final respondents/participants of the sample is summarised in Table 1. The result of the study also shows a word cloud generated from the names of the entered superfoods that our participants referred to as their most recently consumed superfoods. As shown in Figure 2, ghee, seeds, amla, makhana, oats, turmeric, etc., were the most recent superfood consumed by the participants. Further Table 2 is providing information regarding various items and shows Cronbach's alpha

Table 1: Demographic Profiles of the Respondents

Demographic Range		*Frequency*	*Percentage (%)*
Gender	Male	216	59%
	Female	149	41%
	Other	0	0%
Age	Under 18	3	1%
	18–24	249	68%
	25–31	68	19%
	32–38	12	3%
	39–45	27	7%
	46–52	3	1%
	Above 52	3	1%
Education level	Lower than secondary level	3	1%
	Secondary level	12	3%
	Bachelor's degree	163	45%
	Master's degree	154	42%
	Doctorate degree	33	9%
Marital status	Single, never married	304	83%
	Married	46	13%
	Widowed	0	0%
	Separated	3	1%
	Divorced	5	1%
	Cohabiting with a significant other or in a domestic partnership	7	2%
Annual income	Less than 25000	58	16%
	25001–50000	78	21%
	50000–75000	21	6%
	75000–100000	90	25%
	100000–200000	73	20%
	More than 200000	45	12%

Source: Author's Compilation

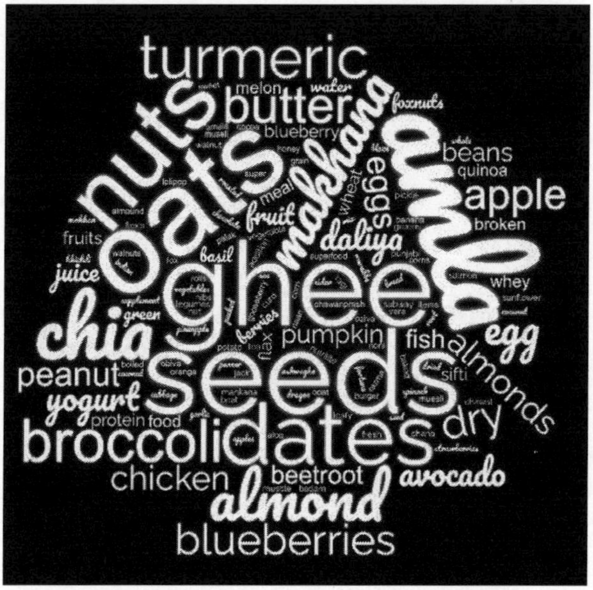

Fig. 2: Word Cloud of Superfoods
Source: Author's Compilation

(α) value for each of the constructs in the study is ranging from 0.717 to 0.922. The range of the α values thereby ensures a high degree of reliability.

Data Analysis and Results: (N = 365)

The designed conceptual model was tested along with the proposed hypothesis using the technique of structural equation modeling (SEM) in Amos version 25.0. Estimation of the significance level of causal relationships between various distinguished constructs was measured for the structural model. The results of the various required values are also shown in Table 2. All of the measured values in Table 3 are meeting the cutoff values required for successful model validation (Bagozzi & Yi, 1988; Brown, 2015). Convergent validity, as well as discriminant validity of the various distinguished constructs, was also measured. Composite reliability and Average variance extracted values were analysed to check the composite reliability (Hair et al., 2013).

Table 2: Results of Confirmatory Factor Analysis

Index	*Value*
X^2/df	1.647
Root mean square error of approximation (RMSEA)	0.055 (*PCLOSE of 0.285*)
Goodness of Fit Index (GFI)	0.922
Comparative Fit Index (CFI)	0.962
Tucker-Lewis Index (TLI)	0.952
Incremental Fit Indices (IFI)	0.962

Source: Author's Compilation

Table 3: Constructs Items with Descriptive Statistics, Factor Loading, Reliability Score and Interclass Correlation

Item	*M*	*SD*	*FL*	*α*	*ICC* 95% CI (Lower, Upper), $p < 0.001$
Functional Consumption Value (Func) (adopted from Sweeney & Soutar, 2001)					
Superfood products have consistent quality	5.12	1.395	0.784	0.84	.840 (0.802, 0.873)
Superfood products are well made	5.18	1.262	0.680		
Superfood products have an acceptable quality standard	5.41	1.191	0.608		
Superfood products perform consistenly	5.18	1.283	0.576		
Emotional Consumption Value (Emon) (adapted from Sweeney & Soutar, 2001)					
Superfood products are the ones I would feel relaxed about using	5.39	0.086	0.65	0.874	.874 (0.844, 0.900)
Having superfood products would make me feel good	5.56	0.081	0.744		
Having superfood products will give me pleasure	5.09	0.089	0.728		
I enjoy consuming superfood products	5.40	0.087	0.670		
Epistemic Consumption Value (Epis) (adopted from Hirschman, 1980)					
Before buying the products, I would acquire a great deal of information about the differences it makes	5.37	0.088	0.619	0.744	0.744 (0.678, 0.799)
I always try to seek out new or novel information about new products	5.31	0.087	0.685		
I like to search for new and innovative product	5.34	0.093	0.662		
Social Consumption Value (Soci) (adapted from Sweeney & Soutar, 2001)					
Consuming superfood products would help me feel more accepted in society	4.12	0.113	0.818	0.922	0.922 (0.903, 0.938)
Consuming superfood products would improve the way I am perceived among others	4.28	0.113	0.820		
Consuming superfood food would make a good impression on other	4.18	0.113	0.778		
Consuming superfood products would provide me with social approval	3.98	0.119	0.840		
Conditional Consumption Value (Cond) (adapted from Rahnama and Rajabpour, 2016)					
I would buy superfoods rather than conventional food products if there will be a subsidy on buying those superfood	4.98	0.105	0.697	0.807	0.807 (0,761, 0.846)
I would buy superfoods if they are available at a discounted price in the market discounted price in the market	5.41	0.093	0.693		

Item	*M*	*SD*	*FL*	*α*	*ICC* 95% CI (Lower, Upper), $p < 0.001$
I would buy superfoods in lieu of conventional food products if they are vvailable in the common market	5.08	0.090	0.612		
I would buy superfood products when there are promotional activities being done for their promotion	6.62	0.104	0.575		
Relative Advantage (Rel) (adopted from Leckie et al., 2017; Müller-Stewens et al., 2017)					
Superfoods surpass other food items in the benefit they provide	5.37	0.086	0.56	0.859	0.859 (0.826, 0.888)
Best dietary styles include superfoods in them	5.31	0.095	0.516		
The quality of superfoods exceeds those of normal foods	5.22	0.096	0.518		
Unique benefits are offered by superfoods	5.34	0.094	0.697		
Health Consciousness (Cons) (adapted from Wang and Yu, 2020)					
I carefully use food products to ensure good health	5.55	0.079	0.73	0.831	0.831 (0.787, 0.867)
I think I am a consumer with health-conscious behaviour	5.24	0.094	0.809		
I often think about health-related issues	5.45	0.084	0.754		
Perceived Cost (Cost) (adapted from Sweeney & Soutar, 2001)					
Superfood products offer back value for the money spent on them	5.19	0.093	0.616	0.717	0.717 (0.643, 0.777)
Superfood products are good products for the price being paid for them	5.1	0.087	3.624		
Buying superfood products will be very economical	4.47	0.099	0.551		
Impulse Purchasing Behaviour (Imp) (adapted from Beatty & Ferrell, 1998; Rook & Fisher, 1995)					
I am the type of person who makes unplanned purchases for my food products	4.67	0.113	0.795	0.85	0.850 (0.815, 0.880)
I feel excited to buy superfoods spontaneously	4.61	0.101	0.636		
I usually go by the saying 'Just Do It'	4.7	0.106	0.754		
'Buy now, think about it' later is the way that describes me	4.09	0.127	0.735		
I buy my food products things according to how I fee at the moment	4.93	0.113	0.707		

Note: M = mean, SD = standard deviation, FL = standardised factor loadings, α = Cronbach's alpha, ICC = intracless correlations, CI = confidence interval
Source: Author's Compilation

CR values in Table 4 falling in the range of .759 and .916 are satisfying the required cut-off values thereby ensuring the construct reliability of various constructs. The AVE values as shown in Table 4 are exceeding the required standard of 0.5 thereby ensuring the necessary reliability and convergent validity of various distinguished constructs. Three different criteria for confirming the discriminant validity of constructs were assessed. The correlation between the pairs of distinct constructs is lower than the sq. root of AVE for each of the constructs and MSV also having a lower value than AVE for all constructs also shows clear evidence of discriminant validity for various constructs (Fornell & Larcker, 1981).

Table 4: Convergent Validity for Constructs of the Study

	CR	*AVE*	*MSV*	*1*	*2*	*3*	*4*	*5*	*6*	*7*	*8*	*9*
Soci	0.894	0.737	0.441	0.859								
Cond	0.863	0.678	0.555	0.590***	0.824							
Func	0.813	0.592	0.590	0.466***	0.624***	0.769						
Cost	0.891	0.731	0.615	0.499***	0.695***	0.731***	0.855					
Rel	0.836	0.631	0.615	0.458***	0.745***	0.768***	0.784***	0.794				
Epis	0.907	0.764	0.654	0.611***	0.680***	0.607***	0.644v	0.591***	0.774			
Emon	0.876	0.639	0.536	0.454***	0.732***	0.718***	0.711***	0.705***	0.602***	0.800		
Cons	0.916	0.785	0.624	0.362***	0.574***	0.528***	0.543***	0.667***	0.891***	0.503***	0.786	
Imp	0.759	0.759	0.441	0.664***	0.539***	0.448***	0.510***	0.535***	0.368***	0.487***	0.655***	0.871

Note: CR = composite reliability, AVE = average variance extracted, MSV = meximum shared squared variance, Func = Functional consumption value, Emon = Emotional consumption value, Soci = Social consumption value, Epis = Epistemic consumption value, Cond = Conditional consumption value, Rel = Relative advantage, Cost = Perceived costs, Cons = health consciousness, Imp = Impulse purchase intention. Significance of correlations: * = $p < .050$, ** = $p < .010$, *** = $p < .001$

Source: Author's Compilation

Table 5: Results of Hypothesis Testing

Hs	*Path Direction*		*Std. β*	*SE*	*t-value*	*p-value*	*Result*
H_{1a}	Functional value	→ Relative Advantage	0.430	0.133	3.233	0.001**	Supported
H_{1b}	Emotional value	→ Relative advantage	0.032	0.141	0.226	0.821ns	Not supported
H_{1c}	Social value	→ Relative advantage	−0.009	0.065	−0.139	0.89ns	Not supported
H_{1d}	Epistemic value	→ Relative advantage	−0.017	0.161	−0.108	0.914ns	Not supported
H_{1e}	Conditional value	→ Relative advantage	0.371	0.119	3.129	***	Supported
H_2	Relative advantage	→ Impulsive purchase	0.520	0.081	6.396	***	Supported
H_3	Relative advantage × Health consciusness	→ Impulsive purchase	−0.109	−0.100	−1.090	0.276ns	Not supported
H_4	Relation advantage × Perceived cost	→ Impulsive purchase	0.399	0.150	2.652	0.002**	Supported

** = $p < .010$, *** = $p < .001$, ns = not significant

Source: Author's Compilation

Furthermore, the relationship was examined between the different value perceptions and relative advantage (H1a-e). The final findings of the study suggest that the function values(H1a) and conditional value (H1e) collectively contribute to the perceptions of the consumers in terms of relative advantage towards superfoods. The findings in Table 5 and Fig. 3 indicate that the functional values positively influence the relative advantage of superfoods as consumers are more inclining towards functional foods for living a better and healthy lifestyle (Çakiroğlu & Uçar, 2017). The findings of the study also suggest that conditional values also influence the perception of the consumer towards the relative advantage of the superfoods. Consumers, nowadays don't just focus on the product but also rely on the dynamics of the consumer-product relationship. With having accustomed to the benefits that can be obtained from discounts, coupons, etc, this value perception is more context-specific as consumers build stronger perceptions relative advantage of a product in presence of discounts or by seeing the promotional activities done for the superfood products (Estay, 2022).

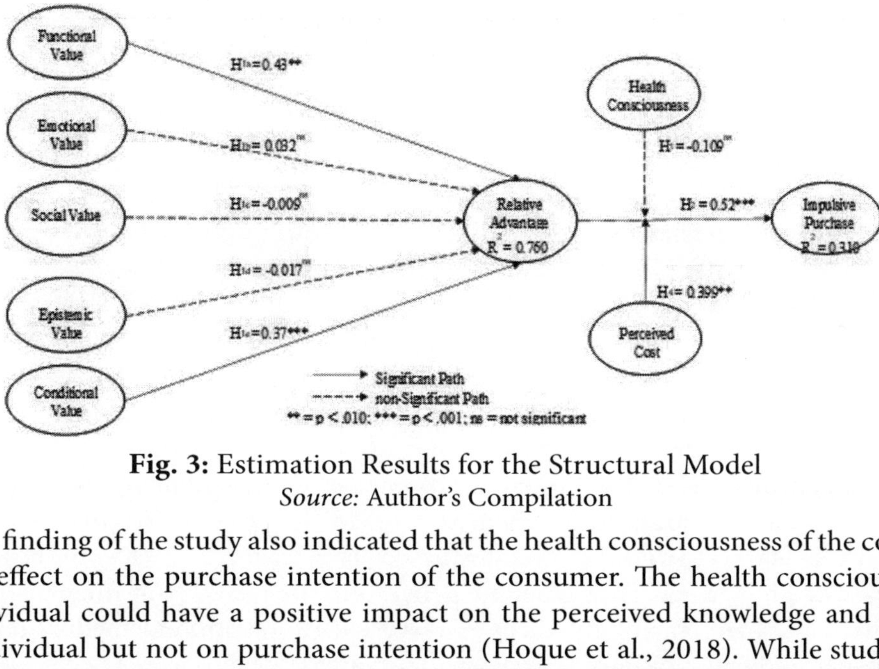

Fig. 3: Estimation Results for the Structural Model
Source: Author's Compilation

The finding of the study also indicated that the health consciousness of the consumer has no effect on the purchase intention of the consumer. The health consciousness of an individual could have a positive impact on the perceived knowledge and belief of that individual but not on purchase intention (Hoque et al., 2018). While studying the moderating effect of perceived cost on the impulse buying of consumers, perceive cost has shown a positive influence. Perceived cost in terms of fixed price helps in eliciting a more positive effect than discounted price format. Price fairness has been a prominent motivator in encouraging impulse buying behavior (Haryanto et al., 2019; Suri et al., 2002).

Discussion and Implications

This study explicates how relative advantages of the dietary product (a superfood in this study) are developed over the perceived values and how they influence their buying behavior. Functional Values about a food product such as how good that food product is and how much quality that food product possesses and how that product can provide a consistent quality contributes to the relative advantage of the towards as compared to other items available in the same product category. According to a report by Future market insight, Amla extract is being globally accepted for its various nutrient-rich properties and thereby gaining the universal name of superfruit. This global acceptance has been achieved by growing awareness of the product among the consumer and consumers becoming knowledgeable about the functional capabilities of the amla 'super fruit'. Because of this awareness growth about the functional capabilities, the AMLA extract market has gained a total market share of more than 42 per cent in Europe (*Amla Extract Market*, 2022). Availability of the food products so that they come into the eyes and sight of the customer and promotional activities such as advertisement and discount offers can contribute to the relative advantage of the product by providing a conditional value edge to them. Conditional values in this study can be extended to the context of making consumers known through marketing messages and forums how superfoods can be consumed to alleviate their health-related problems. Marketing messages concentrating on how certain foods can improve the health of an individual and how they address health-related issues could give superfoods a necessary boost to upscale their sales. As per a real story of an Indian startup, Alpino, co-founder said that the company went around various fitness events and health exhibitions showcasing the product thereby persuading potential customers to actually impulsively sample the product (Krishna, 2019). This study also highlights the positive effect of perceived cost between relative advantage and impulse buying. This study contributes by expanding the context of the present theory of consumption values, thereby, highlighting the significant influence of price in the impulsive buying of certain items such as groceries. Many studies from the past have differentiated and compared the discounted and fixed-price strategies of brands. Fixed-priced strategies have stronger positive effects on the mind of the consumer than discounted prices (Suri et al., 2002). Hence, we suggest that superfood companies should lower their margins in the price of the products thereby penetrating the market to a greater extent and also using direct selling techniques to make their customer know the product thereby generating the relative advantage perception in their mind and then playing the cards of lower price perception to encourage impulse buying then and there. Not only in India, India's various desi food products such as tea and herbs have gained validation from various renowned celebrities across the US, UK, and regions of Canada (Alves, 2022).

In addition to the various implications suggested for the market practitioners in the food product category with special reference to superfoods, this study also suggests some measures for policymakers. The term super in the superfood has no medical or scientific backing and the way super is perceived in the minds of the customer is not standardised. There is no sufficient research to give a steady base to the health claims by different companies about their products. This has led to a greater extent of confusion than a problem solver. Policymakers should try to solve this problem by taking the help of market practitioners and mainstream media by educating the customer and providing them with accurate information and credible sources to guide the consumers in their dietary food consumption decisions.

Limitation and Future Research

This study contributes to the present theory of consumption values by extending it in the direction of superfoods. What are those factors that contribute to the impulsive buying of superfoods when compared to other products in the same category? This study focuses on potential superfood customers. The moderation effect of perceived cost is also studied in the study as to how it influences impulsive purchases. Future research can also focus on social media influencers and talk about their impact on encouraging impulse buying behavior. A bigger sample size from more versatile geographic locations could be beneficial for further strengthening the constructs. Cross-culture studies can also help in extending the present study to other different relevant directions.

References

[1] Alves, G. (2022, August 10). *Why homegrown brands are flaunting their Indianness abroad.* ETBrandEquity.com. Retrieved December 6, 2022, from https://brandequity.economictimes.indiatimes.com/news/business-of-brands/why-homegrown-brands-are-flaunting-their-indianness-abroad/93461662

[2] *Amla Extract Market.* (2022, August). Future Market Insights. Retrieved December 9, 2022, from https://www.futuremarketinsights.com/reports/global-amla-extract-market

[3] Bagozzi, R. P., & Yi, Y. (1988). On the evaluation of structural equation models. *Journal of the Academy of Marketing Science, 16*(1), 74–94. https://doi.org/10.1007/bf02723327

[4] Bagozzi, R. P., Yi, Y., & Phillips, L. W. (1991). Assessing Construct Validity in Organizational Research. *Administrative Science Quarterly, 36*(3), 421. https://doi.org/10.2307/2393203

[5] Barsby, J. P., Cowley, J. M., Leemaqz, S. Y., Grieger, J. A., McKeating, D. R., Perkins, A. V., Bastian, S. E. P., Burton, R. A., & Bianco-Miotto, T. (2021). Nutritional properties of selected superfood extracts and their potential health benefits. *PeerJ, 9*, e12525. https://doi.org/10.7717/peerj.12525

[6] Brown, T. A. (2015). *Confirmatory Factor Analysis for Applied Research (Methodology in the Social Sciences)* (Second). The Guilford Press.

[7] Burton, J. L., Gollins, J., McNeely, L. E., & Walls, D. M. (2018). Revisiting the Relationship between Ad Frequency and Purchase Intentions. *Journal of Advertising Research, 59*(1), 27–39. https://doi.org/10.2501/jar-2018-031

[8] Çakiroğlu, & Uçar. (2017). Consumer attitudes towards purchasing functional products. *Journal of Nutrition and Internal Medicine, 20*(2), 257–262. https://doi.org/10.23751/pn.v20i2.5859

[9] Cummins, E., Hospido, A., & Van Impe, J. F. (2019). Quantitative tools for sustainable food and energy in the food chain. *Food Research International, 115*, 126–127. https://doi.org/10.1016/j.foodres.2018.08.026

[10] de Regt, A., Montecchi, M., & Lord Ferguson, S. (2019). A false image of health: how fake news and pseudo-facts spread in the health and beauty industry. *Journal of Product &Amp; Brand Management, 29*(2), 168–179. https://doi.org/10.1108/jpbm-12-2018-2180

[11] Estay. (2022, March 10). *How to Use Customer Discounts to Boost Sales (2022).* The BigCommerce Blog. Retrieved December 3, 2022, from http://www.bigcommerce.com/blog/customer-discount/

[12] Franco Lucas, B., Alberto Vieira Costa, J., & Brunner, T. A. (2022). How Information on Superfoods Changes Consumers' Attitudes: An Explorative Survey Study. *Foods, 11*(13), 1863. https://doi.org/10.3390/foods11131863

[13] Fornell, C., & Larcker, D. F. (1981). Evaluating Structural Equation Models with Unobservable Variables and Measurement Error. *Journal of Marketing Research, 18*(1), 39–50. https://doi.org/10.1177/002224378101800104

[14] Gogoi, B. J. (2020). Do Impulsive Buying Influence Compulsive Buying? *Academy of Marketing Studies Journal, 24*(4), 1–15.

[15] Graeff-Hönninger, S., & Khajehei, F. (2019). The Demand for Superfoods: Consumers' Desire, Production Viability and Bio-intelligent Transition. *Food Tech Transitions*, 81–94. https://doi.org/10.1007/978-3-030-21059-5_5

[16] Hair, J. F., Ringle, C. M., & Sarstedt, M. (2013). Partial Least Squares Structural Equation Modeling: Rigorous Applications, Better Results and Higher Acceptance. *Long Range Planning, 46*(1–2), 1–12. https://doi.org/10.1016/j.lrp.2013.01.001

[17] Hansen, H. (2013). Price Consciousness and Purchase Intentions for New Food Products: The Moderating Effect of Product Category Knowledge when Price Is Unknown. *Journal of Food Products Marketing, 19*(4), 237–246. https://doi.org/10.1080/10454446.2013.724363

[18] Haryanto, H., Wiyono, W., & Hastjarja KB, D. (2019). Impulse Buying: The Effect of Price Fairness, in Store Promotion, Merchandise and Time Availability. *KnE Social Sciences, 3*(13), 924. https://doi.org/10.18502/kss.v3i13.4257

[19] Hoque, M., Alam, M., & Nahid, K. (2018). Health Consciousness and Its Effect on Perceived Knowledge, and Belief in the Purchase Intent of Liquid Milk: Consumer Insights from an Emerging Market. *Foods, 7*(9), 150. https://doi.org/10.3390/foods7090150

[20] Jagdale, Y. D., Mahale, S. V., Zohra, B., Nayik, G. A., Dar, A. H., Khan, K. A., Abdi, G., & Karabagias, I. K. (2021). Nutritional Profile and Potential Health Benefits of Super Foods: A Review. *Sustainability, 13*(16), 9240. https://doi.org/10.3390/su13169240

[21] Jaidev, P. U. A. P. K. M. (2022, March 1). *Price Perception & Continued Intention To Buy Organic Food: A Mediated Moderation Model.* https://www.abacademies.org/articles/price-perception--continued-intention-to-buy-organic-food-a-mediated-moderation-model-14507.html

[22] Joshi, A., Kale, S., Chandel, S., & Pal, D. (2015). Likert Scale: Explored and Explained. *British Journal of Applied Science &Amp; Technology, 7*(4), 396–403. https://doi.org/10.9734/bjast/2015/14975

[23] Krishna, V. (2019, May 3). *[Startup Bharat] How Surat-based Alpino turned a Rs 5 lakh investment into a Rs 5 Cr turnover by selling peanu.* YourStory.com. https://yourstory.com/2019/05/startup-bharat-surat-alpino-peanut-butter-amazon

[24] Kotler, P., Armstrong, G., & Opresnik, M. O. (2020). *Principles of Marketing, Global Edtion.* Pearson Education Limited.

[25] Labay, D. G., & Kinnear, T. C. (1981). Exploring the Consumer Decision Process in the Adoption of Solar Energy Systems. *Journal of Consumer Research, 8*(3), 271. https://doi.org/10.1086/208865

[26] Leckie, C., Nyadzayo, M. W., & Johnson, L. W. (2017). Promoting brand engagement behaviors and loyalty through perceived service value and innovativeness. *Journal of Services Marketing, 32*(1), 70–82. https://doi.org/10.1108/jsm-01-2017-0035

[27] Liang, R. D. (2016). Predicting intentions to purchase organic food: the moderating effects of organic food prices. *British Food Journal, 118*(1), 183–199. https://doi.org/10.1108/bfj-06-2015-0215

[28] Long, M. M., & Schiffman, L. G. (2000). Consumption values and relationships: segmenting the market for frequency programs. *Journal of Consumer Marketing, 17*(3), 214–232. https://doi.org/10.1108/07363760010329201

[29] Loyer, J. (2016, October 13). *The social lives of superfoods.* Adelaide Research & Scholarship. https://digital.library.adelaide.edu.au/dspace/handle/2440/101777

[30] Loyer, J., & Knight, C. (2018). Selling the 'Inca superfood': nutritional primitivism in superfoods books and maca marketing. *Food, Culture &Amp; Society, 21*(4), 449–467. https://doi.org/10.1080/15528014.2018.1480645

[31] Link. (2020, July 6). *An Apple a Day Keeps the Doctor Away — Fact or Fiction?* Healthline. Retrieved December 2, 2022, from https://www.healthline.com/nutrition/an-apple-a-day-keeps-the-doctor-away

[32] Liu, H., Meng-Lewis, Y., Ibrahim, F., & Zhu, X. (2021). Superfoods, super healthy: Myth or reality? Examining consumers' repurchase and WOM intention regarding superfoods: A theory of consumption values perspective. *Journal of Business Research, 137*, 69–88. https://doi.org/10.1016/j.jbusres.2021.08.018

[33] Lucas, B. F., Costa, J. A. V., & Brunner, T. A. (2021). Superfoods: Drivers for Consumption. *Journal of Food Products Marketing, 27*(1), 1–9. https://doi.org/10.1080/10454446.2020.1869133

[34] Lucas, B. F., Alberto Vieira Costa, J., & Brunner, T. A. (2022). How Information on Superfoods Changes Consumers' Attitudes: An Explorative Survey Study. *Foods, 11*(13), 1863. https://doi.org/10.3390/foods11131863

[35] Meena, S. (2018). Consumer Psychology and Marketing. *International Journal of Research and Analytical Reviews, 5*(3), E-ISSN 2348-1269, P-ISSN 2349-5138.

[36] MacGregor, C., Petersen, A., & Parker, C. (2018). Promoting a healthier, younger you: The media marketing of anti-ageing superfoods. *Journal of Consumer Culture, 21*(2), 164–179. https://doi.org/10.1177/1469540518773825

[37] Oude Groeniger, J., van Lenthe, F. J., Beenackers, M. A., & Kamphuis, C. B. M. (2017). Does social distinction contribute to socioeconomic inequalities in diet: the case of 'superfoods' consumption. *International Journal of Behavioral Nutrition and Physical Activity, 14*(1). https://doi.org/10.1186/s12966-017-0495-x

[38] Pacho, F. T., & Batra, M. M. (2021). Factors influencing consumers' behaviour towards organic food purchase in Denmark and Tanzania. *Studies in Agricultural Economics, 123*(2), 62–75. https://doi.org/10.7896/j.2127

[39] Pentikäinen, S., Arvola, A., Karhunen, L., & Pennanen, K. (2018). Easy-going, rational, susceptible and struggling eaters: A segmentation study based on eating behaviour tendencies. *Appetite, 120*, 212–221. https://doi.org/10.1016/j.appet.2017.09.001

[40] PROESTOS, C. (2018). Superfoods: Recent Data on their Role in the Prevention of Diseases. *Current Research in Nutrition and Food Science Journal, 6*(3), 576–593. https://doi.org/10.12944/crnfsj.6.3.02

[41] Rana, J., & Paul, J. (2017). Consumer behavior and purchase intention for organic food: A review and research agenda. *Journal of Retailing and Consumer Services, 38*, 157–165. https://doi.org/10.1016/j.jretconser.2017.06.004

[42] *Relative Advantage*. (2018, February 7). Monash Business School. https://www.monash.edu/business/marketing/marketing-dictionary/r/relative-advantage

[43] Santeramo, F., Carlucci, D., De Devitiis, B., Seccia, A., Stasi, A., Viscecchia, R., & Nardone, G. (2018). Emerging trends in European food, diets and food industry. *Food Research International, 104*, 39–47. https://doi.org/10.1016/j.foodres.2017.10.039

[44] Sheth, J. N., Newman, B. I., & Gross, B. L. (1991). Why we buy what we buy: A theory of consumption values. *Journal of Business Research, 22*(2), 159–170. https://doi.org/10.1016/0148-2963(91)90050-8

[45] Sohn, Y. S., & Ko, M. T. (2021). The impact of planned vs. unplanned purchases on subsequent purchase decision making in sequential buying situations. *Journal of Retailing and Consumer Services, 59*, 102419. https://doi.org/10.1016/j.jretconser.2020.102419

[46] Suri, R., Manchanda, R. V., & Kohli, C. S. (2002). Comparing fixed price and discounted price strategies: the role of affect on evaluations. *Journal of Product &Amp; Brand Management, 11*(3), 160–173. https://doi.org/10.1108/10610420210430051

[47] Tanrikulu, C. (2021). Theory of consumption values in consumer behaviour research: A review and future research agenda. *International Journal of Consumer Studies, 45*(6), 1176–1197. https://doi.org/10.1111/ijcs.12687

[48] Turel, O., Serenko, A., & Bontis, N. (2010). User acceptance of hedonic digital artifacts: A theory of consumption values perspective. *Information &Amp; Management, 47*(1), 53–59. https://doi.org/10.1016/j.im.2009.10.002

[49] Venkatraman, M. P. (1991). The Impact of Innovativeness and Innovation Type on Adoption. *Journal of Retailing, 67*(1), 51–67. https://link.gale.com/apps/doc/A11102218/AONE?u=googlescholar&sid=bookmark-AONE&xid=7f61e466

[50] Wang, J., Pham, T. L., & Dang, V. T. (2020). Environmental Consciousness and Organic Food Purchase Intention: A Moderated Mediation Model of Perceived Food Quality and Price Sensitivity. *International Journal of Environmental Research and Public Health, 17*(3), 850. https://doi.org/10.3390/ijerph17030850

[51] Ware, M. R. (2019, January 7). *What are superfoods and why should you eat them?* Retrieved December 2, 2022, from https://www.medicalnewstoday.com/articles/303079

[52] Wright, A. (2020, September 14). *Consumer interest in superfoods is booming*. New Hope Network. Retrieved December 2, 2022, from https://www.newhope.com/products-and-trends/consumer-interest-superfoods-booming

[53] Wiedenroth, C. F., & Otter, V. (2021). Who Are the Superfoodies? New Healthy Luxury Food Products and Social Media Marketing Potential in Germany. *Foods, 10*(12), 2907. https://doi.org/10.3390/foods10122907

[54] Yeboah, A., & Owusu-Prempeh, V. (2017). Exploring the Consumer Impulse Buying Behaviour from a Range of Consumer and Product Related Factors. *International Journal of Marketing Studies, 9*(2), 146. https://doi.org/10.5539/ijms.v9n2p146

[55] Zeithaml, V. A. (1988). Consumer Perceptions of Price, Quality, and Value: A Means-End Model and Synthesis of Evidence. *Journal of Marketing, 52*(3), 2–22. https://doi.org/10.1177/002224298805200302

Antecedents of Service Quality in Online Shopping Behaviour: An Exploratory Study

Dr Biranchi Narayan Swar

Dean and Professor – Marketing, Management Development Institute, Murshidabad

Abstract

Purpose: The online population of India is growing at a rapid pace and as a result many consumers want to shop online. So, in this context, it is inevitable for today's marketers to understand the online shoppers' behaviour and also the antecedents of service quality in online shopper behaviour. Hence, the objective of the paper is to identify the antecedents of service quality in online shopper behaviour.

Design/ methodology/ approach: For this purpose, the study has used both qualitative and quantitative research approach. In this regard, the data were collected from 220 online shoppers and analysed to meet the objectives of the study.

Findings: The results of the study showed that male shoppers spend less time than female shoppers while evaluating the products and shopping online. The factors which influenced the service quality in online shopping behaviour were safety, security, discounts, pricing, product reviews and product availability.

Implications: The insights drawn from the study showed that the findings may be useful for today's online retailers to formulate their online retailing strategies. The growth and availability of the internet has encouraged the shopper to shop online and also the retailers to provide better service quality to have a competitive edge. This will help in understanding the online shopper behaviour in a better way and will also to enhance customer satisfaction and loyalty.

Keywords: *Shopping Behaviour, Customer Satisfaction, E-Service Quality, Customer Loyalty, Online Shopping*

Introduction

With ever increasing competition and globalisation in today's market the only way the retailers can compete is to find the psychology behind online shopper behaviour. One area that needs to be focused on while understanding online shopper behaviour is the impact of different stages of evolution of internet, i.e. the World Wide Web (WWW). The internet is omnipresent in today's business.

The impact on shopper behaviour with evolution of Internet:

- In the early stages of Web 1.0, online shopper behaviour was the same as the traditional consumer, it was just complimentary. It was just seen as a channel where consumers could gather information and look for knowledge with respect to various products and services.

- Web 2.0 provided a platform to collaborate. It enabled social interaction and collaboration across the globe with anyone who had internet access. This stage created a value by new communities that was not there and could be accessed through internet only. Web 2.0 helped in building a two-way direction relation between people who provided goods and services and the consumers.
- The third step, Web 3.0 or what is known as Semantic Web: The combination of Artificial Intelligence and humans is the key feature of this stage. With the help of AI technologies, the information was easily accessible and more relevant of specifically targeted consumers on a real time basis. With the amount of information that was available on a real time basis, it accounted to the way the consumers took decisions in the interactive way. Information about the consumers decisions for psychological variables could easily be gathered which was difficult to be gathered previously.
- The fourth step, Web 4.0, that is based on wireless and mobile communications: It is called Symbiotic Web. It has the ability to connect with people, objects and places anytime and anywhere in the virtual or physical world on a real time basis.
- Web 5.0 stage referred to as the Emotive or Sensory Web: This is in line with marketing of Web 4.0 with emphasis on the individual shopper experiences, journey of shopping behaviour and decision making process. This stage is to make the technologies have emotional sensitivity. The main aim of this stage is to develop the computers that interact with human beings and become a part of their life.

Thus, the evolution of Internet creates possibilities of more interaction with the shoppers and understanding the shopper behaviour in a better way.

Online buying behaviour is the behaviour that reflects a shopper act in the process of purchasing online. It starts from the step when shopper starts browsing the website for the purpose of searching, selection and finally purchasing goods and services, in order to fulfil their wants and needs.

Shoppers prefer online shopping compared to the traditional shopping due to various benefits such as ability to view and shop at anytime from anywhere, features like gathering knowledge about products, placing a query or placing a purchase order. Apart from this, there were also other reasons like convenience, lower price which attracts shoppers to purchase online.

Different Online Consumer Purchase Stages

- **Stage 1:** The pre-purchase stage is the most important stage in the decision-making process as it helps online consumers to compare various options and select as per their choice and get better clarity about the products or services they are looking for.
- **Stage 2:** During the purchasing stage, the most critical things which help online customers to decide what product they should choose, or from which retailer they should buy, this may be on the basis of certain criteria like product assortment, sale services and information quality.

- **Stage 3:** Post-purchase behaviour becomes more important after consumers' purchase online. Sometimes, it may happen that consumers are not happy with the existing purchase and as a result they want to return or exchange the products. Hence, in such cases return and exchange services become more important.

Service Quality and Online Consumer Behaviour

Service Quality

Service quality is commonly characterised as the distinction between anticipated assistance and perceived. Accordingly, the e-service quality of retail can be characterised as the impression of how much the service meets the customer's desires. Great assistance quality pulls in and fulfils customers, increases an organisation's profit successfully, and a real piece of the overall industry. It is particularly significant for online retail sites because of the generally various attributes of web-based marketing from conventional marketing, for example, the inability to come in contact with items, view of comfort, danger, and shopping delight. Online customers are increasingly more dependent on the administrations offered by sites. Consequently, a significant build getting critical exploration consideration is E-service quality. First, it is essential to establish the privacy/ security of online customers because of more prominent vulnerability and danger in making on the web purchase in contrast with conventional marketing. Second, wellbeing is additionally the essential reason of each arrangement, and customers will possibly buy when they have a sense of safety. Consequently, today, online shoppers give more importance to the safety and security of the websites. Moreover, convenience is another viewpoint that is imperative to most customers. Furthermore, right order fulfilment and bill (reliability), fast reactions to online requests (responsiveness), and improving the effectiveness of internet shopping. This will furnish online shoppers with a charming and fulfilling experience of shopping.

Customer Satisfaction

Customer satisfaction is simply the mid-stage in the guideline cycle of online shopping. Basically, it is an emotional reaction of the customer. In the market hypothesis, consumer loyalty is a key proportion of whether retailers are satisfying the advertising idea. It is the level of addressing customers' needs during online purchases. Fulfilling online based shopping experience can initiate customer dependability. Numerous internet advertising contemplates recommending that delightful customers should be an essential objective for firms since customer satisfaction prompts profitability. For online retailers, offering the blend of items, administrations and encounters improves customer satisfaction.

Consumer satisfaction is meeting consumer desires for administrations by contrasting and perceived expectations. Customers are fulfilled if the apparent presentation coordinates their desires, and disappointed in the event that it doesn't. Furthermore, numerous examinations found that e-service quality has a critical beneficial outcome on customer satisfaction.

Customer Loyalty

Customer loyalty is one of critical elements in online shopping. Building customer dedication is a significant methodology for the accomplishment of any retailers. Most advertisers centre around customer loyalty due to its constructive outcome on long haul productivity. The most widely recognised meaning of customer loyalty is by, who portrayed it as a one-sided (non-arbitrary), behavioural response (purchase), communicated after some time, by some dynamic unit, as for at least one elective brand out of a lot of such brands, and is an element of psychological processes. Numerous accept that reliability can bring about monotonous purchasing, notwithstanding promoting or situational impacts. This is particularly significant for the proceeded with the progress of an online retailer confronting furious competition. Nonetheless, client faithfulness is hard to characterise and gauge; along these lines, researchers will in general utilise social and attitudinal measures to evaluate it, Buyers assess the administration nature of sites they buy from before. Whenever fulfilled, the hours of continue purchasing are high since this experience build loyalty.

Factors Influencing Service Quality in Online Consumer Behaviour

Venkatesh, V., Speier-Pero, C. and Schuetz, S. (2022) conducted a longitudinal survey and validated the data among 9,992 respondents to identify the antecedents to online purchase. The study found the antecedents such as risk, impulse buying behaviour, value consciousness, local shopping, shopping enjoyment, and browsing enjoyment. Miao, M., Jalees, T., Zaman, S.I., Khan, S., Hanif, N.-U. and Javed, M.K. (2022) surveyed 415 online shoppers and explored that service delivery affects satisfaction and services quality effect trust.

Tata, S.V., Prashar, S. and Parsad, C. (2021) collected data from 367 respondents and revealed that there was a significant influence of service quality, company's sincerity, and price transparency on shoppers' satisfaction. Saad, A.T. (2021) analysed 177 consumers from Bangladesh and found that price, service quality, delivery time, and condition of food delivered comprised of first factor influencing the success of online food delivery. The second factor consists of menu, variety and number of restaurants, attitude, and delivery tracking service of a delivery person.

Wang, W. and Kim, S. (2019) examined 330 online consumers in China and revealed that efficiency was the first element of service quality, the second one was responsiveness and reliability dimensions. They concluded that service quality affect customer satisfaction and customer satisfaction influences customer loyalty.

Dang, V.T. and Pham, T.L. (2018) collected data from 221 consumers in Vietnam. The outcomes of the study showed that shoppers' perception of web design is positively related to perceptions towards privacy, customer service, purchase intention, and reliability. They also found that, shoppers' perception of service is positively associated with purchase intention. Han, B., Kim, M. and Lee, J. (2018) concluded that e-service quality positively affect attitudes towards shopping online, which in turns positively affect purchase intention of the shoppers. Self-efficacy also influenced online purchasing positively and that affects the behavioural intentions of the shopper.

Urumsah, D. (2015) examined the 819 Indonesian respondents and found that motivation has the strongest influence towards the usage of e-service. Wang, H. (2011) found that customer perceived value and e-service quality influence customer satisfaction, and then in turn it influences customer loyalty. Also high customers' perceived value have a stronger association with satisfaction and customer loyalty. Park, C. and Kim, Y. (2003) surveyed with 602 Korean online customers and revealed that user interface quality, security, information quality, and user interface quality influence satisfaction and relational benefit and in turn actual purchase behaviour.

Objectives of the Study

1. To know the different stages of shoppers' decision-making process.
2. To understand the relationship between service quality and online shopper behaviour.
3. To identify the factors influencing service quality in online shopper behaviour.

Research Methodology

The paper has used both qualitative and quantitative research to collect the data from 220 online shoppers. Then, the data were analysed to achieve the objective of the research. On the basis of the analysis the conclusions are drawn with respect to service quality and online shopper behaviour.

Analysis and Findings

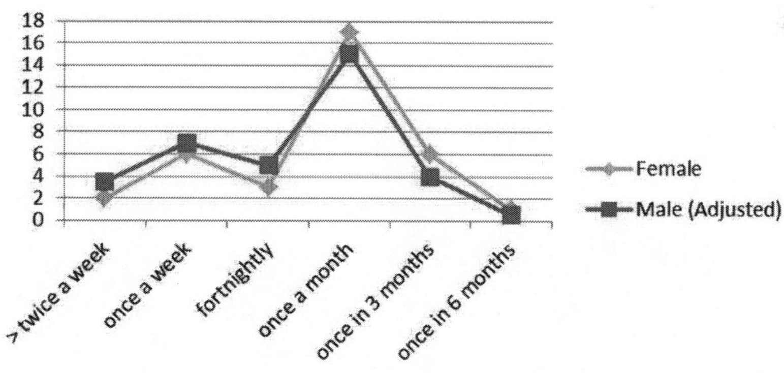

Fig. 1: Frequency of Online Purchase

As observed through the analysis of primary data, Male members of society do online shopping more frequently as compared to females. Although the difference in purchasing frequency is not vast. But, a considerate portion of spending is from Male end. We can observe that Males prefer the online shopping mode more often, the reason behind this can be observed as males prefer to spend less time on their shopping chores rather than females who like to compare, assess and bargain more.

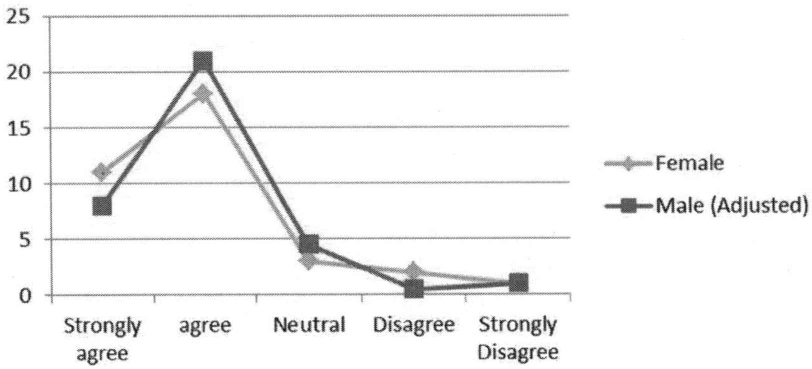

Fig. 2: Ease of Selecting and Making Comparisons

Both the Genders, either Male or female, feel that they experience ease of selecting and making comparisons while shopping through online mode. Experience and ease don't vary across male and female.

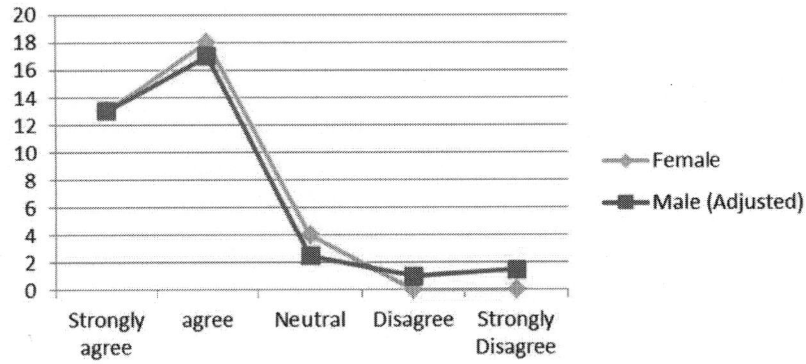

Fig. 3: Effects of Website UX on Gender for Online Shopping

Both males and females feel that the user interface plays a major role for navigation in Online shopping. Thus, the company doesn't need to change its website design, they can aim at providing a user-friendly website for a better UX.

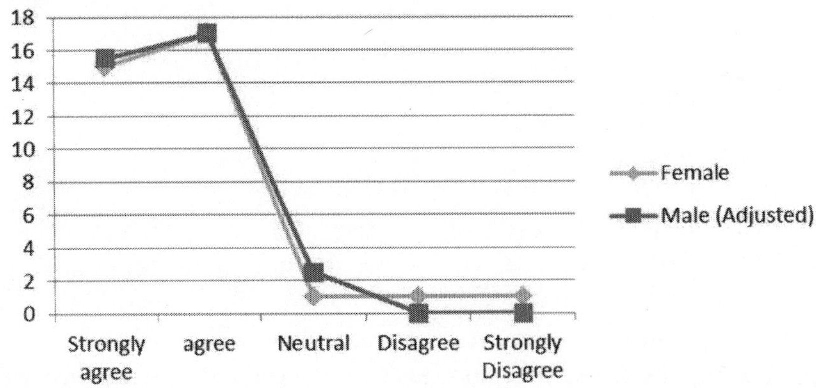

Fig. 4: Impact of Safety and Trust of Website on Purchase Decision

Website safety and security plays a critical role during any purchase decision and this is rightly depicted from above graph wherein we see majority of respondents from both the genders strongly agreeing/agreeing to the above facts.

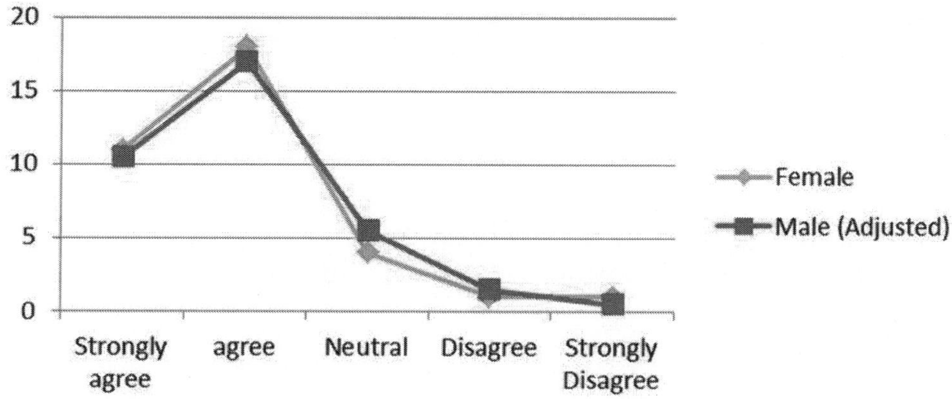

Fig. 5: Impact on Purchase with Familiarity with Respect to the Website

As we can see both the genders believe that impact on purchase with respect to online shopping strongly associates with the familiarity with the nuances of the website. More number of female shoppers agree that familiarity with respect to the website has impact on purchase decision. Hence a very user-friendly UI and UI experience should be available and navigation and information sharing to the customer should be as easy as is possible.

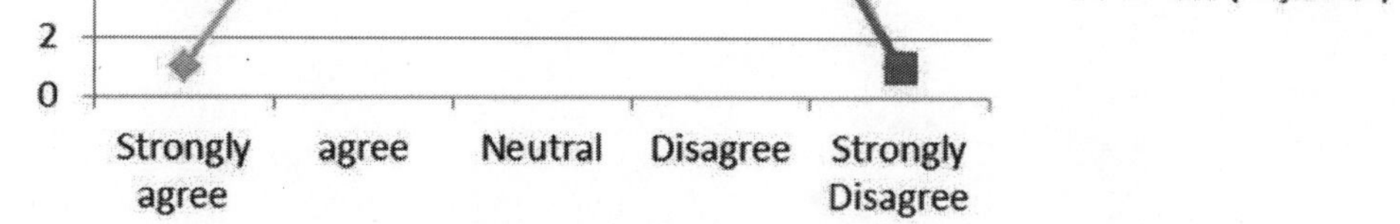

Fig. 6: Impact of Gender on Time to Evaluate and Select a Product while Shopping Online

From this we can interpret that male shoppers have higher affiliation or thought that online shopping takes less time when compared with female shoppers, yet a considerate portion of respondents from both the gender feel that to evaluate and select a product one has to spend time in surfing net. Hence, the e-tailers websites should be made in such a way that a consumer can have their desired product without wasting their valuable time.

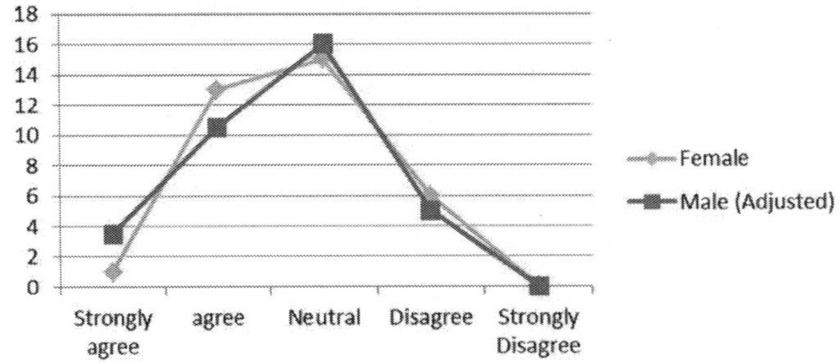

Fig. 7: Perception about Safety and Security of the Websites

Here both the gender thinks the same way. They both expect safety and security while shopping online, but they are not sure about the safety and security when it comes to online shopping.

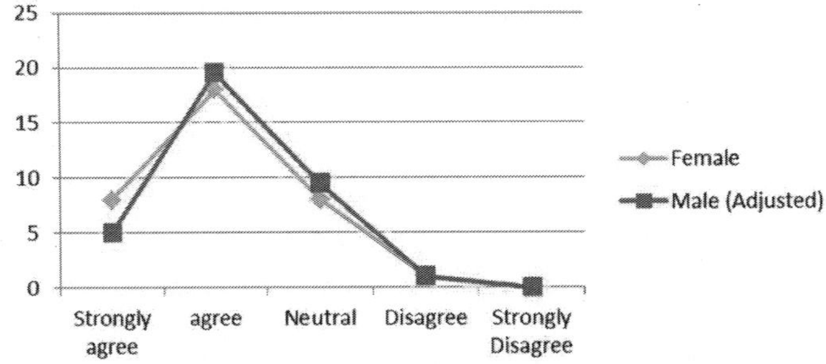

Fig. 8: Impact of Discount Coupons and Offers and Online Purchase

A good discount and cash back schemes are important to increase the sales and both the genders agree to these promotional schemes. Female shoppers buy more when there is offers or discount than male shoppers, this may be due to more buying power lies with male than female with respect to Indian consumers. So, the retailers should focus more on the promotion and schemes related activities to be more customers centric in their approach.

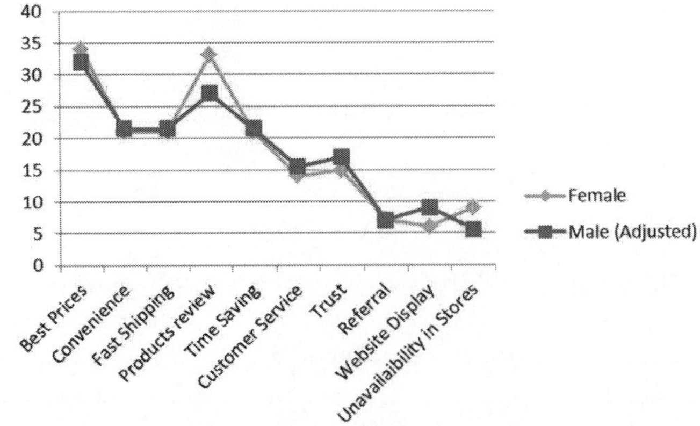

Fig. 9: The Crucial Factors which Effects the Shopper Decision Making during Final Selection of the Product

It is clear from the above figure that best prices are needed by both the gender to decide on the product and buying it from online platform.

The next factor for Female is the product review, by comparing both gender and the correlation between them it can be inferred that females buy the product by emphasising more on the reviews by other customers and this factor effects them the most, the higher the customer satisfaction reviews more likely that product is/ will be bought by the female shoppers. Thus, the online retailers should provide better customer service to create happy customers to get positive reviews which will help to bring new customers and will increase the sales in the long run.

Product unavailability in the store is a reason which makes the female shoppers to look for online options. Hence, it's very important for the online retailers to have product in their inventory and replenishment of stocks becomes the norm to have the best customer service quality.

Conclusion

The purpose of the above study was to basically find out the antecedents of service quality in online shopper behaviour. Throughout the study we have tried to list down all the factors that affect service quality in online consumer behaviour. We came across a lot of factors that could affect online consumer behaviour. One of the most prominent factors in it was the gender role and hence we conducted a primary research to find out the role of gender. During the research we had to undergo a lot of limitations the top being a limited sample size and also the sample size mostly consisted of college students. In our analysis we found out that gender plays a very minimal role in online decision-making. On the whole what we see that the factors which influence service quality were customer satisfaction, customer loyalty, etc. And the factors influencing service quality in online shopping behaviour were safety and security, discounts, pricing, product availability and product reviews.

The followings were the most important conclusions drawn from the study:

- To enhance customer satisfaction and customer loyalty, the retailers have to give more importance to service quality elements like reliability, responsiveness etc.
- Gender plays a very important role in the online shopper behaviour; men and women both have different needs and desires. They both look into things with a different perspective and have different ways to react to the things happening in around them and this can be very well seen with the decision they make while shopping online. Where men generally look see the visual side of it, women see the reviews/feedback part. And the e-commerce sites have to keep this fact in mind when portraying their products for different segments of shoppers.
- To ensure service quality in online shopper behaviour, the online retailers should consider factors such as safety and security, discounts, pricing, product availability and product reviews.

Thus, we conclude that the shopping behaviour differs across different segments, so it is critical for the service providers to devise a strategy by taking into account all the recommendations and suggestions given in this paper to ensure service quality in online shopping behaviour.

References

[1] Dang, V.T. and Pham, T.L. (2018), 'An empirical investigation of consumer perceptions of online shopping in an emerging economy: Adoption theory perspective', *Asia Pacific Journal of Marketing and Logistics*, Vol. 30 No. 4, pp. 952–71.

[2] Han, B., Kim, M. and Lee, J. (2018), 'Exploring consumer attitudes and purchasing intentions of cross-border online shopping in Korea', *Journal of Korea Trade*, Vol. 22 No. 2, pp. 86–104.

[3] Hsin Chang, H. and Wang, H. (2011), 'The moderating effect of customer perceived value on online shopping behaviour', *Online Information Review*, Vol. 35 No. 3, pp. 333–59.

[4] Miao, M., Jalees, T., Zaman, S.I., Khan, S., Hanif, N.-u. and Javed, M.K. (2022), 'The influence of e-customer satisfaction, e-trust and perceived value on consumer's repurchase intention in B2C e-commerce segment', *Asia Pacific Journal of Marketing and Logistics*, Vol. 34 No. 10, pp. 2184–206.

[5] Park, C. and Kim, Y. (2003), 'Identifying key factors affecting consumer purchase behaviour in an online shopping context', *International Journal of Retail & Distribution Management*, Vol. 31 No. 1, pp. 16–29.

[6] Saad, A.T. (2021), 'Factors affecting online food delivery service in Bangladesh: an empirical study', *British Food Journal*, Vol. 123 No. 2, pp. 535–50.

[7] Tata, S.V., Prashar, S. and Parsad, C. (2021), 'Examining the influence of satisfaction and regret on online shoppers' post-purchase behaviour', *Benchmarking: An International Journal*, Vol. 28 No. 6, pp. 1987–2007.

[8] Urumsah, D. (2015), 'Factors Influencing Consumers to Use e-services in Indonesian Airline Companies', *E-services Adoption: Processes by Firms in Developing Nations* (Advances in Business Marketing and Purchasing, Vol. 23B), pp. 5–254.

[9] Venkatesh, V., Speier-Pero, C. and Schuetz, S. (2022), 'Why do people shop online? A comprehensive framework of consumers' online shopping intentions and behaviours', *Information Technology & People*, Vol. 35 No. 5, pp. 1590–1620.

[10] Wang, W. and Kim, S. (2019), 'Lady first? The gender difference in the influence of service quality on online consumer behaviour', *Nankai Business Review International*, Vol. 10 No. 3, pp. 408–28.

Section II

Reinventing Management through Sustainability, Innovation and Analytics: Finance and Accounting

Key Predictors for Acceptance of Cashless Transactions: Survey of Small Retailers

Dr Sunita Bishnoi[1], Dr Deepak Kumar[2] and Apeksha[3]

[1]*Associate Professor, DAV Institute of Management, Faridabad*
[2]*Assistant Professor, DAV Institute of Management, Faridabad*
[3]*Government P.G. Nehru College, Jhajhar*
E-mail: Bishnoi.sunita@rediff.com; apeksha0993@gmail.com

Abstract

The intention of the study is to uncover key predictors for acceptance of cashless transactions. The paper also focuses on relevance and importance of predictors which are impacting acceptance of cashless transactions by small retailers. A self-structure questionnaire was used to collect perception of 500 small retailers during October–January 2022. The methodology used is PLS-SEM. The finding of study revealed that 'safety & security', 'customer services', 'time saving' and 'business promotion' are the significant predictors for acceptance of cashless transactions. The measurement model and structural model has been assessed and results are found significant. The study provides implications for different stakeholders participating in cashless transactions. It will be helpful for fintech companies as well as financial institutes as the study provides an insight of small retailers related to their perception about acceptance of cashless transactions. The study will help future researchers to explore additions in the number of predictors. Further, they can increase the scope of research area as well as sample size. This study unfolds a novel theoretical model to understand the relevance and importance of predictors, which impact acceptance of cashless transactions.

Keywords: *Cashless Transactions, Safety and Security, Convenience, Digital Payments, Measurement Model, Path Analysis, Small Retailers*

Introduction

Digitisation is rapidly changing the retail landscape. E-commerce, which is central to digitisation, is growing steadily in developing countries such as India (Seethamraju & Diatha (2019). The concept of cashless transactions in a cashless economy is created using digital currency, where money is exchanged and recorded only in electronic digital form. The impact of digital trading presents numerous challenges and opportunities (Singhraul & Yogita Satish Garwal, 2018).

The development of cashless literature is indicating that convenience, easy maintenance of financial records, achieving customer satisfaction through online payment options, real time money transfer, government initiatives regarding digital and cashless India, technological developments, user friendly apps and software's, complementary software's for business, digital reach, technological and banking infrastructural developments, etc., are the motivating force at the back of cashless India.

Smaller retailers have poor adoption of mobile and information technology as they have basic infrastructure, poor accounting and administrative processes, rely heavily on cash and credit-based transactions. They are therefore vulnerable to the previously identified destructive tendencies (Sinha, Gokhale & Rawal, 2015). In order to combat the black economy, boost overall retail sector efficiencies, and reduce leakages in government subsidy programmes, governments in India are also promoting the adoption of digital technology including cashless transactions and digitalised retail procedures. Aadhaar-based biometric systems, the PMJDY, the government-supported BHIM app, Bharat QR codes, RuPay cards, and the 'Digital India' initiative are some of the programme and policies targeted towards digitising small size merchants (Observer Research Foundation, 2021). Based on a tailored TOE framework, Ravi Seethamraju Krishna Sundar Diatha (2019) identified adoption factors for small retailers; external/environmental (technology as well as other environmental factors such as inefficient processes, physical infrastructure, tax implications and industry characteristics, and government regulations) and internal factors (perceived risks, costs, personal characteristics, and loss of control).

A cashless economy can be realised by implementing suitable digital payment mechanisms. It can be achieved with the help of full established new financial policies, regular monitory attention on the bankers, centralised administrative control, government agencies and other private services. Safe and secured services like clear statement of their accounts, immediate certification of payments, no hidden charges, shorten process of transaction by fulfil of mandatory information and full control on money (Singhraul & Garwal, 2018).

Government policies, digital India campaign have positive and significant impact on cashless transactions (Kurane T.S., Salunkhe, Pawar P. A., Prakash S. & Chougule (2020). The present paper explores a novel set of predictors which impact acceptance of cashless transaction by small retailers during their daily business activities. The study mainly addresses two research questions:

1. What are the key predictors for small retailers to accept cashless transactions?
2. What is the relevance and importance of key predictors?

The present paper has been divided into 6 sections. Section 1 introduces the importance of cashless transactions, section 2 explain the review of important studies which are related to the selected topic. Section 3; clarify the objectives, hypotheses and methodology adopted. Section 4 addresses data analysis and in section 5 discussions are presented. Last section (6) of study covered implications and future research directions for future researchers.

Review of Literature

There is paucity of research articles related to perception of small retailers regarding cashless transactions/digital transactions. Podile V. & Rajesh P. (2017) study revealed that there are some problems faced by retailers/merchants like lack of network, lack of willingness, high transaction cost, lack of digital literacy, failure of transactions, financial limits etc. Besides of these problems users feel comfortable with the cashless methods. Mahajan P. and Singla A. (2017) talked about that small retailers are not equipped with latest technological advancements. Chattopadhyay et al. (2018) studied awareness level of small retailers. They included modes of cashless transactions, convenience and extent of usage of cashless methods. Their result found that small retailers were significantly aware about cashless transaction. Prakasam, Jose S. & Karthigai (2019) studied awareness level among users (384) of cashless payments methods and retailers (384) accepting cashless payments. They concluded that awareness level of both the groups was significantly high. Seethamraju R. & Diatha K.S. (2019) studied TOE framework and investigated the impact of digitalisation on small retail store. They found low adoption level of technologies because of high cost, inadequate access & poor reliability, insufficient processes and lack of infrastructure. Lele U. (2019) conducted a survey of retailer in Pune city to find out the status of adoption of cashless payments. Out of the survey retailers 85 per cent doing small business accepting cashless payment and further retailers admitted that 45 per cent of transactions belong to cashless category, and contribution of mobile app was 48 per cent as a cashless mode. Kapuria & Nalawade (2021) have found the fact that demonetisation and COVID-19 pandemic have positively increased the use of cashless transaction. By using digital technology and e-commerce models, small retailers can expand their customer base. Additionally, through POS devices, cashless methods enhance creditworthiness, and debit and loan payments generate data that helps retailers enlarge credit. Singh and Sinha (2020) conducted an online survey of 315 Indian traders. The study concluded that customer perceived value creation had the greatest impact on merchant intent, followed by perception of technology usefulness. Small retailers can increase their customer base with the help of digital advancements. Additionally, digital payments help lenders extend credit.

The journey from cash to cashless is not free of challenges and problems. Some problems are common for all at macro level, while others are for some selective segment. Important among macro level are digital divide, lack of financial literacy, lack of infrastructural facilities, banks stages in technological development, security and safety, regulatory aspects, financial inclusion of population, banking habits of people, internet reach (speed and connections), etc.

As far as subjective problems are concerned, it is mostly observed that people are not willing to opt cashless transactions as they feel that cash is more convenient to deal with. Rural and regional matured people are not adopting cashless methods. Online payment frauds, lack of safety and security, lack of awareness are other important challenges for cashless transactions.

Research Methodology

To answer the research questions pointed out in the introduction, the following objectives of study have to be achieved.

- To confirm reliability and validity of the proposed key indicators.
- To find out the direction of relationship between key indicators and acceptance of cashless transaction by small retailers; and to find out significant predictors for small retailers, which motivate them to accept cashless transactions.
- To investigate the predictive relevance of the proposed retailers' model.

Data Collection and Analysis

To extract factors which motivate small retailers to accept cashless transactions 20 statements (Likert scale) were developed. Firstly, EFA was applied to extract factors by using SPSS software. The 5 extracted factors were then analysed using Smart–PLS Software (free trail version).

In total 500 respondents were surveyed out of which 125 from District Hisar, 135 from District Faridabad, 110 from District Bhiwani and 130 from District Gurugram. The questionnaire was distributed using the convenience sampling method during October 2021–January 2022. With the help of paired sample t test non-response bias was also tested. Sample size was suggested by members of Departmental Research Committee, (Maharishi Dayanand University, Rohtak) at the time of research proposal approval.

On the bases of proposed model following hypotheses are formulated. Hypotheses H_1 to H_5 are related to find out the significant impact of the individual construct on acceptance of cashless transactions by small retailers. Hypotheses H_6 to H_{10} are related to find out the direction of relationship between dependent and independent constructs.

- H_1: There is no significant impact of safety and security, on acceptance of cashless transactions.
- H_2: There is no significant impact of time saving, on acceptance of cashless transactions.
- H_3: There is no significant impact of convenience, on acceptance of cashless transactions.
- H_4: There is no significant impact of customer services associated with cashless transactions, on acceptance of cashless transactions.
- H_5: There is no significant impact of business promotion, on acceptance of cashless transactions.
- H_6: Impact of safety and security, is positively related to acceptance of cashless transactions.
- H_7: Impact of time saving, is positively related to acceptance of cashless transactions.
- H_8: Impact of convenience, is positively related to acceptance of cashless transactions.
- H_9: Impact of customer services is positively related to acceptance of cashless transactions.

- H_{10}: Impact of business promotion, is positively related to acceptance of cashless transactions.

Data Analysis

The explanation of the results is categorised in three sections: (a) measurement model; (b) structural model, and (c) Predicative analysis of model. From review of article written by Hair et al., 2019, 2020 and PLS manual were referred for statistical methods to asses formative model. Table 1 represents the sample distributional statistics.

Table 1: Preferred Methods of Cashless Transactions

Modes of Cashless Transactions	*Frequency*	*Percentage*
Banking Cards (Credit, Debit Card, etc.)	210	42.0
AEPS (Aadhaar enabled Payment System)	230	46.0
UPI (Unified Payment interface)	359	71.8
PoS (Point of Sale)	240	48.0
Mobile wallets	347	69.4
Micro ATMs	72	14.4

Source: Primary Data collected by Researcher

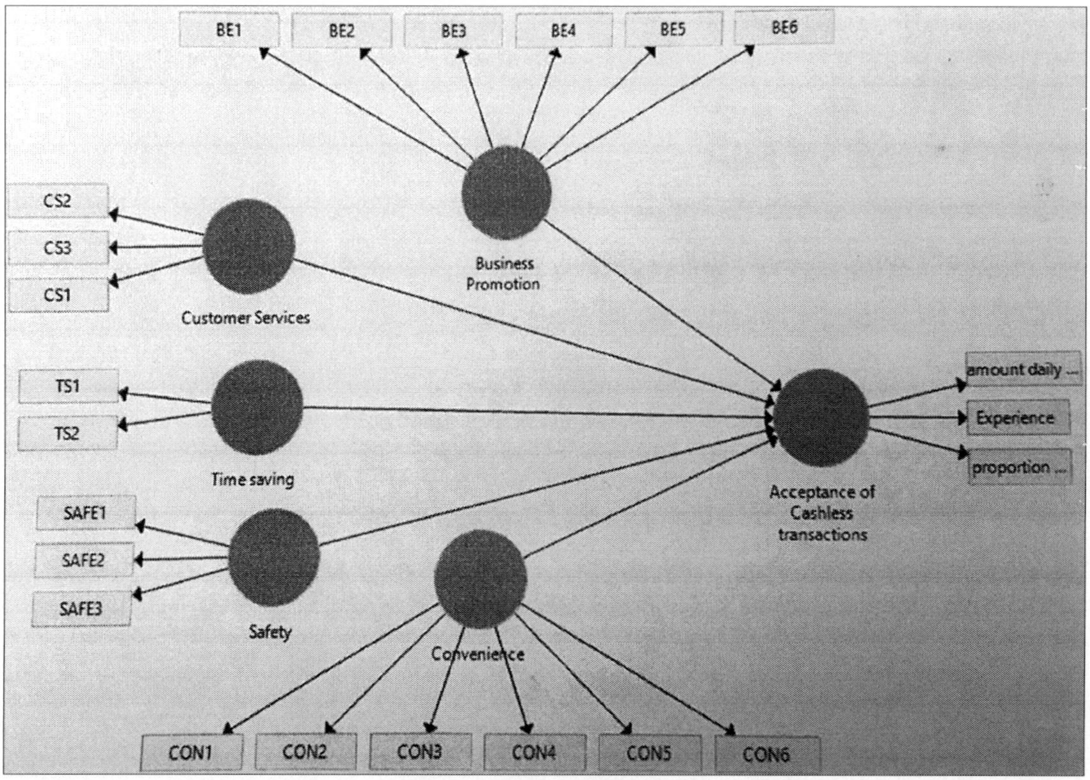

Fig. 1: Proposed Model

Table 2: Small Retailers Surveyed in Study

Type of Retailer	*Frequency*	*Percentages*
Grocery shops (Kirana)	55	11
Fruit/vegetable vendors	30	6
Pharmacies/medical shops	40	8
Bakery	50	10
Street food joints	42	8.4
Stationery and variety store	45	9
Mobile repair shops	49	9.8
Garment shops	45	9
Tailors	35	7
Hair dressers or beauty parlour	45	9
Shoe shop	34	6.8
Miscellaneous other shops	30	6
Total	500	100

Source: Survey data

Measurement Model (Construct Reliability and Validity)

- **Construct Reliability:** Table 3 reflected that value of Cronbach's alpha for each construct is greater than 0.70 which is considered as excellent by researchers. Current researches have shown that there are other methods in comparison to Cronbach's alpha. The threshold value for Jöreskog's Rho is 0.70 and our proposed model has achieved higher values than required to establish the integrity and homogeneity of the model. The table related to construct reliability is showing that all construct namely benefits, convenience, records and maintenance; safety & security, time saving have scored values higher than the threshold values explained by various researchers in the studies. Hence the constructs are reliable. The construct reliability values for acceptance of cashless transactions (daily amount received as cashless, proportion of daily cashless transactions & experience about cashless transactions) have just touched the threshold values decided by the researchers.
- **Validity (Convergent Validity and Construct Validity):** Convergent validity is a criterion used to assess how closely actual construct measures match those that would, in theory, be related. When the AVE value is above 0.50, statistically convergent validity is confirmed. Table 3 reflected that AVE values are much higher than the threshold value. Hence, the scale which is prepared to measure the impact of business promotion, convenience, customer services, safety & security and time saving (predictors) on acceptance of cashless transactions (dependent) is valid, as it has the convergent validity.

The results related to cross loading are reflecting that cross loading values for the variables associated with benefits are higher in comparison to other factors. Similarly cross loading values for all the statements are highest in relation to their respective factors.

Table 3: Cross Loadings

Factors	*Items*	*Construct Reliability*				*Convergent Validity*
		Factor Loadings/ Weights	*Cronbach's Alpha*	*Rho A*	*CR*	*AVE*
Threshold limits		.708	.70	.70	.70	.50
Business Promotion	BE1	**0.831**	0.948	0.967	0.958	0.794
	BE2	**0.898**				
	BE3	**0.938**				
	BE4	**0.915**				
	BE5	**0.872**				
	BE6	**0.888**				
Convenience	CON1	**0.846**	0.955	0.961	0.964	0.816
	CON2	**0.897**				
	CON3	**0.927**				
	CON4	**0.941**				
	CON5	**0.930**				
	CON6	**0.876**				
Customer Services	CS1	**0.918**	**0.895**	1.011	0.930	0.817
	CS2	**0.931**				
	CS3	**0.861**				
Safety and Security	SAFE1	**0.842**	0.896	**0.907**	0.936	0.830
	SAFE2	**0.958**				
	SAFE3	**0.929**				
Tie Saving	TS1	**0.900**	0.747	0.749	**0.888**	0.798
	TS2	**0.887**				
Acceptance of Cashless Transactions	Amount daily transaction	**0.652**	0.690	0.679	0.770	**0.529**
	Experience	**0.726**				
	Proportion total revenue	**0.797**				

Source: Model Calculation

The results of 'Fornell and Larcker Criterion' in table 4 showed that correlation values of construct business promotion is 0.891 which is highest among all correlation values in the specific column. Similarity the correlation values of columns related to convenience, customer services, safety& security and timesaving are highest. All the values mentioned in table have established discriminant validity. Hence, discriminant validity of all construct used in study has been found satisfactory.

Table 4: Discriminant Validity (Fornell and Larcker Criterion)

	Business Promotion	*Convenience*	*Customer Services*	*Safety*	*Time Saving*	*Acceptance of Cashless Transactions*
Business promotion	**0.891**					
Convenience	0.184	**0.903**				
Customer services	0.13	0.251	**0.904**			
Safety	0.214	0.354	0.241	**0.911**		
Time saving	-0.077	0.299	0.075	0.232	**0.893**	
Acceptance of cashless transactions	0.157	0.237	0.297	0.442	0.241	**0.727**

Source: Model Calculation

Table 5: Heterotrait–Monotrait (HTMT Ratio)

	Business Promotion	*Convenience*	*Customer Services*	*Safety*	*Time Saving*
Business promotion					
Convenience	0.189				
Customer services	0.120	0.275			
Safety	0.227	0.384	0.241		
Time saving	0.093	0.356	0.104	0.290	
Acceptance of cashless transactions	0.204	0.348	0.391	0.614	0.378

Source: Model Calculation

The HTMT estimates (Table 5) tell us about how similar the latent variables are. All the tabulated values related to measured constructs are less than 0.85, hence HTMT of correlations are established for the proposed model.

Structural Model Assessment

Assessing the structural model comes next in comparing PLS-SEM effects once the measurement model assessment is found to be satisfactory. Standard assessment criteria, include:- Coefficient of determination (R^2), redundancy degree Q^2, and the relevance of the direction coefficients.

It is advised to examine the constructs and their predictive relevance while assessing structural model. Re-sampling techniques are used in bootstrapping to determine the importance of PLS coefficients. In bootstrapping, subsamples are generated from the original set of data using randomly chosen observations (with replacement, using sub-sample). To calculate the 95 per cent confidence intervals for significance testing, the parameter estimates calculated from the subsamples are used (e.g., original PLS-SEM results are significant when they are outside the confidence interval). Additionally, the estimates' standard errors are provided by bootstrapping, allowing t-values to be computed to determine the significance of each estimate. To get the necessary p-values for the study's proposed hypotheses, the bootstrapping procedure was used (Hair et al., 2020).

To ensure that co-linearity is not affecting the regression results, it must be checked before evaluating the structural correlations. Hence it is must to check co linearity (Becker et al., 2015). As per guidelines values in Table 8 reflected that the constructs have no collinearity issues as the values of VIF in relation to all measured constructs is less than 3. Hence the data set and constructs are fit to run regression model.

Results of (R^2)

The value of $R^2 = 0.258$ which is acceptable and support the weak model. R^2 value indicates that the constructs namely benefits, convenience, records & maintenance, safety & security and time saving explain 26 (approx.) per cent of variance in usage of cashless transactions.

Table 6: Results of (R^2)

Variable (Dependent)	*R^2*	*R^2 Adjusted*
Usage of Cash less Transactions	0.258	0.250

Source: Model Calculation

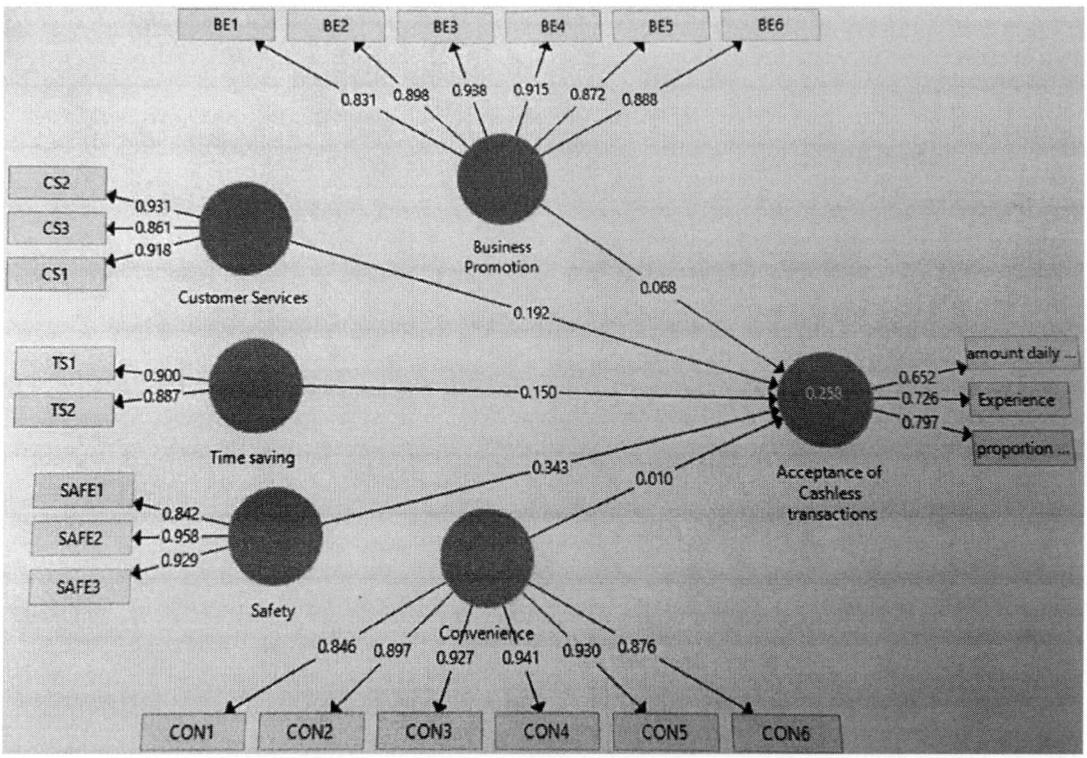

Fig. 2: Structural Model (Path Coefficient Values)

In Fig. 2, it is mentioned in the construct frequency of usage of cashless transaction is well explained by the predictive construct included in this research.

Structural Model Assessment (Bootstrapping Method)

The current study has performed bootstrapping method for assessment of structural model by running 5000 subsamples (using bootstrapping calculate method). The results of assessment of structural model are presented in the following explanation. The coefficient of determination of usage of cashless transactions was found significantly high at 0.258 (25.8 per cent). Hence acceptance of cashless transactions are significantly determined the factors namely business promotion, customer services, convenience, records & maintenance, safety & security and time saving (predictors).

Table 7: Bootstrapping Run (R^2)

R^2	*(O)*	*(M)*	*(STDEV)*	*(|O/STDEV|)*	*P values*
Acceptance of cashless transactions	0.258	0.269	0.029	8.794	0
Bootstrapping results (interval confidence)					
	(O)	(M)	Limit 2.50%	Limit 97.50%	Impact
Acceptance of cashless transactions	0.258	0.269	0.214	0.327	Significant

Source: Model Calculation

To evaluate the importance of coefficients and their values, which normally range between '1 and –1, researchers must do bootstrapping (Nitzl, 2016).

Table 8: Structural Model Assessment

Factors	*Beta Values (Sig.)*	*2.50%*	*97.50%*	*VIF*	*Null Hypothesis as Per t Value Sig. Level*	*Interval Limits*
		Interval Limits				
Business Promotion → Acceptance of cashless transactions	0.072 (0.039*)	0.011	0.136	1.098	Significant	Within limit
Convenience → Acceptance of cashless transactions	0.013 (0.833)	-0.081	0.113	1.281	Not Significant	Outside the limit
Customer Services → Acceptance of cashless transactions	0.193 (0.000*)	0.106	0.278	1.103	Significant	Within limit
Safety → Acceptance of cashless transactions	0.342 (0.000**)	0.25	0.431	1.239	Significant	Within limit
Time saving → Acceptance of cashless transactions	0.151 (0.000**)	0.077	0.223	1.153	Significant	Within limit

Source: Model Calculation

Note: ** Significant at 1 per cent and * significant at 5 per cent

Table 9: Summary Table of Hypotheses Results

Hypotheses	*Results*	*Remarks*
H_1: There is no significant impact of safety and security, on the acceptance of cashless transactions	Rejected	Significant
H_2: There is no significant impact of time saving, on the acceptance of cashless transactions.	Rejected	Significant
H_3: There is no significant impact of Convenience, on the acceptance of cashless transactions.	Fail to reject	Not significant
H_4: There is no significant impact of customer services associated with cashless transactions, on the acceptance of cashless transactions.	Rejected	Significant
H_5: There is no significant impact of business promotion, on the Acceptance of cashless transactions.	Rejected	Significant
H_6: Impact of safety and security, is positively related to the acceptance of cashless transactions.	Fail to reject	Positively related
H_7: Impact of time saving, is positively related to the acceptance of cashless transactions.	Fail to reject	Positively related
H_8: Impact of Convenience, is positively related to the acceptance of cashless transactions.	Fail to reject	Positively related
H_9: Impact of customer services is positively related to the acceptance of cashless transactions.	Fail to reject	Positively related
H_{10}: Impact of business promotion, is positively related to the acceptance of cashless transactions.	Fail to reject	Positively related

Source: Model Calculation

Model Fit and Predictive Importance and Relevance

Model fit: The SRMR global fit index was examined for goodness-of-fit criteria. In the current era of research using PLS-SEM models to assess model quality, global model fit measures such as SRMR are essential (Hair et al., 2020). His SRMR value for this study was 0.066 for the estimated model, well below the 0.08 threshold, indicating that the model considered has excellent explanatory power (Henseler et al., 2016).

Estimation with Blindfolding

Table 10: Construct Cross-Validated Redundancy (Q^2 value)

Factors	*Acceptance of Cashless Transactions (f^2 value) and P Values*		*SSO*	*SSE*	*Q^2 (=1-SSE/SSO)*
Business promotion	0.006	0.363	3000	3000	
Convenience	0.000	0.978	3000	3000	
Customer services	0.045*	0.032	1500	1500	
Safety	0.128**	0.001	1500	1500	
Time saving	0.026***	0.064	1000	1000	
Acceptance of cashless transactions			1500	1312.979	0.125

Source: Model Calculation

Note: *5 per cent, ** 1 per cent, *** 10 per cent level of Sig.

Table 10 reflects that Q^2 value is 0.125 it shows that the proposed model has moderate predictive value. Redundancy is only calculated for endogenous variables in the model (here, Acceptance of cashless transactions).

f^2 **Effect Sizes:** Table 10 is reflecting f^2 values based on bootstrapping is reflecting that in prediction model customer services (0.045), safety & security (0.001) and time saving (0.026) have significant impact on acceptance of cashless transactions.

Importance Performance Map Analysis (IMPA)

Purpose of using IMPA in study is to decide the crucial factor for influencing the performance of the target construct for cashless transaction methods (www.smartpls.com). With a relatively high importance construct in the investigation, the strong overall effects towards the target construct were detected in this approach (Ringle and Sarstedt, 2016).

Figure 3 reflecting that the entire predictive construct have higher performance importance as all constructs are clustered between app. 40.00 to 55.00 scores out of 100 performances on usage. Interestingly safety & security has shown high importance

Fig. 3: Importance Performance Map

Table 11: Importance – Performance Map

Constructs	*Importance*	*Performance*	*Importance Change*	*Performance Change*
Business promotion	0.074	45.620	By 1%	45.620 + 0.074 = 45.694
Convenience	0.01	55.697	By 1%	55.697 + 0.001 = 55.707
Customer service	0.224	53.679	By 1%	53.679 + 0.224 = 53.903
Safety and security	0.425	40.607	By 1%	40.607 + 0.425 = 41.032
Time saving	0.186	54.603	By 1%	54.603 + 0.186 = 54.789
Acceptance of cashless transactions		45.356		45.356

Source: Model Calculation

Table explain about the importance and performance of measured constructs in relation to acceptance of cashless transactions. Performance score is highest in relation to the Convenience but importance attached is very less. If convenience is increased by 1 per cent the performance will increase from 55.697 to 55.707. The importance of performance indicator namely safety & security, customer service and time saving has shown high importance value. The highest change in performance is due to safety & security followed by customer services and time saving.

Discussions

Our study explored five factors namely customer services, convenience, business promotion, safety & security and time saving, which are positively motivating small retailers to accept cashless transactions. As mentioned earlier in introduction section research papers, reports/project work completed by IIMB (2017), PWC report (2020, Indian payment Handbook 2020–2025), BSP Digital Payments Transformation Roadmap 2020-2023, Ravi Seethamraju & Krishna Sundar Diatha (2019), Lele (2019), Observer Research Foundation (2021) paper by Kapuria & Nalawade have also found the fact that demonetisation and COVID-19 pandemic have positively increased the use of cashless transaction. The factors covered under current study explained 26 per cent impact on small retailers to accept cashless transactions. Further it was observed that customer services, safety and security, time saving and business promotion are the significant factors which contribute positively in the acceptance of cashless transactions by small retailers.

Implications and Future Research Directions

The current paper proposes imperative insights about acceptance of cashless transactions by the small retailers. Firstly the study contributes to find out the important factors which motivate small retailers to accept cashless transaction via various methods. Secondly study concluded that safety & security is the utmost important factor which impact acceptance of cashless transactions. As the managerial implications are concerned the study observed that acceptance of cashless transaction methods by small retailers is positively affected by safety & security, customer services, time saving and business promotion. This result can help the fin-tech companies to developed such techniques that how to provide more customer service-based applications/ softwares which provide benefits and security to users. The practical implications were strengthened with the applications of importance map analysis (IPMA). Safety and security has scored highest importance value among all constructs, followed by customer service and time saving. Although convenience and business promotion have less importance values but in future these constructs can help financial partners to recognise the important areas.

This study is not free from limitations. Firstly, the study is based on self-structured questionnaire. Future researchers can incorporate certain latest developments in their study and can include more factors which impact usage of cashless transactions. Secondly, this study is conducted in four district of Haryana state; future researchers can cover other areas of India with a larger sample size. Thirdly, researchers can study moderating and mediating factors to add more clarity about the usage of cashless methods.

References

[1] Becker J.M., Ringle C.M., Sarstedt M. & Völckner F. (2015), 'How Collinearity Affects Mixture Regression Results', *Marketing Letters*, Vol. 26, No. 4, pp. 643–59.

[2] Chattopadhyay S., Bose I. & Gulati P. (2018), 'Awareness and Participation of Small Retail Businesses in Cashless Transactions: An Empirical Study', *Management Dynamics in the Knowledge Economy*, Vol. 6, No. 2, pp. 209–25.

[3] Hair J.F. Jr, Howard M.C. & Nitzl C. (2020), 'Assessing Measurement Model Quality in PLS SEM Using Confirmatory Composite Analysis', *Journal of Business Research*, Vol. 109, pp. 101–10.

[4] Hair J.F., Sarstedt M. & Ringle C.M. (2019), 'Rethinking Some of the Rethinkingof Partial Least Squares', *European Journal of Marketing*, Forthcoming.

[5] Henseler J., Hubona G. & Ray P.A. (2016), 'Using PLS Path Modeling in New Technology Research: Updated Guidelines', *Industrial Management and Dat Systems*,Vol. 116, No. 1, pp. 2–20.

[6] Kapuria & Nalawade (2021), 'Digitising Indian Retail: Analysing Challenges and Exploring Growth Models', ORF Occasional Paper, No. 304.

[7] Kurane T.S., Salunkhe, Pawar P.A., Prakash S. & Chougule (2020), 'A Study of Impact of Cashless Transaction on Society Using Statistical Methods', *IJISRT*, Vol. 5, No. 7.

[8] Lele U. (2019), 'Adoption of Cashless Payments by Small Retailers in Pune City: An Empirical Study', *International Journal of Research in Engineering, IT and Social Sciences*, Vol. 09, No. 09, pp. 20–26.

[9] Mahajan P. & Singla A. (2017), 'Effect of Demonetisation on Financial Inclusion in India', *International Journal of Science Technology and Management*, Vol. 6, No. 1, pp. 338–43.

[10] Nitzl C. (2016), 'The Use of Partial Least Squares Structural Equation Modelling (PLS-SEM) in Management Accounting Research: Directions for Future TheoryDevelopment', *Journal of Accounting Literature*, Vol. 37, pp. 19–35.

[11] Podile V. & Rajesh P. (2017), 'Public Perception on Cashless Transactions in India', *Asian Journal of Research in Banking and Finance*, Vol. 7, No. 7, pp. 63–77.

[12] Prakasam, Jose S. & Karthigai (2019), 'Consumers' and Retailers' Kinds of Awareness of Cashless Payment System', *Journal of Emerging Technologies and Innovative Research*, Vol. 6, No. 1.

[13] Ringle C.M. & Sarstedt M. (2016), 'Gain More Insight from Your PLS-SEM Results the Importance Performance Map Analysis', *Industrial Management and Data Systems*, Vol. 16, No. 9, pp. 1865–886.

[14] Seethamraju R. & Diatha K.S. (2019), 'Digiatilsation of Small Retail Store – Challenges in Digital Payments', *Proceedings of the 52nd Hawai International Conference on System Sciences*.

[15] Singhraul B.P. & Garwal Y.S. (2018), 'Cashless Economy – Challenges and Opportunities in India' , *Pacific Business Review International*, Vol. 10, No. 9, pp. 55–63.

[16] Sinha P.K., Gokhale S. & Rawal S. (2015), 'Online Retailing Paired with Kirana – A Formidable Combination for Emerging Markets,' *Customer Need and Solutions*, Vol. 2, pp. 317–24.

[17] Singh & Sinha (2020) 'How Perceived Trust Mediates Merchant's Intention to Use a Mobile Wallet Technology', *Journal of Retailing and Consumer Services*, Vol. 52, January 2020.

[18] PwC, The Indian Payment Handbook – 2020–2025.

Financial Distress Analysis of the Steel Industry using Altman's Z-Score Model

Shikha Yadhav[1], Shrey Srivastava[1] and Dr Pinku Paul[2]

[1]*Student (Batch 2022-2024), MDI Murshidabad*
[2]*MDI Murshidabad, West Bengal, India*

Abstract

One of the major reasons for the financial sustainability of firms is to understand when they enter the financial distress zone. Therefore, understanding the financial distress level and the factors affecting the same are highly important for firms. The purpose of the study is to examine the financial distress level of the firms in the steel industry of India by employing the Altman's Z-Score. The study used the empirical model of Altman's Z-Score (Altman,1984) and applied it to 124 steel companies. The study's findings indicated that most companies are in the green zone with a Z-Score higher than 2.99, i.e. 77 companies out of 124. 22 companies were found to be in the distress zone, contributing to 18 per cent of the entire sample. The results of the study can be used to suggest that financially distressed companies work on the variables in which they are suffering and overcome the distress zone.

Keywords: *Financial Distress, Altman's Z-Score, Steel Industry, Debt Level, Equity, Liabilities*

Introduction

Insolvency is a state of the financial crisis in which a person or corporation is unable to pay its debts. The state of financial distress may result in the liquidation of the assets of the entity and also legal obligations. Business owners can restructure debts into more managed instalment by dialog with creditors directly. Since creditors want to be paid back, even if it is on a delayed schedule, they are often open to this strategy. In order to make a drastic change in the financial structure of the company the capital structure of the firm has to undergo changes. The business can also work on its cost optimisation and maintain a sustainable line of business. The cost optimisation plans require proper differentiating and classifying of the cost into value-added and non-value-added activities to ensure proper cash flow of profits for the business. Insolvency is significantly exacerbated by rising vendor expenses. Lack of income causes bills to go unpaid and creditors to demand money that is owed to them. Some businesses fail because their products or services don't change to meet the shifting demands of their customers. If a company doesn't change to the market as consumers start looking for alternatives that offer a wider range of goods and services, it will lose money. Revenues fall short of expenses, and invoices go unpaid.

All of the aforementioned factors result in a company becoming insolvent, which then results in bankruptcy, which has a significant negative influence on the economy, market crashes, and other things. Well-known scholars have created a number of models to investigate, comprehend, and stop these occurrences. The Altman's Z-Score model is one of these models; it essentially serves as a tool to analyse the financial status of a business in light of insolvency.

Steel was chosen as the research topic because India produced 103 MT of crude steel globally in FY21, ranking second in the world. One of the main forces behind the industrial revolution has been metals (Ministry of Steel, India-a, 2022). Steel has traditionally had a leading position among metals. Steel production and consumption are frequently used as measures of a country's economic development because it is both a raw material and an intermediary product. Since the steel industry is the foundation of every economy, it would not be an exaggeration to argue that it has always been at the forefront of industrial progress.

Research Gap

Any organisation's ability to satisfy its existing obligations and maintain a healthy level of profitability is directly related to its financial soundness, whether measured in terms of liquidity, profitability, solvency, or growth. Since insolvency affects not only the company's stockholders but also the overall economy of the nation. Therefore, every stakeholder is interested in a company's financial situation. For management, owners, creditors, the government, auditors, suppliers, employees, and other entities, predicting a financial crisis is a big problem. To identify businesses that may file for bankruptcy and to give an early warning of a large bankruptcy risk, bankruptcy prediction models can be created. A frequently employed strategy in literature is the creation of bankruptcy prediction models, such as the Altman's Z-Score model. Numerous academics from all around the world have come to the conclusion that models for predicting bankruptcy may frequently forecast possible economic and financial issues in a company's operations with a year to go before filing for bankruptcy.

Steel is utilised in practically every part of our life, including vehicles, refrigerators, washing machines, highways, bridges, ships, and airplanes, as well as widely in engineering and building projects, so it was chosen as the industry for research purposes. As a result, the socioeconomic development of many large countries can be closely correlated with the production and consumption of steel. The growth of the Indian economy has benefited greatly from the use of steel. To maintain operating capacity, this industry needs contemporary technology, and to do so, businesses need large funds, which they raise from the debt market. And businesses that make investments between economic booms and busts, or during cyclical crises, frequently fail.

From 22 million tonnes in 1990 to 105 million tonnes in 2018, India consumed more crude steel. The Ministry of Steel estimates that steel and related industries employ about 25 lakh people and contribute about 2 per cent of the nation's GDP. Given that it has one of the strongest economic ties to the nation's GDP, it is clear that the steel sector is significant. Therefore, it is crucial to comprehend the financial situation of an industry that contributes significantly (Ministry of Steel, India-b, 2022).

Another major reason for conducting the study was that there is a significant gap in the quantity of research that is currently available and that no research article could be located with such a big number of organisations employing the Altman's Z-Score.

Indian Steel Industry

The Indian steel sector contributes roughly 2 per cent of the nation's GDP and supports 6.8 times as many jobs as it does in terms of employment and output. Through the blast furnace (BF) or direct reduced iron (DRI) routes, it is primarily iron-based. The domestic availability of raw materials like iron ore and affordable labour has been major contributor to the growth of the steel industry. As a result, the steel industry has contributed significantly to India's manufacturing output. Being a core industry, it also long-term tracks the expansion of the entire economy. Steel's success is reliant on the development of these end-user industries because steel demand comes from other industries including transportation, consumer goods, and infrastructure. The domestic steel sector benefits greatly from this in terms of costs. Domestic steel prices are becoming more in line with international export pricing as markets balance domestic demand and imports. South Asian and European demand for Indian steel could be threatened by China's declining consumption and the resulting increase in exports. The movement of currencies relative to the US dollar also has a big impact on the pricing of raw materials and steel around the world. In recent years, there has been a lot of investment in the steel business. In the steel industry, 100 per cent FDI is permitted through the automatic method. In the period between April 2000 and March 2020, the Indian metallurgical industries garnered Foreign Direct Investment (FDI) of US$13.4 billion, (IBEF, 2022)

Literature Review

Cristi et al. (2021) highlighted in their study the financial distress model by using the Altman score for the Indian textile industry. The findings of the study stated that the majority of the firm out of 161 were financially distressed. In a study like the one described in this paper, two prominent aviation companies—Indigo and Jet Airways—were subjected to the Altman Z-Score model, with the results showing that while Indigo had a low likelihood of becoming insolvent soon, Jet Airways was in a precarious position and thus might become an insolvent (Rao et al., 2013). Another study Saifuddin (2017), examined the Indian steel industry's capacity, production and consumption, imports and exports, price fluctuations, and wholesale price index. It was determined that there has been a declining tendency in output growth. Because of the sluggish industrial expansion, consumption growth lagged. India grew to be a significant net importer and exporter. The steel industry's installed capacity overall rose. Domestic steel prices have seen a downward trend partly due to lowering iron ore prices and pressure from slumping steel prices globally. Retail pricing showed a similar pattern of declining prices. Bhatia (2017), Z-Score was used to know the insolvency of listed power generation and distribution companies in India. In order to examine the financial position of the industries, the researchers calculated the mean of all the ratios for 19 power generation/distribution businesses, did ratio analysis and utilised Altman's Z-Score model. The Z score was also utilised to get the conclusion that most of the companies—18 out of 19—were in a distress zone Azhar & Ramesh (2017). Another study offered a straightforward method for using a series of financial ratios as inputs to calculate an overall bankruptcy index (ABI). This index's value ranges from 0 to 1, and it essentially assesses the companies according to how financially distressed they are. According to their research, ABI can forecast a firm's bankruptcy more effectively than Z-Score. They claim that ABI has quite a strong predictive potential, allowing it to be used in conjunction with other models to anticipate company insolvency (Liao and Mehdian, 2016*)*. A study on the financial performance of the steel business was conducted to better understand the steel industry in India. It was based on the financial performance of 10 Indian steel companies and looked at the industry's growth, profitability, and short- and long-term solvency. They have examined which company is operating better utilising the instruments of the quick ratio, current ratio, inventory turnover ratio, debtor turnover ratio, and fixed assets turnover ratio. They have utilised the log-linear multiple regression model (Balakrishnan, 2016*)*.

Another study was carried out to comprehend the same thing, and the financial health of the sector was examined using a sample of 5 organisations. The positions of the selected units' liquidity, solvency, activity, and profitability were taken into account in order to assess their financial performance. The alternate hypothesis and a few hypotheses based on whether there is a difference between the ratio value and financial success of the various companies were both proven by Arab, Masoumi, and Barati (2015). Twenty of the big and medium steel units that are listed were selected in order to assess the implications of the Altman's Z-Score model for the steel industry and the viability of the sector. The study's sample period was chosen to be between 2001 and 2010. Using Altman's Z-Score model, which has been widely utilised by researchers and practitioners in the past, the financial performance of the steel sector was tracked and measured. This study employs the Z-Score model to reasonably and accurately analyse the likelihood of business failure. The study's findings show that apart from two enterprises during the study period the steel industry had strong financial performance despite the effects of weak demand and the global economic slump (Chavali 2012).

Altman's Z-Score

The probability that a company would file for bankruptcy during the next two years is predicted using a metric known as Altman's Z-Score. The model was developed in 1968 by American finance professor Edward Altman to evaluate the financial health of organisations (Altman, 1984). The primary financial ratios were combined to create the model's sole index. Prior to being insolvent, it made a clear distinction between enterprises that were bankrupt and those that were not. It bases its judgment on ratios for profitability, leverage, liquidity, solvency, and activity. The better the company's health, the higher the Z-Score (Altman 1984).

Altman's Z-Score model is a commonly used tool in research papers. Arab, Masoumi & Barati (2015), Azhar & Ramesh (2017), Safiuddin (2017) have all used the Altman's Z-Score model to study specific industries as mentioned.

Research Methodology

It is an analytical study primarily conducted to comprehend the state of the steel sector and to identify companies that may be at risk of going bankrupt. The Objectives of the study are:

- examine the existing steel industry from the perspective of bankruptcy.
- provide a Z-Score model overview of the steel industry; and
- identify the companies that may be at risk of going bankrupt soon.

The study is largely based on information and data extracted from various *secondary data* sources such as Annual reports, online articles, journals issued by various research institutes, official NSE, BSE & SEBI websites, previously conducted and published papers, and international studies.

The Research paper has used an empirical model, i.e. the Altman's Z-Score model by Edward Altman (Altman, 1984). The data of 124 companies in the steel industry have been taken as a sample through the stratified random sampling method and they have been studied and subsequent observations have been made. The model uses 5 financial ratios to determine the Z-Score of any company.

- X1 = working capital/total assets
- X2 = retained earnings/total assets
- X3 = earnings before interest and tax/total assets
- X4 = market value of equity/total liabilities
- X5 = sales/total assets

Altman's Z-SCORE = (1.2) X1 + (1.4) X2 + (3.3) X3 + (0.6) X4 + (1.0) X5

Zone of Discrimination

Z > 2.99 – 'SAFE ZONE'
1.81 < Z < 2.99 – 'GREY ZONE'
Z < 1.81 – 'DISTRESS ZONE'

A company has a high likelihood of going bankrupt within two years if its Z-Score is less than 1.81. Companies that have a score of at least 3 are relatively safe and have a low likelihood of going bankrupt. A grey zone is defined as a score between 1.81 and 3. Small, non-manufacturing or privately held businesses should not use Altman's initial model. Altman uses statistical information from publicly traded manufacturing businesses to create the model. Altman's Z-Score model is one of the more widely used and accepted models for checking the likeliness of a company to go bankrupt. It provides the investors with clear and easy-to-interpret signals for them to take informed decisions. A Z-Score of 3 (green zone) means that the company is not likely to go bankrupt in the near future. A score between 2.99 – 1.81 (grey zone) means that there is a possibility of a company going bankrupt as, the lower the Z-Score, the higher the probability of the organisation suffering from insolvency. Finally, a Z-Score below 1.8 (distress zone) indicates that a company is closer to bankruptcy. Therefore, based on the Z-Score, the investor can decide whether to invest in a particular company or not (Altman, 1984).

Findings

Table 1: Descriptive Analysis

	X1	*X2*	*X3*	*X4*	*X5*
Mean	0.25867	–1.3071	0.16902	32.3143	1.48072
Standard dev	0.59515	13.8214	1.13501	310.562	1.35063
Max	0.9325	0.90777	12.2904	3475	11.0848
Min	–5.0615	–152.5	–2.75	0.00403	0
Range	5.994035	153.4078	15.04042	3474.996	11.08477

Source: Authors' Calculation

After calculation of the descriptive statistics of the respective variables for all 124 companies, the mean, standard deviation, and range of the variables were found. It was observed that mean of X4 (32.3143) is the highest among all the variables on the other hand the mean of X2 (–1.3071) is the lowest. X4 also has the highest standard deviation amongst the variables of 310.562 and X1 has the lowest standard deviation of 0.59515. X4 also has the highest range amongst all the variables – 3474.996 on the other hand X1 has the lowest range – 5.994035.

Table 2: Correlation Analysis

	X1	*X2*	*X3*	*X4*	*X5*
X1	1	0.250987	0.136794	0.005975	0.262962
X2	0.250987	1	0.221227	0.012426	0.111206
X3	0.136794	0.221227	1	-0.01269	0.670736
X4	0.005975	0.012426	–0.01269	1	–0.10136
X5	0.262962	0.111206	0.670736	-0.10136	1

Source: Authors' Calculation

The correlation between the X3 and X5 is 0.670736 which indicates that they have a positive correlation. Among all other financial ratios, only X3 and X5 have a significant positive correlation between them. A change in the value of X3 will affect the value of X5. The correlation between the X3 and X4 is -0.01269, indicating that they have a weakly negative correlation. The correlation between the X4 and X5 is -0.10136, indicating that they have weakly negative correlation.

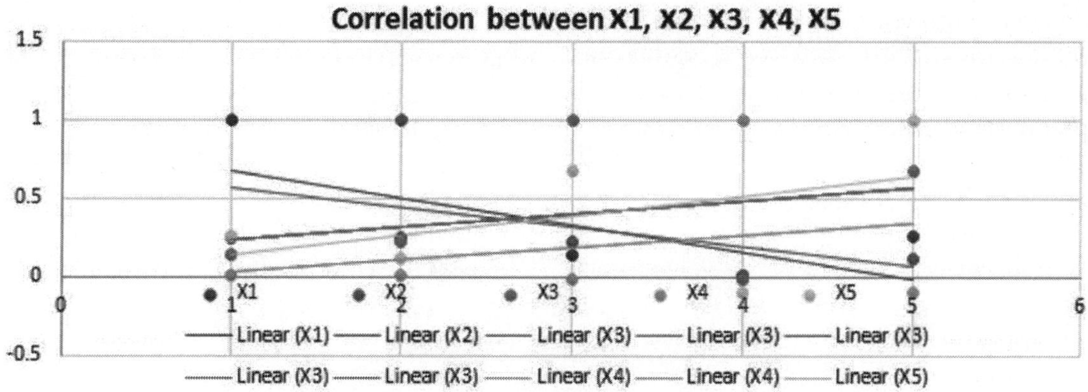

Fig. 1: Correlation Analysis
Source: Authors' Calculation

From the above table, we can see that X1 and X2, X1 and X3, X1 and X4, X1 and X5, X2 and X3, X2 and X4, X2 and X5, have a weakly positive correlation. But there will not be e significant change in value, with the change in other values.

Table 3: Analysis of the Z-SCORE

Name	*Z-score*	*Name*	*Z-score*
JSW Steel	2.439615449	Tata Metaliks	4.148651105
Tata Steel	2.422307717	JTL Infra	10.72675886
Jindal Steel	3.065859443	Technocraf.Inds.	4.011467126
S A I L	2.176680338	Mukand	2.924953253
APL Apollo Tubes	10.48744592	Sunflag Iron	2.901516124
Ratnamani Metals	14.94008335	Gallantt Ispat L	8.097751602
Jindal Stain.	3.129149523	Venus Pipes	8.884964328
Lloyds Metals	7.103738615	ISMT	3.729884692
Shyam Metalics	4.287098628	JSW Ispat Speci.	1.493926716
Jindal Stain. Hi	4.256549821	Rama Steel Tubes	6.355801504
Apollo Tricoat	22.13539342	Kalyani Steels	3.416870209
Welspun Corp	1.874301615	Lloyds Steels	8.780422515
Mah. Seamless	4.75778711	Goodluck India	4.361899117
Rajratan Global	10.36608859	Vardhman Special	4.579032549
Mishra Dhatu Nig	4.281241616	Raghav Product.	23.82955701
Kirl. Ferrous	3.079760205	Prakash Industri	2.542871158
Usha Martin	4.874709906	Salasar Techno	3.463166042
Godawari Power	5.248725231	Welspun Special.	1.076548857
Sarda Energy	3.458258509	Pennar Industrie	2.466901289
Tata Steel Long	0.761961435	Hi-Tech Pipes	4.661087741
Jindal Saw	2.067540508	Beekay Steel Ind	4.426012252
Surya Roshni	5.191173675	Hariom Pipe	6.72465458

Name	*Z-score*	*Name*	*Z-score*
Bharat Wire	3.257340658	Zenith Steel	-1.807347065
Gandhi Spl. Tube	30.3488576	Hisar Met.Inds.	4.074358088
BMW Industries	2.748726107	Metal Coatings	7.065745156
D P Wires	13.15665099	Vaswani Industri	3.240232466
Jai Balaji Inds.	1.037315564	Remi Edelstahl	3.357086671
Man Industries	2.862649252	Chennai Ferrous	6.25532759
Alliance Integ.	-2.003862565	Aanchal Ispat	2.803915628
Kamdhenu	4.394487514	Uttam Galva Stee	-2.535632599
Bajaj Steel Inds	3.412949109	Rathi Bars	4.629655634
MSP Steel & Pow.	2.002008152	Gujarat Intrux	11.1331224
Rhetan TMT Ltd	6.249669454	Gyscoal Alloys	-0.715917084
Mangalam World.	6.660044041	Supreme Engg.	1.314672775
Panchmahal Steel	5.101718786	Sharda Ispat	6.138011363
Manaksia Steels	5.679438572	Ashirwad Steels	2086.609361
Rudra Global	2.68519655	Unison Metals	1.952006291
Bedmutha Indus.	2.35525036	Ashiana Ispat	4.427062904
Swastik Pipe	3.611067117	Surani Steel Tub	4.303106595
Visa Steel	-2.054261995	Modern Steels	50.25220187
Sh. Bajrang All.	3.642568571	Garg Furnace	5.508458336
Scan Steels	3.715138265	Natl. Steel&Agro	-3.884241783
Kritika Wires	4.719198677	Bombay Wire	48.93526037
Ahlada Engineers	3.157291525	Grand Foundry	-38.00639175
Suraj	4.804843383	Sathavaha. Ispat	-1.721007236
Guj.Nat.Resour.	2.44598579	Rish.Digh.Steel	6.51160238
Natl. Gen. Inds.	14.43106359	Pact Industries	2.582371946
Shah Alloys	4.179865354	Sh. Steel Wire	7.000672809
Manaksia Coated	2.141692468	Mukat Pipes	-2.881267692
Mahamaya Steel	4.856686898	Rajas. Tube Mfg	3.686557153
Incredible Indus	5.431255854	Umiya Tubes	1.849480351
Bonlon Industrie	7.063379099	Ahm. Steelcraft	17.25933676
Suraj Products	4.028452286	P.M. Telelinnks	7.040481475
S.A.L Steel	2.044034168	Aryavan Enter.	6.537160268
Oil Country	2.478945063	Heera Ispat	-216.5216667
Electrotherm(I)	0.78765567	Aditya Ispat	1.822006534
Ankit Met.Power	-0.582373835	Mahalaxmi Seam.	0.380736966
Prakash Steelage	2.136445773	T N Steel Tubes	4.069106702
Bansal Roofing	6.052972863	Narayani Steels	2.617370404
India Steel	-0.275556203	Vallabh Steels	-0.664750202
Bihar Sponge	-0.143132543	Indian Bright St	5.007407407
Kanishk Steel	5.128009425	Gopal Iron Stl.	-1.034885165

Source: Authors' Calculation

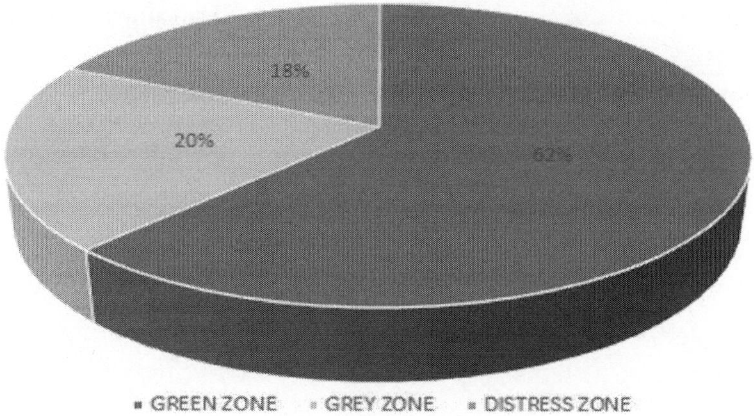

Fig. 2: Z-Score Distribution and Zone Classification
Source: Authors' calculation

The above pie chart shows the percentage of companies that were in the green, grey, and distress zones according to the model. The pie chart was derived from the above table. The majority of the companies are in the green zone (62 per cent) i.e.; they are not likely to go bankrupt under normal circumstances 20 per cent of the companies are in the grey zone which means that there is a chance that they might face insolvency in the future. 22 companies (18 per cent) are in the distress zone meaning they are heading towards bankruptcy. Overall, the majority of the top performer in the industry are in the green and grey zone.

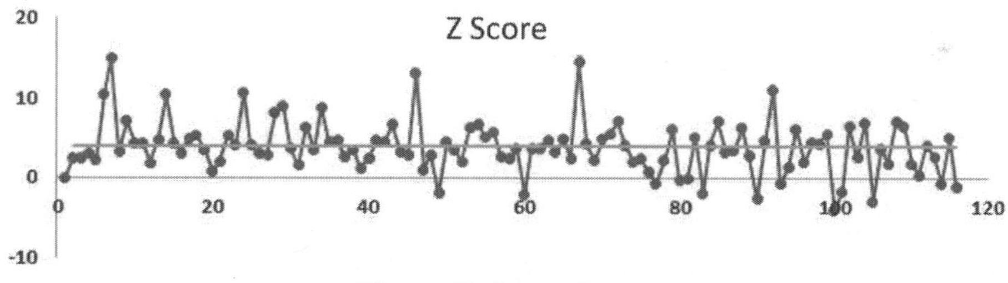

Fig. 3: Z-Score Range
Source: Authors' calculation

Table 4: Analysis of Z-Score with Level of Distress

Zone of Discrimination			*Number of Companies*
Z > 2.99		Green Zone	77
1.81 < Z < 2.99		Grey Zone	25
Z < 1.81		Distress Zone	22

Source: Authors' Calculation

After an analysis of 124 businesses in the steel industry, it is observed that 77 companies are in the 'green zone,' which indicates that they will not go insolvent very soon. There are 25 companies and 22, respectively, that are in the grey and distress zones. This indicates that these businesses face the possibility of going bankrupt soon.

The top 10 companies in the steel industry are based on market share. None of the leading companies (top 10) are in the distress zone. Only 30 per cent of the companies might go insolvent.

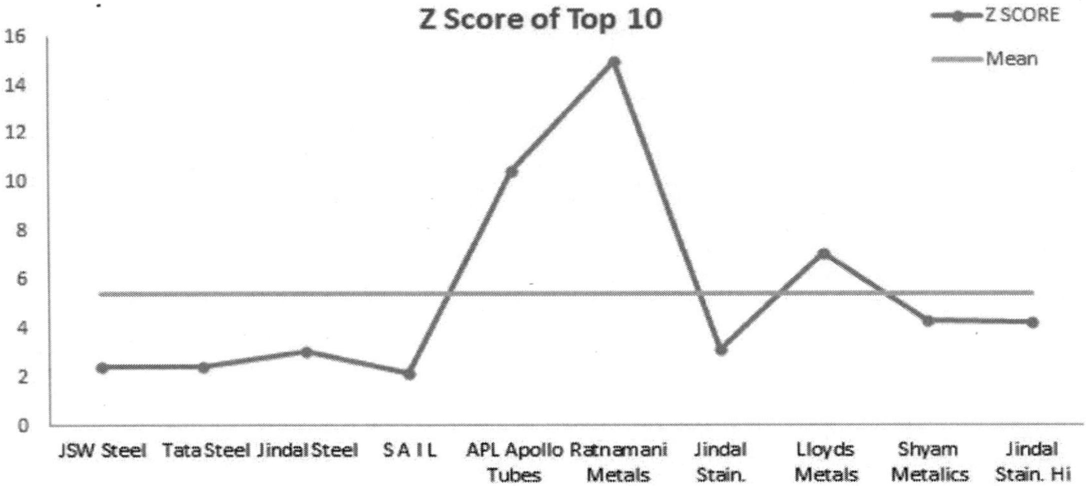

Fig. 4: Z-Score and Mean Range of Top Ten Companies
Source: Authors' calculation

Three of the companies with the lowest share capital (bottom 10) are in the distress zone. 50 per cent of the companies might go insolvent.

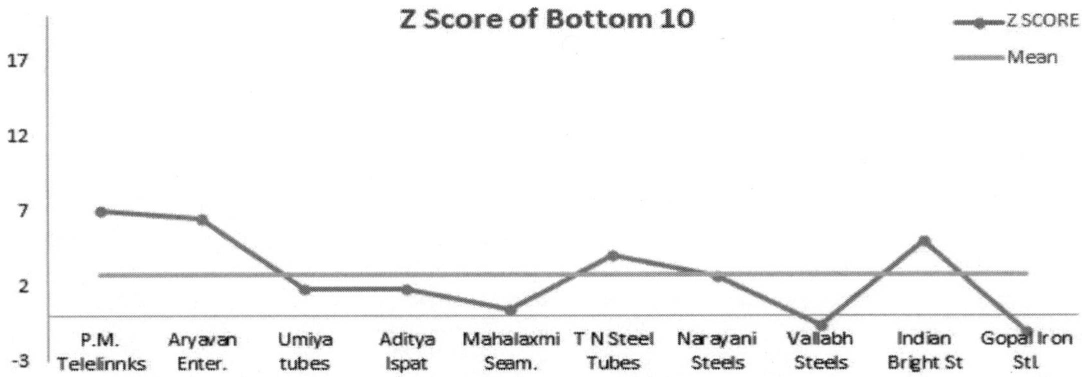

Fig. 5: Z-Score and Mean Range of Bottom Ten Companies
Source: Authors' calculation

Discussion

Poor financial management leads to insolvency. Loss of revenue, loss of cash flow, and loss of capital –are the major reason for the company to fall into insolvency. Excessive borrowing for the future growth of the company will lead to insolvency. Dependencies on particular or fewer investors/customers. When a company is dependent on fewer investors, and that investor decides to no longer support your company, then the company will have the risk of insolvency. At times company fails to evolve according to the changing needs and desires of the customer. In this case, the customer tends to lose interest and shift to another company.

Suggestions for Companies to Avoid Insolvency

- **Improve liquidity** – Companies heading towards insolvency must take into consideration whether their current assets are able to cover their current liabilities. The business should increase its working capital. Current assets including debtors, receivables, marketable securities, and prepaid expenses should be monitored continuously.
- **Work on core operation activities** – There should be a proper team that can concentrate on the core operations of the business, work on cost reduction, and works on a solid supply chain because sometimes inadequate financing prevents a firm from being able to earn more income. Handheld analysers, grapple monitoring systems, and automatic scrap monitoring portal systems are available to assist steel manufacturing facilities that use scrap metal in the identification of orphan sources and radiation-contaminated commodities. In order to help companies, meet the tightest tolerances, they need to make sure that products meet the most exact specifications, and make the best use of raw materials, non-contact thickness gauges for hot- and cold-rolling mills provide accurate, real-time measurements during high-speed production of steel plate and sheet.
- **Manage debt and long-term borrowings** – The companies in the grey and red zone should also prioritise reducing their liabilities. Large loans and borrowing might eventually hurt a firm. It had been seen that India's top steel makers JSW Steel, Tata Steel, SAIL and JSPL, and ArcelorMittal Nippon Steel had lowered their debt by 15 per cent, or Rs 35,000 crore, between the fiscal years 2021 and 2022 by leveraging the increased operating profits generated for prepayment.
- **Raise capital using equity** – For companies who are looking to expand in the market should focus on raising capital through options like bootstrapping, crowdfunding, and Angel investment rather than taking loans and long-term liabilities.
- **Focus on switching markets** – If the company is at a high risk of becoming bankrupt soon, the only option the company has is to shut down its operations in the current industry and try to enter another market. This will provide the company with a possible opportunity to grow.

Conclusion

For our study, we took all 124 listed companies in the steel industry as our sample. After analysing and studying the companies we were able to conclude that the Steel industry is one of the most important industries in the country contributing around 2 per cent to the GDP and employing more than 25 lac people. Through a review of various literature on the subject, we understood how insolvency models are used to predict the financial distress of an industry whether that be the power generation industry or the textile industry or etc. The data was collected from various secondary sources, and it was studied using the Altman's Z-Score model for private manufacturing companies to identify the overall financial health of the companies in the steel industry. The mean, standard deviation, and range of all the variables were observed. After conducting a correlation between the variables, it was concluded that there was a positive correlation between X3 and X4. It was concluded that few of the variables had a weakly positive correlation between them but there would be no significant change in the value of one variable with the change in another. While looking at the overall position of the steel industry, it was concluded that overall, it is in a healthy position as most of its companies are in the green zone with their Z-Score higher than 2.99 i.e., 77 companies out of 124. 22 companies were found to be in the distress zone, contributing to 18 per cent of the entire sample. The top companies and bottom companies based on market share were observed and it was found that none of the top companies were in the distress zone. On the other hand, 3 out of the bottom 10 companies were in the distress zone, signalling a link between market share and chances of going Keeping all of this in mind major suggestions for companies in the grey and red zone were to improve their liquidity position, work on improving operations for maximum productivity, manage debt and long-term borrowings, raise capital using equity, or switch markets to look for an opportunity elsewhere.

References

[1] Altman, E. (1984). The Success of Business Failure Prediction Models. *Journal of Banking and Finance*, 8, 171-198. https://doi.org/10.1016/0378-4266(84)90003-7

[2] Arab, Ollah Rooh, Seyed Saadat Masoumi, Saadat Seyed and Barati, Azadeh, (2015). Financial Performance of the Steel Industry in India: A Critical Analysis, *Middle-East Journal of Scientific Research* 23 (6): 1085-1090, 2015 ISSN 1990-9233 doi :10.5829/idosi.mejsr.2015.23.06.22197

[3] Azhar, Syed and Ramesh, B., (2017). Predicting Financial Insolvency of Listed Power Generation/Distribution Companies in India Using Z–Score. *IOSR Journal of Business and Management* (*IOSR-JBM*) (2017).

[4] Balakrishnan, C, (2016). A Study on Financial Performance of Steel Industry in India, Vol-2 Issue-4 2016 IJARIIE-ISSN(O)-2395-4396.

[5] Bhatia,Shipra, (2017). Crisis in Indian Steel Industry: Issues and Challenges, *International Journal of Scientific and Research Publications*, Volume 7, Issue 8, August 2017 ISSN 2250-3153.

[6] Chavali, Kavita (2012). Application of Z Score Analysis in evaluating Steel Industry in India. *Asia Pacific Journal of Research in Business Management*, 3(1).

[7] Cristi, Spulbar & Birau, Ramona & Hawaldar, Iqbal & Vaswani, Anju & Soni, Rashmi & Mendon, Suhan & Minea, Elena & Criveanu, Maria (2021). Predicting financial distress in the Indian textile sector. *Industria Textilă*. 72. 503-508. 10.35530/IT.072.05.20214.

[8] IBEF, 2022, available at https://www.ibef.org/industry/steel

[9] Ministry of Steel, India-a, 2022, available at https://steel.gov.in/make-india

[10] Ministry of Steel, India-b, 2022, available at https://steel.gov.in/overview-steel-sector

[11] Liao, Q., & Mehdian, S.M. (2016). Measuring Financial Distress and Predicting Corporate Bankruptcy: An Index Approach. *Review of Economic and Business Studies*, 9, 33–51.

[12] Rao N V, Atmanathan G, Shankar M, & Srivatsan R, (2013). Analysis of Bankruptcy Prediction Models and Their Effectiveness: An Indian Perspective. *Great Lakes Herald*, Vol 7, No 2, pp. 3–17.

[13] Safiuddin, S.K. (2017). Prediction of Insolvency-A Study of Select Companies in Indian Aviation Industry. *International Research Journal of Management Science & Technology*, Vol. 8 No. 10, pp. 304–09.

Issues and Challenges of Sustainable Agriculture in India: A Policy Analysis

Dr Salma Begum[1] and Guna Durga R.[2]

[1]Assistant Professor, [2]MBA, 2022–24
CMS Business School, Faculty of Management Studies,
JAIN (deemed-to-be University), Bangalore

Abstract

The agricultural sector is one of the important pillars of India's economic growth and development. Majority of the population is engaged in agriculture, and sustainability in agriculture is very important for the overall growth of the sector as well as the economy. This paper focuses on the importance of sustainable agriculture in India and the challenges faced. The government has been working towards sustainability by implementing several policies. The paper is based on secondary data analysis to measure the trend of agricultural development and discuss the challenges and policy implications. The finding of the paper shows the private expenditure and investment in the sector has increased over the period as the FDI inflow has increased. Further, in the policy for agroforestry and rainfed, there has been a shortfall in the funding during COVID-19. The study does not elaborate on the success of the policy implemented by the government due to time constrain. However, it is evident that sustainability in agricultural sector is necessary for the development of the sector and the economy as it captures for major share of total employment.

Keywords: *Sustainability, Agriculture, FDI Inflow, Policy, Rainfed*

Introduction

Agriculture is the primary source of livelihood for a majority of the Indian population and accounts for a significant portion of the country's GDP. The sector supports the livelihood of almost half of India's workforce and is estimated to employ more than 550 million people. Agriculture also contributes to the country's export earnings. India is the world's second-largest producer of food and spices and a major exporter of agricultural products. This sector is a major source of income for small and marginal farmers, who comprise the bulk of India's rural population. In such a way, the agriculture sector plays an important role in India but now, farmers are facing many problems due to using fertilizer. Fertilizer aids in the growth of crops but it causes many problems to the soil. It contains a high amount of nitrogen and phosphorus which are essential for plant growth but it can also lead to excessive growth of algae in water bodies. The increased nutrients in water may lead to water pollution and decrease the water quality. Fertilizer runoff may also lead to soil erosion and loss of soil fertility. The runoff can also contaminate drinking water sources and cause health problems. To overcome these problems, farmers should use organic fertilizers such as compost, manure, and green manure. These organic fertilizers are rich in nutrients and can improve soil fertility. They also help to conserve water and reduce the risk of water pollution. Therefore, sustainable development is important in the Agricultural sector.

Sustainable agriculture has been widely adopted in India in recent decades as a means of improving the country's agricultural productivity and reducing the environmental impact of traditional farming practices. Sustainable agriculture is based on principles of conservation, sustainability, and self-sufficiency. It focuses on the development of agricultural systems that are resilient, diverse, and more productive than traditional methods. Sustainable agriculture can be implemented using different methods, such as crop rotation, intercropping, composting, and integrated pest management, as well as the use of renewable energy sources and efficient water management techniques. In India, the government has implemented several initiatives to promote sustainable agriculture, including the National Mission on Sustainable Agriculture, and the Pradhan Mantri Fasal Bima Yojana. These initiatives are helping to ensure that India's agricultural sector remains profitable and sustainable in the long term.

Literature Review

Raliya, R. (2021), reviewed the benefits of nano fertilizer towards improving the quality and productivity of crops under sustainable agricultural development in the paper. The paper discussed the importance of nano fertilizers using pilot study and secondary data analysis and provide suggestions to implement the same for sustainable agricultural development. Paoletti, M.G. (2011), examines how contemporary agricultural methods affect the environment. One of the most urgent challenges with regard to agriculture sustainability is soil loss (along with soil fertility), rising water demand from agricultural practices, and environmental contamination brought on by the extensive use of agrochemicals. Concerns include biodiversity loss brought on by changes in land use and greenhouse gas emissions from agricultural activities. Further, the author pointed on an opportunity for an alternative, a more ecological form of agriculture and that research should be conducted to more accurately evaluate the advantages and disadvantages of the many options. Despite the 'Green Revolution's' significant successes, there will be a 70–100 per cent increase in global food demand by 2050. In order to feed nine billion people while protecting natural resources and soil fertility, a new hurdle must be overcome. Velten, L and et al (2015) conducted a study to measure the issues in implementing the methods of sustainable agriculture through a structured literature review and a cluster analysis. The findings of their study support different aspects of implementing sustainable agricultural development as proposed in prior literature which includes adapting to interdisciplinary approach. Shekhawat, R. S., (2020), evaluates public spending on agricultural inputs and support services both at the state and federal levels. The combined finance and revenue accounts of the Indian government and the financial accounts of several states have been used to produce panel data on public agricultural expenditures. A comparative geographical analysis showed that the irrigation sector received the majority of attention in the western and southern areas while rural development received greater attention in the eastern region. Crop husbandry has grown in importance with a bigger expenditure percentage share during the period when compared to the total expenditure on agricultural inputs and services. In eleven years, state spending on agricultural supplies and support services has increased more than thrice, which will indirectly contribute to raising rural incomes and reducing the rural-urban income gap. In order to attain the goal of inclusive growth in Indian agriculture, the study found disparities in the inter-state allocation of public expenditure in agriculture.

Dwivedi, N.U. (2015): The purpose of the paper is to investigate the significance of sustainable development in the agricultural sector. Since a substantial portion of India's population lives in rural areas and relies on agriculture for their survival, agriculture is the country's primary occupation. The goal of sustainable development in the agricultural industry is to boost output, effectiveness, and employment levels while also reducing the overuse of natural resources to safeguard and maintain them. Additionally, it offers ways to lessen soil degradation through various agricultural techniques, deforestation, and various other reasons.

Objective

1. To understand the issues and challenges of sustainability in agricultural sector.
2. To analyse the trend pattern and policies under sustainable agricultural development.

Methodology

The current study is based on secondary information gathered from various sources. To analyse trend of agricultural development, information on FDI equity flow, capital formation, development expenditure and minimum support pricing was compiled from the Agricultural Statistics (Ministry of Agriculture, 2021), Reserve Bank of India and different sources are used.

Sustainable Development in Agriculture

Sustainable development in agriculture is the process of developing agricultural systems that are both economically viable and environmentally sustainable. This includes practices such as conservation agriculture, integrated pest management, agroforestry, precision agriculture, and organic farming, among others. Sustainable agriculture seeks to improve yields, build soil fertility, reduce pollution, conserve water, and promote biodiversity while also considering the economic and social aspects of the system.

Sustainable agriculture practices should be promoted in India through the use of organic fertilizers, improved irrigation, crop rotation, and integrated pest management. Organic fertilizers provide an effective, natural way to enrich soil and control pests. They do not contain harmful chemicals that can damage the environment and are often more affordable than other fertilizers. Cover crops are a form of green manure, which is a form of agriculture that uses plants to protect and enrich the soil. They can also reduce soil erosion, and reduce the need for chemical fertilizers and pesticides. No-till farming uses minimal soil disturbance, reducing the need for tilling, while still allowing farmers to increase yields. This can reduce erosion, improve water retention, and build soil fertility

Importance of Sustainability in Agriculture in India

Sustainability in agriculture is essential to India's long-term economic and social stability. In India, agriculture is the main source of livelihood for about 50 per cent of the population and contributes 16–17 per cent to the country's GDP. The sector is also a major provider of raw materials for industry. To ensure that these vital economic and social contributions continue, India must take greater steps toward sustainability in agriculture. Sustainability in agriculture is important for India for several reasons. First, it can help to reduce the nation's dependence on imported food, fuel, and other agricultural products. This reduced dependence can help to strengthen India's economy, especially during times of economic hardship. Second, sustainability in agriculture can help to improve the availability of water and other natural resources, which are essential inputs for agricultural production. Third, sustainability in agriculture can help to reduce the environmental impact of agricultural practices, such as soil erosion, water pollution, deforestation, and climate change. Finally, sustainable agricultural practices can help to reduce the costs of production and improve the profitability of agricultural operations. sustainability in agriculture is essential for India's long-term economic and social stability. It can help to reduce the nation's dependence on it.

Challenges of Sustainable Agriculture

- *Resistance to adoption:* Many farmers and agricultural businesses may be resistant to adopting sustainable practices due to the difficulty and cost associated with making changes to their operations. This resistance can be due to a lack of understanding of the benefits associated with sustainable practices, or a lack of resources to make the necessary changes.
- *Lack of financing:* Affordable financing for sustainable agriculture projects can be difficult to find, as many lenders and investors may not understand the potential benefits of such initiatives. Without access to the necessary financing, farmers and agricultural businesses may be unable to make the necessary investments to adopt sustainable practices. The Indian government is trying to help these farmers by providing financial support through initiatives like Pradhan Mantri Krishi Sinchayee Yojana (PMKSY), and National Mission for Sustainable Agriculture (NMSA).
- *Limited access to education and training:* Many farmers and agricultural businesses may lack the education and training necessary to understand and implement sustainable agriculture practices. This lack of knowledge can be a barrier to adoption,

as it can lead to the mismanagement of resources and a lack of understanding of the benefits associated with sustainable practices.

- *Market barriers:* The recent trend says that consumers are increasingly conscious of the environmental impact of the products they purchase. As such, they are often willing to pay a premium for sustainably produced products. However, in many cases, they are not willing to do so. This can put farmers in a difficult situation, as they may not be able to access the necessary markets for their products. Furthermore, this lack of demand for sustainably produced products means that farmers are not incentivised to invest in sustainable practices, which can have a long-term negative impact on the environment. It is also important to recognise that, for many farmers, access to these markets is limited due to financial constraints or a lack of necessary resources. Ultimately, in order to ensure that farmers are able to access these markets and are incentivised to invest in sustainable practices, it is important that consumers be willing to pay a premium for sustainably produced products. Therefore, it is important that consumer education around the importance of sustainable practices be increased, and that access to these markets be improved.
- *Environmental challenges:* The climate of India has a major influence on the agriculture of the country. The monsoons are the most important climatic factor in India and determine the timing and amount of rainfall, which is essential for the growth of crops. The monsoons are also responsible for determining the temperature, humidity, and cloudiness, which all have an impact on the crops. Long periods of drought can lead to crop failure and famine, while too much rain can cause flooding and damage to crops. Other climatic factors such as wind, temperature and humidity also play a role in the success of Indian agriculture. Therefore, adopting sustainable development in agriculture is difficult.
- *Socio-cultural factors:* Social and cultural norms can influence the adoption of sustainable agricultural practices, and the attitudes of local communities towards sustainable agriculture must be taken into consideration. For example, in some areas, there is a strong cultural belief that natural methods of farming are the only way to cultivate crops. This can lead to more people adopting sustainable farming practices, such as using organic fertilizers, avoiding synthetic chemicals, and using crop rotation. In other areas, there may be a strong cultural belief that technology can help improve agricultural practices. This can lead to more people adopting new technologies, such as precision agriculture and automated irrigation systems. In either case, cultural norms can have a significant influence on how people view and adopt sustainable agricultural practices.
- *Lack of government support:* Governments may be reluctant to provide financial or other incentives to encourage the adoption of sustainable agricultural practices. This can be due to a lack of understanding of the potential benefits associated with sustainable agriculture, or a lack of resources to make the necessary investments. The Indian government faces several challenges when it comes to developing

sustainable agriculture. One of the major challenges is allocating sufficient funds for it, as the government has to spend on many other expenses. This challenge is further compounded by the fact that agriculture is a low-priority sector in India. To address this challenge, the government needs to prioritise sustainable agriculture and allocate more funds to it. Additionally, the government needs to enhance its financial and technical support to farmers and agricultural research and development initiatives to promote sustainable agriculture. Furthermore, it needs to implement policies that encourage and incentivise sustainable agricultural practices. Finally, the government needs to raise awareness and educate people about the importance of sustainable agriculture in order to get more support for it.

Trend in Agricultural Development

Figure 1 shows the financial year-wise percentage change of FDI equity inflows from 2010 to 2021 in the agriculture services sector. The FDI equity inflows show a positive change from 2010–11 to 2011–12 with 11.66 per cent. This percentage decreased in 2012–13 to 229.40 per cent. Further, there was a fall of 43.64 per cent in 2013–14 followed by a decrease of 34.13 per cent in 2014–15. The percentage changed to 41.20 per cent in 2015–16 and there was a decrease of 9.71 per cent in 2016–17. However, in 2017–18, the percentage increased to 44.17 per cent followed by a decrease of 19.45 per cent in 2018–19 and 41.20 per cent in 2019-20. The FDI equity inflows showed a significant rise of 124.37 per cent in 2020–21.

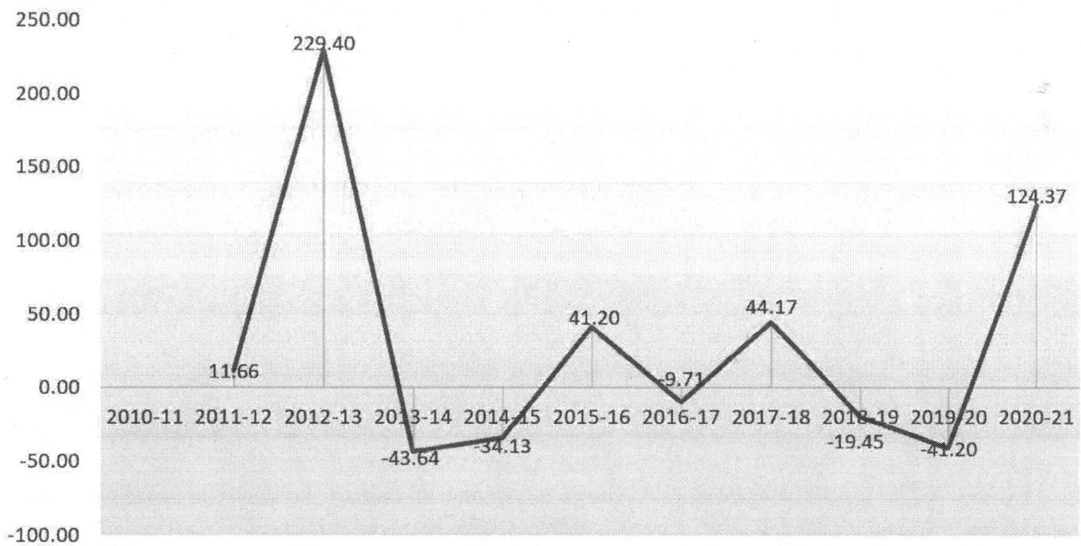

Fig. 1: Financial Year-wise Percentage Change of FDI Equity Inflows from 2010 to 2021 in the Agriculture Services Sector

Source: Ministry of Agriculture and Farmer Welfare Government of India, National Accounts Statistics and Agricultural Statistics at a Glance (2021)

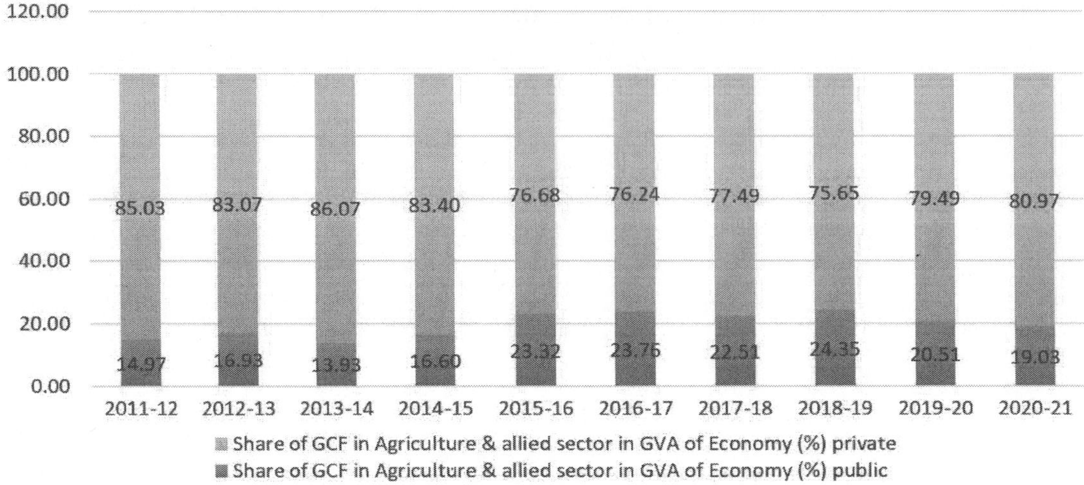

Fig. 2: Share of Gross Capital Formation (GCF) in Agriculture and Allied Sector in GVA of Economy at Current Price

Source: Ministry of Agriculture and Farmer Welfare Government of India, National Accounts Statistics and Agricultural Statistics at a Glance (2021)

The share of Gross Capital Formation (GCF) in the agriculture & allied sector in the Gross Value Added (GVA) of the Indian economy over the last decade. The data is provided in figure 2. In 2011–12, the share of GCF in the Agriculture & allied sector in the GVA of the economy was 14.97 per cent, with the private sector accounting for the majority of this share at 85.03 per cent. This share has fluctuated

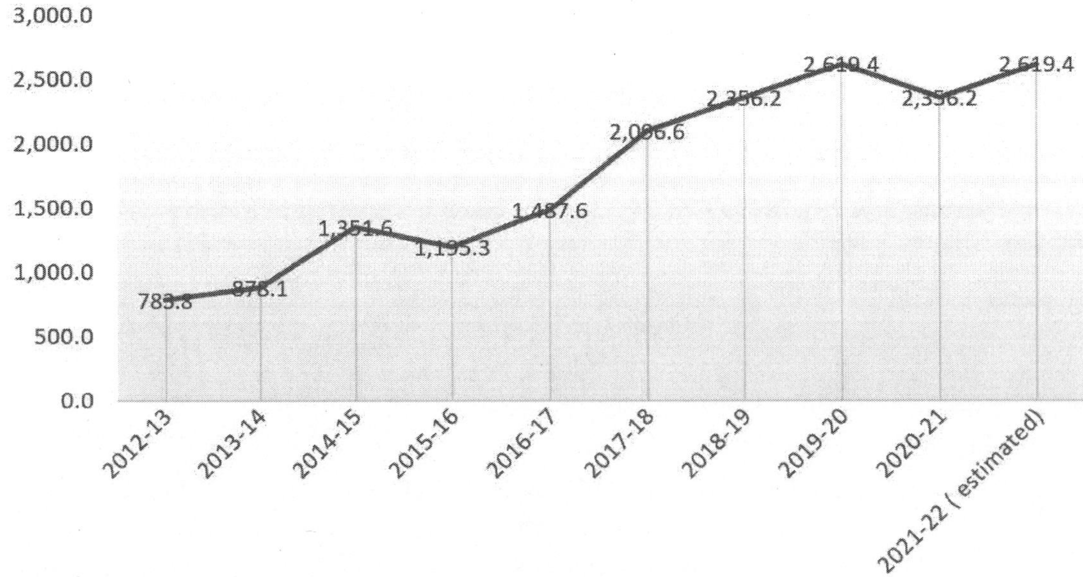

Fig. 3: Agriculture and Allied Activities (Development Expenditure)

Source: Reserve Bank of India (in billions)

over the last decade, with the highest share being in 2015–16 at 23.32 per cent, and the lowest in 2019–20 at 20.51 per cent. In 2020–21, the share of GCF in the Agriculture & allied sector in the GVA of the economy was 19.03 per cent, with the private sector accounting for the majority of this share at 80.97 per cent. This figure is important in understanding the contribution of the agriculture & allied sectors to the GVA of the Indian economy, and the importance of private investment in this sector.

Figure 3 reveals the expenditure in billions on Agriculture and Allied activities in India from 2012–13 to 2021–22. It is evident that the expenditure has been on the rise over the years, with the highest increase being seen between 2014–15 and 2015–16. The expenditure in 2021–22 is estimated to be 2,619.4 billion, which is a considerable increase from 2012–13 when the expenditure was 783.8 billion. The rising expenditure on Agriculture and Allied activities is an indication that the government is taking the sector seriously and investing more resources in it. This will likely result in improved productivity and better yields, which will benefit the farmers and the rural population of India. The government should continue to invest in the agricultural sector and come up with innovative and effective policies that will help the farmers and ensure the sector's growth.

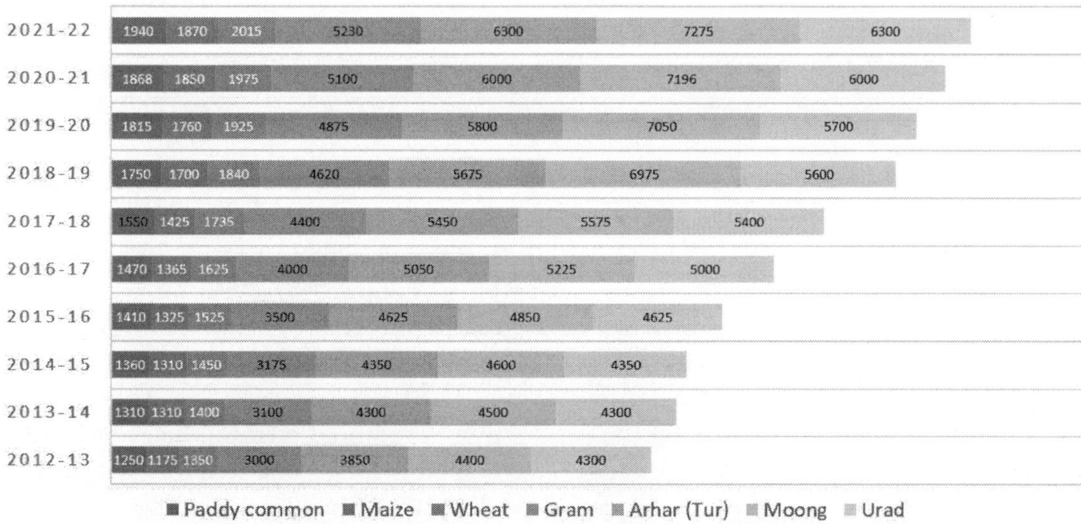

Fig. 4: Minimum Support Price For Foodgrains According to Crop Year
Source: Reserve Bank of India (Rs per quintal)

As per Figure 4, it is evident that the MSP for food grains has been increasing steadily over the years. The MSP of paddy, maize, wheat, gram, arhar (tur), moong, and urad has risen from 2012–13 to 2021–22. For instance, the MSP for Paddy Common was Rs 1,250 in 2012–13 and has gone up to Rs. 1940 in 2021–22. Similarly, the MSP for Arhar (Tur) was Rs. 3850 in 2012–13 and has increased to Rs 6,300 in 2021–22. This is a positive step taken by the government to ensure the welfare of farmers in India. The increasing MSP will help farmers increase their income, which will eventually help in the economic development of the country. However, along with the increasing MSP, the government should also take necessary steps to ensure that the farmers get the right price for their produce in the markets. This will help the farmers earn a fair remuneration for the hard work they put in. minimum support price for foodgrains according to the crop year, as mentioned in Figure 4.

Policy by the Indian Government

National Mission for Sustainable Agriculture

National Mission for Sustainable Agriculture (NMSA) is one of the eight Missions included in the National Action Plan on Climate Change, is where NMSA gets its authority (NAPCC) implemented in September 2010 with the aim to promote sustainable agriculture in terms of livestock and fish cultures, crops seeds, efficient uses of water, nutrient management and pest management. The NMSA objectives:

- To increase agriculture's output, sustainability, profitability, and resiliency to climate change by promoting Integrated/Composite Farming Systems tailored to specific geographic regions.
- To protect the environment by taking suitable soil and moisture conservation measures.
- Adopting thorough soil health management techniques based on soil fertility maps, applying macro- and micronutrients based on soil tests, and using fertilisers wisely, among other things.
- To achieve 'more produce per drop' by maximising the use of water resources through effective water management.
- To increase the capacity of farmers and other stakeholders in the field of climate change adaptation and mitigation strategies, in conjunction with other ongoing Missions such as the National Mission on Agriculture Extension & Technology, National Food Security Mission, National Initiative for Climate Resilient Agriculture (NICRA), etc.
- To check models for increasing the productivity of rainfed farming in a few blocks by mainstreaming rainfed technologies developed through NICRA and by utilising funds from other programmes/missions like the Mahatma Gandhi National Rural Employment Guarantee Scheme (MGNREGS), the Integrated Watershed Management Programme (IWMP), the RKVY, etc.;
- Establishing efficient departmental and ministerial coordination for carrying out the main objectives of the National Mission for Sustainable Agriculture under the auspices of NAPCC

Sub-Mission on Agroforestry

This mission, which was started in 2016 when the National Agroforestry Policy was adopted, intends to boost tree planting while integrating it with crop production

(MoAFW 2016). Agroforestry, an alternative to traditional agriculture that is more climate-adaptive, entails planting fruit-bearing or timber trees around fields. Long-term, the approach could have an impact on raising farmer revenues and enhancing soil health. In India, it is seen to be especially advantageous for the ability of marginal and small farmers to generate money. The planned increase in tree cover also aligns with India's nationally defined commitment to the Paris Agreement, which aims to improve tree cover in order to create an additional 2.5–3 billion tonnes of carbon sinks.

Table 1: Allocation, Release and Achievement of Funds Under Sub-Mission on Agroforestry (amount in Rs)

Year	*General*	*SCSP*	*TSP*	*Total*	*Achievement*
2016-17	16,59,00,000	3,82,00,000	2,11,00,000	22,52,00,000	1,72,19,459
2017-18	31,14,25,700	5,98,40,000	5,53,74,500	42,66,40,200	8,32,88,436
2018-19	20,29,25,760	3,72,69,000	4,55,60,000	28,57,54,760	6,79,60,268
2019-20	10,32,67,000	2,74,20,000	94,85,000	14,01,72,000	4,34,01,115
2020-21	6,61,98,000	1,34,06,000	2,53,96,000	10,50,00,000	3,30,33,523

Source: National Mission for Sustainable Agriculture (NMSA), Department of Agriculture & Farmers Welfare, Ministry of Agriculture & Farmers Welfare, Government of India.

Table 1 provides information about the Allocation, Release & Achievement of Funds Under Sub-Mission on Agroforestry. As we can see from the data provided, the General, SCSP, and TSP funds have increased from 2016-17 to 2020-21. However, the overall achievement in terms of funds released has followed an irregular trend. In 2016-17, the total fund allocated was 22.52 crore, out of which only 1.72 crore was achieved. On the other hand, in 2018-19, the allocated funds were 28.57 crores, out of which 6.79 crores were achieved. This data indicates that there is an urgent need to review the existing policies and procedures related to funding allocations and releases.

Rainfed Area Development

The programme encourages integrated agricultural systems in rainfed regions of the nation that use mixed cropping techniques with horticulture, livestock, fisheries, etc., to increase farmer incomes and lessen the effects of extreme weather events like floods and drought. The importance of the programme can be understood by the fact that 68.3 million hectares of the 140.1 million hectares of cultivated land used to produce food grains are irrigated, while the remaining 71.7 million hectares are rainfed. Rainfed regions are characterised by low production, low farmer earnings, and a high danger of harsh weather conditions. They also lack irrigation infrastructure. It is evident by examining the coverage target and funding allocation for the programme over time that the programme continuously fails to meet the goals set.

Table 2: Allocation, Release and Achievement of Funds Under Rainfed Area Development

Year	*General*	*SCSP*	*TSP*	*Total*	*Achievement*
2015-16	1,48,70,78,000	32,58,00,000	16,82,57,000	1,98,11,35,000	80,19,59,868
2016-17	1,47,75,32,000	27,00,00,000	25,43,68,000	2,00,19,00,000	1,04,83,69,621
2017-18	1,56,41,27,319	26,82,87,600	25,99,99,800	2,09,24,14,719	1,21,09,44,615
2018-19	1,42,43,15,000	31,88,89,800	35,80,30,200	2,10,12,35,000	1,28,82,38,399
2019-20	31,67,70,000	8,18,28,000	2,30,04,000	42,16,02,000	90,53,15,873

Source: National Mission for Sustainable Agriculture (NMSA), 2021 Ministry of Agriculture & Farmers Welfare, Government of India.

Table 2 provided above relates to the allocation, release, and achievement of funds under Rainfed Area Development from 2015-16 to 2019-20. The General fund is the largest contributor to the total fund allocation, with an average of around 94 per cent. The Scheduled Caste Sub-Plan fund is the second biggest contributor, with an average of around 14 per cent. The Tribal Sub-Plan fund is the smallest contributor, with an average of around 3 per cent. Despite the funds being allocated, the achievement rate is low. In 2015-16, the achievement rate was only 40 per cent, while in 2019-20 it was only 21 per cent. This is an indication that the funds are not being utilised in an efficient and effective manner. Therefore, there is a need to identify the reasons for the low achievement rate and take the necessary steps to ensure that the funds are utilised in a more effective manner. This will help in ensuring the efficient utilisation of the funds and the effective implementation of rainfed area development projects.

Soil Health Management

This important programme aims to 'promote location- and crop-specific sustainable soil health management, creation and connection of soil fertility maps with macro-micro nutrient management, prudent application of fertilisers and organic agricultural techniques'. The Soil Health Card (SHC) programme, which was introduced in 2015, is the centrepiece policy of this programme. The SHCs, which are given to farmers every three years, advise them on the nutritional quality of their land, the ideal crops to choose for the crop cycle, and the correct nutrient dosage required to improve soil fertility. The idea behind the plan is that farmers will spend significantly less on inputs, see improved production, and have a lower probability of suffering losses if they know what to cultivate and how to improve the soil's health. Additionally, with continued use of this technique, soil nutrients and organic content improve. 66 per cent of farmers, according to an effective assessment study of the SHC scheme, are able to comprehend the SHC's content, although there is potential for improvement in the farmers' participation in meetings and exposure visits (Reddy 2017b). The study also demonstrates that, despite being advantageous to marginal farmers, the creation of the SHC requires the findings of soil sample analysis to be completed well in advance of the sowing season.

Pradhan Mantri Krishi Sinchayee Yojana (PMKSY)

The Government of India has been implementing the Centrally Sponsored Scheme on Micro Irrigation with the goal of increasing water use efficiency in the agricultural sector by supporting appropriate technological interventions like drip and sprinkler irrigation technologies and motivating the farmers to employ water-saving and conservation technologies. The Centrally Sponsored Scheme on Micro Irrigation was introduced by the Department of Agriculture & Cooperation, Ministry of Agriculture, in January 2006. (CSS). It was expanded to become the National Mission on Micro Irrigation (NMMI) in June 2010, and it ran through 2013–2014. The OFWM Micro Irrigation component has been included in the Pradhan Mantri Krishi Sinchayee Yojana as of April 1, 2015. It was put into action as a Centrally Sponsored Scheme on Micro Irrigation for the fiscal year 2015–16 in accordance with the same aid and cost rules as were in place under OFWM, up until they are revised. As of April 1, 2014, NMMI was integrated into the National Mission on Sustainable Agriculture (NMSA), and during the 2014–15 fiscal year, it was implemented as 'On Farm Water Management' (OFWM).

The main objective of PMKSY is to increase the use of precision irrigation and other water-saving technologies (more crop per drop), increase recharging of aquifers, establish convergence of irrigation investment at the field level, expand cultivable land under assured irrigation, improve on-farm water use efficiency to decrease water wastage, and promote sustainable water conservation techniques by investigating the viability of reusing treated municipal wastewater.

The scheme consists of four major parts that each address a different problem with regard to agricultural water use:

- *Accelerated Irrigation Benefit Programme (AIBP)* – This programme aims to complete medium- and large-scale irrigation projects more quickly.
- *Har Khet ko Paani* – Supporting small-scale irrigation, rainwater collection systems, and groundwater development in abundant regions.
- *Per Drop More Crop (PDMC)* – programme that aims to increase the adoption of water-saving micro irrigation methods including drip irrigation and spray irrigation.
- *Watershed Development* – Rejuvenating conventional water sources and controlling surface runoff (PMKSY n.d.).

Source: Ministry of Jal Shakti, 2022

Pradhan Mantri Fasal Bima Yojana (PMFBY)

In order to protect farmers' losses from unavoidable natural risks, PMFBY was established in 2016. It offers pre-sowing to post-harvest crop insurance coverage. In the plan, crop damage is estimated using crop-cutting experiments (CCE), on the basis of which insurance reimbursements are provided. Earlier, the country's crop insurance programmes were beset by excessive premium rates, delays or non-payment of payments due, insufficient insurance amounts, insufficient government support for premium subsidies, poor coverage of the land area, and a low number of farmers insured. By implementing technical solutions like mobile phone apps for data gathering and communication and digitalised land records connected to farmers bank accounts for better claim settlement, PMFBY hopes to address these problems.

The programme also aims to broaden coverage by requiring crop insurance from farmers who request loans to plant specified crops. However, from the programme's inception, significant implementation problems have plagued it. According to the plan, the federal and state governments are each required to contribute equally to premium subsidies. The majority of states don't pay their portion of the subsidies on time. The delays extend beyond the subsidy share. The programme mandates that governments give insurance companies production and agricultural data based on CCEs within a month of harvesting. However, most states do not finish this procedure on time, which results in payouts that are occasionally low and occasionally delayed.

Table 3: PMFBY and RWBCIS Combined – Year-wise Data

Year	*Farmers Applications Insured (Lakh)*	*Area Insured (Lakh ha)*	*Sum Insured (Rs. crore)*	*Paid Claims (Rs. crore)*	*Farmer Applications Benefitted (Lakh)*
2016-17	583.7	561.1	2,03,110	16,809	156.5
2017-18	532.7	507.7	2,02,282	22,118	176.8
2018-19	577.2	525.8	2,29,598	28,129	222.6
2019-20	612.9	501	2,19,040	25,822	223.6

Source: Pradhan Mantri Fasal Bima Yojana, Ministry of Agriculture & Farmers Welfare, Government of India.

This table highlights the data for the Pradhan Mantri Fasal Bima Yojana (PMFBY) and Restructured Weather Based Crop Insurance Scheme (RWBCIS) combined from 2016–17 to 2019–20.

In 2016–17, the number of farmers' applications insured was 583.7 lakhs, the area insured was 561.1 lakhs hectares, the sum insured was Rs 2,03,110 crores, the paid claims were Rs 16,809 crores, and the farmer's applications benefitted were 156.5 lakhs. In 2017-18, the numbers were 532.7 lakhs, 507.7 lakhs hectares, Rs 2,02,282 crores, Rs 22,118 crores, and 176.8 lakhs respectively. In 2018–19, the numbers were 577.2. Most notably, there has been an increase in farmer applications, area insured, and sum insured from 2016–17 to 2019–20. Furthermore, the paid claims and farmer applications benefitted have also increased. This is an encouraging sign, as it shows that the PMFBY and RWBCIS have been successful in providing insurance and financial assistance to farmers.

Conclusion

The need for sustainable agriculture in India is clear, but the challenges are immense. Farmers must be equipped with the knowledge and resources to adopt sustainable practices, while policymakers must ensure that the right incentives are in place to make them viable. Investment in research and technology is essential to identify and develop cost-effective, sustainable agricultural techniques. Furthermore, transparent and inclusive governance is needed to ensure that farmers, especially small-scale farmer, have access to the resources and benefits of sustainable agriculture. India has the potential to become a leader in sustainable agricultural development. To achieve this, it is essential to implement policies that promote sustainable agricultural practices, such as those that promote water conservation and improved soil health, and to ensure adequate access to inputs and services other than what schemes that they provide. The policies that the Indian government provided are sufficient but not efficient and effective. Additionally, policies should be designed to promote economic opportunities for small-scale farmers and to foster their inclusion in value chains. Finally, policies should recognise the importance of social and environmental sustainability and should strive to reduce the environmental impacts of agriculture. By implementing these policies, India could become a global leader in sustainable agriculture and set an example for other countries to follow.

References

[1] Kumar, Y, Tiwari, K.N., Singh, T., & Raliya, R. (2021). Nanofertilizers and their role in sustainable agriculture. *Annals of Plant and Soil Research*, 23(3), 238–55.

[2] Gomiero, T., Pimentel, D., & Paoletti, M. G. (2011). Is there a need for a more sustainable agriculture?. *Critical reviews in plant sciences*, 30(1-2), 6–23.

[3] Velten, S., Leventon, J., Jager, N., & Newig, J. (2015). What is sustainable agriculture? A systematic review. *Sustainability*, 7(6), 7833–865.

[4] Rajesh, T., PShivaswamy, G., Anuja, A.R., Singh, K.N., Shekhawat, R.S., & HV, H.K. (2020). Public expenditure on agricultural inputs and farm support services in India–An overview.

[5] Shukla, K.H., & Dwivedi, N.U. (2015). Sustainable development in agricultural sector in India. *The Business & Management Review*, 5(4), 220.

[6] Abhay Kumar Singh, 02 Dec 2022, Here is why the world needs regenerative agriculture, *Down-to-earth*, https://www.downtoearth.org.in/blog/agriculture/here-is-why-the-world-needs-regenerative-agriculture-86328

[7] Aksheev Thakur, 20 March, 2022, Public expenditure on agriculture in India declined considerably in past decade: Experts, *The Indian Express*, https://indianexpress.com/article/india/public-expenditure-agriculture-india-declined-past-decade-7828036/

[8] 07 Dec 2022, HarvestPlus wins FICCI Award for outstanding sustainable agricultural development programme, *Agriculture Post*, https://agriculturepost.com/agribusiness/harvestplus-wins-ficci-award-for-outstanding-sustainable-agricultural-development-program/

[9] Sandip Das, 1 December 2022, Farmers & traders hold stocks: Wheat prices a quarter above MSP, *Financial Express*, https://www.financialexpress.com/economy/farmers-amp-traders-hold-stocks-wheat-prices-a-quarter-above-msp/2897068/

[10] Shoba Suri , 24 Nov 2022 , Climate Smart Agriculture for sustainability and food security, *ORF*, https://www.orfonline.org/expert-speak/climate-smart-agriculture-for-sustainability-and-food-security/

[11] Vineet Kumar, 14 Nov 2022, CSE's organic experiment: Challenge starts with procuring right seeds, *Down To Earth,* https://www.downtoearth.org.in/blog/agriculture/cse-s-organic-experiment-challenge-starts-with-procuring-right-seeds-85960

[12] Sonali Behera, 21 Nov 2022, Is it time for the Indian Government to Focus on Agri-Startups?, *Krishi Jagran,* https://krishijagran.com/blog/is-it-time-for-the-indian-government-to-focus-on-agri-startups/

[13] Jocelyn Fernandes, 07, Dec 2022, RBI Monetary Policy | Highlights of MPC announcements by Governor Shaktikanta Das, *Money Control,* https://www.moneycontrol.com/news/business/economy/rbi-monetary-policy-highlights-of-mpc-announcements-by-governor-shaktikanta-das-9663271.html

[14] Sanjeeb Mukherjee, Dec 06 2022, Are states with high levels of poverty spending less on MGNREGS?, *Business Standard,* https://www.business-standard.com/article/economy-policy/did-states-with-high-levels-of-poverty-decrease-spending-on-mgnregs-122120500978_1.html

[15] Ani, 6 Dec 2022, India brought 4.78 lakh hectare land under natural farming last year, *The Print,* https://theprint.in/economy/india-brought-4-78-lakh-hectare-land-under-natural-farming-last-year/1250459/

[16] Tribune News Service, 6 Dec 2022, Recast MSP panel: Bathinda MP Harsimrat Badal, *The Tribune,* https://www.tribuneindia.com/news/punjab/recast-msp-panel-sad-458428

[17] Jayanta Bhattacharya, 10t Nov 2022, Minimum support price system is broken, the government should now fix it, *The New Indian Express,* http://newindianexpress.com/web-only/2022/nov/10/minimum-support-price-system-is-broken-the-government-should-now-fix-it-2516988.html

[18] 07 Dec 2022, Towards Effective Soil Management, *Drishti IAS,* https://www.drishtiias.com/daily-updates/daily-news-editorials/towards-effective-soil-management

[19] News Desk, 5 Dec 2022, State secy Abu Bakr Siddique orders speedy implementation of milk production, pisciculture, PMKSY projects, *The Avenue Mail,* https://avenuemail.in/state-secy-abu-bakr-siddique-orders-speedy-implementation-of-milk-production-pisciculture-pmksy-projects/

[20] Nov 25,2022, Atal Dulloo reviews the status of micro irrigation, irrigation for Kharif 2023, *The Kashmir Images,* https://thekashmirimages.com/2022/11/25/atal-dulloo-reviews-status-of-micro-irrigation-irrigation-for-kharif-2023/

[21] Swati Luthra, 01 Dec 2022, Committed to providing comprehensive insurance against crop loss under PMFBY: Centre, *liveMint,* https://www.livemint.com/news/india/committed-to-providing-comprehensive-insurance-against-crop-loss-under-pmfby-centre-11669891969673.html

The Impact of Debt Levels on Inflation in High-Income and Low-Income Countries: An Analysis Based on Data From 157 Countries

C.A. Pranav Dnyaneshwar Mandke

Research Scholar
E-mail: theofficialpranavmandke@gmail.com

Abstract

Under the backdrop of a global recession in 2008, this paper aims to establish the association between the debt-to-GDP ratio levels with inflation rates of an economy. Increasing Debt-to-GDP ratios may lead to a future fall in the value of money. The analysis is conducted on data from 157 countries gathered from World Bank and IMF for a period of 7 years during 2009–2015. It is observed that the association differs between high and low-income countries, while the former shows that there is a negative association, the same for the poorer countries are not significant. However, a logistic regression analysis demonstrates that the likelihood of having a high inflation rate increases with the rise in debt in general. The reason can be pertained to skewed distributions of inflation level.

Keywords: *Debt-to-GDP Ratio, Inflation, High-Income Country, Low-Income Country, Monetary Policy, Money Supply, Inflationary, Recession, 2008 Economic Crisis*

Introduction

The basic requirement for a growing economy would be capital. These capital requirements are in essence the excess funds to aid that growth. This growth can be funded by either issuing debt or equity. Most economists have always maintained that rising debt levels of a country, especially in developing countries may lead to inflation (Kwon et al., 2006). Most Developing countries refrain from raising too much debt with this fear of the debt becoming inflationary.

Several multi-country studies have shown a mixed relationship of public debt vis-à-vis inflation. A study investigating the various effects of public debt on inflation using panel data for 71 countries for a period of 1963 to 2004, showed that the there is strong positive relationship in highly indebted developing countries, weak positive in the case of other developing countries, but generally insignificant for developed countries (Kwon et al., 2006). A study conducted in Germany during 1991 to 2010 stated that public debt causes inflation and vice-versa. Public deficit is inflationary if the money supply is expansive (Nastansky et al., 2014). A similar pattern was found in lowly developed economies. Studies conducted on 15 developing economies of Asia during 1990 to 2012 (van Bon, 2015), involving 52 African countries during 1950 to 2012 (Lopes da

Veiga, Ferreira-Lopes & Sequeira, 2014), and conducted in Kenya during 1996 to 2011 (Harmon, 2012) found weakly positive relationships between public debt and inflation.

However, when looking at a time period since the 1960s, no significant relationship was observed between public debt vis-à-vis inflation in the industrial countries (Giannitsarou and Scott, 2006). A similar association was observed and was concluded that debt predominantly does not lead to high inflation rates in developing countries, since they have a stable financial position (Catao and Terrones, 2005). A negative correlation (-0.19) was observed for 15 OECD countries post the 1980s (Bleaney, 1996).

Theoretical Framework

According to the mainstream, rational or neo-classical economists, debt should have a positive impact on inflation. Contrarily, Heterodox Economists who propounded Modern Money Theory suggest that debt won't have any significant impact on the inflation rates on the country, while the inflation rates depend on the monetary policy tools. L Randall Wrey (1998) talks about a policy that would generate true, full employment. In Understanding Modern Money, he talks about deficits not being inflationary up to the point of full employment.

Hypotheses of the Study

H_0 1: Debt – to – GDP ratio does not have any impact on Inflation of a country.

A_0 1: Debt – to – GDP ratio has an impact on Inflation of a country

Methodology

Conceptual Model

In our basic model inflation is considered to be a function of debt-to-GDP ratio.

Inflation = *f* (*Debt-to-GDP ratio*)

However, for the regression analysis we have also controlled for gross capital formation (G), revenue (R) and money supply (M).

With Control Variables

Inflation = *f* (*Debt-to-GDP ratio, G, R, M*)

In order to understand the association between debt and inflation, besides understanding the chances of recording a specific inflation level, this analysis has considered inflation as a continuous variable, as well as categorical variables (based on accepted criteria or classification).

To analyse the effect of debt-to-GDP ratio on inflation, since the dependant variable is continuous in nature, linear regression models have been used.

$$Inflation = \alpha + \beta_1.D + \beta_2.G + \beta_3.R + \beta_4.M + \varepsilon \qquad (\varepsilon = \text{Error term})$$

However, while examining the likelihood of high inflation with respect to income-debt ratio, we conducted binary logistic regression analysis, where the dependent variable is dichotomous, i.e. acceptable inflation rates, considering low inflation rates as reference category.

$$Pr\ (High\ inflation) / [1 - Pr\ (High\ inflation)] = \alpha + \beta_1.D + \beta_2.G + \beta_3.R + \beta_4.M + \varepsilon$$

Following are the three different classifications of high inflation.

- *Acceptable inflation level of 2 per cent:* The 2 per cent inflation rate is considered as acceptable or normal. This level finds base in the Inflation Target of the US Federal Reserve (FED). This 2 per cent target is based on the Federal Reserve's Federal Open Market Committee (FOMC) recommendations.
- *Acceptable inflation level of 4 per cent:* Four percentage point cut-off for inflation is based on the argument presented in the research paper 'The Case for 4 per cent Inflation' by Laurence Ball (2014). This paper states that a slightly higher normal inflation rate, i.e. till four per cent would be more beneficial in the long run. This gives more margin of safety when recession hits, since rates have more room to fall before hitting zero and increasing chances that policymakers restore full employment. Also, a four per cent target helps to ease the constraints on the Monetary policy that arise from the lower limit of zero interest rate. This means that economic downturns would be less severe.
- *Acceptable inflation level of 5 per cent:* This rate is taken into consideration based on the argument of Lawrence H Summers in the report published in the Hutchins Centre on Fiscal & Monetary Policy Conference in January 2018. In this report, the argument presented is for a nominal Inflation rate of around 5 per cent has the property that the expected rate of inflation rises as the expected real growth in GDP declines. So, a higher Inflation rate is an advantage due to its implicit response to changing conditions.

Before the analysis was conducted, the dataset was checked for missing data and outliers. After data cleaning, the analysis was done using Minitab.

Nature of Data

The data analysed for this study is a short and unbalanced panel data. The time period considered for this study was post the global financial crisis of 2008, i.e., during 2009 and 2015.

Source of Variables

All the data required for the study was obtained from the publicly available downloadable records from the International Monetary Fund (IMF) and the World Bank. The data on inflation, Debt-to-GDP ratio, revenue, and money supply has been collected from International Monetary Fund (IMF), while the data for gross capital formation (GCF) has been collected from World bank, for the concerned time period.

This paper also presents a comparative analysis of the associations between debt and inflation in the case of low-income and high-income countries. World Bank categorizes economies into four income groups: high, upper-middle, lower-middle, and low. The classification is done based on Gross National Income (GNI) per capita of a country, which is estimated using the Atlas method. Such classification was introduced in the first World Development Report (1978), where 'low income' and 'middle income' countries were classified with a cut-off GNI of $250 per capita. The report after five years split 'middle income group' into 'lower middle' and 'upper middle' groups, and in 1989 a 'high income' country group was defined using US$ 6000 per capita threshold (in 1987 prices). From then on, the thresholds that define the income groups, are periodically adjusted for prices.

All the GNI per capita is calculated using the World Bank Atlas method.

Table 1.1: GNI per Capita

Sr. No.	*Category for this Study*	*Category of Economies as per World Bank*	*GNI per Capita ($) Range*
1.	High Income Countries	High Income	> $ 12375
2.		Upper Middle Income	$ 3996 to $ 12375
3.	Low Income Countries	Lower Middle Income	$ 1026 to $ 3995
4.		Low Income	$ 0 to $ 1025

Source: Author's Compilation

Results

Table 1.2: Descriptive Statistics of Inflation

Income	*Mean (Inflation)*	*Sd (Inflation)*	*Mean (Debt-to-GDP ratio)*	*Sd (Debt-to-GDP ratio)*
Low	4.92	5.83	42.04	23.06
High	4.11	5.17	52.08	36.56
Pooled	4.33	5.36	49.37	33.73

Source: Author's Compilation

Table 2 shows the regression results of continuous inflation variable interacting with other independent variables. While in high income countries there is a negative (inverse) association between debt-to-GDP ratio and inflation, in low-income countries we did not find any statistically significant relationship between them. In the economically underprivileged states inflation significantly increases with rise in GCF and revenue. However, with pooled data, debt-to-GDP ratio demonstrates an inverse association with the level of inflation with p-value of 0.08, while no other variable could define inflation statistically significantly.

However, even with the weak positive relationship, the R-squared values are 1.61 per cent for low-income countries, 4.22 per cent for high income countries and 3.83 per cent for the pooled data of countries. These values indicate that less than 5 per cent of the variation in inflation is explained by debt. The rest is explained by variables outside the scope of this study. These results would lead to the same conclusion that debt has no significant influence or impact on inflation.

The correlation analysis demonstrated through scattered diagrams state that there is no distinct pattern of association between inflation and debt-to-GDP ratio. Even if the association is weak (r = −0.096) for high-income countries, it shows statistical significance.

Table 2: OLS Regression Results for the Continuous Inflation Variable

Variables		*Coefficient*	*SE Coefficient*	*p-value*
Low Income				
Debt-to-GDP Ratio		-0.0166	0.0201	0.41
GCF		0.2231	0.0737	0.00
Money Supply		0.0042	0.0104	0.68
Revenue		0.1125	0.0476	0.02
R-squared values	Unadjusted	0.45%		
	Adjusted	5.88%		
High Income				
Debt-to-GDP Ratio		-0.01415	0.00723	0.05
GCF		0.0162	0.0342	0.63
Money Supply		-0.00909	0.00723	0.20
Revenue		-0.0119	0.0283	0.67
R-squared values	Unadjusted	0.92%		
	Adjusted	0.50%		
Pooled				
Debt-to-GDP Ratio		-0.01169	0.00655	0.07
GCF		0.0409	0.0307	0.18
Money Supply		-0.00598	0.00589	0.31
Revenue		0.0089	0.0243	0.71
R-squared values	Unadjusted	0.47%		
	Adjusted	0.52%		

Source: Author's Compilation

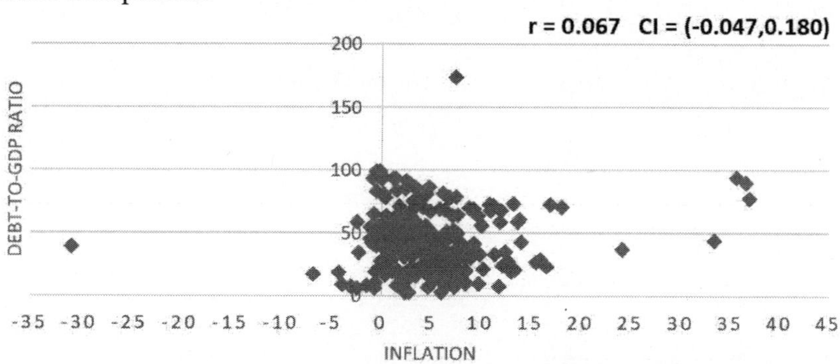

Fig. 1: Correlation Analysis for Low-Income Countries (Inflation, Debt-to-GDP ratio)
Source: Author's Compilation

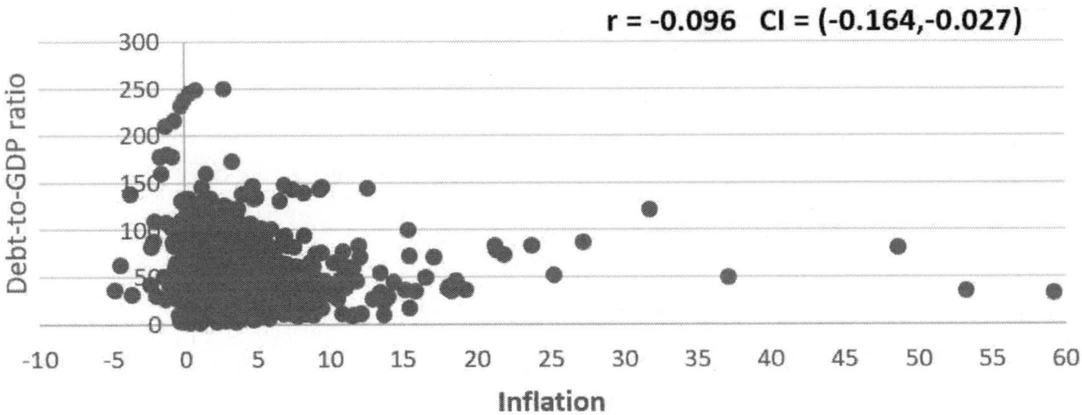

Fig. 2: Correlation Analysis for High-Income Countries (Inflation, Debt-to-GDP ratio)
Source: Author's Compilation

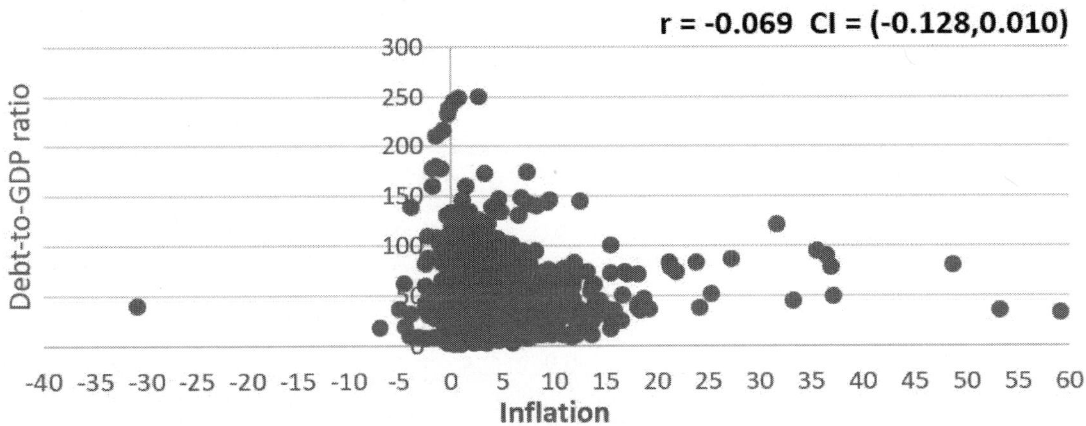

Fig. 3: Correlation Analysis for Pooled Data (Inflation, Debt-to-GDP ratio)
Source: Author's Compilation

Table 3 provides a detailed number of observations under different inflation categories.

Table 3: Number of Observations under Different Inflation Categories

Category	*Number of Observations*
Greater than 2%	741
Lesser than 2%	367
Greater than 4%	462
Lesser than 4%	646
Greater than 5%	368
Lesser than 5%	740

Source: Author's Compilation

Acceptable Inflation Level of 2 Per cent

Table 4: Logistic Regression Results with Normal Inflation Rate of 2 Per cent

Variables	*Low Income*			
	Unadjusted		*Adjusted*	
	Odds Ratio	*95% CI*	*Odds Ratio*	*95% CI*
Debt	1.012	(1.0010, 1.0231)	1.0239	(1.0026, 1.0458)
GCF			0.8814	(0.8159, 0.9523)
Money Supply			0.987	(0.9764, 0.9978)
Revenue			0.9115	(0.8620, 0.9639)
High Income				
Debt	1.0119	(1.0077, 1.0162)	1.0089	(1.0037, 1.0141)
GCF			0.981	(0.9563, 1.0064)
Money Supply			1.0053	(1.0003, 1.0102)
Revenue			1.0071	(0.9870, 1.0276)
Pooled				
Debt	1.0123	(1.0084, 1.0162)	1.0083	(1.0035, 1.0131)
GCF			0.969	(0.9452, 0.9934)
Money Supply			1.0019	(0.9977, 1.0061)
Revenue			0.9959	(0.9778, 1.0144)

Source: Author's Compilation

According to Table 4, statistical significance and directions associated with the likelihood of having an inflation level above 2 per cent with respect to the control variables, is similar to the results of OLS regression. However, in low-income countries, if debt-to-GDP ratio rises by one percentage point, probability of having an inflation above 2 per cent level is likely to rise by 2 per cent, whereas the odds ratios are 1.0089 and 1.0083 for high income countries and pooled data respectively. Unlike low-income countries, high income countries portray a positive association between the odds of more than 2 per cent inflation level and money supply. Nevertheless, even if the association between GCF and inflation is inconsequential among high income countries, for low-income nations (OR = 0.8814) and for pooled data (OR=0.969) they are inversely related.

Acceptable Inflation Level of 4 Per cent

Table 5: Logistic regression results with a normal inflation rate of 4 per cent

Variables	*Low Income*			
	Unadjusted		*Adjusted*	
	Odds Ratio	*95% CI*	*Odds Ratio*	*95% CI*
Debt	1.0119	(1.0015, 1.0224)	1.0218	(1.0028, 1.0411)
GCF			0.8746	(0.8161, 0.9374)
Money Supply			0.9911	(0.9821, 1.0002)

Variables	*Low Income*			
	Unadjusted		*Adjusted*	
	Odds Ratio	*95% CI*	*Odds Ratio*	*95% CI*
Revenue			0.9514	(0.9101, 0.9947)
High Income				
Debt	1.0097	(1.0052, 1.0143)	1.0049	(0.9997, 1.0102)
GCF			0.9836	(0.9618, 1.0060)
Money Supply			1.0067	(1.0014, 1.0120)
Revenue			0.9865	(0.9684, 1.0050)
Pooled				
Debt	1.0109	(1.0067, 1.0151)	1.0057	(1.0009, 1.0106)
GCF			0.9702	(0.9496, 0.9913)
Money Supply			1.003	(0.9988, 1.0073)
Revenue			0.9866	(0.9704, 1.0032)

Source: Author's Compilation

Considering an inflation rate of 4 per cent, similar association can be observed for low-income countries (in Table 5), where there is a 2 per cent increase in inflation when there is a one hundred basis points increase in debt-GDP ratio. Debt-GDP ratio is found to be ineffective for 4 per cent inflation rate in high-income countries. However, unlike low-income countries, rise in money supply can potentially increase the chances of inflation rate breaching 4 per cent mark. With a pooled data the pattern of association remains same for all explanatory variables, where the odds ratio is 1.0086 for unit rise in debt.

Acceptable Inflation Level of 5 Per cent

Table 6: Logistic Regression Results with a Normal Inflation Rate of 5 Per cent

Variables	Low Income			
	Unadjusted		Adjusted	
	Odds Ratio	95% CI	Odds Ratio	95% CI
Debt	1.0136	(1.0029, 1.0244)	1.0204	(1.0010, 1.0403)
GCF			0.8516	(0.7917, 0.9160)
Money Supply			1.0048	(0.9933, 1.0163)
Revenue			0.9577	(0.9161, 1.0011)
High Income				
Debt	1.0082	(1.0033, 1.0132)	1.0072	(1.0014, 1.0131)
GCF			0.9937	(0.9709, 1.0170)
Money Supply			1.0041	(0.9987, 1.0096)
Revenue			0.9858	(0.9671, 1.0048)
Pooled				

Debt	1.0102	(1.0058, 1.0146)	1.0086	(1.0031, 1.0142)
GCF			0.9781	(0.9574, 0.9992)
Money Supply			1.0043	(0.9997, 1.0090)
Revenue			0.9856	(0.9690, 1.0024)

Source: Author's Compilation

According to Table 6, pattern of association between debt-GDP ratio and chances of high inflation remains unchanged for a pooled data, even if the cut-off inflation rate is 5 per cent here. There are significant associations between debt and risk of high inflation in both groups of countries. While in low-income countries only debt and GCF are found to be significantly associated with risk of 5 per cent inflation, for high income countries it is only debt which shows a statistical significance with OR = 1.0072.

R-squared values for a bivariate regression analysis between inflation and debt-GDP ratio were 0.45 per cent for low-income countries, 0.92 per cent for high income countries and 0.47 per cent for the pooled data, which indicate that only less than 1 per cent of the variation in inflation is explained by debt. However, controlling for the rest three factors we observed that GCF, money supply and revenue have stronger impact on inflation in low-income countries, while high income countries show a different picture.

The reason for positive association between likelihood of having a high inflation rate and debt can be attributed to skewed distributions of inflation level.

Discussion

A difference is observed in the pattern of association between inflation and the explanatory factors when the dependent variable is considered as continuous and as categorical ones.

When inflation is considered as a continuous variable, we observe a negative association between inflation and debt. The association is observed in high-income, low-income countries and the pooled data. This would imply that a unit rise in debt would not lead to a rise in inflation. This can further be supported with the use of the R-squared values of the OLS regression. A low R-squared value signifies that there are other factors explaining inflation which have more significance than debt.

Even if most economists (Lopes da Veiga, Ferreira-Lopes & Sequeira, Harmon etc.) claim that debt has a negative impact on inflation, our results considering inflation as a categorical variable show that there is hardly a 1 per cent chance of increase in inflation with a unit rise in debt. This 1 per cent probability of increase in inflation does not hold significant in high-income countries with an inflation threshold level of 4 per cent. This indicates that debt has no significant impact on inflation.

So, inflation taken as a continuous variable is showing a negative association which indicates that the countries can borrow debt without risking their economy towards inflation. This leads to the conclusion that debt has no significant impact on inflation. Hence, we fail to reject H_0 1.

When inflation is taken as a categorical variable (inflation levels – 2 per cent, 4 per cent and 5 per cent), a rise in debt increases the chance to fall into an abnormally high inflation rate (categorical inflation variable). The reason can be attributed to the skewed distributions of inflation level. This could mean that if inflation crosses the threshold limit of 5 per cent, there is a chance that it could lead to an abnormally high debt trap.

When we look at the relationship between inflation and money supply, a negative relation is observed (OR=0.987). This would indicate that inflation would not be affected by money supply in low-income countries. However, this association is not observed in high-income countries (OR=1.005). A similar association was found by Muritala (2011). When the pooled data is considered, this association becomes inconsequential and the association in low-income countries is masked. With these associations, it can be inferred that with an increase in money supply (an expansive monetary policy in terms of money supply) there would not be high inflation in low-income countries unlike as observed in high-income countries.

Potential Implications

These results suggest that a country can utilise debt and money supply, especially in low-income countries, without the fear of it becoming inflationary in the future. Since low-income countries typically need funds to grow, this study could potentially help them in raising debt and having an expansive monetary policy without the fear of it becoming inflationary.

Conclusion

With the signs of an economic slowdown and a possible recession, nations are concerned of their debt levels. An analysis was required to examine the effects of debt post the global financial crisis and economic meltdown of 2008.

This study has highlighted that the impacts of debt on inflation have been overemphasized in the past. While these results would be shown in a pooled analysis, when a clear differentiation into low- and high-income countries is done, it has elucidated that this association is indecisive.

A peculiar association is also seen in the case of revenue. Revenue holds a negative association in high-income countries, while this association fails to be seen in low-income countries and the pooled analysis.

This study clearly highlights upon the differential relationships existing between inflation and debt in high-income and low-income countries. A pooled analysis may mask the inconsequential association between these two variables in poorer economies.

A peculiar association is seen in the case of money supply in low-income countries where it has been observed to have an inverse relationship.

This study concludes that debt has shown no significant impact on inflation. This study also concludes that a low-income country can afford to have an expansive monetary policy in terms of money supply. The findings of this study could further shed light on the Modern Money Theory (MMT) and its claims of debt not becoming inflationary in the future.

References

[1] Nguyen Van Bon, 2015. 'The relationship between public debt and inflation in developing countries: Empirical evidence based on difference panel GMM,' *Asian Journal of Empirical Research, Asian Economic and Social Society*, vol. 5(9), pages 128-142, September.

[2] Harmon, E.Y., 2012, The impact of public debt on inflation, GDP growth and interest rates in Kenya (Doctoral dissertation).

[3] Kwon, G., McFarlane, L. and Robinson, W., 2006, Public debt, money supply, and inflation: A cross-country study and its application to Jamaica, International Monetary Fund.

[4] Lopes da Veiga, J., A. Ferreira-Lopes and T. Sequeira, 2014, Public Debt, Economic Growth, and Inflation in African Economies, MPRA Paper No. 57377, posted 17. July 2014.

[5] Nastansky, A., Mehnert, A. and Strohe, H.G., 2014, A Vector Error Correction Model for the Relationship between Public Debt and Inflation in Germany (No. 51), Universität Potsdam, Wirtschafts-und Sozialwissenschaftliche Fakultät.

[6] Bleaney, M. (1996), Inflation and Public Debt. Australian Economic papers, 35: 141-155. Doi:10.1111/j.1467-8454.1996.tb00043.x

[7] Chryssi Giannitsarou, A.S. (2006). Inflation Implications of Rising Government Debt. National Bureau of Economic Research.

[8] Catao, Luis & Terrones, Marco (2003). Fiscal Deficits and Inflation. International Monetary Fund, IMF Working Papers. 52. 10.1016/j.jmoneco.2004.06.003.

[9] The Federal Reserve of the United States, target/ acceptable Inflation rate. https://www.federalreserve.gov/faqs/economy_14400.htm

[10] Laurence M. Ball, 2014. 'The Case for a Long-Run Inflation Target of Four Percent,' IMF Working Papers 14/92, International Monetary Fund.

[11] Lawrence H. Summers, D. W. (2018). Rethinking the Fed's 2 percent inflation target. Hutchins Center On Fiscal & Monetary Policy.

[12] Muritala, T. (2011). Investment, Inflation and Economic Growth: Empirical Evidence from Nigeria. *Research Journal of Finance and Accounting*, Vol 2, No 5.

Performance Analysis of Hindustan Unilever Limited by using the DuPont Model

Dr Pinku Paul

Management Development Institute Murshidabad, West Bengal, India

Abstract

The performance analysis of the company is an important parameter to understand its sustainability and growth prospects. The present case has tried to conduct a multilayer performance analysis of HUL which is one of the largest players in the fast-moving consumer goods sector. As a manufacturing firm, it should focus on all the parameters of profit, asset utilisation, and leverage of the firm. For this purpose, the DuPont model was used. The findings of the case reflect and justify the five-factor DuPont Model with the parameters of profit margin, asset utilisation, leverage, interest cover, and tax cover for HUL. The case concludes that the total asset base of the company and as well as the equity base affect the ROE and ROA of the company.

Keywords: *Asset Utilisation, DuPont Model, Interest Cover, Leverage, Profit Margin, Tax Cover*

Introduction

India has a rising middle-class population with more than the total USA population. This gives ample opportunities for fast-moving consumer goods (FMCG) companies to grow and capture the market. The FMCG sector is the fourth major sector in the economy. It has been rising at a rapid rate due to the increase in the disposable income of the population of India, the youth population, and the growing awareness of the use of brands. In the FMCG sector, 50 per cent of sales come from the household and personal care division. The FMCG sector is predicted to expand at a CAGR of 14.9 per cent to achieve US$ 220 billion by 2025. The big players in this sector are Johnson & Johnson, Himalaya, Hindustan Unilever, ITC, Lakme, and other companies.

Hindustan Unilever Limited (HUL)

HUL came into existence with the unification of three companies: Hindustan Vanaspati Manufacturing Company(1931), Lever Brothers India Limited (1933), and United Traders Limited (1934) as an overseas company with 10 per cent shareholding to the Indian public. HUL then subsequently started acquiring the companies and brands such as Brooke Bond (1984), Lipton (1977), and Ponds (1986). The liberalisation of trade in the year 1991 gave a new beginning to HUL with respect to mergers and acquisitions. The companies which got associated with HUL were Tata Oil Mills Company (1993),

Lakmé Limited (1998), Kotex Sanitary Pads and Huggies Diapers(1994), Kissan company (1994), and Dollops Icecream (1994). After that HUL went for a strategic partnership with Kwality Icecream Group. In a historic decision in January 2000, the government agreed to give HUL a 74 per cent equity stake in Modern Foods. And later on in the year 2002, HUL purchased Modern Foods. In 2001 HUL started its rural project Shakti which was an exemplary move for human wellbeing with a business plan and connecting rural India. The Pureit water filter was added to the basket of HUL in the year 2004.

Moving forward with the Unilever Sustainable Living Plan (USLP), HUL launched the 'Prabhat' (Dawn), in the year 2013 which connected the regional community to the production facility. In the year 2020 HUL acquired the female intimate hygiene product VWash which is the industry leader in this segment. The historic merger of GSK Consumer Healthcare with HUL in 2020 made the entry of HUL in the Health drink category with the brands Horlicks and Boost. In 2022, HUL opened the first gender-

Table 1: Summery of Income Statement (2018–22)

Annual (Rs. in Cr.)	*2022*	*2021*	*2020*	*2019*	*2018*
Sales	52,446	47,028	39,783	39,310	35,545
Other Income	258	410	632	550	384
Total Income	52,704	47,438	40,415	39,860	35,929
Total Expenditure	40,724	36,715	31,124	31,223	28,599
EBIT	11,980	10,723	9,291	8,637	7,330
Interest	106	117	118	33	26
Tax	2,987	2,606	2,409	2,544	2,079
Net Profit	8,887	8,000	6,764	6,060	5,225

Source: Annual Report HUL

Table 2: Summery of Balance Sheet (2018–22)

Annual (Rs. in Cr.)	*2022*	*2021*	*2020*	*2019*	*2018*
Equities & Liabilities	44,621	44,256	43,891	43,525	43,160
Share Capital	235	235	216	216	216
Reserves & Surplus	48,826	47,439	7,998	7,627	7,065
Total Equity	49,061	47,674	8,214	7,843	7,281
Current Liabilities	11,280	11,103	9,317	8,667	8,887
Other Liabilities	10,176	9,980	2,622	2,119	1,694
Total Liabilities	70,517	68,757	20,153	18,629	17,862
Assets					
Fixed Assets	35,389	34,791	5,959	5,004	4,908
Current Assets	15,522	14,217	12,321	11,914	11,660
Other Assets	19,606	19,749	1,873	1,711	1,294
Total Assets	70,517	68,757	20,153	18,629	17,862

Source: Annual Report HUL

balanced plant and a zero-carbon facility of Unilever South Asia as the new Home Care factory and an automated distribution center for Unilever India Limited. A quick glance at the financial performance of HUL for five years (2018–22)

Multilayer Performance analysis of HUL

The multilayer performance analysis is conducted by using the DuPont Model.

Two-Factor DuPont Analysis

An important tool for understanding the performance of any firm is to conduct a DuPont analysis, first conceptualised by F. Donaldson Brown in 1912. Brown proposed the DuPont analysis using two factors, one to describe the profitability of the firm and the second factor used is asset utilisation of the firm (Paul, 2021). This formulation of the DuPont analysis is referred to as the two-factor DuPont model. Profitability is determined by the return on total assets (ROA) of the firm and is computed by the expression.

$$\text{ROA} = \frac{\text{Net Income or Profit After Tax}}{\text{Total Sales}} \times \frac{\text{Total Sales}}{\text{Total Assets}}$$

Net profit margin is estimated by dividing the profit after tax by the total sales of the firm. The ratio on the right side of the above equation, the total sales divided by the total assets of the firm, is equivalent to the asset turnover. The assets turnover ratio indicates the assets utilisation with respect to the sales of the firm. In the two factors model, the performance of the firm is determined in terms of return on assets (ROA). It was a composition of Net Profit Margin (NPM) and Assets Turnover (AT).

The two factor DuPont analysis of HUL has been presented in TN: Table 3. It was found that over the period from 2018 to 2022, the NPM of HUL increased from 20.40 per cent to 22.73 per cent. While analysing the second factor of the model, it was observed that the asset utilisation has reduced and from 2.0115, it has become 0.7474. The trend depicts a fall. ROA is the result of the product of profit margin and asset utilisation. The values of these ratios compensate each other and one of the high values of the ratio is supplemented by the other ratio. A similar trend was observed in HUL also. So overall the profitability of HUL has seen a huge change from 41.04 per cent in 2018 to 16.99 per cent in 2022.

Table 3: Two-Factor DuPont Analysis

Year	*ROA*	*NPM*	*AT*
2022	0.1699	0.2273	0.7474
2021	0.1560	0.2260	0.6899
2020	0.4610	0.2299	2.0054
2019	0.4636	0.2167	2.1397
2018	0.4104	0.2040	2.0115

Source: Authors' computation

Three-Factor DuPont Analysis

The second version of the DuPont Model described the profitability of the firm with respect to the leverage, asset utilisation, and profit margin of the firm. That is, the three-factor DuPont model. The profitability is measured by the return on equity (ROE) of the firm.

$$\text{ROE} = \frac{\text{Profit After Tax}}{\text{Total Sales}} \times \frac{\text{Total Sales}}{\text{Total Assets}} \times \frac{\text{Total Assets}}{\text{Equity}}$$

With the net profit margin and asset turnover, leverage is incorporated. Leverage measures the use of equity to finance the total assets of the firm. The three-factor model provides insight into the performance of the company in terms of Net Profit Margin (NPM), Assets Turnover (AT), and Leverage (LEV).

The three-factor DuPont analysis of HUL. has been presented in Table 4. The first two factors of the model, i.e. NPM and AT are not dependent on the capital structure of the company. Therefore, financial leverage was incorporated into the model to understand its impact on the profitability of the company. The ROE of HUL for the year 2022 was 18.11 per cent, which was far less than the ROE of 2018 which was reported as 71.76 per cent. So, as the asset utilisation has reduced over the period from 2018 to 2022 and it was found that the leverage has reduced over the period, as the total assets were 2.4532 times of total equity of the company in 2018, which has become 1.4373 times in 2022. The NPM has increased from 2018 to 2022. Therefore, less asset utilisation and use of debt in the capital structure over the period resulted in the decline of the overall profitability of the company.

Table 4: Three-Factor DuPont Analysis

Year	*ROE*	*NPM*	*AT*	*LEV*
2022	0.1811	0.2273	0.7474	1.4373
2021	0.1678	0.2260	0.6899	1.4422
2020	0.8235	0.2299	2.0054	2.4535
2019	0.7727	0.2167	2.1397	2.3752
2018	0.7176	0.2040	2.0115	2.4532

Source: Authors' computation

Five-Factor DuPont Analysis

The final DuPont model is the latest version of these models inspired by Brown's early work and is the five-factor DuPont model. It measures the profitability by the ROE of the firm. ROE is a function of five factors: tax cover, interest cover, leverage, asset utilisation, and the profit margin of the firm. ROE is the product of these five parameters; that is

$$\text{ROE} = \text{Profit Margin} \times \text{Asset Turnover} \times \text{Leverage} \times \text{Interest Cover} \times \text{Tax Cover}$$

or

$$\text{ROE} = \frac{\text{Profit Before Interest and Tax}}{\text{Total Sales}} \times \frac{\text{Total Sales}}{\text{Total Assets}} \times \frac{\text{Total Assets}}{\text{Equity}}$$

$$\times \frac{\text{Profit Befor Tax}}{\text{Profit Before Interest and Tax}} \times \frac{\text{Profit After Tax}}{\text{Profit Before Tax}}$$

In this five-factor model, the compound leverage factor ,ROA and tax cover is used to describe the decomposition of ROE, wherein, the compound leverage factor is product of leverage and interest cover, and ROA is the product of asset turnover and profit margin.

$$\text{Compound Leverage Factor} = \frac{\text{Profit Befor Tax}}{\text{Profit Before Interest and Tax}} \times \frac{\text{Total Assets}}{\text{Equity}}$$

$$\text{ROA} = \frac{\text{Profit Before Interest and Tax}}{\text{Total Sales}} \times \frac{\text{Total Sales}}{\text{Total Assets}}$$

Therefore, the decomposition of ROE is as follows:

$$\text{ROE} = \text{ROA} \times \text{Compound Leverage Factor} \times \text{Tax Cover}$$

The financial health and performance ITC has been reflected through the five factor DuPont Model, wherein, the ROE has been decomposed into five factors, profit margin (NPM), asset turnover (AT), interest cover (IC), tax cover (TC) and leverage (LEV).

Table 5: Five-Factor DuPont Analysis

Year	*ROE*	*NPM*	*IC*	*TC*	*AT*	*LEV*
2022	0.1811	0.2273	0.9912	0.7484	0.7474	1.4373
2021	0.1678	0.2260	0.9891	0.7543	0.6899	1.4422
2020	0.8235	0.2299	0.9873	0.7374	2.0054	2.4535
2019	0.7727	0.2167	0.9962	0.7043	2.1397	2.3752
2018	0.7176	0.2040	0.9965	0.7154	2.0115	2.4532

Source: Authors' computation

The five-factor DuPont analysis of HUL. was presented in Table No-5. Let us first focus on factors NPM and AT and the product of both gives the ROA of the firm. The factor NPM is the company's operating profit margin, which equals operating profit per rupee of sales. HUL's operating profit margin has improved over the period from 20.4 per cent to 22.7 per cent. The next factor AT, which is the association of sales to total assets, is known as total asset turnover ratio. The ratio is used to measure the productivity of the firm's use of assets with respect to annual sales generated by each rupee of assets. It was found that from 2018 to 2020 for HUL the AT was more than 2 which means that per rupee of asset generates twice one rupee of sales, which is good sign for the company. But from 2021 to 2022, it declined below 1, which indicated that the assets of the company were not utilised to its optimum capacity to generate the sales. The factors NPM and AT are not dependent of the financial leverage of the company. Therefore, it can be inferred that the ROA of the company is not affected by financial leverage of the company. So as the factor TC, the ratio of profit after taxes to profit before tax of the company is called as tax cover ratio. This ratio indicates the government's tax rate and the policies adopted by the company to reduce its tax load. As it was indicative in the model that factors NPM, AT and TC are not affected by the capital structure of the company but, the factors IC and LEV are affected. The factor IC is ratio of profit before tax to profit before interest and tax. The firm's profit before tax will be highest when there are no interest expenses to be made to debtholders or no debt in the capital structure. So, the highest possible value 1 is given to company having no debt. In case of HUL, the IC values are nearing to one over the period, which indicates minimum dependency on leverage by the company. The next factor LEV is the ratio of assets to equity, which is a gauge of the firm's degree of financial leverage. In all the years from 2018 to 2020, HUL had a LEV greater than 2, which indicates, the use of debt in the capital structure. The presence of financial leverage helps to increase ROE only if ROA is greater than the interest rate on the firm's debt. So, to understand the impact of financial leverage, further analysis of compound leverage factor which is the product of IC and LEV is done. The compound leverage factor is greater than 1 in all the years for HUL, indicating the positive contribution of financial leverage to ROE. But over the years the ratio reduces, reflecting the fact that ROE falls with use of debt in the capital structure. The trend analysis of the components of DuPont model was presented in Figure 1.

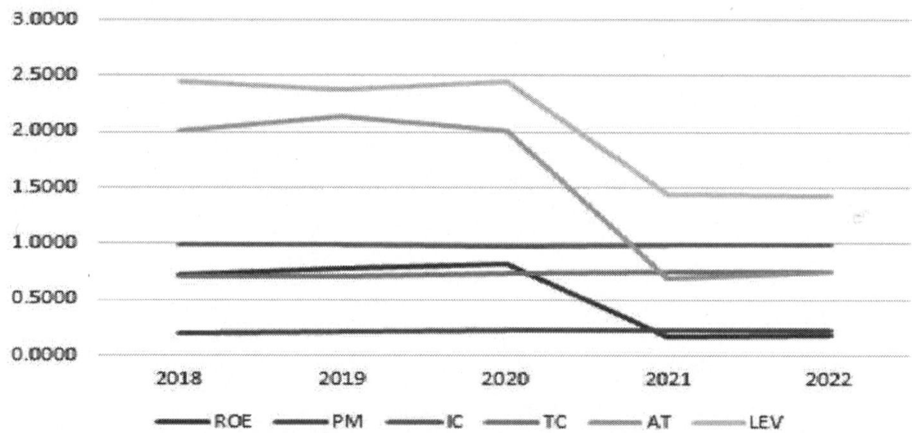

Figure 1: Performance Analysis

Source: Authors' computation

Discussion and Conclusion

The trend predicted in the analysis of Dupont reflected that the performance of the company from 2018 to 2020 was improving whereas during 2021 and 2022 there was a Steve fall in the performance with respect to the ROE of the company. The reason for the same was HUL in the year 2020-21 successful merger with GSK Consumer Healthcare to get a very robust position in the Nutrition and Health food drink category. This was reflected in the total asset base of the company and as well as the equity base which has substantially increased and thus affected the ROE and ROA of the company. Therefore, for the company now to improve the performance must focus on the asset utilisation of the company and the leverage parameters. The company should improve the productivity of the firm's use of assets. The compound leverage factor of the firm is more than one which indicates that positive contribution of financial leverage to the profitability of the firm. The presence of financial leverage helps to increase ROE only if ROA is greater than the interest rate on the firm's debt. Hence the overall position of the company seems to be in a very sound and healthy. The company aims to be to deliver steady, competitive, and sustainable growth and profitability through purpose led and future fit business model.

References

[1] https://www.hul.co.in/our-company/hul-history/

[2] https://www.hul.co.in/investor-relations/annual-reports/

[3] Paul, P. (2021), 'A Study of Multilayered Profitability Analysis by Using DuPont Model: Evidence from Indian Pharmaceutical Industry', Global Business Review, Online first on March 21, 2021, https://doi.org/10.1177/0972150921993056.

What Matters More in Sustaining Healthcare Performances?: Evidence from Multi-branched Hospitals in India

Dr Ashutosh Dash

Associate Professor, MDI Gurgaon, Sukhrali, MG Road, Gurugram
E-mail: ashutosh@mdi.ac.in

Abstract

Healthcare organisations encounter problems that are either inherent to the evolution of care demand and supply or are the result of surprises that occur outside the health system, like economic shocksor disease outbreaks. The challenges, be it internal or external, often necessitate a paradigm shift in governance and structure, as well as financing and resource allocation, accountability frameworks and public health system solutions. To keep up with the changing environment performance manage systems must change. This paper will help understand the impacts of cost and quality performances of the healthcare organisations on sustenance of their financial performance. With help of data collected through a survey from employees of large hospitals located in the national capital region of India and multivariate path analysis model, the study examines the relationship between cost performances, quality performances and the financial performances. The research piece identifies high correlations between cost and quality indicators that significantly impact the financial metrics of the hospitals. The results of this study reveal that quality performance mediates the interrelationships between cost and financial results metrics. Healthcare organisations can improve their business viability by focusing on the quality of care they provide to the public.

Keywords: *Performance Management, Healthcare Sector, Path Analysis, Cost Performances, Quality Performances, Financial Performances*

Introduction

Research on corporate sustainability and corporate social responsibility has taken a front seat in the millennium and has been multifaceted by spreading across a variety of fields. One of the most contentious issues looked at by various researchers is how does sustainability initiatives affect company performance and vice-versa (Artiach et al., 2010; Bodhanwala and Bodhanwala, 2018; Chang and Kuo, 2008; Choi et al., 2010; do Prado et al., 2020; Feng et al., 2017; Goyal et al., 2013; Lin et al., 2015; Lourenço and Branco, 2013; Nguyen et al., 2022; Pham et al., 2021; Velte, 2017; Weber, 2017; Yang and Wang, 2022). Many authors concluded that the appropriate use of performance management systems (PMS) can support strategy implementation and push organisations toward sustainability objectives (Baumgartner, 2014; Gond et al., 2012). Therefore, organisations need to embrace sustainability concerns and embed it in to their internal performance management systems to get maximum benefits for themselves while creating imprints for the society, and the environment (Lankoski, 2016; Sroufe, 2017; Wijethilake and Upadhaya, 2020). The internal disconnect in the management control system becomes a hinderance for firms in developing sustainability strategies and report on sustainability issues. Without developing a PMS that specifically monitors sustainability objectives it is difficult for firms to collect data and evaluate the sustainable strategies (Bebbington and Unerman, 2018).

Performance management system (PMS) is a way of management that lets managers to track and analyse the performance of their staff members. The prime objective of PM system is to help people achieving their full potential and accomplish their work in the most efficient and effective way feasible. A systematic PMS ensures that employees at all levels of the organisation must be on the same page when it comes to mission and vision of the organisation and must ensure that their individual's work is goal congruent to fit into the company's overarching vision. In order to create a clear knowledge of expectations, PMS is built on the principle that Individuals must be considered in the context of the larger workplace system and necessitates responsibility and transparency.

From performance management point of view healthcare sector is considered to be an important area as the task of measuring performance of healthcare institutions becomes increasingly complex when such organisations gradually evolve into integrated service providers comprising of hospitals for in-patient treatment, outdoor patient clinics and specialised surgical units, and home health services (Curtright et al, 2000). Health care systems face tremendous challenges because of many external factors occurrence such as economic shocks or epidemic outbreaks (Vaineire et, al, 2020). Coping such challenges often require a paradigm shift in governance, corporate financing and resource allocation in the organisations without compromising on their accountability and compliance to health regulatory systems.

Though it is imperative for health organisations to develop a methodology and system that align organisational strategies and core principles with performance measurement and management indicators, many healthcare organisations still consider profit as the sole yardstick of measuring performance aligned to the NPM movement ideals of 1980s. As a result of unexpected effects and new concepts about performance in healthcare over the past four decades (from 1980s to 2021), healthcare sector encouraged the creation of multidimensional performance assessment systems. The capability of a healthcare organisation to progress towards one or more numerous desired outcomes while paying close attention to either the integrity of its action and the degree of its successes is referred to as performance. The emergence of PMS within the healthcare sector is intrinsically tied to the 'evolution of the notion of health performance'.

Besides the key performance indicators used the success of performance measurement system largely depends on the behavioural traits of the superiors evaluating the performance of subordinates. As a result, it's not an exaggeration to suggest that one's performance is molded by the eyes of the beholder. Managers may abandon rational analysis in favouriof heuristics while making complex decisions. When evaluating organisational performance, managers are opportunistic and seek organisational benefits. Similarly, when several or multiple indicators are employed to assess the performance of an individual, the allocation of weights may be subject to the biases of the evaluator rather than the sensitivity of the indicators (Dai, Kuang & Tang 2018). The behavioural biases or opportunistic behaviour is purely a psychological and can be explained by the agency theory.

Literature Review

A PMS is a strategic and cohesive approach for sustained success of an organisation through individual human capital development that improves both team and individual performances in the interest of the organisation (Armstrong and Baron, 1998). Therefore, organisations employ PMS to shape employee behaviour aligned to organisational interest to achievea specific result. Because of the goal congruency at the core, the PMS has a considerable impact on organisation's performances, be it financial and productivity. Management of performance is a critical tool that assists supervisors in efficiently managing human resources (Armstrong and Baron, 2004). PMS by considering employees is as one of the most valuable assets in any corporation plays a critical role for improving organisational performance and assisting corporations in achieving their business objectives.

Since the business objectives are linked to the financial performance that can be achieved through employee efficiency, organisations including healthcare institutions link a rewards-based approach to performance management of employees. It has been observed that the reward-based systems are not successful in many organisations, thereby necessitating a different and unique approach to manage and sustain the organisational performance (Bhattacharjee and Sengupta, 2011). Devising an ideal PMS for an organisation is a continuous and gradual process that involves several trials for an effective design and successful implementation. PMS adoption is not a simple task as it necessitates a thorough understanding of workplace human behaviour and its influence on the commercial objectives of the organisation in a specific desired way.

A section of literature that looked into the association between the financial outcomes and performance management conclude that PMS has a favorable impact on financial performance indicators. The PMS helps in improving the operating and financial performances by enhancing the quality of products and services and improving the market share (Damanpour et al., 1989; Subramanian and Nilakanta, 1996; Han et al., 1998; Langerak et al 2000; York and Miree, 2004). The rich experience and exclusivity of services, facilitates the healthcare organisations in retaining their existing consumers and build stronger customer loyalty that can help grow their market share and profits. Further, the increase in size of operation due to higher market share may assist cutting costs through scale economies and coping the uncertainties that the organisations face in their operating environment (Langerak et al., 2000; York and Miree, 2004).

In the context of healthcare sector, cost measures have an indirect impact on hospital financial performance, while quality measures have a direct impact on the performance indicators (Chaudary, Zafar & Salman, 2015). In hospitals, costs are incurred in order to meet the quality criteria of healthcare (Uyar and Neyis, 2018). Cost and quality performances in a healthcare organisation are intricately interwoven as high-quality services reduce waste and waste reduction reduces the cost. Quality performances also avoid malpractices at the time of rendering, hence enhances a hospital's financial performance.

Quality is a complex and multidimensional entity that gets influenced by a variety of circumstances (Cefalu, Elliot, Setodji, Cleary, and Hays, 2018) within and beyond an organisation. It is considered to be an operational performance indicator in the organisations and in case of healthcare organisations clinical quality and patient satisfaction levels are the true indicators of their service quality. For that reason, healthcare executives divert all their efforts on increasing the clinical quality in order to provide maximum satisfaction to their patients (Tsai, Orav & Jha, 2015). Clinical quality is termed as the ability of healthcare organisations to attain high standards in medical services such as proper diagnosis, procedure and treatment, and managing the aftermath physical and physiological consequences on patients (Marley, Collier & Goldstein, 2004). In reality, hospitals with high patient satisfaction are found to deliver efficient clinical care to the patients with shorter stays and lower inpatient costs because of which governing boards of the large hospitals centers their focus on improving clinical quality (Tsai, Orav & Jha, 2015).

Cost performance is measured by various indicators like inpatient expenses, labour productivity, and capacity utilisation (Li, Benton & Keong Leong, 2002). Labour productivity is considered as the foremost indicator of cost performance; hence cost performance entails extra attention to the healthcare workforce (Hofmarcher, Festl & Bishop-Tarver, 2016). Patient flow is linked to revenue, which has a substantial impact on a hospital's financial performance (Singh & Wheeler, 2012). Therefore, financial performance is another important factor that can have an indirect impact on patient perceptions of care quality by increasing profitability (Cleven, Mettler, Rohner, & Winter, 2016). Besides the cost and quality performances, other structural restrictions of healthcare organisations such as location, size, and teaching status, appear to be linked to financial and market share features (Kaufman et al., 2016).

The most typical metrics used to assess an organisation's financial performance are market share and operating profitability (Li, Benton & Leong, 2002). Individual hospitals have varying degrees of market share since hospitals with highest clinical quality may not have unlimited capacity to address the needs of the entire patients in a particular market (Mougeot & Naegelen, 2005). Since the quality of care provided by a hospital has an impact on its future market share, the individual small hospitals can get future financial success by focusing on care quality and a feedback effect from the patients (Sari, 2002).

The second measure of financial performance of a healthcare organisation is its operating profit margin that considers revenue, patient care costs and other operating expenses to calculate profit from the hospital operations (Reiter & Song, 2011). The financial viability of health care organisations and sustainable financial performance is often evaluated through the quantity, quality and consistency of the operating profits (Rauscher & Wheeler, 2008). To increase operating profitability, create value to equity holders, and stay financially sustainable in the long run, successful management of the patient revenue cycle also become vital for the healthcare entities. Given the importance of revenue cycle, hospitals must devise mechanism that can handle higher number of patients while ensuring patient access to financial data (Singh & Wheeler, 2012).

Management control process is an important part in the Finance department. Though most of the work in this department revolves around budgetary planning and control, now Performance management System (PMS) has become an integral part of it. But performance management systems at health care organisations in India is not explored in its length and breadth so far. Therefore, the study intends examine whether quality or cost measures of the performance management system can lead to long term sustainable financial performances. The paper intends to shed light on previously unexplored areas of performance management and may suggest performance improvement solutions. The outcomes of this study will offer policymakers with a frame work to guide health care worker planning and management in the region and extrapolating to India and other developing countries. The research will also help to link those parameters to financial performance indicators in healthcare sector with the changes in the performance management.

With an intent to examine the research objective that the operational performance measures such as costs and quality performances have a substantial impact on the financial performance of healthcare organisations, the study proposed the following hypotheses:

- H1: Improving clinical quality improves patient satisfaction, market share and operating profit
- H2: Holding down in-patient cost, attaining labour productivity and maintaining capacity utilisation led to better clinical quality and higher patient satisfaction

Research Design

In order to examine the relationship between cost performance, quality performance and financial performances the following framework is proposed in Figure 1:

The study gathered data from large hospitals that dominate the healthcare industry with multiple branches with multicity presence to examine the model. The reason behind such selection is that the concept of performance management is ideally suited to large scale healthcare industry as it is very hard to find the options to improve their productivity and thereby increase their financial performance. Also, the study considers some of the management control practices like Incentive Control (Incentivising based

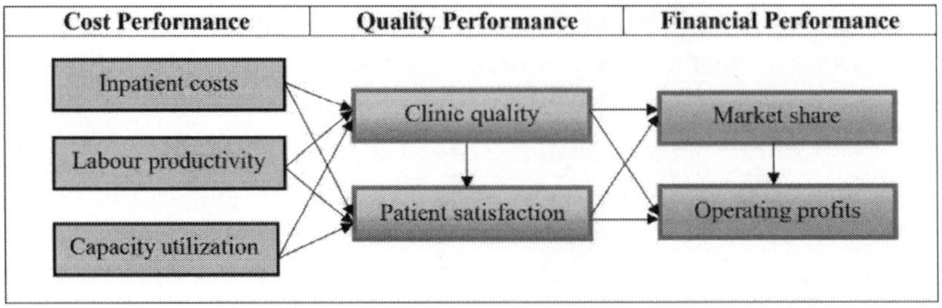

Fig. 1: Relationship Framework of the Performance Indicators
Source: Author Compilation

on high labour activity, patient satisfaction in the form of feedbacks), Result Control (by checking the high utilisation of the hospitals) initiatives togauge the implementation of Performance Management in the hospital. The data has been collected through a primary survey during a time frame of six months staring from April 2022 through September 2022 given the fact that the abnormal earnings owing to COVID pressure on the hospitals had gone down substantially by the beginning of the financial year 2022-23.

In this survey, hospital executives were asked to evaluate their facilities to competitors in terms of cost, quality, and financial performance. Data was gathered using a five-point scale. The response categories for most statements ranged from (1) significant lower to (5) significantly higher. Scheduled interviews were conducted with around 90 hospital managers from 5 different public and private hospitals in the national capital region of the country. Physicians, head of the departments, nursing staff, administrative staff, management personnel like directors and assistant directors were among the hospital executives interviewed. Before the surveys were conducted, ethical approval was obtained from the hospitals'ethical committees.

To establish the relationships among the performance indicators in the model, the Pearson correlation coefficients are used to identify the multicollinearity, if any and illuminating the model-building process further. The study used the path analysis approach to empirically establish the relationship among the variables. Path analysis is a type of multivariate regression analysis that takes into account numerous dependent (and typically multiple independent) variables at the same time to evaluate causal theories (Geiser, 2013). This method is used to determine the degree and importance of causal relationships between the performance indicators. The foremost advantage of path analysis is that it clarifies correlation among the variables and indicates the strength of a causal hypothesis. The study did not prefer the Structured Equation Modelling (SEM) over path analysis because SEM doesn't help prioritise the relationships that are important to the analysis but path analysis has that added advantage.

Data Analysis

The demographic statistics of the respondents show a balanced gender ratio within the hospitals with 56.4 per cent males and 43.6 per centfemales. 74.5 per cent of doctors are married, and majority of respondents are graduate and above. Furthermore, there is a balance amongst hospital manager vocations, with 25.5 per cent working asa manager, 29.8 per cent as a doctor, and 21.3 per cent as an assistant director. The assessment of the values obtained from the respondents, we will formulate the mean and standard deviation for every performance indicator whichis presented in Table 1.

Table 1: Descriptive Statistics

Hospital Performance Indicators	*Mean*	*Standard Deviation*
Cost Performance		
Lowering the inpatient costs	2.90	1.28
Achieving high labour activity	4.02	0.64
Trying to maintain high-capacity utilisation	4.35	0.70
Quality Performance		
Clinical Quality	4.48	0.63
Patient Satisfaction	4.37	0.66
Financial Performance		
Market Share Growth	4.31	0.69
Operating Profit	4.41	0.72

Source: Author Compilation

A cursory look at these number convey that lowering the inpatient costs is not much welcomed by the managers in the healthcare sector. Rather, high priorities have been assigned to the various indicators of the quality like clinical quality and patient satisfaction. The low variance in the quality performance indicators show a consistent mindsetof various interviewed managers on quality consciousness.

Table 2: Correlation Matrix

Variables	*C1*	*C2*	*C3*	*Q1*	*Q2*	*F1*	*F2*
C1	1.000						
C2	0.114	1.000					
C3	0.281	0.807*	1.000				
Q1	0.145	0.564	0.627	1.000			
Q2	0.106	0.694*	0.623	0.643*	1.000		
F1	0.137	0.505	0.529	0.564	0.530	1.000	
F2	0.201	0.702*	0.662*	0.657*	0.654*	0.640*	1.000

Source: Author Compilation

Whereas C1 – Inpatient costs, C2 – Labour productivity, C3 – Capacity utilisation, Q1 – Clinical quality, Q2 – Patient satisfaction, F1 – Market share, and F2 – operational profits

* Significant at 5 per cent level

Table 2 presents the correlation matrix that shows the Pearson correlation coefficients among the variables under study. The table highlights that capacity utilisation and labour productivity had the highest correlation score. Both the variables have a high association with operating profits of the hospitals.

The covariance matrix is produced in Table 3 because it is a valuable tool for isolating structured relationships from random variables in a matrix. This can be applied as a transformation toother parameters or used to decorrelate variables.

Table 3: Covariance Matrix

Covariance Matrix	*C1*	*C2*	*C3*	*Q1*	*Q2*	*F1*	*F2*
C1	1.618						
C2	0.101	0.494					
C3	0.252	0.400	0.498				
Q1	-0.165	0.639	0.221	0.462			
Q2	0.087	0.315754	0.284	0.933	0.419		
F1	0.123	0.249321	0.262	0.269	0.781	0.494	
F2	0.188	0.362155	0.343	0.327	0.311	0.900	0.539

Source: Author Compilation

Results and Analysis

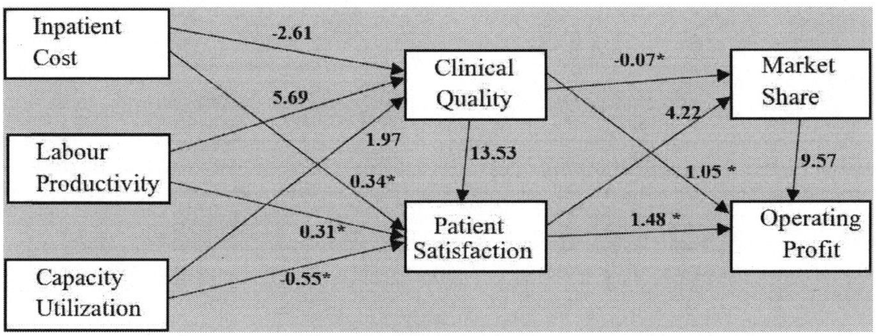

Fig. 2: t-Test Values Network
*Significance at 5 per cent level; *Source:* Author Compilation

The final figure after elimination shows out to be what is conquered from the final path model. The path model highlights that the t values obtained from six paths are meaningful as the p values are found to be less than 0.05.

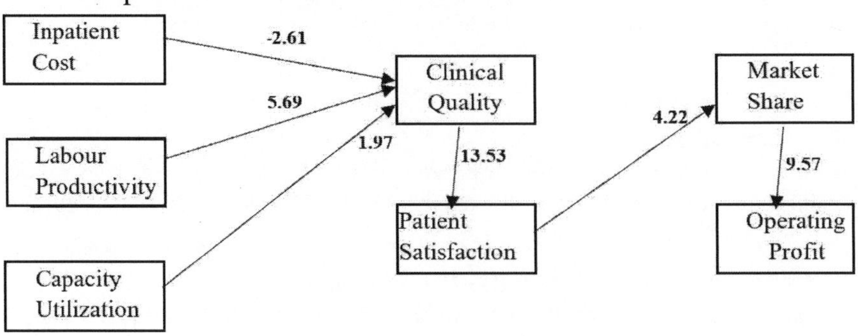

Fig. 3: The Path Model
Source: Author Compilation

Figure 4 shows the completed model standard path coefficients which show that the model's overall goodness of fit indices is satisfactory. The root mean square error value is 0.124; the goodness of fit index (GFI) value is 0.92; and the adjusted GFI (AGFI) value is 0.84. As a reminder, these values are higher than the suggested RMSEA, GFI, and AGFIvalues ofi0.05–0.10, 0.90, and 0.81, respectively (Bentler, 1990).

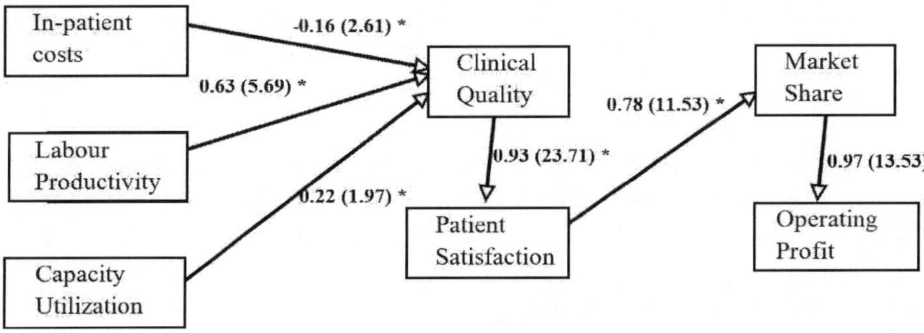

Fig. 4: Standard Path Coefficient Network
*Significance level = 5 per cent; *Source:* Author Compilation

The path coefficients determined in the path coefficient network are found to be statistically significant at 5 per cent level of significance. Clinical quality is directly and negatively affected by efforts to reduce inpatient costs indicating that the efforts to reduce inpatient cost does not necessarily reduce the clinical quality. Clinical quality is directly affected by increasing labour productivity. It is expected that increasing labour productivity would result in better clinical outcomes. Clinical quality is also found to be directly influenced by excessive capacity use. The findings of the study suggest that better cost management improves clinical quality by increasing labour productivity and maximising capacity utilisation.

The findings of the study confirm a positive association between clinical quality and patient satisfaction. The results also reveal that patient satisfaction improves the hospital market share directly and positively. This goes in tandem with the well-established fact that increasing patient happiness leads to increased market share,which is backed up by these findings. Growing market share directly influence the operating earnings of the healthcare organisations. The results back the assertion that increasing market share has the potential to enhance operating profit. The findings that quality performance has a favourable and considerable effect on market share, according to this supporting theory. The study's final finding adds to our understanding by demonstrating that marketshare has a favourable and significant impact on operating profits. The beneficial interrelationships among financial performance metrics are supported by this result.

Conclusions

The financial performance of a hospital is a necessary condition for its survival. Existing research does not provide adequate subjective assessments of hospital employees perceptions of the relationships between various hospital performance metrics like cost, quality and financial performances. Despite an increasing understanding of the interrelationships between hospital performance metrices, a closer look at the elements that influence financial success deserves greater attention.

Based on the survey data on employees of large hospitals in national capital region of India and using a path model, the research has found high correlations between cost and quality indicators and their influence upon the financial metrics. According to this study, quality performance mediates the interrelationships between the cost and financial results metrics. Hospitals can improve their business viability by focusing on labour productivity and capacity utilisation for improving the quality of care they give. Attempts to reduce cost can not be considered strategic as it negatively impacts the clinical quality. The effect of clinical quality on patient satisfaction creates a strong link between quality performance and financial performance measures like market share and operating profits.

The study's strength is that it empirically proved the correlation between cost and quality indicators impact the financial metrics from the perspective of hospital executives. The study's original contribution is to advocate for a different viewpoint on how to comprehend the factors that influence hospital financial performance. In this regard, the findings of the study are useful in attracting top hospital executives' attention to the multifaceted dynamics of financial performance. This effect brings to light the fact that financial performances are not just driven by numerical assessments but also by the perceptions of hospital executives on cost and quality indicators.

References

[1] Armstrong, M., and Baron, A. (1998), Performance Management, The new realities, Inst. Personnel Dev., London.

[2] Armstrong, M., and Baron, A. (2004), Managing performance: Performance management in action, CIPD, London.

[3] Bhattacharjee, S., and Sengupta, S. (2011), 'A study of Performance Management System in a Corporate Firm', *VSRD International Journal of Business and Management Research*, Vol. 1, No. 8, pp. 496–513.

[4] Bilqees, G., Khalid, M., and Afaq, A.K. (2018), 'Restructuring the relationship between performance management and employee engagement', *Pakistan business review*, Vol. 20, No. 1, pp. 99–109.

[5] Chin, W.W., Gopal, A. and Salisbury, W.D. (1997), 'Advancing the theory of adaptive structuration: the development of a scale to measure faithfulness of appropriation', *Information Systems Research*, Vol. 8, No. 4, pp. 342–67.

[6] Curtright, Jonathan W.; Stolp-Smith, Steven C. FACHE; Edell, Eric S. M.D. (January 2000), 'Strategic Performance Management: Development of a Performance Measurement System at the Mayo Clinic', *Journal of Healthcare Management*, Volume 45, Issue 1, pp. 58–68.

[7] Dai Narisa Tianjing, Xi (Jason) Kuang & Guliang Tang (2018), Differential Weighting of Objective Versus Subjective Measures in Performance Evaluation: Experimental Evidence, *European Accounting Review*, 27: 1, 129–148, DOI: 10.1080/09638180.2016.1234402

[8] Edward, M., Christina, E., Kathryn, G., Bennett, P., and Carolyn, S. (2011), 'Performance Management at the Wheel: Driving Employee Engagement in Organisations', *Journal of Business and Psychology*, Vol. 26, pp. 205–12.

[9] Fornell, C., and Larcker, D.F. (1981), 'Evaluating structural equation models with unobservable variables and measurement error', *Journal of Marketing Research*, Vol. 18, No. 1, pp. 39–50.

[10] Gachengo, V., and Wekesa, S. (2017), 'Influence of motivation on employee performance: A case of national bank of Kenya', *International Journal of Business, Management and Social Research*, Vol. 03, No. 02, pp. 179-185.

[11] Goh, S.C. (2012), 'Making performance measurement systems more effective in public sector organisations', *Measuring Business Excellence*, Vol. 16, No. 1, pp. 31–42.

[12] Gruman, J.A., and Saks, A.M. (2011), 'Performance management and employee engagement', *Human Resource Management Review*, Vol. 21, No. 2, pp. 123–136. https://doi.org/10.1016/j.hrmr.2010.09.004

[13] Lutwama G.W., Roos J.H., Dolamo B.L. (2013), Assessing the implementation of performance management of health care workers in Uganda. *BMC Health Serv Res.* 13: 355, doi:10.1186/1472-6963-13-355

[14] Vainieri, Milena, Guido Noto, Francesca Ferre, and Laura C. Rosella (2020). 'A Performance Management System in Healthcare for All Seasons?' *International Journal of Environmental Research and Public Health* 17, no. 15: 5590. https://doi.org/10.3390/ijerph17155590

Section III

Reinventing Management through Sustainability, Innovation and Analytics: SCM & ITM

Circular Economy Practices in Hospitality Industry – Current Research Trends

Sharad Sharma[1] **and Rajesh Kumar Singh**[2]

Management Development Institute Gurgaon, India
E-mail: efpm22sharad_ss@mdi.ac.in; rajesh.singh@mdi.ac.in

Abstract

Accounting for about 15 per cent of GDP and providing for almost 10 per cent of employment, hospitality is one of the growing sectors in the world economy. The concepts of Circular Economy (CE), Net Zero and Decarbonisation are among the top focus areas for hospitality sector as well. This paper summarises the current research in the field of Circular Economy and related practices within the hospitality sector using Bibliometric analysis. The findings include descriptive and thematic analysis. Overall, key themes emerging are use of Corporate Social Responsibility (CSR) initiatives in driving CE agenda along with effort on reducing emission caused due to energy and food consumption. The drivers and challenges for implementing CE practices from the literature indicate a need for all the stakeholders to work in tandem to achieve the objectives of CE.

Introduction

The hospitality market comprises of organisations engaged in providing accommodation as well as food services, often at the same premises. It is one of the fast growing section in the world economy, accounting for approx 4.5 trillion USD of consumer spend in the year 2022, the sector roughly accounts for 10 per cent of global GDP and is growing at CAGR of 15 per cent. (Aksoy et al., 2022; Businesswire, 2022). The industry being manual labour intensive (ILO, 2010), also accounts for more than 313 million jobs, approx. 10 per cent of total global employment. In India, this sector accounts for about 80 million jobs through direct and indirect means, accounting for more than 15 per cent of jobs and at the same time earning valuable foreign exchange. (Ministry of Tourism, 2022).

It is not just the direct contribution to GDP that makes hospitality important for the economy, this industry also contributes to local economies by way of spends in retail, dining, entrance fee for amusement parks, entertainment venue, etc., enabling even funding for local infrastructure (impoff.com, 2020). With such significant contribution to economy and society, hospitality sector like all others, is getting impacted by the outcome of the Paris Agreement (Legrand Willy, n.d.). Consequently, sustainability in operations, reduction in GHG emissions, addressing climate change and water conservations are some of the upcoming trends in academic research (Aksoy et al., 2022).

Circular Economy is the rapidly evolving concept, popular within both the researcher as well as practitioner communities. At the core, Circular Economy is the practice of moving away from a linear flow of energy and material (extract -> produce -> use -> dump) to a circular flow involving repair, reuse, refurbishment and recycling. (Ellen MacArthur Foundation, 2012).

CE is defined as: '....an economic system that is based on business models which replace the "end-of-life" concept with reducing, alternatively reusing, recycling and recovering materials in production/distribution and consumption processes....' (Kirchherr et al., 2017)

Similar to the CE is the concept of Net Zero economy – the number zero signifying carbon emissions. A large number of countries have already committed to reaching Net Zero by 2050, which means a net balance in emissions released and those captured from atmosphere. (Mishra et al., 2022). Efforts to achieve Net Zero thus have to focus on both the legs of activities—reducing the carbon emissions being generated from economic activities (also called Decarbonisation) as well as absorbing carbon through sustainable efforts in forestation, carbon sumps and promotion of carbon positive economic activities. Overall, all the three concepts—Circular Economy, Net Zero and Decarbonisation—are now key constituents of sustainability practices across the world. Adopting sustainable business practices is no longer an option for the industry today. Continual focus from the governments, investors and regulatory authorities on sustainability is forcing firms to adopt it as one of their core strategy, to remain relevant in the current times. Through the 2021 Glasglow declaration, the tourism sector has recommitted itself to be 'climate neutral' by 2050 (Scott & Gössling, 2022).

In addition, with the constant messaging, especially in social media on the ill effects of climate change, the damage caused by industrialisation, customers of businesses are also demanding sustainable business practices. Multiple studies have highlighted that sustainability and environmental friendly practices result in favourable customer attitude at the time making a booking in the hospitality sector (Martínez et al., 2019; Tanford et al., 2020; Vinzenz et al., 2019)While there is a lot of research under the Circular Economy theme from a tangible perspective, the same is not true for service dominated industries (Sorin & Sivarajah, 2021) . The concept of Circular Economy from a hospitality perspective is the focus of this paper. The aim of this paper is to study the existing academic research done on Circular Economy in Hospitality Sector and identify future research directions by examining documents published between 2010 and 2021.

The current publication on Circular Economy for Hospitality Industry is limited in quantity and to the best of our knowledge, there has been no systematic / bibliometric review completed so far. This study aims to bridge this gap and help put together a comprehensive status of the existing literature in this field. The research question that we want to answer in this study is –

RQ: What are the current trends in academic research in the field of Circular Economy for Hospitality Industry?

The remainder of this paper is organised as follows. Section 2 introduces the research methods. In Section 3, we present the descriptive analysis of the publications in detail. In Section 4, we discuss the thematic inferences. Section 5 closes the paper with some interesting concluding remarks and directions for future.

Research Methods

Bibliometrics methods have been widely used to analyse existing research across all kind of domains including sustainability. (Bhatt et al., 2020; Ogunmakinde et al., n.d.; Tang et al., 2018). This method involves an analysis of publishing pattern over multiple dimensions such as authors, key words, citations, location etc bringing out a holistic picture of the current status of academic literature in the given field.

We followed a 3 steps approach to conduct this study:

- *Step 1 – Identifying the articles:* A nested search query consisting of all the key terms was designed. All articles with the with the terms 'Circular Economy' or 'De-carbonisation' or 'Net Zero' along with 'hospitality' in Title, abstract or key word section were shortlisted. Additional filters on date, type, subject area and language of publication were added.

  The query designed in step 1 was executed on Scopus data base and it yielded a result of 35 papers. After a careful reading of the Abstract for assessing relevance of the papers, 2 papers were removed and the rest of 33 papers were taken to the next stage.

Table 1: Paper Search Criteria

Source	*Search Term*
Scopus	TITLE-ABS-KEY (('Circular Economy' OR de-carbonisation OR 'Net Zero') AND (hospitality)

Table 2: Filter Criteria

Filter	Inclusion Criteria
Time	2012 -22 (Last 10 years)
Type of Publication	Journal Article
Subject Area	• Business & Management • Environmental Science • Social Sciences
Language	English

- *Step 2 – Conducting Bibliometric Analysis:* To collect data for this study, a bibliometric analysis was performed using Biblioshiny tool package (Aria & Cuccurullo, 2017). The tool was selected based on the ease of usability and availability (comes free of costs).
- *Step 3 – Drawing Inferences and Future Direction:* Based on the quantitative analytics and insights provided by the software, inferences were crafted and appended to the output of the tool. At this stage, the researcher also tried to

Descriptive Analysis

Structure of Available Research

Annual Trend

While we conducted the search for all articles since 2012, the first time these search terms appeared was in 2017, indicating the recency of this research subject. As shown in the Figure 1, 60 per cent of the articles have been published only in the last two years.

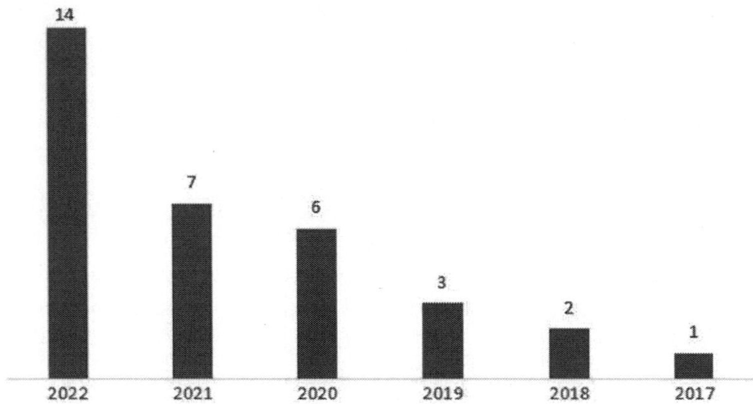

Fig. 1: Annual Research Trend

Source of Research

Maximum no of articles have been published in Sustainability (Switzerland) journal (see Figure 2). The sources are a mix of Journals focusing on sustainability as well as hospitality and tourism also have contribution in this field.

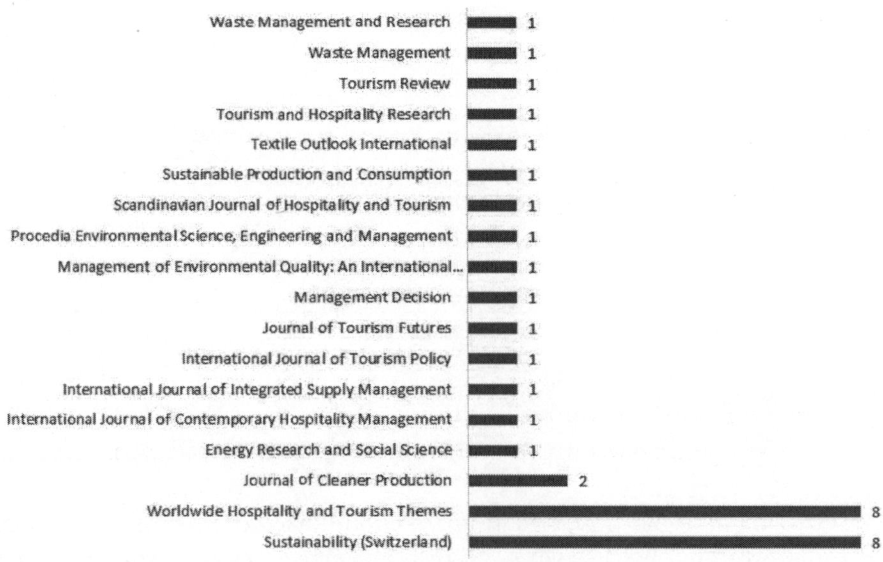

Fig. 2: Article Sources

Citation Statistics

Table 3 shows the Citation information for all the papers included in the review. The review article by Jones & Whynn (Jones & Wynn, 2019) has been citied the maximum no of times among all the articles included in this study.

Table 3: Citations per Article

Paper	*Total Citations*
Jones & Wynn, 2019	39
Fieschi & Pretato, 2018	30
Voukkali et al., 2021	18
Rodríguez-Antón & Alonso-Almeida, 2019	16
Pablo-Romero et al., 2019	11
Gretzel et al., 2020	7
Xu et al., 2022	6
Camilleri, 2021	6
Saura et al., 2022	6

Country of Study

Looking at the country of origin of these studies, as shown in Figure 3, we discover that there is a lot of interest in European regions (including UK) in the concepts of CE for hospitality industry.

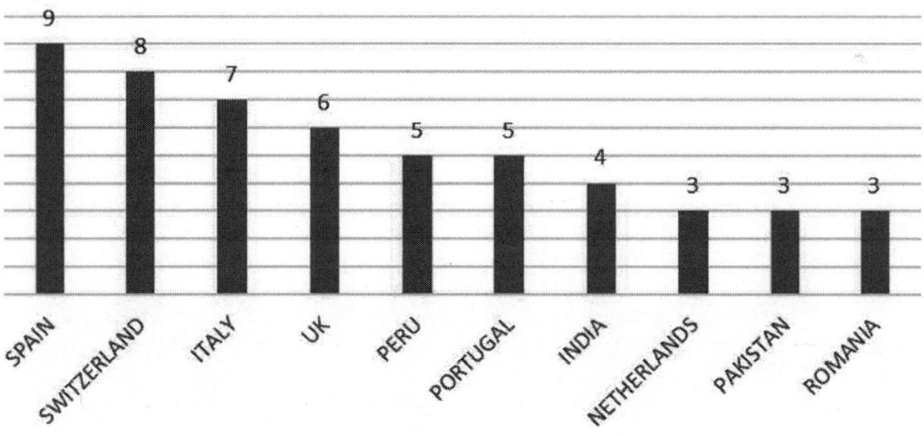

Fig. 3: Publications by Country

Word Cloud

The word cloud maps shown in Figure 4 indicates importance of sustainability and food waste as frequently occurring keywords in the set of papers in the study. With the names of countries appearing frequently, we can understand the focus on CE and sustainability in European region.

Fig. 4: Word Cloud

Study Methods

A detailed analysis on the methods deployed in the selected papers is included in Figure 5. Majority of the studies have been qualitative in method with a significant number of studies carried out using Case Study method.

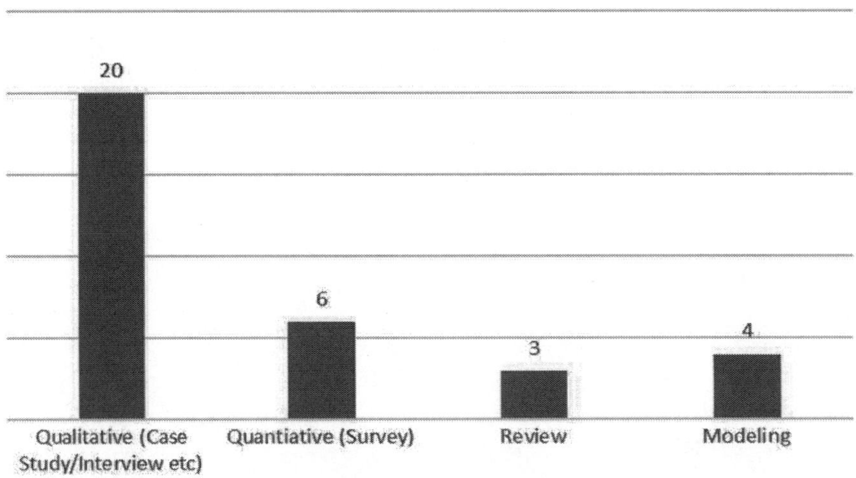

Fig. 5: Publications by Research Method

Thematic Analysis

Key Themes and Discussion

Based on the analysis of the papers in the study, there are a number of clear themes that emerge. These themes are can be looked at as areas of research interest being pursued and published in the academia in the field of Circular Economy within the Hospitality industry. The summary of theme is included in Table 4.

Table 4: Categorisation of Articles by Top 3 Themes

Theme	References
CSR	(Bhagtani, 2022; Davies & Egas, 2022; Fu et al., 2022; Matteucci, 2020; Pham et al., 2022; Rivera Aguilar et al., 2022; Xu et al., 2022; Zheng, 2022)
Food and Food Waste	(Cordova-Buiza et al., 2022; Fieschi & Pretato, 2018; Filimonau & Ermolaev, 2022; Gretzel et al., 2020; Gruia et al., 2021; Serra et al., 2021; Voukkali et al., 2021)
Energy & Energy Efficiency	(Kenington et al., 2020; Pablo-Romero et al., 2019)

The first theme that emerges prominently is the role of *CSR – Corporate Social Responsibility* in driving Circular Economy agenda. When firms choose to run with CSR initiatives, it's not just excellent corporate citizenship, but they also pursue their economic interests. The benefits realised include improved image and reputation as well as enhanced employee satisfaction and commitment (Stombelli, 2020). CSR initiatives can help in driving employee behaviour towards pro-environment, sustainable behaviour. It is primarily driven by self motivation experienced by the employees on account of the socially and environmentally relevant initiatives driven by the organisation (Xu et al., 2022). This relationship has been reported by multiple researchers and empirically tested for energy specific pro environmental behaviour of employees (Fu et al., 2022).

A recent special issue by the Journal Worldwide Hospitality and Tourism Themes had multiple papers linking Quality of Life provisions with sustainability in hospitality industry (Bhagtani, 2022; Davies & Egas, 2022; Pham et al., 2022; Rivera Aguilar et al., 2022; Zheng, 2022). These papers examined the relationship between Quality of Life, work life balance and behaviour and actions towards sustainability in hospitality sector. The findings are mixed with Pham et al (2022) and Davis & Egas (2022) finding positive relationship between CSR and QOL where as Bhagtani (2022) on the other hand, reporting that a hotel general manager's own well-being does not necessarily translate into high levels of CSR activity.

The second theme appearing in this set of research papers is about *food and handling food wastage*. It is estimated that food systems contribute to approx. one third of the total GHG emission (European Union, 2020). In hospitality, specifically in tourism, food is not just nourishment, but also adds to the experience and attraction for the customer, during festivals and holidays, oversized portions and bountiful buffets lead to excess food wastage (Gretzel et al., 2020). Efficient Circular Economy practices to address this source have been reported by scholars. Local procurement of food products and raw material through flexible contracts which enables 'just in time' procurement and reduced inventories are methods that can be deployed (Camilleri, 2021).

Just by preventing wastage in food systems can reduce GHG emission by 6-8 per cent (World Wide Fund for Nature, 2021). Hotels, caterers and restaurants can deploy innovative means to reduce wastage of raw material as well as prepared food to reduce this wastage. 'Sustainable Menu' can be designed which limiting portion size and number of items to reduce wastage. Utilising a sharing economy, reusing and recycling surplus food by offering customers to carry with them, giving away surplus food to under privileged communities and food banks are some of the options being exercised (Camilleri, 2021).

For handling inedible food waste, composting and converting to compost and feeding to fishes and animals at the Hotel are also utilised (Camilleri, 2021). A model based on Industrial Symbiotic principles has been proposed in Russia for a win-win situation for farms as well as hotels to reduce cost on solid waste management and arrange for compost and animal feed from food waste (Filimonau & Ermolaev, 2022).

In order to achieve recovery of food for either human, animal or plant consumption, the primary requirement to segregate waste according to the type of waste. In absence of correct segregation, the only option left is to dump the waste at landfills, which is the least recommended method. Dumping organic waste at landfill is most recurring method requiring least amount of effort, as per a study conducted in Peru (Cordova-Buiza et al., 2022). Use of bio degradable tableware and recycling the same is another lever to drive sustainability, specifically in case of Quick Service Restaurants (QSRs), catering and other events (Fieschi & Pretato, 2018).

The next prominent theme emerging in literature is about *Energy*. Electricity is one of the most common cause of Green House Gases (GHG) emission – as much as 35 per cent of global emissions are caused by electricity. (UN, n.d.). In order to address the carbon emission produced by electricity consumption, organisations have to work on two fronts simultaneously – first on the demand side, reduce the electricity consumption and second on the supply side generate and use renewal energy. Only by simultaneously working on both the aspects, can a firm aim to reach 'Net Zero' in emissions.

Hotels, essentially running 24 hours have a high demand of electricity for heating and cooling among other uses. (Fu et al., 2022). The effect of change in temperature on electricity consumption in hospitality thus assumes significance, more so in light of overall Global warming. A panel data study on effects of temperature on electricity consumption indicated non-linear relationship between the two for hospitality sector, forecasting a higher consumption pattern due to increase in global temperatures (Pablo-Romero et al., 2019).

The financial implication of driving efficiency in energy consumptions are also important for examination, a study of Scandinavian hotel industry highlighted energy consumption costs, being the main operating cost to mitigate as one of the key drivers for sustainability (Sorin & Sivarajah, 2021). The need to drive efficiency assumes significance as there is no effect of electricity prices on the consumption of electricity in hotels (Pablo-Romero et al., 2019).

Overall researchers recommendation to address the carbon footprint from energy use include using energy efficient lighting and other appliances, alternative energy supplies, maximising use of sunlight, green construction to reduce need of cooling, automatic switch offs, installing heat pumps and energy automations (Ahmed et al., 2021; Menegaki, 2018; Prakash et al., 2022; Rodríguez-Antón & Alonso-Almeida, 2019).

Drivers and Inhibitors to Circular Economy Practices

Drivers for Circular Economy in hospitality sector as mentioned by researchers is summarised in Table 5. One of the key drivers of moving towards Circular Economy is the financial incentive to do so – the cost of operations. In addition, employees and management's motivation and overall regulatory environment are also driving CE practices.

Table 5: Drivers for Circular Economy

Drivers	*References*
Costs of Operations – Covering raw material, utilities (water and electricity), waste management, upkeep and refurbishing costs	(Gretzel et al., 2020; Julião et al., 2020; Kenington et al., 2020; Prakash et al., 2022; Sorin & Sivarajah, 2021; Voukkali et al., 2021)
Employee and Management motivation towards sustainability	(Davies & Egas, 2022; Fu et al., 2022; Pham et al., 2022; Prakash et al., 2022; Xu et al., 2022)
Increasing regulatory focus locally and marco drive for sustainability (eg Paris declaration)	(Ahmed et al., 2021; Gretzel et al., 2020; Julião et al., 2020; Pablo-Romero et al., 2019; Prakash et al., 2022; Rodríguez-Antón & Alonso-Almeida, 2019; Voukkali et al., 2021)
Customer Demand for sustainability	(Julião et al., 2020; Menegaki, 2018; Prakash et al., 2022; Sorin & Sivarajah, 2021; Voukkali et al., 2021)

As shown in Table 6, some of the challenges that are emerging in research are lack of infrastructure and supply chain and practical knowledge about CE practices.

Table 6: Challenges for Circular Economy

Inhibitors / Challenges	*References*
Investments & Assets required to be owned	(Kenington et al., 2020; Münster et al., 2022; Sorin & Sivarajah, 2021)
Eco-System of sustainable supply chain	(Filimonau & Ermolaev, 2022; Münster et al., 2022; Sorin & Sivarajah, 2021)
Deploying sustainable measures at the Design stage – often conflicting with market requirements	(Münster et al., 2022)
Practical Knowledge about deploying CE throughout the value chain	(Münster et al., 2022; Sorin & Sivarajah, 2021)

Conclusion

We have seen in this study, the research in the field of CE for hospitality is limited and very recent, with mostly coming in the last 4 years. The research is concentrated in Europe with key themes emerging are around Decarbonisation in energy and food consumption and CSR.

Firms in this sector are experiencing a nudge to move to sustainable practices both from the customers as well as regulators. While currently a lot of effort is being spent on deploying sustainability initiatives, there is also an increasing focus on Circular Economy practices in Hospitality as highlighted by this paper. Hospitality firms have started to link their CE efforts with CSR to get a better alignment between these initiatives, as reported by many researchers, this is also helping the firm to improve the engagement with their employees.

Like all other service sector firms, electricity is one of the prime driver of GHG emission for Hospitality as well. Firms are trying to address this in multiple ways – improving efficiency to reduce consumption, sourcing green energy and other automation initiatives to reduce waste. Food, specifically food wastage is a much highlighted area that the firms are working on. There are efforts being made on reducing carbon footprint by local sourcing, reduce wastage by multiple means and trying to utilise the food by way of donation to needy etc.

Overall, the concept of CE in Hospitality is at a nascent stage and is still being looked at from a pure sustainability view point. While all the articles reviewed have mentioned either Circular Economy or Decarbonisation, there is no literature talking about the total carbon emissions or any efforts to reach Net Zero. Future research can be conducted with a focus to bring the net carbon emission in Hospitality to zero. As highlighted by the summary of challenges in this paper, any effort to reach Net Zero will require efforts from all the stakeholder groups – the customers, firms as well as regulators.

References

[1] Ahmed, M.F., Mokhtar, M. bin, Lim, C.K., Hooi, A.W.K., & Lee, K.E. (2021). Leadership roles for sustainable development: The case of a malaysian green hotel. *Sustainability (Switzerland), 13*(18). https://doi.org/10.3390/su131810260

[2] Aksoy, L., Choi, S., Dogru, T., Keiningham, T., Lorenz, M., Rubin, D., & Bruce Tracey, J. (2022). Global trends in hospitality. *Journal of Business Research, 142*, 957–73. https://doi.org/10.1016/J.JBUSRES.2021.12.068

[3] Aria, M., & Cuccurullo, C. (2017). bibliometrix: An R-tool for comprehensive science mapping analysis. *Journal of Informetrics, 11*(4), 959–75. https://doi.org/10.1016/j.joi.2017.08.007

[4] Bhagtani, N. (2022). Hotel general managers' quality of life and its impact on organisational sustainability and corporate social responsibility initiatives. *Worldwide Hospitality and Tourism Themes, 14*(3), 286–99. https://doi.org/10.1108/WHATT-02-2022-0022

[5] Bhatt, Y., Ghuman, K., & Dhir, A. (2020). Sustainable manufacturing. Bibliometrics and content analysis. *Journal of Cleaner Production, 260*, 120988. https://doi.org/10.1016/j.jclepro.2020.120988

[6] Businesswire (2022). *Hospitality Markets Analysis & Forecast.* https://www.businesswire.com/news/home/20220131005793/en/Global-3952.87-Billion-Hospitality-Markets-Analysis-Forecasts-2016-2021-2021-2026F-2031F---ResearchAndMarkets.com

[7] Camilleri, M.A. (2021). Sustainable production and consumption of food. Mise-en-place circular economy policies and waste management practices in tourism cities. *Sustainability (Switzerland), 13*(17). https://doi.org/10.3390/su13179986

[8] Cordova-Buiza, F., Paucar-Caceres, A., Quispe-Prieto, S.C., Rivera-Garré, A.P., Huerta-Tantalean, L.N., Valle-Paucar, J.E., de León-Panduro, C.V.P., & Burrowes-Cromwell, T. (2022). Strengthening Collaborative Food Waste Prevention in Peru: Towards Responsible Consumption and Production. *Sustainability (Switzerland), 14*(3). https://doi.org/10.3390/su14031050

[9] Davies, S.J., & Egas, J.L. (2022). Do social corporate responsibility initiatives help to promote circular economic activity and quality of work life for employees? *Worldwide Hospitality and Tourism Themes, 14*(3), 221–235. https://doi.org/10.1108/WHATT-02-2022-0018

[10] Ellen MacArthur Foundation. (2012). *Towards the Circular Economy: Economic and business rationale for an accelerated transition*. https://www.werktrends.nl/app/uploads/2015/06/Rapport_McKinsey-Towards_A_Circular_Economy.pdf

[11] European Union. (2020, May 20). *Farm to Fork Strategy for a Fair, Healthy and Environmentally-Friendly Food System*. Communication from the Commission to the European Parliament, the Council, the European Economic and Social Committee and the Committee of the Regions. https://eur-lex.europa.eu/legal-content/EN/TXT/HTML/?uri=CELEX:52020DC0381&from=EN

[12] Fieschi, M., & Pretato, U. (2018). Role of compostable tableware in food service and waste management. A life cycle assessment study. *Waste Management, 73*, 14–25. https://doi.org/10.1016/j.wasman.2017.11.036

[13] Filimonau, V., & Ermolaev, V.A. (2022). Exploring the potential of industrial symbiosis to recover food waste from the foodservice sector in Russia. *Sustainable Production and Consumption, 29*, 467–478. https://doi.org/10.1016/j.spc.2021.10.028

[14] Fu, Q., Ghardallou, W., Comite, U., Siddique, I., Han, H., Arjona-Fuentes, J.M., & Ariza-Montes, A. (2022). The Role of CSR in Promoting Energy-Specific Pro-Environmental Behavior among Hotel Employees. *Sustainability (Switzerland), 14*(11). https://doi.org/10.3390/su14116574

[15] Gretzel, U., Murphy, J., Pesonen, J., & Blanton, C. (2020). Food waste in tourist households: a perspective article. *Tourism Review, 75*(1), 235–238. https://doi.org/10.1108/TR-05-2019-0170

[16] Gruia, R., Florescu, G.I., Gaceu, L., Oprea, O.B., & Ţane, N. (2021). Reducing environmental risk by applying a polyvalent model of waste management in the restaurant industry. *Sustainability (Switzerland), 13*(11). https://doi.org/10.3390/su13115852

[17] ILO, G. (2010). Developments and challenges in the hospitality and tourism sector. www.ilo.org/publns.

[18] impoff.com (2020). *Importance of Hospitality Industry*. https://impoff.com/importance-of-hospitality-industry/

[19] Jones, P., & Wynn, M.G. (2019). The circular economy, natural capital and resilience in tourism and hospitality. *International Journal of Contemporary Hospitality Management, 31*(6), 2544–2563. https://doi.org/10.1108/IJCHM-05-2018-0370

[20] Julião, J., Gaspar, M., & Alemão, C. (2020). Consumers' perceptions of circular economy in the hotel industry: Evidence from Portugal. *International Journal of Integrated Supply Management, 13*(2–3), 192–209. https://doi.org/10.1504/IJISM.2020.107849

[21] Kenington, D., Chiu, L.F., Janda, K.B., & Ruyssevelt, P. (2020). Encouraging energy efficiency in united kingdom independent retail? The case of the butcher, fishmonger and cycle-shop. *Energy Research and Social Science, 62*. https://doi.org/10.1016/j.erss.2019.101347

[22] Kirchherr, J., Reike, D., & Hekkert, M. (2017). Conceptualizing the circular economy: An analysis of 114 definitions. In *Resources, Conservation and Recycling* (Vol. 127, pp. 221–232). Elsevier B.V. https://doi.org/10.1016/j.resconrec.2017.09.005

[23] Legrand Willy (n.d.). *Hospitality stakeholders: Why is COP26 important?* Retrieved 15 October 2022 from https://www.hospitalitynet.org/viewpoint/125000135.html

[24] Martínez, P., Herrero, Á., & Gómez-López, R. (2019). Corporate images and customer behavioral intentions in an environmentally certified context: Promoting environmental sustainability in the hospitality industry. *Corporate Social Responsibility and Environmental Management, 26*(6), 1382–1391. https://doi.org/10.1002/CSR.1754

[25] Matteucci, V. (2020). How can the hospitality industry increase corporate value aligned with sustainable development goals? Case examples from Hilton, Meliá and Sun. *Worldwide Hospitality and Tourism Themes, 12*(5), 509–523. https://doi.org/10.1108/WHATT-06-2020-0043

[26] Menegaki, A.N. (2018). Economic aspects of cyclical implementation in Greek sustainable hospitality. *International Journal of Tourism Policy, 8*(4), 271–302. https://doi.org/10.1504/IJTP.2018.098896

[27] Ministry of Tourism, G. of I. (2022, July 21). *Press Release.* https://pib.gov.in/PressReleasePage.aspx?PRID=1843507

[28] Mishra, R., Singh, R., & Govindan, K. (2022). Net-zero economy research in the field of supply chain management: a systematic literature review and future research agenda. In *International Journal of Logistics Management.* Emerald Group Holdings Ltd. https://doi.org/10.1108/IJLM-01-2022-0016

[29] Münster, M.B., Sönnichsen, S.D., & Clement, J. (2022). Retail design in the transition to circular economy: A study of barriers and drivers. *Journal of Cleaner Production, 362.* https://doi.org/10.1016/j.jclepro.2022.132310

[30] Ogunmakinde, O.E., Egbelakin, T., Sher, W. (n.d.). *Circular Economy in Africa's Built Environment: A Conceptual Bibliometric Analysis.* https://www.researchgate.net/publication/363071591

[31] Pablo-Romero, M.D.P., Pozo-Barajas, R., & Sánchez-Rivas, J. (2019). Tourism and temperature effects on the electricity consumption of the hospitality sector. *Journal of Cleaner Production, 240.* https://doi.org/10.1016/j.jclepro.2019.118168

[32] Pham, Q.M., Dhir, M., & Carrier Guillomet, T. (2022). How do corporate charitable and economic social responsibility practices help to improve the quality of work life for employees? *Worldwide Hospitality and Tourism Themes, 14*(3), 300–311. https://doi.org/10.1108/WHATT-02-2022-0021

[33] Prakash, S., Sharma, V.P., Singh, R., Vijayvargy, L., & Nilaish. (2022). Adopting green and sustainable practices in the hotel industry operations- an analysis of critical performance indicators for improved environmental quality. *Management of Environmental Quality: An International Journal.* https://doi.org/10.1108/MEQ-03-2022-0090

[34] Rivera Aguilar, J.E., Zang, L., & Fushimi, S. (2022). Towards sustainability in hospitality operations: How is quality of life and work–life balance related? *Worldwide Hospitality and Tourism Themes, 14*(3), 274–285. https://doi.org/10.1108/WHATT-02-2022-0019

[35] Rodríguez-Antón, J.M., & Alonso-Almeida, M. del M. (2019). The circular economy strategy in hospitality: A multicase approach. *Sustainability (Switzerland), 11*(20). https://doi.org/10.3390/su11205665

[36] Scott, D., & Gössling, S. (2022). Destination net-zero: what does the international energy agency roadmap mean for tourism? *Journal of Sustainable Tourism*, *30*(1), 14–31. https://doi.org/10.1080/09669582.2021.1962890

[37] Serra, M., Antonio, N., Henriques, C., & Afonso, C.M. (2021). Promoting sustainability through regional food and wine pairing. *Sustainability (Switzerland)*, *13*(24). https://doi.org/10.3390/su132413759

[38] Sorin, F., & Sivarajah, U. (2021). Exploring Circular economy in the hospitality industry: empirical evidence from Scandinavian hotel operators. *Scandinavian Journal of Hospitality and Tourism*, *21*(3), 265–285. https://doi.org/10.1080/15022250.2021.1921021

[39] Stombelli, V.M. (2020). Corporate Social Responsibility in hospitality: Are sustainability initiatives really sustainable? Case examples from CitizenM, Lefay and Six Senses. *Worldwide Hospitality and Tourism Themes*, *12*(5), 525–545. https://doi.org/10.1108/WHATT-06-2020-0041

[40] Tanford, S., Kim, M., & Kim, E.J. (2020). Priming social media and framing cause-related marketing to promote sustainable hotel choice. *Journal of Sustainable Tourism*, *28*(11), 1762–1781. https://doi.org/10.1080/09669582.2020.1760287

[41] Tang, M., Liao, H., Wan, Z., Herrera-Viedma, E., & Rosen, M. (2018). Ten Years of Sustainability (2009 to 2018): A Bibliometric Overview. *Sustainability*, *10*(5), 1655. https://doi.org/10.3390/su10051655

[42] un.org (n.d.). *Act Now*. United Nation. Retrieved 7 October 2022, from https://www.un.org/en/actnow/facts-and-figures

[43] Vinzenz, F., Priskin, J., Wirth, W., Ponnapureddy, S., & Ohnmacht, T. (2019). Marketing sustainable tourism: The role of value orientation, well-being and credibility. *Journal of Sustainable Tourism*, *27*(11), 1663–1685. https://doi.org/10.1080/09669582.2019.1650750

[44] Voukkali, I., Loizia, P., Navarro Pedreño, J., & Zorpas, A.A. (2021). Urban strategies evaluation for waste management in coastal areas in the framework of area metabolism. *Waste Management and Research*, *39*(3), 448–465. https://doi.org/10.1177/0734242X20972773

[45] World Wide Fund for Nature (2021). *Fight Climate Change by Preventing Food Waste*. https://www.worldwildlife.org/stories/fight-climate-change-by-preventing-food-waste

[46] Xu, L., Mohammad, S.J., Nawaz, N., Samad, S., Ahmad, N., & Comite, U. (2022). The Role of CSR for De-Carbonization of Hospitality Sector through Employees: A Leadership Perspective. *Sustainability (Switzerland)*, *14*(9). https://doi.org/10.3390/su14095365

[47] Zheng, J. (2022). How can aspects of quality of life be incorporated into corporate social responsibility strategies to achieve work life balance? *Worldwide Hospitality and Tourism Themes*, *14*(3), 210–220. https://doi.org/10.1108/WHATT-02-2022-0025

Decarbonisation in Energy Sector: A Bibliometric Analysis

Anil Kumar Sharma[1] **and Rajesh Kumar Singh**[2]

Management Development Institute Gurgaon, India
E-mail: efpm22anilkumar_s@mdi.ac.in; rajesh.singh@mdi.ac.in

Abstract

Decarbonisation has great impact on sustainability and climate change. One of the main ways to reduce effect of the carbon emission is to decarbonise the energy sector process itself. This has gained importance in recent years and researchers are motivated to research in this domain. This paper aims to analyse recent research in this domain using bibliometric analysis and highlight the trends of research focusing on areas related to decarbonisation like carbon dioxide emission control, fossil fuel, alternate energy, energy policy, global warming, sustainable development, renewable energy, etc. This paper uses R software to find publication pattern for last ten years. Further, the paper also highlights the challenges being faced currently for decarbonisation of energy sector and finally provides future directions for research.

Keywords: *Decarbonisation, Energy Sector, Sustainable Development, Renewable Energy, Global Warming*

Introduction

Energy utilities have been contributing to a safe energy supply and decarbonisation by playing a key role in energy transition. There has never been so much focus and debate on the importance of sustainability in three dimensions of society, economy, and environment. The Governments focusing on regulations while investors showing their urge to invest in companies working towards climate protection and sustainability. This will force energy utilities for approaching comprehensively towards sustainability (Pricewaterhouse Coopers, 2022).

The Indian power sector is one of the most diversified in the world. In electricity generation, India is on third position in the world while in consumption its second largest worldwide. Total All India Installed Electricity Generating Capacity as on 31.08.2022 is 405773.22 MW comprising of Thermal 236065.42 MW, Hydro 46850.17 MW, Nuclear 6780.00 MW and 116077.64 MW from Renewable Energy Sources (Central Electricity Authority – CEA) The growth in the population and per capita usage increase will further lead to rise in demand for electricity. As per the national infrastructure pipeline 2019-25, energy sector projects accounted for the highest share of this demand, which further poses challenges for decarbonisation challenges.

The historic (The Paris Agreement | UNFCCC, 2015) on climate change in 2015 has been adopted by 196 countries to reduce global warming and build resilience to climate change. Its overall goal is to limit warming to no more than 1.5 °C. Currently, the earth is already about 1.1°C warmer than it was in the late 1800s and emissions continue to rise.

The humans have triggered climate change responsible for global warming which is a massive threat to the planet earth. To limit global warming to 1.5 °C, it needs global net human-caused carbon dioxide emissions (CO_2) to reduce by around 45 per cent from 2010 levels by 2030 and thus reach net zero by around 2050 (Masson-Delmotte et al., 2018), also any remaining emissions in the atmosphere will have to be well-adjusted by taking out CO_2 from the atmosphere. The electricity sector emitted 12.3 Gt CO_2 in 2020 (36 per cent of all energy-related emissions), which is more than any other sector. Coal remains the largest single source of electricity worldwide, and by far the largest source of electricity sector emissions: it contributes just over one-third of electricity supply but is responsible for nearly three-quarters of electricity sector CO_2 emissions. and therefore, holds the key to preventing the worst effects of climate change ('World Energy Outlook 2021', 2021).

As per ('International Institute for Sustainable Development (IISD),' 2008), forty-five countries, including major emitters such as China and the US, have net zero goals reflected in policy documents, and almost 80 are considering targets. Frontrunners include Finland, which undertakes to be carbon neutral by 2035, and Austria and Iceland, which aim to achieve net zero emissions by 2040. Indian Prime Minister recently at COP-26 announced that as a nation, we would reach net zero emissions by 2070. Suriname and Bhutan are the only two countries that are currently net negative.

Due to the predicted population growth Energy consumption is going to increase drastically by 2050. As per this anticipated rise there is great amount of focus is being put on the smart technologies to meet this demand, however decarbonisation should be a fundamental component of the solution provided (Razmjoo et al., 2021). Decarbonisation and net zero commitments are linked to national priorities, these priorities can be related to energy for all and sustainable development. Thus, every country has its own considerations depending on its limits, constraints, and capabilities for accelerating decarbonisation, therefore has its own set of technology priorities and policies (Dahal et al., 2018).

This decarbonisation is possible through comprehensive deployment of advanced low-carbon technologies as well as measures that increase investments in low-carbon infrastructure and decrease investments in fossil fuel-based technologies in the power and transport sectors. Therefore, it is important to thoroughly understand the sectoral transition pathways under different climate targets in order to coordinate inter-sectoral actions and resources in a cost-effective manner (Liu et al., 2021). To reduce the effect of climate change, Energy sector decarbonisation is possible by means of wide-ranging new actions in the energy sector. Electricity market being complex and having dynamic environment requires manifold views with all round approach (Ćorović et al., 2022).

The contribution of renewable energy has increased as primary energy source, this has been made possible due to the focus on climate change and worldwide efforts on carbon dioxide emissions reduction pledge. However, in the future also, all countries must extensively focus towards decarbonisation of energy sector (Papadis & Tsatsaronis, 2020). Wind and solar energy technologies will definitely have a vital role to play in eliminating energy generated by coal and also in decarbonising the power sector in future (Vats & Mathur, 2022).

This paper produces bibliometric analysis of the research done over the period 2013–22 on decarbonisation and highlights the challenges towards de-carbonisation of energy sector through review of selected articles. The research questions being answered by this paper are:

- RQ-1: What are the publication pattern over time in the field of decarbonisation of power sector?
- RQ-2: What are de-carbonisation challenges of power sector globally?

This paper is divided into different sections. Section 2 describes about the data and research methodology steps followed for this analysis. Section 3 covers about the details of findings of bibliometric analysis and highlights the challenges of decarbonisation. Future research directions are mentioned under section 4 and conclusion of study is in section 5.

Research Methodology

This research paper studies articles indexed in Scopus database. Bibliometric analysis has been conducted as per the steps explained below steps and shown in Fig.1; Bibliometric analysis classify bibliographic material by framing representative summaries of published literature (Donthu et al., 2021). This analysis helps in understanding patterns of citing a document and other elements of study such as annual articles published, relevant affiliation, relevant source, evolution of key words, co-occurrence of keywords, descriptive and thematic map of published articles. A flow diagram is shown in Fig. 1 mentioning the steps followed:

- **Step 1: Developing the search Criteria** – We developed a search criterion to meet our first study's goal 'To identify the publication pattern in the field of de-carbonisation of power sector' We have critically examined the publication pattern following bibliometric analysis and then identifying de-carbonisation challenges by review of selected article.
- **Step 2: Searching the database and the keywords** – To search the literature, we have used keywords such as 'barrier' or 'challenge' or 'restriction' and 'decarbonisation' and 'Power sector' or 'Energy Sector'. The syntax used for this study is TITLE-ABS-KEY [('barrier' OR 'challenge' OR 'restriction') AND ('decarbonization' AND ('Power sector' OR 'Energy Sector')]. We wanted to focus only on de-carbonisation this study; so we ignored using keywords like sustainability, circular economy, net zero economy, etc. We have used Scopus data base since it is one of the most chosen databases for systematic literature review. Scopus provides superior quality documents, contains more global content, combats predatory publishing, and make

the research work flow more efficient and effective (Why Choose Scopus – Scopus Benefits | Elsevier Solutions, 2021). At this stage we got 157 documents as of 7 October 2022.

- **Step 3: Selecting the study dimensions** – At this stage, limitations are used to further refine this study. Language is selected as English; the time period of the past 10 years (2012—22) is selected for the study. In order to get the holistic view of this research, we consider only articles for this study. By applying these limitations, we got 90 documents.
- **Step 4: Assessing the relevant literatures** – At this stage, by focusing on the abstract and the full length of the document, we assessed the quality and relevance of the document pertaining to the second research objective.
- **Step 5: Extracting main content** – After reviewing the relevant research papers, the barriers towards decarbonisation of energy sectors have been identified as shown in Fig. 9.

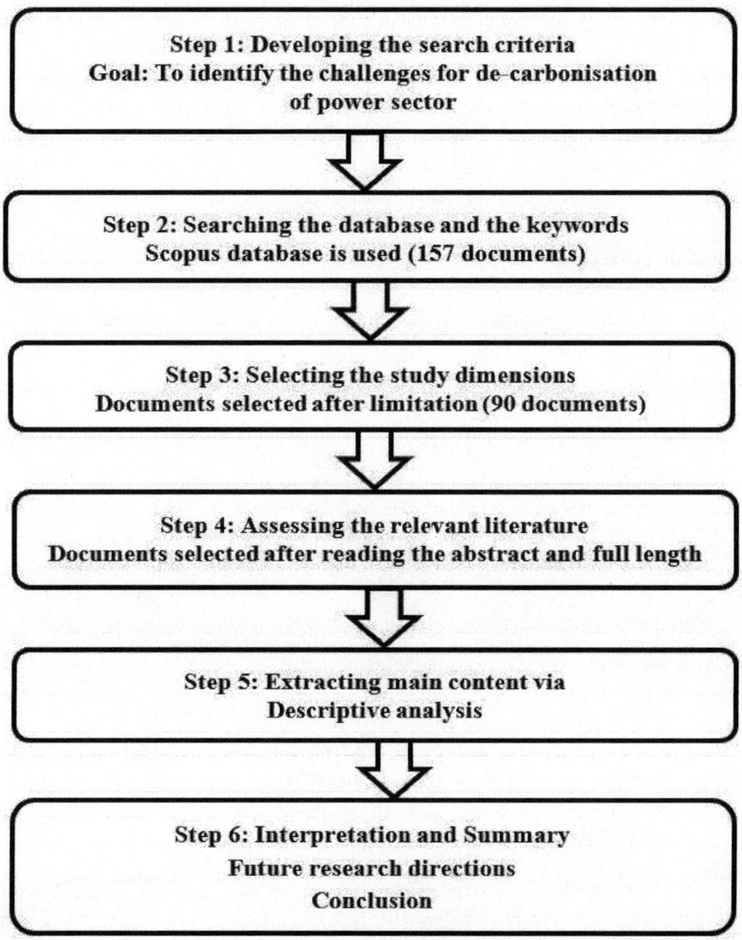

Fig. 1: Flow Chart of Research Methodology (Pare et al., 2016)

Descriptive Analysis and Findings

Overview of Bibliometric Analysis

Main information about the Scopus dataset used for analysis is mentioned under table 1. This dataset is within the time span of 2013-2022 containing 90 articles with growth rate of 42.35 per cent having document average age of 1.64. Total number of references mentioned in these 90 documents are 5759. This dataset contains 719 keywords with 339 as author's keywords. As far as Authors collaboration is concerned, there are 9 single authors, 4.2 co-authors per documents and international co-authorships is 37.78 per cent.

Table 1: Main information of the Scopus Dataset

Description	Results
Timespan	2013: 2022
Document Type: Article	90
Document	90
Annual Growth Rate %	42.35
Document Average Age	1.64
Average citations per doc	13.29
References	5759
Document Contents	
Keywords Plus (ID)	719
Author's Keywords (DE)	339
Authors	
Authors	358
Authors of single-authored docs	9
Authors Collaboration	
Single-authored docs	9
Co-Authors per Doc	4.2
International co-authorships %	37.78

Publication by Year

As depicted in Fig. 2, The publications have increased significantly, from almost nil during 2013-15 to 12 in 2021 and 30 in 2022. This indicate that decarbonisation in energy sector has been gaining visibility as means for sustainable development and therefore drawn attention of scholars to work on this domain.

Publishing Activity by Country

Figure 3 shows the network of countries affiliated with JBEF authors. It is clear that the authors are affiliated with the United States, Germany and China are prominent on the network. While, at the same time, Poland, United Kingdom, Australia, Norway,

Denmark, and Italy are significant. Also, countries, like Austria, Chile, Hong Kong, Spain, Sweden and Ukraine, play an essential role.

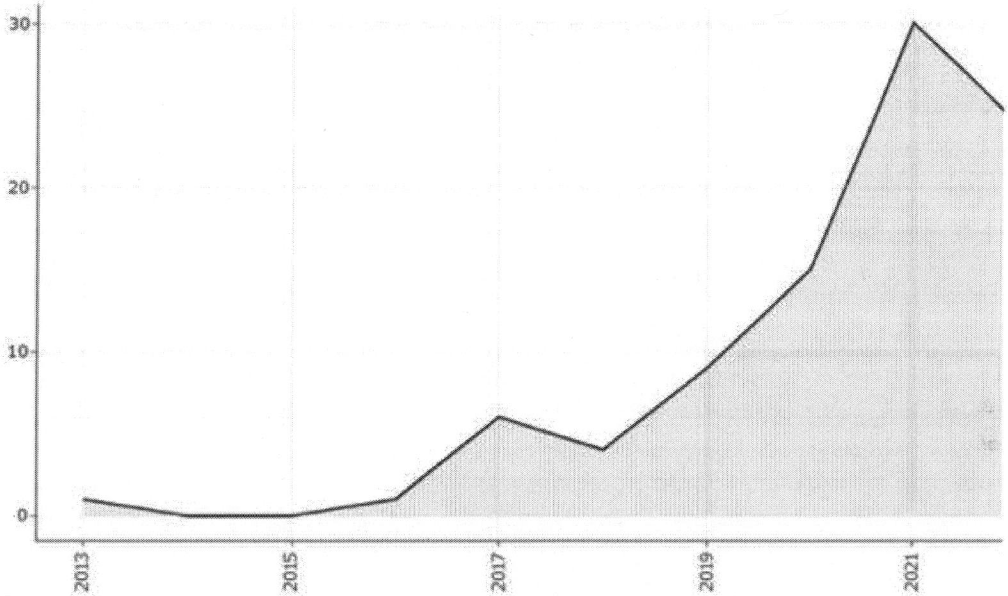

Fig. 2: Annual Distribution of Number of Articles on Decarbonisation of Energy Sector Based on Scopus Database

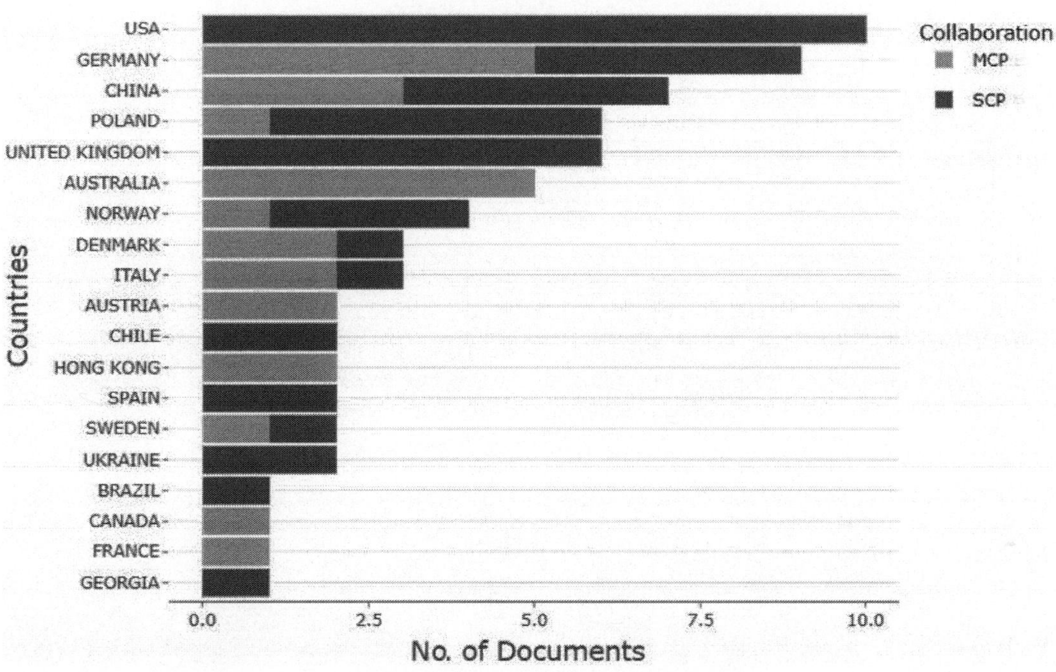

Fig. 3: Publication by Country

Figure 4 depicts the grid of top 10 institutions affiliated with authors. The institutions such as the Imperial College of London, The University of Tokyo are the front runners with 5 authors from each institute while Electric power research Institute, Pontificia University Catolica De Chile and University college London are not behind having four authors from each. The other five institutes have 3 authors from each.

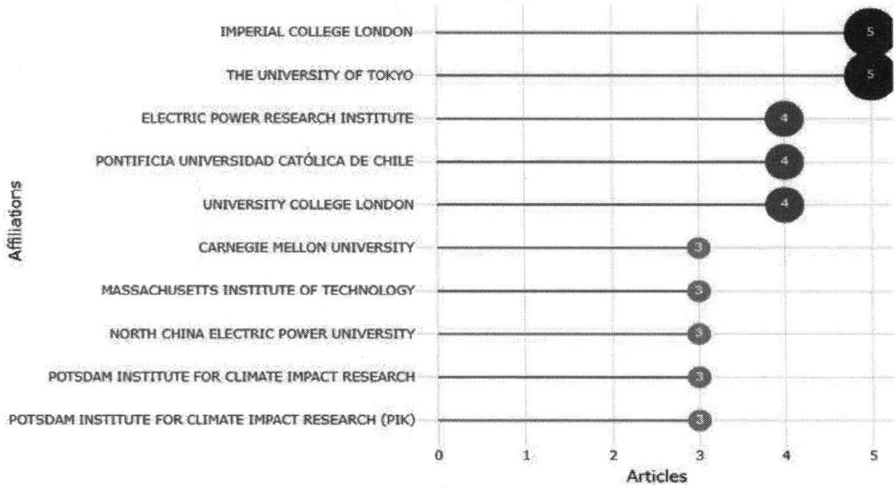

Fig. 4: Most Relevant Affiliations

Publishing Activity by Journal

Figure 5 shows the journals with most relevant source being *Climate Policy* followed by *Energies, Energy, Renewable and Sustainable Energy Review*, *Energy Economics*, *Energy Policy*, *Sustainability* (Switzerland), etc. This clearly shows that the research work focusing on energy, environment and climate related issues is being prominently published in the relevant journals.

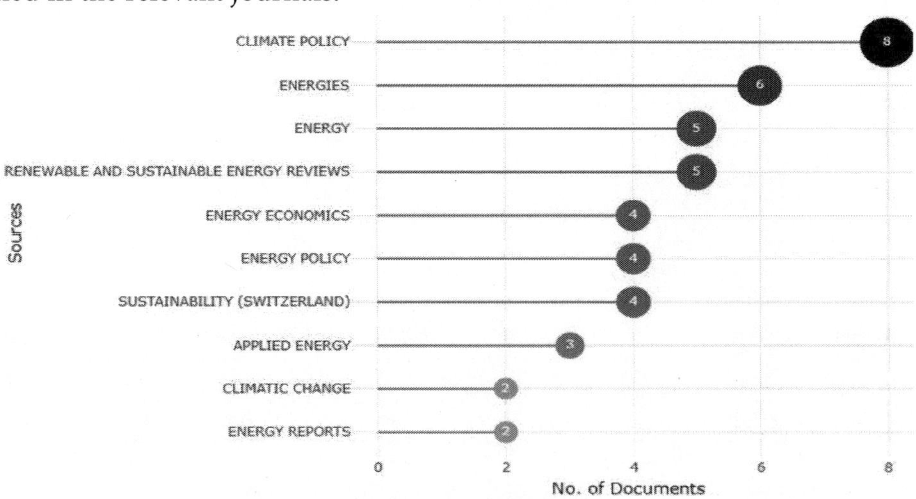

Fig. 5: Most Relevant Sources (Publishing Journals)

Keyword and Co-occurrence Analysis

Figure 6 shows top keywords from the research papers considered for the study along with frequency and percentage occurrence. Carbon dioxide, decarbonisation or decarbonisation and energy policy has frequency of 25, 42 and 24 respectively and percentage of occurrence as 5 per cent, 9 per cent and 5 per cent respectively. Next keywords occurring being alternate energy, emission control and investments with 4 per cent, 3 per cent and 3 per cent respectively with frequency of 18, 18 and 14 respectively.

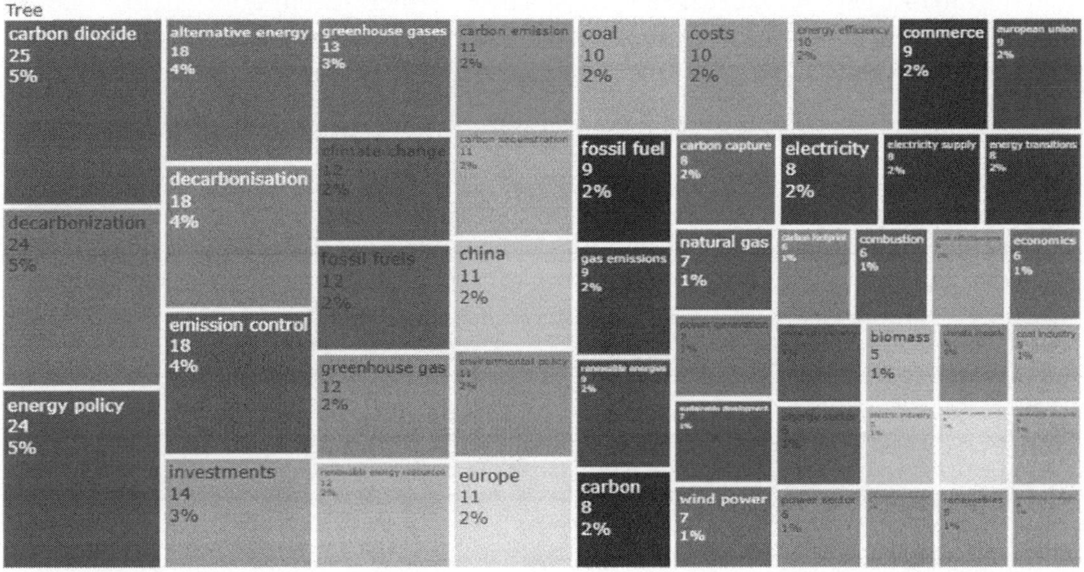

Fig. 6: Top Keywords by the Frequency and Percentage of their Occurrence

Thematic Evolution

Figure 7 below is showing theme which have evolved from 2013 to 2022. It shows that keywords like greenhouse gases, power generation, gas emission which were evolved

Fig. 7: Evolution of Keywords, 2013–22

between 2013-2021 were main themes for research during this period. Recently, themes are shifting to decarbonisation and alternative energy in 2022. Energy policy is also being evolved under decarbonisation and alternative energy. China as country is shown because most alternate energy related research papers are reported from China.

Cluster Map

Cluster map shown in Fig. 8 contains 90 articles. The prominent clusters formed are from the motor themes like decarbonisation, energy policy, greenhouse gas, greenhouse emission, climate change, carbon footprints, energy policy, alternate energy, etc. There are emerging themes of solar power, variable renewable energies, hydrogen fuel, block chain, etc.

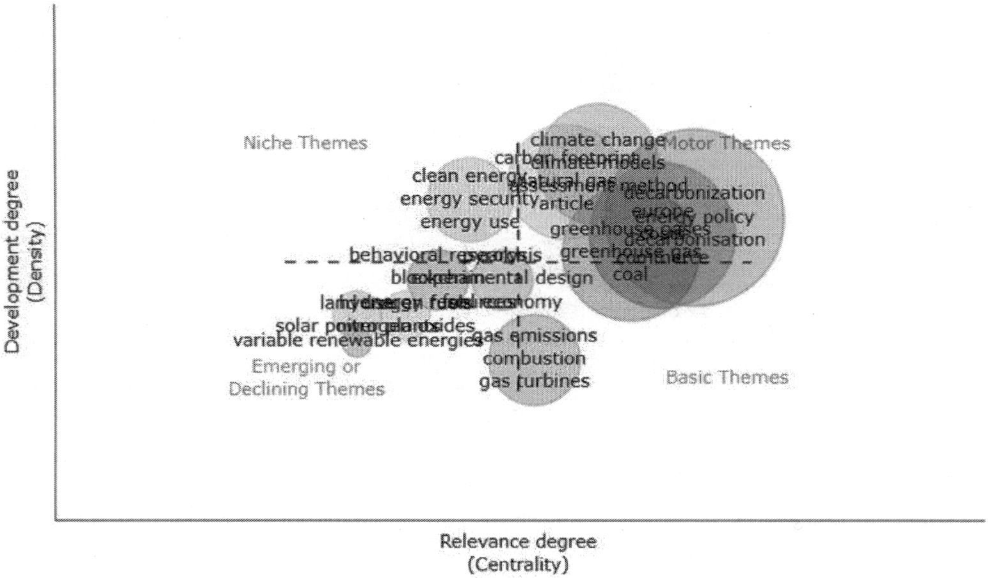

Fig. 8: Cluster Map

Challenges for Decarbonisation

There are many challenges with energy sector globally and India is not left alone. The challenges are several and of variety, and there is not a single shot solution of these challenges towards energy sector transition (Vats & Mathur, 2022). China is ambitiously moving towards 'carbon emission peak' and 'carbon neutral' targets, and the power sector is in the frontline. However, limited by technology, cost, environment, society, and other factors there are few application projects (Wu et al., 2022). Economic viability and political barriers frequently reduce the ample technical potential.(Löffler et al., 2022).

Based on the finding of the research, the challenges towards decarbonisation of energy sector can be broadly classified under three buckets Technological, Policy and Economical challenges. These has been shown in Fig. 9.

Technological Challenges

Sustainable energy transition requires a combination of many basic elements comprising of a strong focus on research & development for cutting across key fuels and materials of the future, smooth phasing out its fossil-based infrastructure and workforce, and using its advantages of existing infrastructure to discover prospects in renewable energy area for both domestic and global market. The current situation is that the new technologies like Hydrogen cell, Energy storage, Hydrogen as a fuel for power plants are not matured enough for full commercialisation. The other technologies for carbon capture for existing power generation units are also have challenges for retrofitting and on the other hand the power generation by Wind and solar needs reliable and affordable energy storage solution.

The cost effective and large capacity electricity storage technologies need to be developed and implemented for reaching full decarbonisation of energy sector. This electricity storage is essential for 100 per cent renewable electrical to be efficient and inexpensive. (Bonilla et al., 2022).

Policy Challenges

Lack of relevant regulations and standards along with lack of investment incentives to new technologies are the main barrier. Thus to confirm timely change of energy system and achieve set climate target, the policy makers must focus on these key issues (Löffler et al., 2022). In spite of many top-class publications focusing on the need for decarbonisation and on the challenges of it, the worldwide policies are way behind in meeting the target. The recommendations as per the researchers conducted are talks about very tight control on the carbon emission by the way of imposing carbon tax. The political interfere, lobbying efforts, corruption make imposing of policies difficult and cause delay or lapse in the progress of decarbonisation (Papadis & Tsatsaronis, 2020). Policymakers should take into consideration that energy plans at domestic or global level must not define impractical targets regarding the decarbonisation of the electricity sector (Bonilla et al., 2022).

As per the current energy sector situation, the environmental restrictions should be in place for environmental protection and sustainability to be followed, up to the mandatory level. There shall be monetary reward as incentive to develop sustainable energy sector (Papadis & Tsatsaronis, 2020).

Economic and Social Challenges

The new technologies which have potential to substitute the fossil fuel-based plants are very expensive and has very long gestation period and low ROI which makes them unaffordable for developing countries. The current economic conditions are responsible for the energy supplied.

The main focus should be on serving the socio-ecological system rather than on the profitability, since need for energy is basic for well-being of humans (Papadis &

Tsatsaronis, 2020) the carbon dioxide emissions associated with the energy sector need to be reduced. Significant reductions can be achieved by using appropriate technologies and policies. In the context of recent discussions about climate change and energy transition, this article critically reviews some technologies, policies and frequently discussed solutions. The options for carbon emission reductions are grouped into (1. Community renewable energy models can be a platform for collaboration with socially and economically marginalised people (Ramirez, 2021).

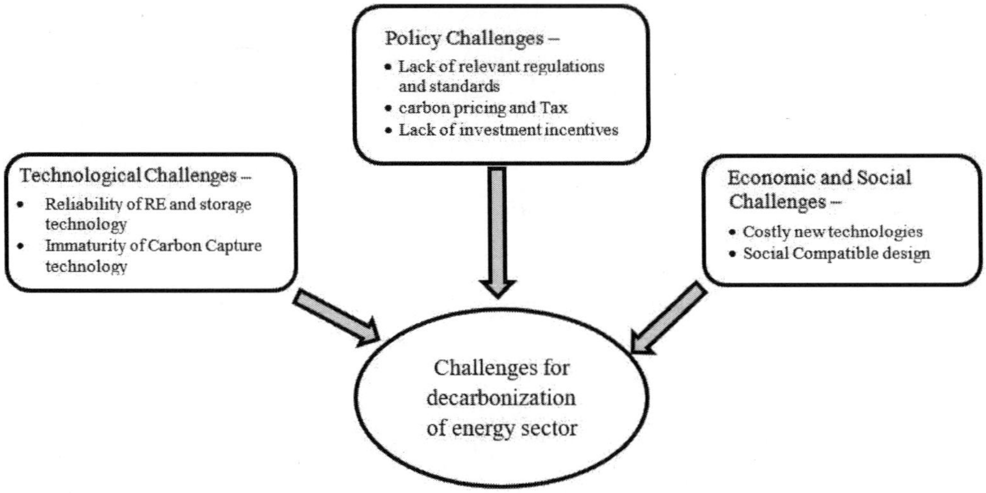

Fig. 9: Challenges for Decarbonisation of Energy Sector

Future Research Direction

The research trends clearly shows that the focus is on the decarbonisation with the use of alternate energy means to fossil fuels such as solar, wind, hydrogen, and by the improvement of performance of existing technology to reduce carbon emission, capturing carbon emission at the source. Efforts are also on to provide decarbonisation friendly policies and infrastructure for reliable and affordable energy. This bibliometric analysis has been conducted only for decarbonisation of energy sector. The challenges for decarbonisation are also identified for energy sector only. However, there are other sectors which are contributing to greenhouse gases. For future scope of study, the sectors like transport, industry, residential, agriculture can be taken up for analysis of research done on these sectors for decarbonisation and to identify challenges. The other future research direction which comes out from the analysis are the areas which less researched like hydrogen fuels, bio energy, energy storage and research to overcome the challenges for decarbonisation highlighted in this research paper.

Conclusion

From the bibliometric analysis it is apparent that research has been done with the focus on decarbonisation of energy sector. The first research question 'What are the publication pattern over time in the field of decarbonisation of power sector' has been answered through this analysis. It has been found that the focus towards decarbonisation is global and almost all countries developed or developing are concerned due climate change. The focus is multi-dimensional whether it is about adopting new technologies like hydrogen or choosing renewable sources, the improvement in the operational aspects such as efficiency improvement, mixing of renewable energy and fossil fuel-based generation are also in focus. Despite all these efforts there are challenges to decarbonisation pertaining to economic, technological as well from policy perspective which needs to be tackled. The management of renewable power generation and energy storage can improve energy utilisation rate, promoting the deep decarbonisation of power industry and realising energy cascade utilisation. Thus, policy makers should focus on dealing with the challenges highlighted so as to timely achieve transformation of energy systems and also achieve net zero target as part of sustainability. We need to rapidly recognise that sooner the decarbonisation happen better it will be for environment and the generations to come. There must be a balance between regulations, government policies, technology, and consumer behaviours to tackle the challenges for decarbonisation.

References

[1] Bonilla, J., Blanco, J., Zarza, E., & Alarcón-Padilla, D. C. (2022). Feasibility and practical limits of full decarbonization of the electricity market with renewable energy: Application to the Spanish power sector. *Energy, 239*, 122437. https://doi.org/10.1016/j.energy.2021.122437

[2] *Central Electricity Authority—CEA*. (n.d.). Central Electricity Authority. Retrieved October 19, 2022, from https://cea.nic.in/

[3] Ćorović, N., Urošević, B. G., & Katić, N. (2022). Decarbonization: Challenges for the electricity market development — Serbian market case. *Energy Reports, 8*, 2200–2209. https://doi.org/10.1016/j.egyr.2022.01.054

[4] Dahal, K., Juhola, S., & Niemelä, J. (2018). The role of renewable energy policies for carbon neutrality in Helsinki Metropolitan area. *Sustainable Cities and Society, 40*, 222–232. https://doi.org/10.1016/j.scs.2018.04.015

[5] Donthu, N., Kumar, S., Mukherjee, D., Pandey, N., & Lim, W. M. (2021). How to conduct a bibliometric analysis: An overview and guidelines. *Journal of Business Research, 133*, 285–296. https://doi.org/10.1016/j.jbusres.2021.04.070

[6] International Institute for Sustainable Development (IISD). (2008). In S. Philander, *Encyclopedia of Global Warming and Climate Change*. SAGE Publications, Inc. https://doi.org/10.4135/9781412963893.n343

[7] Liu, J., Yin, M., Xia-Hou, Q., Wang, K., & Zou, J. (2021). Comparison of sectoral low-carbon transition pathways in China under the nationally determined contribution and 2 °C targets. *Renewable and Sustainable Energy Reviews, 149*, 111336. https://doi.org/10.1016/j.rser.2021.111336

[8] Löffler, K., Burandt, T., Hainsch, K., Oei, P.-Y., Seehaus, F., & Wejda, F. (2022). Chances and barriers for Germany's low carbon transition—Quantifying uncertainties in key influential factors. *Energy, 239*, 121901. https://doi.org/10.1016/j.energy.2021.121901

[9] Masson-Delmotte, V., Pörtner, H.-O., Skea, J., Zhai, P., Roberts, D., Shukla, P.R., Pirani, A., Pidcock, R., Chen, Y., Lonnoy, E., Moufouma-Okia, W., Péan, C., Connors, S., Matthews, J.B.R., Zhou, X., Gomis, M. I., Maycock, T., Tignor, M., & Waterfield, T. (2018). *An IPCC Special Report on the impacts of global warming of 1.5°C above pre-industrial levels and related global greenhouse gas emission pathways, in the context of strengthening the global response to the threat of climate change, sustainable development, and efforts to eradicate poverty*. 630.

[10] Papadis, E., & Tsatsaronis, G. (2020). Challenges in the decarbonization of the energy sector. *Energy, 205*, 118025. https://doi.org/10.1016/j.energy.2020.118025

[11] PricewaterhouseCoopers. (2022). *Sustainability in the energy sector*. PwC. https://www.pwc.de/en/sustainability/sustainability-in-the-energy-sector.html

[12] Ramirez, J. (2021). Governance in energy democracy for Sustainable Development Goals: Challenges and opportunities for partnerships at the Isthmus of Tehuantepec. *Journal of International Business Policy*, *4*(1), 119–135. https://doi.org/10.1057/s42214-020-00077-3

[13] Razmjoo, A., Nezhad, M.M., Kaigutha, L.G., Marzband, M., Mirjalili, S., Pazhoohesh, M., Memon, S., Ehyaei, M.A., & Piras, G. (2021). Investigating Smart City Development Based on Green Buildings, Electrical Vehicles and Feasible Indicators. *Sustainability*, *13*(14), 7808. https://doi.org/10.3390/su13147808

[14] *The Paris Agreement | UNFCCC*. (2015, December). https://unfccc.int/process-and-meetings/the-paris-agreement/the-paris-agreement

[15] Vats, G., & Mathur, R. (2022). A net-zero emissions energy system in India by 2050: An exploration. *Journal of Cleaner Production*, *352*, 131417. https://doi.org/10.1016/j.jclepro.2022.131417

[16] *Why choose Scopus—Scopus benefits | Elsevier solutions*. (2021). https://www.elsevier.com/solutions/scopus/why-choose-scopus

[17] World Energy Outlook 2021. (2021). *International Energy Agency*, 386.

[18] Wu, M., Wu, Y., He, J., Xu, M., Zhang, T., & Liu, F. (2022). Barrier identification, analysis and solutions of hydrogen energy storage application in multiple power scenarios based on improved DEMATAL-ISM approach. *International Journal of Hydrogen Energy*, *47*(71), 30329–30346. https://doi.org/10.1016/j.ijhydene.2022.07.009

Managing Sustainability in Construction Industry: An Overview

Arun Kumar Ahuja and Rajesh Kr Singh

Management Development Institute Gurgaon, India
RICSSBE Amity University Noida, India
E-mail: efpm22arunkumar_a@mdi.ac.in; aahuja@ricssbe.edu.in; rajesh.singh@mdi.ac.in

Abstract

Construction industry is one of the largest consumers of raw materials in the form of cement, sand, aggregate, steel, finishing items, etc. The manufacturing process of these ingredients is highly energy centric and requires raw resources mostly unused. The duration and technology adopted for construction of any project affects the surroundings and life stock around in many ways. Researcher are studying different aspects to address sustainability in various other industries keeping many themes in their researches such as concept of carbon neutrality, net zero and circular economy. There is a wide scope for the implementation of various sustainability practice in construction industry by various means. Such as improved designs guidelines, construction materials, and construction technologies, etc... The objective of this paper is to summarise the thematic research using bibliometric analysis on R platform for the recent years. Study has also identified major challenges and strategies for sustainability in construction industry.

Keywords: *Construction Industry, Sustainability, Challenges, Strategies*

Introduction

Industrial revolution and exploiting natural resources has created the need to address the sustainability issues to meet the future generation's demand (Goodland, 1995). For this many groups have been formed. For city level sustainability measures, a group named C40 Cities having a global network of mayors has been founded in 2005. It is represented by 96-member cities that comprises of 20 per cent of global economy based on oxford economics, C40 modelling and world bank GDP 2020 data. These mayors are empowered to take urgent actions for identified climate crisis to make cities livable for the future generations.

Based on a report on C40 cities, Arup (a British MNC design company) and University of Leeds, due to growing demand, building and infrastructure sector is expected to be single largest contributor towards consumption based emissions for C40 cities till 2050. Hence in order to meet target of 1.5 degree centigrade serious actions are needed to control consumption based emissions. Major contributor (almost 60 per cent) towards these consumption emissions are production and delivery of building material from various sources and maintaining supply chain majorly from cement and steel which has high contribution in all construction related activities.

For construction industry, there are various other bodies which are working on sustainability aspect, such as U.S. green building council or WGBC that influence sustainable market place for 90 countries worldwide, is headquartered at Washington D.C. USGBC has its rating system for construction of green building recognised as Leed certification. Indian green building council formed by Confederation of Indian industry (CII) based out in Hyderabad particularly world with almost similar guidelines of USGBC in India. There is another body in India named TERI which provides GRIHA rating which is actively working in Indian context. Both TERI and USGBC came into a strategic collaboration to promote best practices adopted worldwide in deliver efficient design, constructing high performance buildings and maintain them throughout life cycle.

This rating system works on various work practices that affects overall sustainable development such as sustainable site planning, managing construction, energy optimisation, comfort for the end user, water management, solid waste management, sustainable building materials, socio economic strategies, monitoring performance and innovation. These directions in these certification will benefit the society and surroundings by reducing greenhouse gases, air and water pollutions, energy and water consumption, emissions and burden on natural resources and biodiversity with limited waste creation. It will enhance the user productivity, image and marketability.

In 2015, UN member states set agenda for sustainable development by 2030 comprises of 17 Goals which has 169 targets and 231 unique indicators. Construction industry affects most of it, particularly SDG6, i.e. clean water and sanitation, SDG 9, i.e. Industry, innovation and infrastructure, SDG 11, i.e. sustainable cities and communities, SDG 12, i.e. responsible consumption and production and many others.

There could be many research objectives, however for this paper, we will try to explore the of publication pattern based on interest of researchers pertaining to construction industry throughout the timeframe. Since sustainability in construction industry in not an old phenomenon, hence there is no time limit is kept to explore these publications.

We will also try to identify the challenges and area of opportunities for meeting sustainability goals within construction industries globally. Hence following two research questions are attempted to address through this paper to meet the research objectives.

- RQ1: What is the publication pattern in the field of sustainability in construction industry/projects?
- RQ2: What are the challenges to meet sustainability targets and strategies for sustainability in construction industry?

Remaining part of the paper is organised as follows: Section 2 deals with research methodology, section 3 discusses descriptive analysis of findings, section 4 discusses challenges in bring sustainability, section 5 deals with strategies for sustainability and finally section 6 concludes the study.

Research Methodology

In this research paper, articles referred are indexed in the SCOPUS database. Bibliometric analysis has been conducted on shortlisted database, in the following section detailed information from biblioshiney of R package is documented. It helped in getting the main information about the referred research papers such as time span, annual growth rate in publications, document type, and author's insights and collaboration statistics etc. most relevant and cited sources, having local impact, article publication at intra country and inter country level. It also helped to identify most frequent key words, which further helped in tree map and understanding evolution of trend topic with time and co-occurrence network of topics and thematic map as well as thematic evolution. This bibliometric analysis is based on bibliographic material from published articles and review papers (Donthu et al., 2021).

Query Development for Shortlisting the Papers

A systematic way is followed to develop the query and shortlist the papers addressing the sustainability issues in construction industry. Majority of the researchers are referring different key words to address sustainability in construction industry/projects such as circular economy, carbon neutrality, and net zero for construction industry. These key words were used while searching the SCOPUS database to identify the key articles. Query search for articles is given in Table 1.

Table 1: Query Search for Articles

Level	*Query Search*	*Articles Findings*
Level 1	construction AND (industry OR project) AND sustainability	10,580
Level 2	construction AND (industry OR project) AND sustainability AND 'Carbon Neutrality'	21
	construction AND (industry OR project) AND sustainability AND 'Net Zero'	52
	construction AND (industry OR project) AND sustainability AND 'Circular Economy'	302

Keywords and Database Search

In this study, we followed keywords such as carbon Neutrality OR net zero OR circular economy along with sustainability in construction projects and industry.

Table 2 shows the evolution of query resulted. SCOPUS database is mainly used to reach to the final set of papers as SCOPUS is most sought database for systematic literature review (SLR). This database helped us to get the global publication and by avoiding the predatory publications, which keeps this study authentic and relevant for the theme. Query search development is given in Table 2.

Table 2: Query Search Development for Articles

Level	*Query search*	*Articles Findings*
Level 1	construction AND (industry OR project) AND sustainability	10,580
Level 2	construction AND (industry OR project) AND sustainability AND 'Carbon Neutrality'	21
	construction AND (industry OR project) AND sustainability AND 'Net Zero'	52
	construction AND (industry OR project) AND sustainability AND 'Circular Economy'	302
Level 3	construction AND (industry OR project) AND sustainability AND ('Carbon Neutrality' OR 'Net Zero' OR 'Circular Economy')	368

After the application of final filters we were able to find 368 articles as on 29 Oct 2022.

Selecting Study Dimensions

At this stage, filters were applied on this stage of publication as 'final', type of document as 'article or review', limiting language as 'English' and subject area as 'Engineering' and 'Business management and accounting' particularly submitted to 'journals' only. Time span is kept open as these concepts are novice in construction industry. Query search development using final filters for articles is given in Table 3.

Table 3: Query Search Development using Final Filters for Articles

Level	*Query search*	*Articles Findings*
Level 1	construction AND (industry OR project) AND sustainability	10,580
Level 2	construction AND (industry OR project) AND sustainability AND 'Carbon Neutrality'	21
	construction AND (industry OR project) AND sustainability AND 'Net Zero'	52
	construction AND (industry OR project) AND sustainability AND 'Circular Economy'	302
Level 3	construction AND (industry OR project) AND sustainability AND ('Carbon Neutrality' OR 'Net Zero' OR 'Circular Economy')	368
Final filters	TITLE-ABS-KEY (construction AND (industry OR project) AND sustainability AND ('Carbon Neutrality' OR 'Net Zero' OR 'Circular Economy')) AND (LIMIT-TO (PUBSTAGE, 'final')) AND (LIMIT-TO (DOCTYPE, 'ar') OR LIMIT-TO (DOCTYPE, 're')) AND (LIMIT-TO (SUBJAREA, 'ENGI') OR LIMIT-TO (SUBJAREA , 'BUSI')) AND (LIMIT-TO (LANGUAGE, 'English')) AND (LIMIT-TO (SRCTYPE, 'j'))	127

After the application of final filters we were able to find 127 articles as on 29 October 2022.

We examine these articles by using biblioshiney of R package. It helped in finding information from different perspective having statistical information and network related information and we further tried to find out challenges and opportunities of sustainability in construction industries from the selected articles.

Assessing the Relevant Literature

In order to address the objectives, we assessed SCOPUS database to download in bibTex format. This is raw data file used in biblioshiney R package. For the second objective, we selected papers from identified databased and various published reports based on key word as challenge and strategy were identified and referred focusing identified challenges and various strategies for sustainability in construction industry. Flowchart is developed in Fig. 1.

Observe Findings

From the identified papers, finally 127 papers were taken into consideration to perform bibliometric analysis. Outcome of this analysis can be used to gauge the emerging trends and declining themes in this area. This output is more relevant to observe thematic analysis as well. focusing challenges and strategies for sustainability in construction industry, we documented challenges and strategies for construction industries sustainability. Flowchart is developed in Fig. 1.

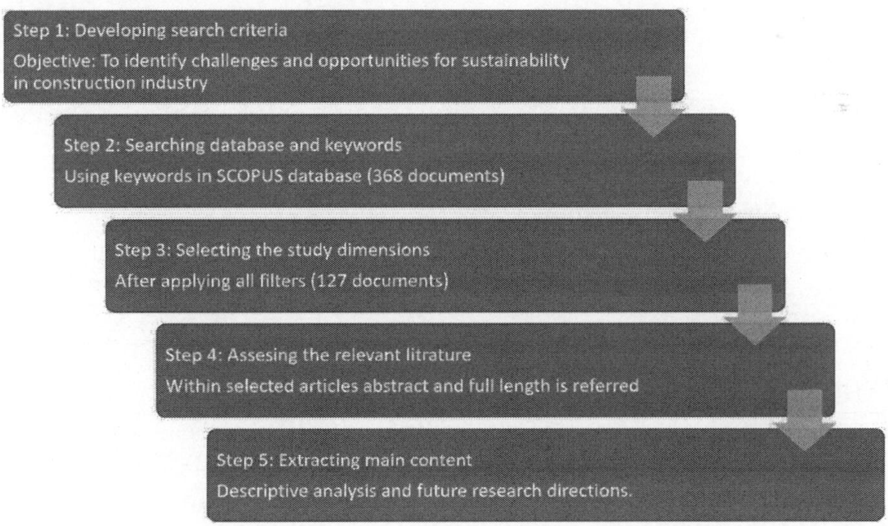

Fig. 1: Flowchart to Shortlist Relevant Articles

Descriptive Analysis

Description of Paper Selection

The Scopus dataset used for analysis is mentioned under Table 4: The timespan of this dataset is 2008:2022 with sources of 53 journals and books. There are 127 documents in this dataset with annual growth rate per cent of 29.91. The average age of document is 1.75 with average citation per doc at 17.84. There are 9495 references in dataset. Regarding the document contents, there are 922 Keyword plus and 514 Authors keywords. Regarding Authors collaboration, there are 462 authors with 6 single authors. Co-authors per doc are 3.73 with 35.73 per cent international coauthor ship. As far as document types are concerned, there are 97 articles and 30 reviews.

Table 4: Information on Scopus Dataset

Description	*Results*
Timespan	2008:2022
Sources (Journals, Books, etc.)	53
Documents	127
Annual Growth Rate %	29.91
Document Average Age	1.75
Average citations per doc	17.84
References	9495
Document Contents	
Keywords Plus (ID)	922
Author's Keywords (DE)	514
Authors	
Authors	462
Authors of single-authored docs	6
Authors Collaboration	
Single-authored docs	6
Co-Authors per Doc	3.73
International co-authorships %	35.43
Document Types	
Article	97
Review	30

Publication by Year

Figure 2 represents the increasing rate of publications per year under the topic of sustainability in construction sector. In 2008, there were null publications on this topic, and it witnessed significant increase in recent times with ~45 publications in 2021. This trend clearly indicates that the topic of sustainability in construction sector is gaining traction among research scholars.

Citations by Year

Figure 3 represents the citations by year. This data indicates the continuous and significant increase in citation per year. In 2008, there were null citations per year which increased significantly to 17-18 citations per year.

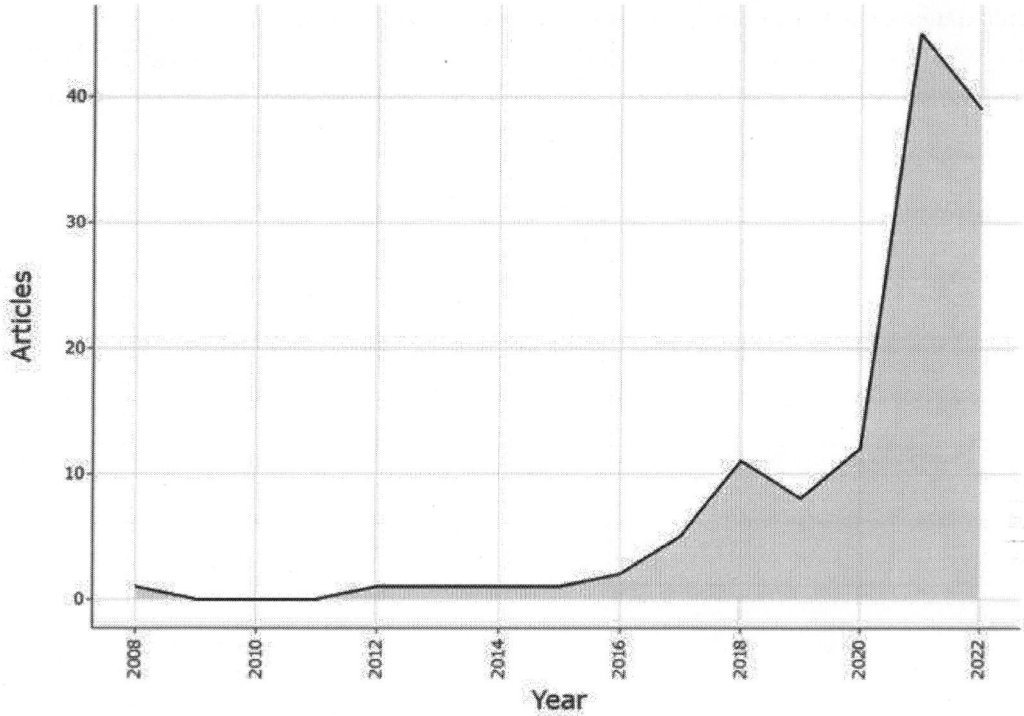

Fig. 2: No. of Articles on Sustainability in Construction Sector

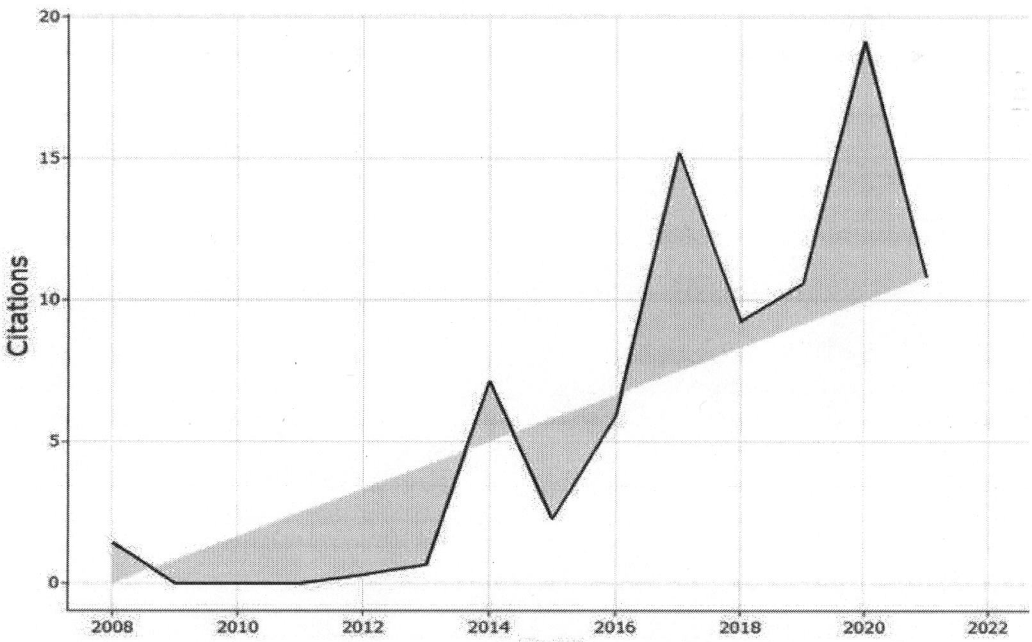

Fig. 3: Citations Per Year on Citations Per Year

Major Publishing Journals

Chart mentioned in Fig. 4 depicts the trend of most relevant sources. The most relevant source is journal of cleaner production followed by Sustainability (Switzerland) and Buildings.

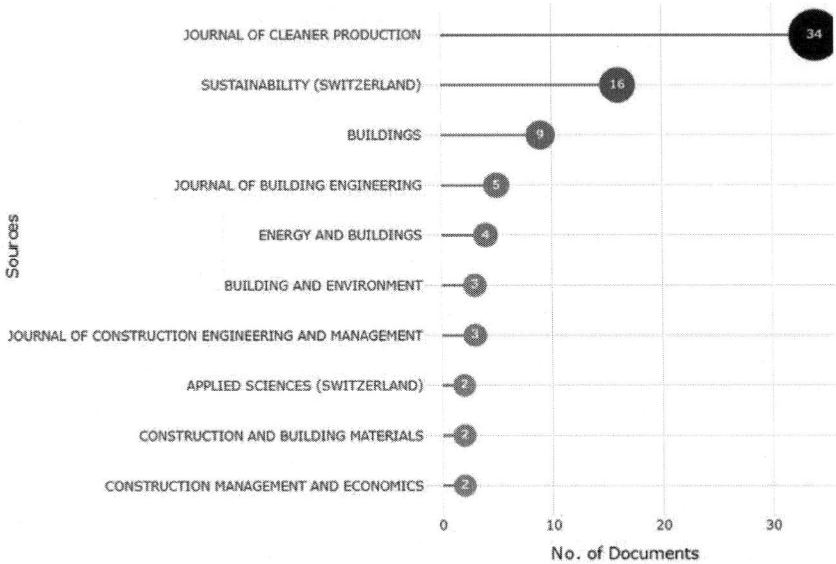

Fig. 4: Most Relevant Sources

Figure 5 represents the most local cited sources, Clean production at 606 number is the most local cited source followed by Resource conserve recycle at 223. Waste Management is the least locally cited source at 95.

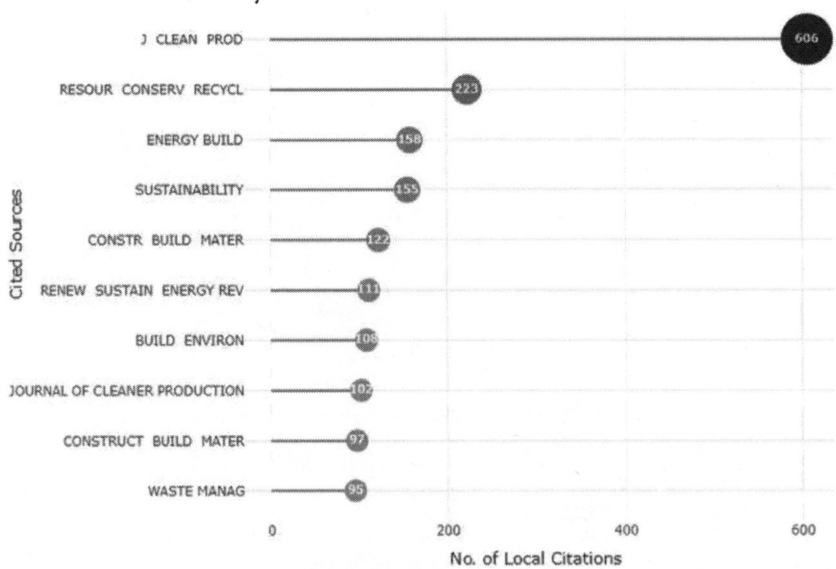

Fig. 5: Most Local Cited Sources (from Reference Lists)

The chart from Fig. 6 indicates the no. of counteries affiliated with JBEF authors. Italy and UK are prominent countries in Intra country and inter country publications. Austria, China, Hong Kong, Netherlands, Portugal and Spain have almost equivalent MCP (Inter country) and SCP (Intra country) publications.

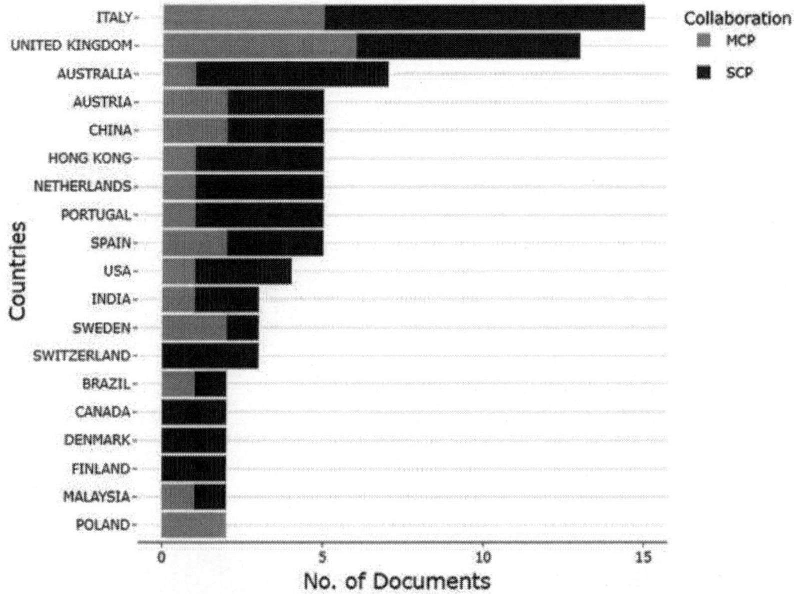

Fig. 6: Corresponding Author's Country

The below chart in Fig. 7 represents the sequnece of citations per country and UK is at the top of the list with 520 citations followed by Italy ar 459 citations. Significant gap in II and III country in this list. India is at the bottom of list with 63 citations only.

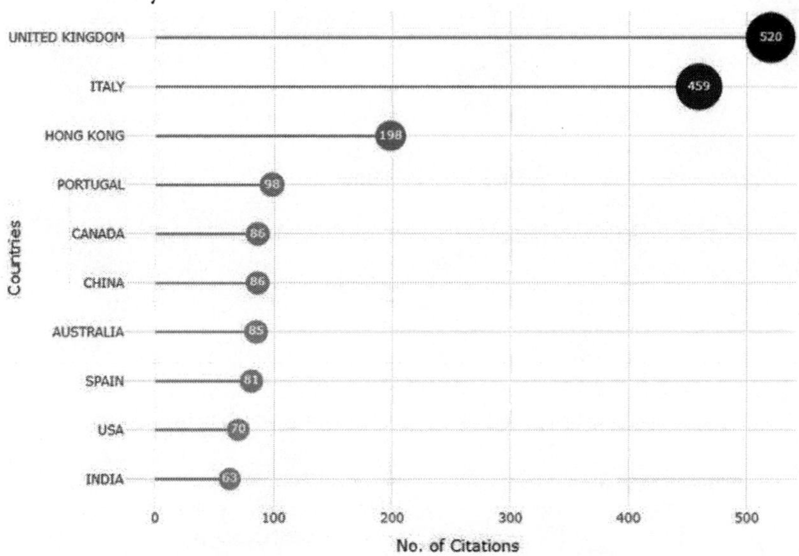

Fig. 7: Most Cited Countries

Figure 8 represents the keywords in journal and the most frequent keyword is construction industry with closely followed by Sustainable development. Circular Economy is at third position in hierarchy list. The least occurred journal is recycling.

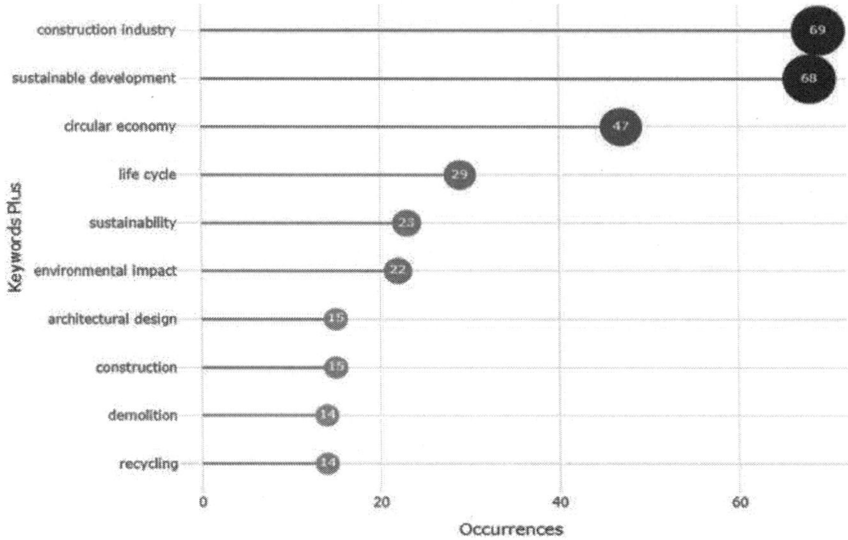

Fig 8: Most Frequent Words

The tree map in Fig. 9 represents the occurrence of keyword and construction industry is at top with 12 per cent frequency followed by sustainable development. A quarter of the frequency of occurrence of keyword is covered by 2 words only which are construction industry and sustainable development. Circular Economy is at 8 per cent frequency.

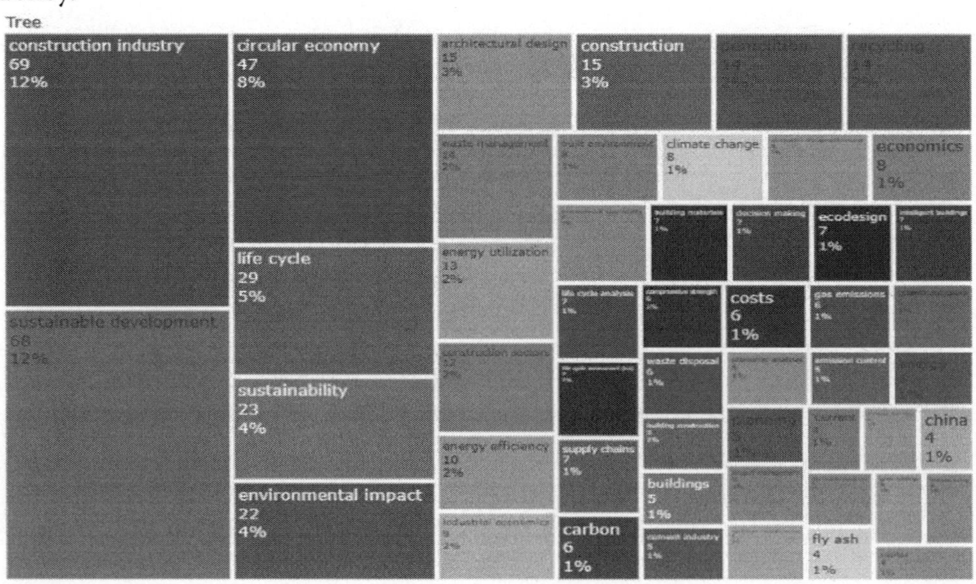

Fig. 9: Tree Map

Figure 10 clearly depicts that waste management and built environment keywords are being used and occurred in 2022; in 2021, the keywords were construction industry, sustainable development and circular economy.

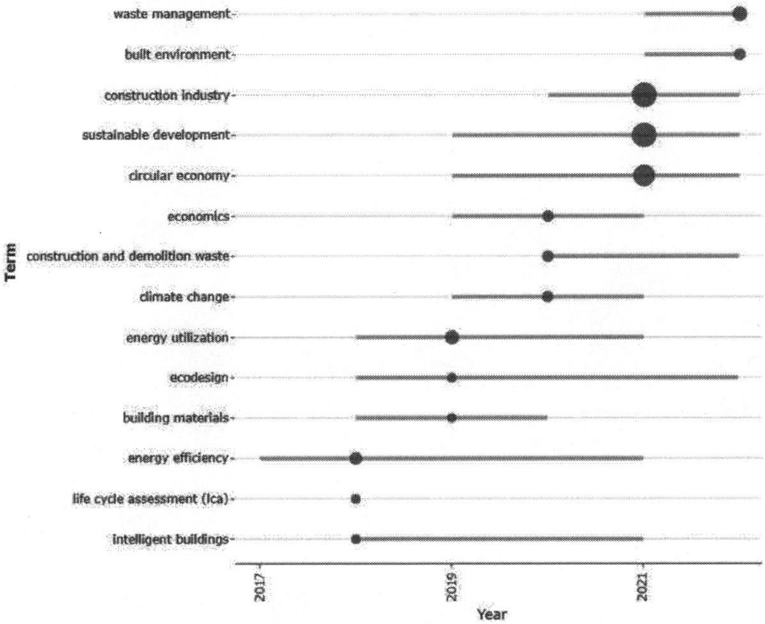

Fig 10: Trend Topic

Co-occurrence Network

In the Fig. 11, the basic theme is sustainability waste management and life cycle analysis, the motor theme is recycling compressive strength fly ash, the niche theme is wastewater treatment and agriculture soil.

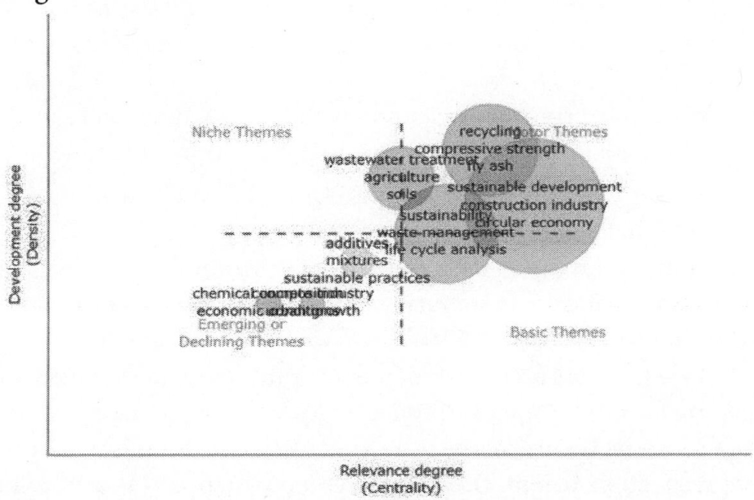

Fig. 11: Thematic Map

Thematic Evolution

The evolution of theme is happening, the term sustainable development is being classified and studied under recycling, environmental impact, construction industry and waste management. Whereas themes such as supply chains, recovery are merged with recycling and structural strength. Refer to Fig. 12.

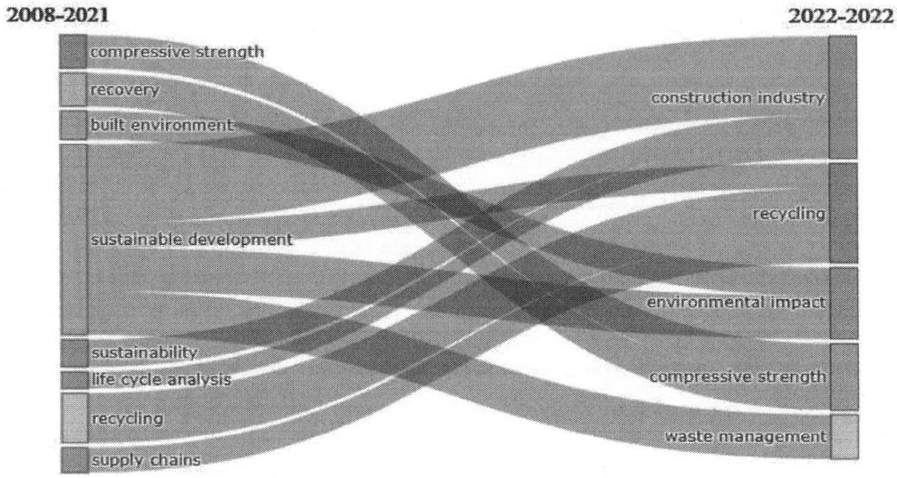

Fig. 12: Thematic Evolution

Challenges for Sustainability in Construction Industry

As per iron triangle, impact on construction projects are mostly studies by time overrun, cost overrun and quality related issues while managing the scope of the project. These research articles talk about time and cost overrun, material wastage, excessive resource utilisation, which are due to following unsustainable practices. Hence, triple bottom line approach is used to relate ESG framework, i.e. environmental, social and governance. It will help to maintain economic, environmental and social sustainability for any organisation.

Based on various reports and researches, following key areas can be taken as challenges for meeting sustainability goal in construction industry.

- Improper planning for the use of a building and dismissal of various retrofitting techniques available for a longer use of existing project.
- Awareness issues by creating demand for high embodied energy materials. It is further affected by sustainable materials availability and newer technology reach to the construction companies.
- Many small-scale projects are constructed without using design and architect expert advice consume extra raw material to serve lessor design load.
- Taking short term decisions to save on expert advice which impact on initial design aspect with respect to orientation and layout, which ultimately affect overall life cycle costing for the project.

- Stakeholder level challenges as the rational of different stakeholders are not aligned, which affects decision making to meet the sustainability.

Strategies for Sustainability in Construction Industry

There are tremendous opportunities to work on at different fronts in construction projects to meet sustainable development. It can be at design and approval level, standardising the demand creation at various stakeholder's level, at material and construction technology level, at policy level.

- **Planning level opportunities:** There are opportunities at planning level by various means such as ensuring utilisation of locally available material, following water conservation practices, planning transit-oriented development, managing better transportation facilities and infrastructure, developing exhaustive water and waste management system.
- **Layout level opportunities:** There are opportunities at layout level by saving top layer of soil, following effective environmental management plan, using sustainable materials throughout and using developing efficient construction management plan, drainage and landscape development, water conservation, rainwater harvesting and waste water management, using solar and wind energy and reduce onsite pollution and its impact.
- **Building level opportunities:** A proper architecture and building orientation can address a lot on life cycle energy requirement in terms of heating, ventilation and air conditioning (HVAC), day light requirement, optimising building services, and use of alternate or local available material to reduce total embodied energy, proper maintenance and safe construction practices can avoid rework and save in terms of extra material. Recycling the waste from demolished project and making best use of it is a key to success in achieving sustainable projects.
- **Policy level initiatives:** Bureau of Indian standard has introduced national building code (NBC) which is a comprehensive code for building construction. The code was first published in 1970 and updated in 1983, 1987 and 1997 and 2005. In recent 2015–16, it was updated again involving 22 expert panels comprises 1,000 expert of respective domain and a chapter on sustainability was introduced for the first time. This policy level input on approach to sustainability addresses embodied energy, environmental impact, indoor air quality, renewable sources, and thermal comfort. According to NBC 2016, to meet the sustainability in construction industry various opportunities lies during planning, design, construction, operation and maintenance of buildings.

Conclusion and Limitations for Study

Through this paper, we tried to find the recent trends on sustainability in construction industry. The findings of the study are summarised by conducting bibliometric analysis on the identified database mainly Scopus. There are limitations to this study as we tried to keep key words relevant to sustainability in construction industry. Many other keywords related to construction industry are not captured in tree map showcasing the frequency. Thematic evolution describes for small period of time and in two frames. Keeping flexible key words and working with a bigger database could be advantageous in such type of studies. For addressing RQ2, i.e. challenges and strategies for sustainability in construction industry an expert interview could have given a better picture on current industry application rather than secondary dataset.

References

[1] Donthu, N., Kumar, S., Mukherjee, D., Pandey, N., & Lim, W. M. (2021). How to conduct a bibliometric analysis: An overview and guidelines. *Journal of Business Research*, 133, 285–96. https://doi.org/10.1016/j.jbusres.2021.04.070

[2] Goodland, R. (1995). The concept of environmental sustainability. *Annual Review of Ecology and Systematics*, 26, 1–24. https://www.jstor.org/stable/2097196

[3] Abadi, M., D.R. Moore, and M.A. Sammuneh. 'A Framework of Indicators to Measure Project Circularity in Construction Circular Economy.' *Proceedings of Institution of Civil Engineers: Management, Procurement and Law* 175, no. 2 (2021): 54–66. https://doi.org/10.1680/jmapl.21.00020.

[4] Alaloul, W.S., M.A. Musarat, M.B.A. Rabbani, M. Altaf, K.M. Alzubi, and M.A. Salaheen. 'Assessment of Economic Sustainability in the Construction Sector: Evidence from Three Developed Countries (the USA, China, and the UK).' *Sustainability (Switzerland)* 14, no. 10 (2022). https://doi.org/10.3390/su14106326.

[5] Beermann, K., and M.C. Austin. 'An Inspection of the Life Cycle of Sustainable Construction Projects: Towards a Biomimicry-Based Road Map Integrating Circular Economy.' *Biomimetics* 6, no. 4 (2021). https://doi.org/10.3390/biomimetics6040067.

[6] Çetin, S., C. De Wolf, and N. Bocken. 'Circular Digital Built Environment: An Emerging Framework.' *Sustainability (Switzerland)* 13, no. 11 (2021). https://doi.org/10.3390/su13116348.

[7] Collivignarelli, M.C., M. Canato, A. Abbà, and M. Carnevale Miino. 'Biosolids: What Are the Different Types of Reuse?' *Journal of Cleaner Production* 238 (2019). https://doi.org/10.1016/j.jclepro.2019.117844.

[8] Cui, X. 'A Circular Urban Metabolism (CUM) Framework to Explore Resource Use Patterns and Circularity Potential in an Urban System.' *Journal of Cleaner Production* 359 (2022). https://doi.org/10.1016/j.jclepro.2022.132067.

[9] Dabaieh, M., D. Maguid, and D. El-Mahdy. 'Circularity in the New Gravity—Re-Thinking Vernacular Architecture and Circularity.' *Sustainability (Switzerland)* 14, no. 1 (2022). https://doi.org/10.3390/su14010328.

[10] Fenner, R., and C. Ainger. 'A Review of Sustainability in Civil Engineering: Why Much More Commitment Is Needed.' *Proceedings of the Institution of Civil Engineers: Civil Engineering* 173, no. 2 (2019): 69–77. https://doi.org/10.1680/jcien.19.00036.

[11] Ghufran, M., K.I.A. Khan, F. Ullah, A.R. Nasir, A.A. Al Alahmadi, A.N. Alzaed, and M. Alwetaishi. 'Circular Economy in the Construction Industry: A Step towards Sustainable Development.' *Buildings* 12, no. 7 (2022). https://doi.org/10.3390/buildings12071004.

[12] Giama, E., and A.M. Papadopoulos. 'Benchmarking Carbon Footprint and Circularity in Production Processes: The Case of Stonewool and Extruded Polysterene.' *Journal of Cleaner Production* 257 (2020). https://doi.org/10.1016/j.jclepro.2020.120559.

[13] Gopinath, A., A. Bahurudeen, S. Appari, and P. Nanthagopalan. 'A Circular Framework for the Valorisation of Sugar Industry Wastes: Review on the Industrial Symbiosis between Sugar, Construction and Energy Industries.' *Journal of Cleaner Production* 203 (2018): 89–108. https://doi.org/10.1016/j.jclepro.2018.08.252.

[14] Hasheminasab, H., S. Hashemkhani Zolfani, M. Kharrazi, and D. Streimikiene. 'Combination of Sustainability and Circular Economy to Develop a Cleaner Building Industry.' *Energy and Buildings* 258 (2022). https://doi.org/10.1016/j.enbuild.2022.111838.

[15] Heesbeen, C., and A. Prieto. 'Archetypical CBMs in Construction and a Translation to Industrialized Manufacture.' *Sustainability (Switzerland)* 12, no. 4 (2020). https://doi.org/10.3390/su12041572.

[16] Honarvar, S.M.H., M. Golabchi, and M.B. Ledari. 'Building Circularity as a Measure of Sustainability in the Old and Modern Architecture: A Case Study of Architecture Development in the Hot and Dry Climate.' *Energy and Buildings* 275 (2022). https://doi.org/10.1016/j.enbuild.2022.112469.

[17] Kneifel, J., E. O'Rear, D. Webb, and C. O'Fallon. 'An Exploration of the Relationship between Improvements in Energy Efficiency and Life-Cycle Energy and Carbon Emissions Using the BIRDS Low-Energy Residential Database.' *Energy and Buildings* 160 (2018): 19–33. https://doi.org/10.1016/j.enbuild.2017.11.030.

[18] Lamptey, T., D.-G. Owusu-Manu, A. Acheampong, M. Adesi, and F.A. Ghansah. 'A Framework for the Adoption of Green Business Models in the Ghanaian Construction Industry.' *Smart and Sustainable Built Environment* 10, no. 3 (2021): 536–53. https://doi.org/10.1108/SASBE-08-2020-0130.

[19] Lei, H., L. Li, W. Yang, Y. Bian, and C.-Q. Li. 'An Analytical Review on Application of Life Cycle Assessment in Circular Economy for Built Environment.' *Journal of Building Engineering* 44 (2021). https://doi.org/10.1016/j.jobe.2021.103374.

[20] Mpofu, A.B., O.O. Oyekola, and P.J. Welz. 'Anaerobic Treatment of Tannery Wastewater in the Context of a Circular Bioeconomy for Developing Countries.' *Journal of Cleaner Production* 296 (2021). https://doi.org/10.1016/j.jclepro.2021.126490.

[21] Munaro, M.R., M.D.C.D. Freitas, S.F. Tavares, and L. Bragança. 'Circular Business Models: Current State and Framework to Achieve Sustainable Buildings.' *Journal of Construction Engineering and Management* 147, no. 12 (2021). https://doi.org/10.1061/(ASCE)CO.1943-7862.0002184.

[22] Nadazdi, A., Z. Naunovic, and N. Ivanisevic. 'Circular Economy in Construction and Demolition Waste Management in the Western Balkans: A Sustainability Assessment Framework.' *Sustainability (Switzerland)* 14, no. 2 (2022). https://doi.org/10.3390/su14020871.

[23] Nijgh, M.P., and M. Veljkovic. 'A Static and Free Vibration Analysis Method for Non-Prismatic Composite Beams with a Non-Uniform Flexible Shear Connection.' *International Journal of Mechanical Sciences* 159 (2019): 398–405. https://doi.org/10.1016/j.ijmecsci.2019.06.018.

[24] Norouzi, M., M. Chàfer, L.F. Cabeza, L. Jiménez, and D. Boer. 'Circular Economy in the Building and Construction Sector: A Scientific Evolution Analysis.' *Journal of Building Engineering* 44 (2021). https://doi.org/10.1016/j.jobe.2021.102704.

[25] Oluleye, B.I., D.W.M. Chan, A.B. Saka, and T.O. Olawumi. 'Circular Economy Research on Building Construction and Demolition Waste: A Review of Current Trends and Future Research Directions.' *Journal of Cleaner Production* 357 (2022). https://doi.org/10.1016/j.jclepro.2022.131927.

[26] Orsini, F., and P. Marrone. 'Approaches for a Low-Carbon Production of Building Materials: A Review.' *Journal of Cleaner Production* 241 (2019). https://doi.org/10.1016/j.jclepro.2019.118380.

[27] Osobajo, O.A., A. Oke, T. Omotayo, and L.I. Obi. 'A Systematic Review of Circular Economy Research in the Construction Industry.' *Smart and Sustainable Built Environment* 11, no. 1 (2022): 39–64. https://doi.org/10.1108/SASBE-04-2020-0034.

[28] Sanchez, B., and C. Haas. 'Capital Project Planning for a Circular Economy.' *Construction Management and Economics* 36, no. 6 (2018): 303–12. https://doi.org/10.1080/01446193.2018.1435895.

[29] Silvestri, L., A. Forcina, C. Silvestri, and M. Traverso. 'Circularity Potential of Rare Earths for Sustainable Mobility: Recent Developments, Challenges and Future Prospects.' *Journal of Cleaner Production* 292 (2021). https://doi.org/10.1016/j.jclepro.2021.126089.

[30] Teisserenc, B., and S. Sepasgozar. 'Adoption of Blockchain Technology through Digital Twins in the Construction Industry 4.0: A PES'S Approach.' *Buildings* 11, No. 12 (2021). https://doi.org/10.3390/buildings11120670.

[31] Thomas, A., C.C. Menassa, and V.R. Kamat. 'A Systems Simulation Framework to Realize Net-Zero Building Energy Retrofits.' *Sustainable Cities and Society* 41 (2018): 405–20. https://doi.org/10.1016/j.scs.2018.05.045.

[32] Abdellah, R.H., and M.A.N. Masrom. 'Exploring the Barriers of Net Zero Energy Buildings (NZEBS) Implementation in Malaysia: Perception of Malaysian Construction Practitioners.' *International Journal of Integrated Engineering* 10, no. 9 (2018): 110–15. https://doi.org/10.30880/ijie.2018.10.09.003.

[33] Ahmed, H.U., A.A. Mohammed, S. Rafiq, A.S. Mohammed, A. Mosavi, N.H. Sor, and S.M.A. Qaidi. 'Compressive Strength of Sustainable Geopolymer Concrete Composites: A State-of-the-Art Review.' *Sustainability (Switzerland)* 13, no. 24 (2021). https://doi.org/10.3390/su132413502.

[34] Akinade, O., L. Oyedele, A. Oyedele, J.M. Davila Delgado, M. Bilal, L. Akanbi, A. Ajayi, and H. Owolabi. 'Design for Deconstruction Using a Circular Economy Approach: Barriers and Strategies for Improvement.' *Production Planning and Control* 31, no. 10 (2020): 829–40. https://doi.org/10.1080/09537287.2019.1695006.

[35] Aktas, C.B., K.C. Ryan, M.E. Sweriduk, and M.M. Bilec. 'Critical Success Factors to Limit Constructability Issues on a Net-Zero Energy Home.' *Journal of Green Building* 7, no. 4 (2012): 100–15. https://doi.org/10.3992/jgb.7.4.100.

[36] Andersson, R., and M. Buser. 'From Waste to Resource Management? Construction and Demolition Waste Management through the Lens of Institutional Work.' *Construction Management and Economics* 40, no. 6 (2022): 477–96. https://doi.org/10.1080/01446193.2022.2081989.

[37] Andrews, T., R. Rapp, E. Ewakil, J.E. Dietz, and S. Baroudi. 'Disaster Response Using the Circular Economy: A Timeline Review of the Literature.' *Journal of Emergency Management (Weston, Mass.)* 20, no. 4 (2022): 365–73. https://doi.org/10.5055/jem.0645.

[38] Asensio, E., C. Medina, M. Frías, and M.I. Sánchez de Rojas. 'Fired Clay-Based Construction and Demolition Waste as Pozzolanic Addition in Cements. Design of New Eco-Efficient Cements.' *Journal of Cleaner Production* 265 (2020). https://doi.org/10.1016/j.jclepro.2020.121610.

[39] Benachio, G.L.F., M.D.C.D. Freitas, and S.F. Tavares. 'Interactions between Lean Construction Principles and Circular Economy Practices for the Construction Industry.' *Journal of Construction Engineering and Management* 147, no. 7 (2021). https://doi.org/10.1061/(ASCE)CO.1943-7862.0002082.

[40] Camba, C., J.L. Mier, L. Carral, M.I. Lamas, J.C. Álvarez, A.-M. Díaz-díaz, and J. Tarrío-saavedra. 'Erosive Degradation Study of Concrete Augmented by Mussel Shells for Marine Construction.' *Journal of Marine Science and Engineering* 9, no. 10 (2021). https://doi.org/10.3390/jmse9101087.

[41] Chaudhary, T., and A. Piracha. 'Effective Contribution of Structural Engineers to Green Buildings and Sustainability.' *Canadian Journal of Civil Engineering* 40, no. 1 (2013): 97–100. https://doi.org/10.1139/cjce-2012-0154.

[42] Fico, D., D. Rizzo, V. De Carolis, F. Montagna, E. Palumbo, and C.E. Corcione. 'Development and Characterization of Sustainable PLA/Olive Wood Waste Composites for Rehabilitation Applications Using Fused Filament Fabrication (FFF).' *Journal of Building Engineering* 56 (2022). https://doi.org/10.1016/j.jobe.2022.104673.

[43] Fregonara, E., and A. Barreca. 'Economics for Sustainability: Impacts on the Real Estate Appraisal and Economic Evaluation of Projects [Economia per La Sostenibilità: Impatti Sull'Estimo e Valutazione Economica Dei Progetti].' *Valori e Valutazioni* 2021, no. 29 (2021): 5–22.

[44] Fregonara, E., R. Giordano, D.G. Ferrando, and S. Pattono. 'Economic-Environmental Indicators to Support Investment Decisions: A Focus on the Buildings' End-of-Life Stage.' *Buildings* 7, no. 3 (2017). https://doi.org/10.3390/buildings7030065.

[45] Ghisellini, P., X. Ji, G. Liu, and S. Ulgiati. 'Evaluating the Transition towards Cleaner Production in the Construction and Demolition Sector of China: A Review.' *Journal of Cleaner Production* 195 (2018): 418–34. https://doi.org/10.1016/j.jclepro.2018.05.084.

[46] Giorgi, S., M. Lavagna, K. Wang, M. Osmani, G. Liu, and A. Campioli. 'Drivers and Barriers towards Circular Economy in the Building Sector: Stakeholder Interviews and Analysis of Five European Countries Policies and Practices.' *Journal of Cleaner Production* 336 (2022). https://doi.org/10.1016/j.jclepro.2022.130395.

[47] Haselsteiner, E., B.V. Rizvanolli, P. Villoria Sáez, and O. Kontovourkis. 'Drivers and Barriers Leading to a Successful Paradigm Shift toward Regenerative Neighborhoods.' *Sustainability (Switzerland)* 13, no. 9 (2021). https://doi.org/10.3390/su13095179.

[48] Hossain, M.U., and S.T. Ng. 'Critical Consideration of Buildings' Environmental Impact Assessment towards Adoption of Circular Economy: An Analytical Review.' *Journal of Cleaner Production* 205 (2018): 763–80. https://doi.org/10.1016/j.jclepro.2018.09.120.

[49] Husgafvel, R., L. Linkosalmi, M. Hughes, J. Kanerva, and O. Dahl. 'Forest Sector Circular Economy Development in Finland: A Regional Study on Sustainability Driven Competitive Advantage and an Assessment of the Potential for Cascading Recovered Solid Wood.' *Journal of Cleaner Production* 181 (2018): 483–97. https://doi.org/10.1016/j.jclepro.2017.12.176.

[50] Kar, A.K., S.K. Choudhary, and V.K. Singh. 'How Can Artificial Intelligence Impact Sustainability: A Systematic Literature Review.' *Journal of Cleaner Production* 376 (2022). https://doi.org/10.1016/j.jclepro.2022.134120.

[51] Khadim, N., R. Agliata, A. Marino, M.J. Thaheem, and L. Mollo. 'Critical Review of Nano and Micro-Level Building Circularity Indicators and Frameworks.' *Journal of Cleaner Production* 357 (2022). https://doi.org/10.1016/j.jclepro.2022.131859.

[52] Krauklis, A.E., C.W. Karl, A.I. Gagani, and J.K. Jørgensen. 'Composite Material Recycling Technology—State-of-the-Art and Sustainable Development for the 2020s.' *Journal of Composites Science* 5, no. 1 (2021). https://doi.org/10.3390/jcs5010028.

[53] Kröhnert, H., R. Itten, and M. Stucki. 'Comparing Flexible and Conventional Monolithic Building Design: Life Cycle Environmental Impact and Potential for Material Circulation.' *Building and Environment* 222 (2022). https://doi.org/10.1016/j.buildenv.2022.109409.

[54] La Scalia, G., M. Saeli, L. Adelfio, and R. Micale. 'From Lab to Industry: Scaling up Green Geopolymeric Mortars Manufacturing towards Circular Economy.' *Journal of Cleaner Production* 316 (2021). https://doi.org/10.1016/j.jclepro.2021.128164.

[55] Lucchi, E., and A.C. Delera. 'Enhancing the Historic Public Social Housing through a User-Centered Design-Driven Approach.' *Buildings* 10, no. 9 (2020). https://doi.org/10.3390/BUILDINGS10090159.

[56] Mantalovas, K., G. Di Mino, A.J. Del Barco Carrion, E. Keijzer, B. Kalman, T. Parry, and D.L. Presti. 'European National Road Authorities and Circular Economy: An Insight into Their Approaches.' *Sustainability (Switzerland)* 12, no. 17 (2020). https://doi.org/10.3390/su12177160.

[57] Mercader-Moyano, P., P. Anaya-Durán, and A. Romero-Cortés. 'Eco-Efficient Ventilated Facades Based on Circular Economy for Residential Buildings as an Improvement of Energy Conditions.' *Energies* 14, no. 21 (2021). https://doi.org/10.3390/en14217266.

[58] Nasir, M.H.A., A. Genovese, A.A. Acquaye, S.C.L. Koh, and F. Yamoah. 'Comparing Linear and Circular Supply Chains: A Case Study from the Construction Industry.' *International Journal of Production Economics* 183 (2017): 443–57. https://doi.org/10.1016/j.ijpe.2016.06.008.

[59] Ng, T.S.K., R.M.H. Yau, T.N.T. Lam, and V.S.Y. Cheng. 'Design and Commission a Zero-Carbon Building for Hot and Humid Climate.' *International Journal of Low-Carbon Technologies* 11, no. 2 (2016): 222–34. https://doi.org/10.1093/ijlct/ctt067.

[60] Pinnegar, S., J. Marceau, and B. Randolph. 'Innovation for a Carbon Constrained City: Challenges for the Built Environment Industry.' *Innovation: Management, Policy and Practice* 10, no. 2–3 (2008): 303–15. https://doi.org/10.5172/impp.453.10.2-3.303.

[61] Rajib, A.I., A. Samieadel, A. Zalghout, K.E. Kaloush, B.K. Sharma, and E.H. Fini. 'Do All Rejuvenators Improve Asphalt Performance?' *Road Materials and Pavement Design* 23, no. 2 (2022): 358–76. https://doi.org/10.1080/14680629.2020.1826348.

[62] Schützenhofer, S., I. Kovacic, H. Rechberger, and S. Mack. 'Improvement of Environmental Sustainability and Circular Economy through Construction Waste Management for Material Reuse.' *Sustainability (Switzerland)* 14, no. 17 (2022). https://doi.org/10.3390/su141711087.

[63] Smitha, J.S., and A. Thomas. 'Integrated Model and Index for Circular Economy in the Built Environment in the Indian Context.' *Construction Economics and Building* 21, no. 3 (2021): 198–220. https://doi.org/10.5130/AJCEB.V21I3.7684.

[64] Sopelana, A., C. Auriault, A. Bansal, K. Fifer, H. Paiva, C. Maurice, G. Westin, J. Rios, A. Oleaga, and A. Cañas. 'Innovative Circular Economy Models for the European Pulp and

Paper Industry: A Reference Framework for a Resource Recovery Scenario.' *Sustainability (Switzerland)* 13, no. 18 (2021). https://doi.org/10.3390/su131810285.

[65] Turner, C., J. Oyekan, and L.K. Stergioulas. 'Distributed Manufacturing: A New Digital Framework for Sustainable Modular Construction.' *Sustainability (Switzerland)* 13, no. 3 (2021): 1–16. https://doi.org/10.3390/su13031515.

[66] Vaidya, U., and J. Hopkins. 'IACMI-the Composites Institute Efforts in Current and Post-Covid-19 Manufacturing Era-Innovations and Sustainability.' *Smart and Sustainable Manufacturing Systems* 5, no. 1 (2021): 113–19. https://doi.org/10.1520/SSMS20200070.

[67] Wijewansha, A.S., G.A. Tennakoon, K.G.A.S. Waidyasekara, and B.J. Ekanayake. 'Implementation of Circular Economy Principles during Pre-Construction Stage: The Case of Sri Lanka.' *Built Environment Project and Asset Management* 11, no. 4 (2021): 750–66. https://doi.org/10.1108/BEPAM-04-2020-0072.

[68] Wijewickrama, M.K.C.S., R. Rameezdeen, and N. Chileshe. 'Information Brokerage for Circular Economy in the Construction Industry: A Systematic Literature Review.' *Journal of Cleaner Production* 313 (2021). https://doi.org/10.1016/j.jclepro.2021.127938.

[69] Zaman, A., Y.-Q. Chan, E. Jonescu, and I. Stewart. 'Critical Challenges and Potential for Widespread Adoption of Mass Timber Construction in Australia—An Analysis of Industry Perceptions.' *Buildings* 12, no. 9 (2022). https://doi.org/10.3390/buildings12091405.

[70] Ahmed, W., and C.W. Lim. 'Production of Sustainable and Structural Fiber Reinforced Recycled Aggregate Concrete with Improved Fracture Properties: A Review.' *Journal of Cleaner Production* 279 (2021). https://doi.org/10.1016/j.jclepro.2020.123832.

[71] Asante, R., M. Agyemang, D. Faibil, and D. Osei-Asibey. 'Roles and Actions of Managers in Circular Supply Chain Implementation: A Resource Orchestration Perspective.' *Sustainable Production and Consumption* 30 (2022): 64–76. https://doi.org/10.1016/j.spc.2021.11.028.

[72] Boschi, G., G. Masi, G. Bonvicini, and M.C. Bignozzi. 'Sustainability in Italian Ceramic Tile Production: Evaluation of the Environmental Impact.' *Applied Sciences (Switzerland)* 10, no. 24 (2020): 1–15. https://doi.org/10.3390/app10249063.

[73] Buyle, M., W. Galle, W. Debacker, and A. Audenaert. 'Sustainability Assessment of Circular Building Alternatives: Consequential LCA and LCC for Internal Wall Assemblies as a Case Study in a Belgian Context.' *Journal of Cleaner Production* 218 (2019): 141–56. https://doi.org/10.1016/j.jclepro.2019.01.306.

[74] Cantù, C.L., D. Schepis, R. Minunno, and G. Morrison. 'The Role of Relational Governance in Innovation Platform Growth: The Context of Living Labs.' *Journal of Business and Industrial Marketing* 36, no. 13 (2021): 236–49. https://doi.org/10.1108/JBIM-02-2020-0114.

[75] Charef, R., E. Ganjian, and S. Emmitt. 'Socio-Economic and Environmental Barriers for a Holistic Asset Lifecycle Approach to Achieve Circular Economy: A Pattern-Matching Method.' *Technological Forecasting and Social Change* 170 (2021). https://doi.org/10.1016/j.techfore.2021.120798.

[76] Chen, Q., H. Feng, and B. Garcia de Soto. 'Revamping Construction Supply Chain Processes with Circular Economy Strategies: A Systematic Literature Review.' *Journal of Cleaner Production* 335 (2022). https://doi.org/10.1016/j.jclepro.2021.130240.

[77] Ferreira, J., M.D. Pinheiro, and J. De Brito. 'Portuguese Sustainable Construction Assessment Tools Benchmarked with BREEAM and LEED: An Energy Analysis.' *Energy and Buildings* 69 (2014): 451–63. https://doi.org/10.1016/j.enbuild.2013.11.039.

[78] Gan, V.J.L., I.M.C. Lo, J. Ma, K.T. Tse, J.C.P. Cheng, and C.M. Chan. 'Simulation Optimisation towards Energy Efficient Green Buildings: Current Status and Future Trends.' *Journal of Cleaner Production* 254 (2020). https://doi.org/10.1016/j.jclepro.2020.120012.

[79] Genc, O. 'SymbioConstruction: A Bibliography-Driven Dynamic Construction Industry Symbiosis Database.' *Journal of Construction Engineering and Management* 147, no. 8 (2021). https://doi.org/10.1061/(ASCE)CO.1943-7862.0002095.

[80] Gencel, O., O. Kizinievic, E. Erdogmus, V. Kizinievic, M. Sutcu, and P. Muñoz. 'Manufacturing of Fired Bricks Derived from Wastes: Utilization of Water Treatment Sludge and Concrete Demolition Waste.' *Archives of Civil and Mechanical Engineering* 22, no. 2 (2022). https://doi.org/10.1007/s43452-022-00396-7.

[81] Ghaffar, S.H., M. Burman, and N. Braimah. 'Pathways to Circular Construction: An Integrated Management of Construction and Demolition Waste for Resource Recovery.' *Journal of Cleaner Production* 244 (2020). https://doi.org/10.1016/j.jclepro.2019.118710.

[82] Goel, G., M.V. Vasić, N.K. Katiyar, S.K. Kirthika, M. Pezo, and P. Dinakar. 'Potential Pathway for Recycling of the Paper Mill Sludge Compost for Brick Making.' *Construction and Building Materials* 278 (2021). https://doi.org/10.1016/j.conbuildmat.2021.122384.

[83] Górecki, J., P. Núñez-cacho, and M. Rutkowska. 'Study on Circular Economy Implementation Propensity of Construction Companies in Context of Prevailing Management Styles.' *Applied Sciences (Switzerland)* 12, no. 8 (2022). https://doi.org/10.3390/app12083991.

[84] Grace, M.A., E. Clifford, and M.G. Healy. 'The Potential for the Use of Waste Products from a Variety of Sectors in Water Treatment Processes.' *Journal of Cleaner Production* 137 (2016): 788–802. https://doi.org/10.1016/j.jclepro.2016.07.113.

[85] Graves, R., and P. Smith. 'Minnesota Sustainable Building Guidelines: History, Effectiveness and Path for the Future.' *Journal of Green Building* 13, no. 2 (2018): 163–80. https://doi.org/10.3992/1943-4618.13.2.163.

[86] Gualeni, P., and M. Maggioncalda. 'Life Cycle Ship Performance Assessment (LCPA): A Blended Formulation between Costs and Environmental Aspects for Early Design Stage.' *International Shipbuilding Progress* 65, no. 2 (2018): 127–47. https://doi.org/10.3233/ISP-180144.

[87] Honic, M., I. Kovacic, P. Aschenbrenner, and A. Ragossnig. 'Material Passports for the End-of-Life Stage of Buildings: Challenges and Potentials.' *Journal of Cleaner Production* 319 (2021). https://doi.org/10.1016/j.jclepro.2021.128702.

[88] Kedir, F., and D.M. Hall. 'Resource Efficiency in Industrialized Housing Construction – A Systematic Review of Current Performance and Future Opportunities.' *Journal of Cleaner Production* 286 (2021). https://doi.org/10.1016/j.jclepro.2020.125443.

[89] Korançe, F. 'Sustainability of the Build Environment and Its Impact on User Performance. Case Study Polis University.' *Vitruvio* 6, no. 1 (2021): 56–71. https://doi.org/10.4995/vitruvio-ijats.2021.15009.

[90] Lederer, J., A. Gassner, J. Fellner, U. Mollay, and C. Schremmer. 'Raw Materials Consumption and Demolition Waste Generation of the Urban Building Sector 2016–2050: A Scenario-Based Material Flow Analysis of Vienna.' *Journal of Cleaner Production* 288 (2021). https://doi.org/10.1016/j.jclepro.2020.125566.

[91] Lekan, A., A. Clinton, and O. James. 'The Disruptive Adaptations of Construction 4.0 and Industry 4.0 as a Pathway to a Sustainable Innovation and Inclusive Industrial

Technological Development.' *Buildings* 11, no. 3 (2021): 1–28. https://doi.org/10.3390/buildings11030079.

[92] Lv, Y., J. Bi, and J. Yan. 'State-of-the-Art in Low Carbon Community.' *International Journal of Energy for a Clean Environment* 19, no. 3–4 (2018): 175–200. https://doi.org/10.1615/InterJEnerCleanEnv.2018025415.

[93] Marzouk, M., A. Elmaraghy, and H. Voordijk. 'Lean Deconstruction Approach for Buildings Demolition Processes Using BIM.' *Lean Construction Journal* 2019 (2019): 147–73.

[94] Matino, I., V. Colla, and S. Baragiola. 'Quantification of Energy and Environmental Impacts in Uncommon Electric Steelmaking Scenarios to Improve Process Sustainability.' *Applied Energy* 207 (2017): 543–52. https://doi.org/10.1016/j.apenergy.2017.06.088.

[95] Merli, R., M. Preziosi, A. Acampora, M.C. Lucchetti, and E. Petrucci. 'Recycled Fibers in Reinforced Concrete: A Systematic Literature Review.' *Journal of Cleaner Production* 248 (2020). https://doi.org/10.1016/j.jclepro.2019.119207.

[96] Mignacca, B., and G. Locatelli. 'Modular Circular Economy in Energy Infrastructure Projects: Enabling Factors and Barriers.' *Journal of Management in Engineering* 37, no. 5 (2021). https://doi.org/10.1061/(ASCE)ME.1943-5479.0000949.

[97] Mikulčić, H., J. Baleta, and J.J. Klemeš. 'Sustainability through Combined Development of Energy, Water and Environment Systems.' *Journal of Cleaner Production* 251 (2020). https://doi.org/10.1016/j.jclepro.2019.119727.

[98] Parigi, D. 'Minimal-Waste Design of Timber Layouts from Non-Standard Reclaimed Elements: A Combinatorial Approach Based on Structural Reciprocity.' *International Journal of Space Structures* 36, no. 4 (2021): 270–80. https://doi.org/10.1177/09560599211064091.

[99] Piispanen, V.-V., S.-T. Suokas, K. Henttonen, and H. Lehtimäki. 'Sustainable Circular Economy in the Wood Construction Industry: A Business Opportunity Perspective.' *South Asian Journal of Business and Management Cases* 11, no. 1 (2022): 27–34. https://doi.org/10.1177/22779779221080570.

[100] Pinho-Lopes, M. 'Sand Reinforced with Recycled Cotton Textiles from Waste Blue-Jeans: Stress–Strain Response.' *International Journal of Geosynthetics and Ground Engineering* 8, no. 5 (2022). https://doi.org/10.1007/s40891-022-00404-z.

[101] Roberts, C.J., and D.J. Edwards. 'Post-Occupancy Evaluation: Identifying and Mitigating Implementation Barriers to Reduce Environmental Impact.' *Journal of Cleaner Production* 374 (2022). https://doi.org/10.1016/j.jclepro.2022.133957.

[102] Ruiter, H., F. De Feijter, and K. Wagensveld. 'Management Control and Business Model Innovation in the Context of a Circular Economy in the Dutch Construction Industry.' *Sustainability (Switzerland)* 14, no. 1 (2022). https://doi.org/10.3390/su14010366.

[103] Saeli, M., D.M. Tobaldi, M.P. Seabra, and J.A. Labrincha. 'Mix Design and Mechanical Performance of Geopolymeric Binders and Mortars Using Biomass Fly Ash and Alkaline Effluent from Paper-Pulp Industry.' *Journal of Cleaner Production* 208 (2019): 1188–97. https://doi.org/10.1016/j.jclepro.2018.10.213.

[104] Schmidt, W., M. Commeh, K. Olonade, G.L. Schiewer, D. Dodoo-Arhin, R. Dauda, S. Fataei, et al. 'Sustainable Circular Value Chains: From Rural Waste to Feasible Urban Construction Materials Solutions.' *Developments in the Built Environment* 6 (2021). https://doi.org/10.1016/j.dibe.2021.100047.

[105] Teisserenc, B., and S. Sepasgozar. 'Project Data Categorization, Adoption Factors, and Non-Functional Requirements for Blockchain Based Digital Twins in the Construction Industry 4.0.' *Buildings* 11, no. 12 (2021). https://doi.org/10.3390/buildings11120626.

[106] Tsui, T., A. Derumigny, D. Peck, A. van Timmeren, and A. Wandl. 'Spatial Clustering of Waste Reuse in a Circular Economy: A Spatial Autocorrelation Analysis on Locations of Waste Reuse in the Netherlands Using Global and Local Moran's I.' *Frontiers in Built Environment* 8 (2022). https://doi.org/10.3389/fbuil.2022.954642.

[107] Vilakazi, A.Q., S. Ndlovu, L. Chipise, and A. Shemi. 'The Recycling of Coal Fly Ash: A Review on Sustainable Developments and Economic Considerations.' *Sustainability (Switzerland)* 14, no. 4 (2022). https://doi.org/10.3390/su14041958.

[108] Wang, H., X. Xu, and G. Zhu. 'Landscape Changes and a Salt Production Sustainable Approach in the State of Salt Pan Area Decreasing on the Coast of Tianjin, China.' *Sustainability (Switzerland)* 7, no. 8 (2015): 10078–97. https://doi.org/10.3390/su70810078.

[109] Xing, M., F. Luo, and Y. Fang. 'Research on the Sustainability Promotion Mechanisms of Industries in China's Resource-Based Cities —— from an Ecological Perspective.' *Journal of Cleaner Production* 315 (2021). https://doi.org/10.1016/j.jclepro.2021.128114.

[110] Yılmaz, Y., and S. Seyis. 'Mapping the Scientific Research of the Life Cycle Assessment in the Construction Industry: A Scientometric Analysis.' *Building and Environment* 204 (2021). https://doi.org/10.1016/j.buildenv.2021.108086.

[111] Zywietz, M., K. Schlesier, and A. Bögle. 'Rethinking Lightweight: Exploration of Circular Design Strategies in Temporary Structures.' *Journal of the International Association for Shell and Spatial Structures* 63, no. 2 (2022): 132–44. https://doi.org/10.20898/j.iass.2022.011.

[112] Amiri, A., and N. Sakeena. 'Towards the Carbon-Neutral High-Rise: The Role of Embodied Carbon.' *CTBUH Journal* 2021, no. 3 (2021): 36–43.

[113] Briga-Sá, A., N. Gaibor, L. Magalhães, T. Pinto, and D. Leitão. 'Thermal Performance Characterization of Cement-Based Lightweight Blocks Incorporating Textile Waste.' *Construction and Building Materials* 321 (2022). https://doi.org/10.1016/j.conbuildmat.2022.126330.

[114] Cross, M. 'Wallasea Island Wild Coast Project, UK: Circular Economy in the Built Environment.' *Proceedings of Institution of Civil Engineers: Waste and Resource Management* 170, no. 1 (2017): 3–14. https://doi.org/10.1680/jwarm.16.00006.

[115] Densley Tingley, D., S. Cooper, and J. Cullen. 'Understanding and Overcoming the Barriers to Structural Steel Reuse, a UK Perspective.' *Journal of Cleaner Production* 148 (2017): 642–52. https://doi.org/10.1016/j.jclepro.2017.02.006.

[116] Eray, E., B. Sanchez, and C. Haas. 'Usage of Interface Management System in Adaptive Reuse of Buildings.' *Buildings* 9, no. 5 (2019). https://doi.org/10.3390/buildings9050105.

[117] Fidanchevski, E., K. Šter, M. Mrak, L. Kljajević, G. Žibret, K. Teran, B. Poletanovic, M. Fidanchevska, S. Dolenec, and I. Merta. 'The Valorisation of Selected Quarry and Mine Waste for Sustainable Cement Production within the Concept of Circular Economy.' *Sustainability (Switzerland)* 14, no. 11 (2022). https://doi.org/10.3390/su14116833.

[118] Hadro, D., J. Fijałkowska, K. Daszyńska-Żygadło, I. Zumente, and S. Mjakuškina. 'What Do Stakeholders in the Construction Industry Look for in Non-Financial Disclosure and What Do They Get?' *Meditari Accountancy Research* 30, no. 3 (2022): 762–85. https://doi.org/10.1108/MEDAR-11-2020-1093.

[119] Larsen, V.G., N. Tollin, P.A. Sattrup, M. Birkved, and T. Holmboe. 'What Are the Challenges in Assessing Circular Economy for the Built Environment? A Literature Review on Integrating LCA, LCC and S-LCA in Life Cycle Sustainability Assessment, LCSA.' *Journal of Building Engineering* 50 (2022). https://doi.org/10.1016/j.jobe.2022.104203.

[120] Liu, T.-Y., S.-J. Ho, H.-P. Tserng, and H.-K. Tzou. 'Using a Unique Retaining Method for Building Foundation Excavation: A Case Study on Sustainable Construction Methods and Circular Economy.' *Buildings* 12, no. 3 (2022). https://doi.org/10.3390/buildings12030298.

[121] Martínez-Corral, A., and D. Cuéllar. 'When Construction Was Linear. Analysis of the Energy Sustainability of Social Housing in Spain (1939-1989).' *Vitruvio* 6, no. 1 (2021): 38–55. https://doi.org/10.4995/vitruvio-ijats.2021.15383.

[122] Meglin, R., S. Kytzia, and G. Habert. 'Uncertainty, Variability, Price Changes and Their Implications on a Regional Building Materials Industry: The Case of Swiss Canton Argovia.' *Journal of Cleaner Production* 330 (2022). https://doi.org/10.1016/j.jclepro.2021.129944.

[123] Moudjari, M., H. Marouf, H. Muhamad, O. Chaalal, M. Mequignon, W. Maherzi, and M. Benzerzour. 'Using Local Materials to Optimize the Eco-Design of a Resilient Urban Environment in Sustainable Urban Project Process.' *Civil Engineering and Architecture* 9, no. 6 (2021): 2084–97. https://doi.org/10.13189/cea.2021.090636.

[124] Newberry, P., P. Harper, and T. Morgan. 'Understanding the Market for Eco Self-Build Community Housing.' *Sustainability (Switzerland)* 13, no. 21 (2021). https://doi.org/10.3390/su132111823.

[125] Phoon, K.-K., J. Ching, and Z. Cao. 'Unpacking Data-Centric Geotechnics.' *Underground Space (China)* 7, no. 6 (2022): 967–89. https://doi.org/10.1016/j.undsp.2022.04.001.

[126] Ramos, A., A. Briga-Sá, S. Pereira, M. Correia, J. Pinto, I. Bentes, and C.A. Teixeira. 'Thermal Performance and Life Cycle Assessment of Corn Cob Particleboards.' *Journal of Building Engineering* 44 (2021). https://doi.org/10.1016/j.jobe.2021.102998.

[127] Sadri, H., P. Pourbagheri, and I. Yitmen. 'Towards the Implications of Boverket's Climate Declaration Act for Sustainability Indices in the Swedish Construction Industry.' *Building and Environment* 207 (2022). https://doi.org/10.1016/j.buildenv.2021.108446.

[128] Shooshtarian, S., T. Maqsood, S. Caldera, and T. Ryley. 'Transformation towards a Circular Economy in the Australian Construction and Demolition Waste Management System.' *Sustainable Production and Consumption* 30 (2022): 89–106. https://doi.org/10.1016/j.spc.2021.11.032.

[129] Tripathy, S.K., J. Dasu, Y.R. Murthy, G. Kapure, A.R. Pal, and L.O. Filippov. 'Utilisation Perspective on Water Quenched and Air-Cooled Blast Furnace Slags.' *Journal of Cleaner Production* 262 (2020). https://doi.org/10.1016/j.jclepro.2020.121354.

Applying Quality Control System in Fly Ash-based Brick Industry for its Sustainability

Madhuri Bhattacharya[1] and Dr. Abhijit Chakraborty[2]

[1]*Research Scholar, Dept. of Management, Maulana Abul Kalam Azad University of Technology*
[2]*Vice Principal (Professor), GIMT, Krishnagar, West Bengal, India*
E-mail: madhuri1103@gmail.com; chakrabortyabhijit100@gmail.com

Abstract

Under the present trend of global market orientation, the fly ash-based brick industries are facing harder challenges every day. At this situation the shift is occurring towards implementation of quality control systems. Most of the fly ash-based brick industry in this state are subjected to poor technical discipline and as a result, there is lack of organised systems for quality improvement. An appreciable quantity of products is rejected due to lack of knowledge and wisdom as the majority of employees are unskilled and their superiors are not applying quality control measures. Quality control is a process aimed at preventing rather than detecting and correcting defects and errors. In fly ash-based brick industry, appropriate importance should be given to quality planning, quality design, quality implementation, quality gap identification, and quality improvement of the product. It will reduce the labour and material costs, optimal use of resources, increased customer satisfaction, improved employee morale, improved employee quality awareness, increased productivity and efficiency in the fly ash-based brick industry. This article describes the quality control of fly ash-based bricks. Several quality tool implementations have been proposed to improve quality management systems. Strategies are suggested for maintaining quality to meet organisational goals. Therefore, it can be said that the fly ash-based bricks industry needs to implement an efficient quality control system in order to remain competitive and survive in the market. Large organisations look to the fly ash-based brick industry for quality assurance. products and services.

Keywords: *Quality, Quality Control, Process Planning, Sustainability, Waste, Fly Ash*

Introduction

Quality is defined as the 'fitness for purpose in totality'. Quality conformance of FAS-C brick is its standard, specifications and procedure of production. A Quality Management system is the method to make sure that the product which will be produced or delivered meet the needs and expectations of customers. Quality control is concerned with preventing defects and errors in a process, rather than detecting the errors at the process end and eliminating them from the process. It is very essential to be concerned about implementation of quality control techniques, while an organisation trails the market.

The present market climate is very much competitive. In this scenario challenges are rapidly growing for the fly ash-based brick industries. They are unable to make proper competitive response and trailing the market. This trail is a result of improper managerial skill to sustain quality. Therefore, implementation of quality control systems is essential for the fly ash-based brick industries to survive in the market competition as the fittest.

Review of Literature

Literature Review on Productivity and Quality Control

Productivity gains can be achieved by systematically arranging operational processes and practices within an organisation. By implementing systematic layout planning patterns (SLP) in production layouts, the fly ash-based brick industry can achieve increased productivity, high product quality, and high customer satisfaction. Systematic Layout Planning (SLP) is a great tool for organising production areas in a factory by placing two commons, logically connected areas close to each other. This process enables the fastest material flow in raw material processing at the lowest cost and shortest throughput time quality is widely recognised as one of the most important areas/ strategies or competitive priorities in organisational development (Sharma and Kodali, 2008). Quality control tools and techniques are practical methods, skills, means or mechanisms that can be applied to specific tasks to promote positive change and improvement (Fotopulos and Psomas, 2009).

Literature Review on Quality

The need to achieve final product quality in the construction of buildings is of great importance. Quality is an integral part of sustainability and customer satisfaction. Quality in its simplest form can be defined as 'meeting customer expectations' or 'meeting customer specifications' (David Kumar, 2015). In a construction project, quality is all about satisfying the customer and meeting the requirements within the set budget (Ahzahar, N., 2011). Quality, like cost and time, plays a key role in any infrastructure development environment (Priyanka, V., 2014).

Literature Review on TQM

According to Mohammed (2006), TQM integrates quality development, quality maintenance and quality improvement efforts of various aspects of the system to enable service at the most economical level and achieve complete satisfaction.

Barriers and Challenges for Fly Ash-based Brick Industry

Fly ash, the coal combustion residue from thermal power plants, is considered a problematic solid waste worldwide. Due to population growth and urbanisation, solid waste treatment from the TPP, such as fly ash, has become a major challenge in many cities in the developing world.

The main problem faced by the fly ash-based brick industries are:

- **Quality of ash:** Different origin of coal and different plant operating conditions leads to variation in quality of fly ash.
- **Disposal system:** Location of power plants being away from the consumption places makes transportation costly.
- **Technology:** Lack of appropriate technology, training regarding fly ash utilisation.
- **Co-ordination:** It is observed that lack of direct interaction among manufacturer of fly ash products and power generation plants.
- **Awareness about fly ash bricks:** Lack of awareness and promotional measure.
- **Marketing organisation:** Non-availability of separate marketing group to promote the fly ash-based brick.

Objective and Methodology

- To do a detail analysis of the different quality improvement techniques in order to illuminate quality issues.
- To develop conceptual quality improvement plans for the fly ash-based bricks manufacturing industry.

The important aspects issue of fly ash-based brick industry is quality issues. Following are the quality improvement methods that can be taken for fly ash-based brick industries:

1. Collection of present plant information and previous records.
2. Planning implementation of quality management.
3. Recommendation of quality tools for current implementation.
4. Continuous improvement programs for sustainability of quality.

Analysis

For the study, the factory was divided into three parts according to the percentage of employees: managers, machine operators, and skilled workers. All employees were personally questioned about company standards. After the completion of this interrogation following problematic issues came in front:

(a) Low-skill managerial practices in terms of quality assurance.
(b) Untrained workforce.
(c) Very less idea about customisation of product.
(d) Very less knowledge about quality tools.
(e) No practice of benchmarking development.

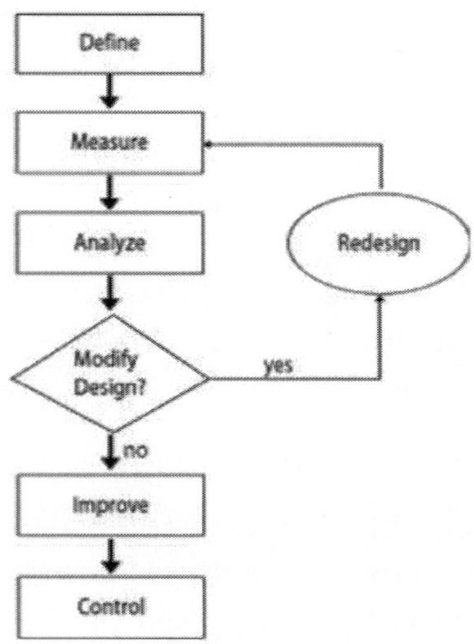

Fig. 1: DMAIC Cycle

To find the actual quality gaps in the system, we looked at the company's past performance against historical records. It was clear from the survey that the company faces viability threats in a highly competitive market.

An attempt has been made by implementing the DMAIC cycle over the fly ash brick manufacturing industry for improving the quality system applying various tools at different stages of the DMAIC cycle. The concern recommended tools have been mentioned in the following Table 1.

Table 1: Recommended Quality Tools According to Phase

Define	*Measure*	*Analyse*	*Implement*	*Control*
Phase 1	*Phase 2*	*Phase 3*	*Phase 4*	*Phase 6*
Identify the Problem	Collect the Data	Analyse the Cause	Plan and Implement Solutions	Standardised results

Phase 1 – Define

The purpose of this phase is to identify product-related defects or problems and reduce the defect rate. This minimises product costs, manages waste and improves brick quality.

In the 'define' stage, whole production process of fly ash brick was analysed deeply. First issue was to know the all relevant elements of the process improvement. For this purpose, the SIPOC diagram is a tool that summarises all inputs and outputs in tabular form. The main requirement of the customer is to have quality fly ash brick. In order to produce high quality fly ash-based bricks, it is essential that the production process run smoothly with greatest quality checking and process checking in steps.

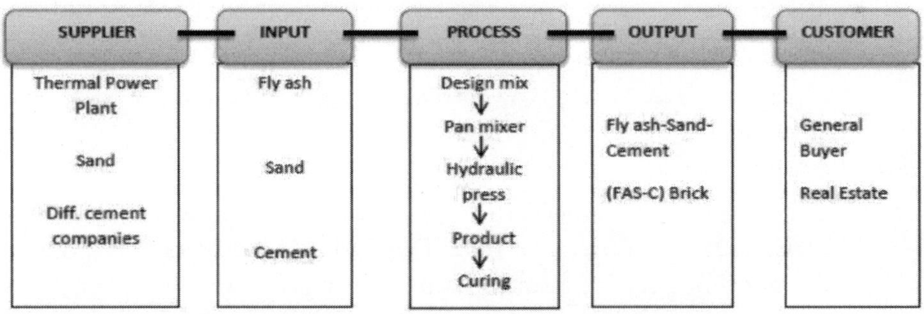

Fig. 2: SIPOC of Fly Ash-based Brick Industry

Phase 2 – Measure

A major issue in the fly ash-based brick industry is the compressive strength of the bricks. This depends on the material quality and brick mix design. The data show that fly ash quality varies with coal quality. Once the problem was identified, we tried to collect relevant data on processes and errors that could be improved. The main objective of the measurement phase is to collect sufficient information about the overall process, current state documentation and comparison test records. After identifying the issue, we attempted to collect relevant process data and troubleshoot.

Baseline performance metrics obtained during the measurement phase of Fly Ash Brick are compared to performance metrics at the end of the business study to objectively determine whether significant improvements have been made. Then decide what and how to measure. Research teams in this group typically make significant efforts to assess the suitability of proposed measurement systems.

Phase 3 – Analyse

The purpose of this procedure is to identify, verify, and select the root cause for remediation. Use fishbone diagrams to identify many potential sources of fly ash. A data collection plan is created and data is collected to determine the relative contribution of each root cause to project metrics. This process is repeated until a 'valid' root cause is identified (Fig. 3).

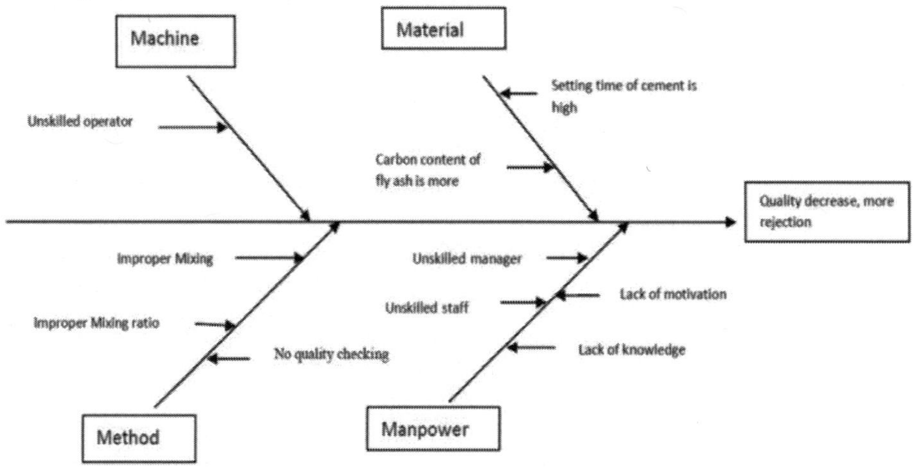

Fig. 3: Root Cause Diagram of Fly Ash-based Brick Industry

Phase 4 – Improve

The purpose of this step is to identify quality issues and test and implement solutions to the issues. Partially or completely free. Depends. Identify creative solutions to troubleshoot and prevent process issues by eliminating the root cause of previous fly ash bricks. Use brainstorming techniques to address these issues. However, the purpose of this step is also to find a solution

- Focus on the simplest and easiest solutions
- Test solutions using plan-do-check-act (PDCA) cycle

In this regard, further the compressive strength of the fly ash bricks at different conditions such as different number of days of different samples/dimensions of different samples have been taken which shows an improvement in the comprehensive strengths with the number of days. It is depicted in the following Table 2, and pictorial representation of the same is shown in Figure 4. Figure 5 is the different sample sizes of fly ash bricks.

Table 2: Compressive Strength of Fly Ash-based Brick

Brick size	*Sample*	*Compressive Strength*			
		15 Days		*28 Days*	
		Weight	*N/mm²*	*Weight*	*N/mm²*
190 mm × 90 mm × 90 mm	First	2.998	3.5	3.000	3.62
		3.054	3.62	2.978	5.86
		3.059	2.92	2.969	7.13
		3.010	4.09	3.010	5.49
		3.100	3.97	3.008	6.19
190 mm × 90 mm × 90 mm	Second	3.003	5.26	2.764	4.21
		2.967	4.21	2.921	5.49
		2.934	4.67	2.957	3.5
		3.018	4.09	2.997	6.43
		3.010	4.44	3.000	5.85
190 mm × 90 mm × 90 mm	Third	2.929	3.04	2.949	5.26
		2.973	3.04	2.965	5.26
		3.065	3.74	3.063	5.96
		3.135	4.67	3.000	5.85
		3.125	4.44	3.047	5.73
230 mm × 110 mm × 70 mm	Four	3.260	3.87	3.251	5.53
		3.177	3.63	2.995	3.55
		3.156	3.55	2.911	3.16
		3.243	2.76	3.104	3.95
		3.266	4.34	2.803	3.87
230 mm × 110 mm × 70 mm	Five	3.222	3.24	3.172	4.82
		3.219	2.76	3.082	4.90
		3.241	3.79	3.100	4.11
		3.067	4.82	3.103	4.98
		3.109	6.24	3.341	7.11
230 mm × 110 mm × 70 mm	Six	3.315	3.79	3.062	6.08
		3.210	3.63	3.118	6.79
		3.178	4.58	3.087	6
		3.137	3.32	2.933	5.13
		2.987	4.18	2.978	4.42
230 mm × 110 mm × 70 mm	Seven	3.089	3.79	3.306	6.40
		3.235	3.51	3.422	5.45
		3.201	3.08	3.257	5.61
		3.152	3.95	3.257	5.84
		3.230	4.03	3.290	6.71
230 mm × 110 mm × 70 mm	Eight	3.092	3.08	3.362	5.92
		3.163	3.47	3.243	5.84
		3.277	2.84	3.486	6.64
		3.105	3.63	3.052	6.71
		3.183	3.55	3.454	6.40

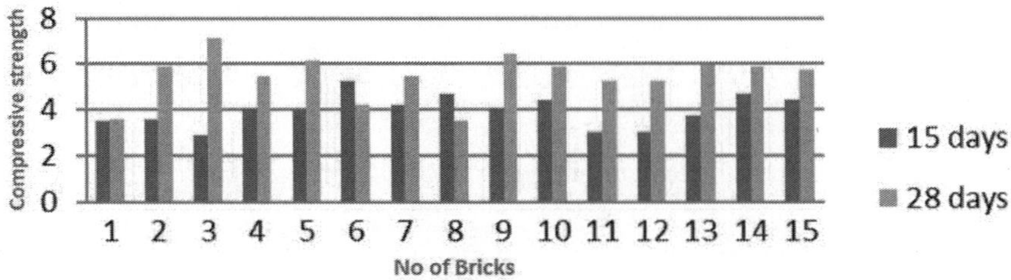

Fig. 4: Compressive Strength for Brick Size 190 mm × 90 mm × 90mm

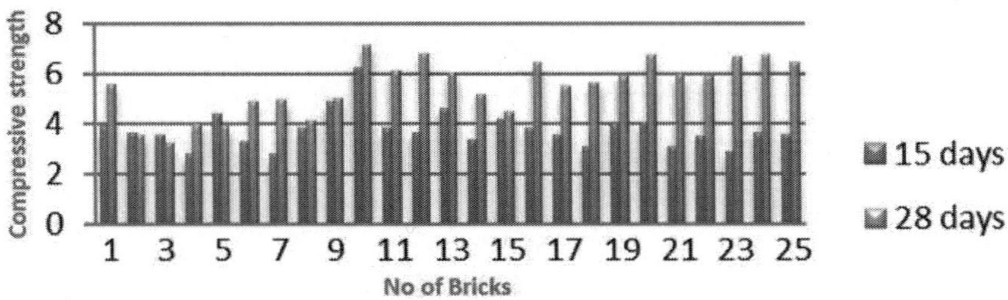

Fig. 5: Compressive Strength for Brick Size 230 mm × 110 mm × 70mm

Phase 5 – Control

To maintain improvement through quality control programmes in the fly ash brick manufacturing industry, statistical process control must be used to monitor and identify performance trends in various fly ash brick manufacturing processes.

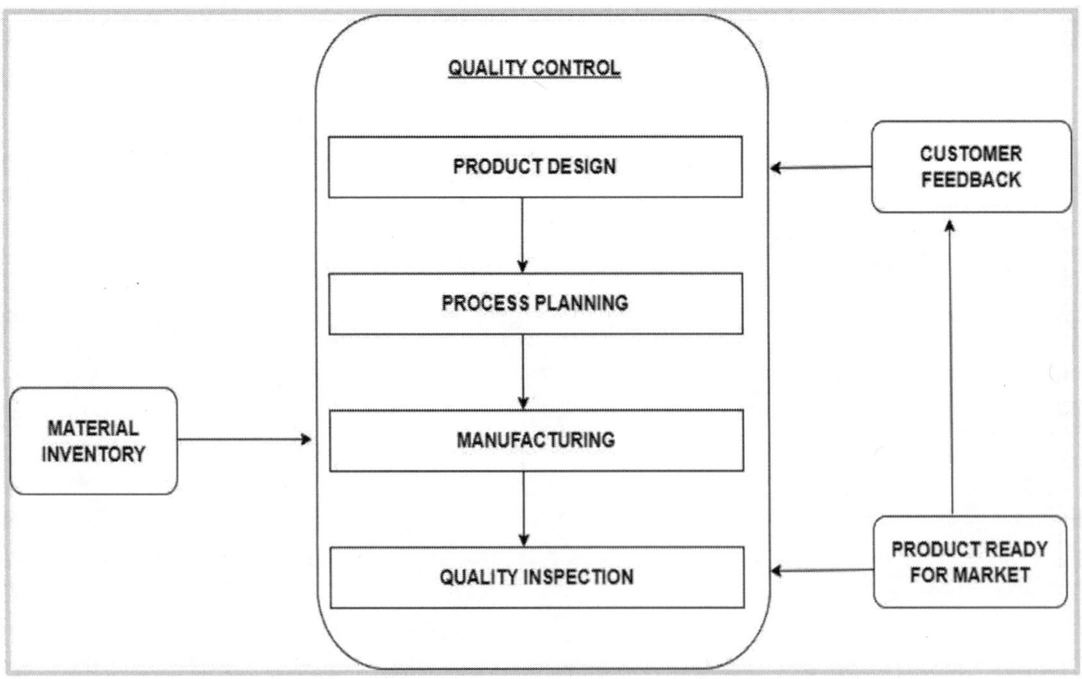

Fig. 6: Quality Control System of Fly Ash-based Brick Industry

In general, fly ash-based industrial production systems are simple and straightforward processes. Several quality control steps need to be taken to detect and improve the process. Figure 1 shows a diagram that can be treated as a process mapping plan for the production of fly ash-based quality brick. In Fly ash-based brick manufacturing system, brick design, production process, and quality inspection are the most important steps to control the quality of the brick.

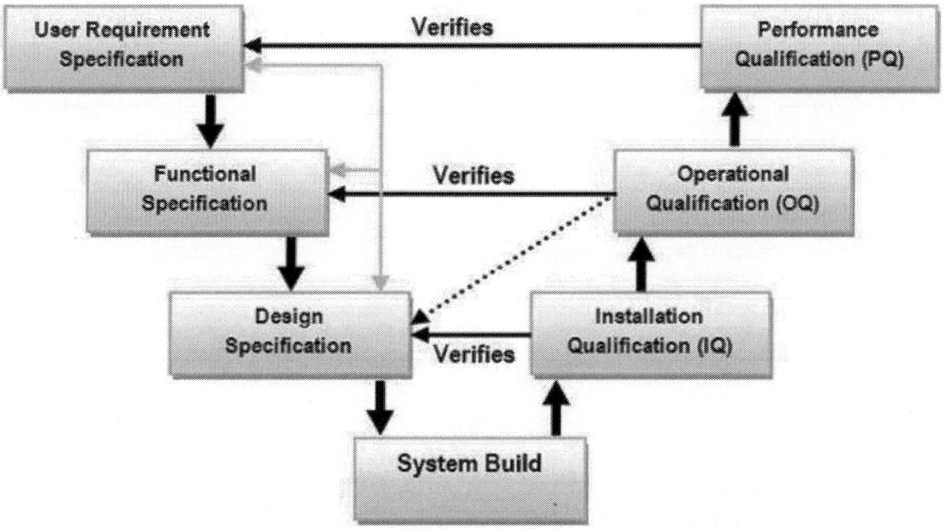

Fig. 7: Proposed Model

The above model reflects the universal idea of factory layout according to specifications, which can solve various problems of fly ash-based brick industry. Developing a quality plan is the key to identifying the right quality plan for your organisation. Proper knowledge and insight into quality is required when planning for each blend. The operator must be able to control the machine and have knowledge of machine operation. The final product is manufactured according to the user's required specifications. A policy of quality improvement has a positive impact on customer satisfaction, lowering prices and increasing productivity as rework/scrap is reduced. This will increase the market share of the fly ash brick manufacturing industry and increase profits. Proper implementation therefore leads to increased productivity and quality.

Conclusion

Fly ash is a waste product of thermal power plants. The fly ash industry uses in making bricks for the development of society in various aspects. Problems facing the fly ash brick manufacturing industry are disposal systems, lack of proper technology, condition and perception of fly ash bricks.

The quality of the fly ash brick can be developed by applying various quality tools phase wise such as workplace organisation, motion and time study, management training, job rotation, cross functional team, quality circle, customisation and continuous improvement. In addition, proper material inventory in the perspective quality control looking at product design, process planning along with quality inspection would give positive thrust in the system of the fly ash brick manufacturing industry. The production system plays a pivotal role having necessary process planning so as to fulfil the quality mission of the fly ash brick manufacturing industry.

References

[1] Abdullah, A. 2010, 'Measuring TQM implementation: a case study of Malaysian SMEs', measuring business excellence, vol. 14, no. 3, pp. 3–15.

[2] Anderberg, S., 2012. Methods for improving performance of process planning for CNC machining - An approach based on surveys and analytical models. Göteborg: Chalmers University of Technology.

[3] Davidkumar.C, Kathirvel.P,' A Study on Factors Influencing Quality of Construction Projects', *International Journal for Research in Applied Science & Engineering Technology (IJRASET),* Volume 3 Issue V, May 2015, IC Value: 13.98 ISSN: 2321-9653.

[4] Gupta, D. P., Gopalakrishnan, B., Chaudhari, S. A. & Jalali, S., 2011. Development of an integrated model for process planning and parameter selection for machining processes. *International Journal of Production Research,* 1 November, 49(21), pp. 6301–319.

[5] Groche, P. et al., 2012. Integration of manufacturing-induced properties in product design. CIRP Annals - Manufacturing Technology, Volume 61, pp. 163–66.

[6] Inman, R. R. et al., 2013. Survey of recent advances on the interface between production system design and quality. IIE Transactions, Volume 45, pp. 557–74.

[7] Mohammad, Z. (2006), 'Nigerian Aviation Sector. Why not a TQM approach?' The voice, www.nanka.org.,30 Sep 2006 last accessed 30/10/2008.

[8] McAdam, R., Stevenson, P. & Armstrong, G. 2000, 'Innovative change management in SMEs: beyond continuous improvement', *Logistic Information Management*, vol. 13, no. 3, pp. 138–49.

[9] N. Ahzahar.N, Karim.N.A, Hassan.S.H, Eman.J, (2011), 'A Study of Contribution Factors to Building Failures and Defects in Construction Industry', Elsevier, Vol.20, pp. 249–255.

[10] Priyanka.V, Ambika.D, (2014), 'Study on factors influencing construction process performance', *International Journal of Advanced Research in Civil, Structural, Environmental and Infrastructure Engineering and Developing*, Vol.2, pp. 85–89.

[11] Sharma, M. & Kodali, R. 2008. 'TQM implementation elements for manufacturing excellence', *The TQM Magazine,* vol. 20, no. 6, pp. 599–621.

[12] Y. Lin, and W. Li, 'Study on the use of SLP in Planning and Designing of Steel Distribution Center,' Chinese and Foreign Architecture, 2007, pp. 124–127.

Forecasting Indian Inflation using Machine Learning Models

Pijush Kanti Das[1] **and Dr Prabir Kumar Das**[2]

[1]Research Scholar, [2]Professor
Indian Institute of Foreign Trade, Kolkata 700100, India
E-mail: pijush_phdmp19@iift.edu; pkdas@iift.edu

Abstract

This study focuses on leveraging fifty explanatory variables from the CMIE database to forecast a macroeconomic parameter, namely the inflation rate in India, using machine learning (ML) models. We chose a large number of features that have not been evaluated earlier. In comparison to existing machine learning (ML) models and benchmark econometric models like ARIMA and linear regression, we found that the Artificial Neural Network (ANN) algorithm can forecast the inflation rate more accurately. The outcomes of this study provide evidence for the advantages of using ML algorithms on forecasting inflation using Indian macroeconomic data.

Keywords: *Inflation Forecasting, Machine Learning, Artificial Neural Network, Random Forest, India*

Introduction

The importance of 'inflation' in economy for any country is well-known and extensively studied to a degree that it is difficult to summarise in a limited space. It plays a salient role in finalising the consumer goods price formation at both wholesale and retail levels. An increase in inflation in goods and services implies a decrease in purchasing power. On the other hand, low inflation will make a country's economic growth slow. These have serious implications, who monitor the monetary policies.

Forecasting inflation is an essential part of policy measures in any economy. Central bankers and policymakers closely track and forecast inflation, to set benchmark interest rates and check 'inflation expectations. Most countries conduct inflationary expectations surveys and use them as an important tool of monetary policy.

Forecasting inflation is one of the most researched topics including the recent developments in big data and statistical learning techniques (Deep and Machine Learning), inflation forecasting has been targeted in mainly three different ways. First, most of the research is based on the development of econometric models and the selection of variables. Machine learning based techniques have improved the accuracy of forecasting to another level. Second, recent approaches to forecasting inflation through the incorporation of high-frequency online prices have yielded promising results. 'Billion Prices Project' by Cavallo and Rigobon (2016) has been crucial in this field.

The last and most recent developments have been through the incorporation of text mining and sentiment analysis, though the efficacy of such methods in improving the performance of forecasting is not yet promising over other methods (Rambaccussing and Kwiatkowski, 2020).

Review of Studies

Traditional econometric approaches in forecasting time series are based on Autoregressive Integrated Moving Average (ARIMA) (Box and Jenkins et al., 2015), Seasonal ARIMA (SARIMA), ARIMA with explanatory variables (ARIMAX), and Vector Auto Regression (VAR). Modern econometric thinking for forecasting inflation may be started with the improvement of Phillips curve-based estimation, using diffusion indexes and the Unobserved Component Stochastic Volatility model (UCSV) (Stock and Watson, 1999; Stock and Watson, 2002). As Stock and Watson (2007) continued their study for the US, many scholars devoted their time to developing improved forecast measures across the globe, e.g. Brouwer and Ericsson(1998) for Australia, and Binner et al. (2005) for the Euro area. Other than traditional approaches, several univariate and multivariate models have been studied for forecasting inflation rates. However, such models have mostly been based on the linearity assumption and do not account for the uncertainty of macroeconomic variables. Linear models usually have poor forecasting performance owing to the inherent non-linearity of the data (Binner et al., 2005). These models are restricted by many limitations and assumptions. With the development of machine learning (ML) and more notably deep learning (DL) algorithms, forecasting has become more data-driven with the capability to fit both nonlinear parametric as well as nonparametric models incorporating a large number of features.

Zhang et al. (1998) explored the promise of artificial neural networks (ANN) and raised several future research questions in terms of improvement over traditional time series models, choice of the best algorithm for a particular forecasting problem and designing of data. In quest of this, several scholars have used several machine learning techniques on macroeconomic data and concluded a better forecasting performance over a benchmark model (in most cases Random Walk [RW] or ARIMA). The algorithms have been studied for both univariate and multivariate setups. On the other hand, after the development of Bootstrap aggregating (Bagging) (Breiman, 1996) and Random Forest Model (Breiman, 2001) along with other ML techniques like Ridge Regression (RR) (Hoerl and Kennard, 1970), Least Absolute Shrinkage and Selection Operator (LASSO) (Tibshirani, 1996), Adaptive Lasso (AdaLASSO) (Zou, 2006), ElasticNet (ElNet) (Zou and Hastie, 2005), forecasting performance has improved.

A vast body of literature has already been contributed to assess the efficiency of ML techniques, some of which may only be discussed as a reference here. Inoue and Kilian (2008) observed Bagging provides more accurate forecasting measures for US CPI-based inflation over median forecasts, shrinkage estimators, and Bayesian model averaging.

Lately, Medeiros et al. (2021), forecasted inflation using ML methods in a data-rich environment. Medeiros et al. (2021) considered RW, AR, and UCSV models as a benchmark and compared them with shrinkage models like RR, LASSO, AdaLASSO, and ElNet; factor models like target factors and factor boosting; Ensembled methods like Bagging, Complete Subset Regressions, Random Forests (RF), Jackknife Model Averaging, and Hybrid Models like (RF/OLS) and (adaLASSO/RF). A data-rich environment has been created in terms of a sample (672 observations, January 1960 to December 2015) and variables. 122 variables and four lags of all variables and hence a total of 508 potential predictors have been used in this analysis. All variables have monthly frequencies and are transformed in year-to-year growth. The models were compared in terms of forecasting performance using root mean square error (RMSE), mean absolute error (MAE) and mean absolute deviation (MAD). Medeiros et al. (2021) concluded that ML methods (LASSO, RF) can produce better forecasts than benchmarks. RF models deserve special attention due to their having the smallest forecasting errors owing to their nonparametric nature and their variable selection mechanism. RF also came out effective as a forecasting method for both economic recession and expansion periods and hence in both low and high uncertainty periods, which is a significant property for any macroeconomic variable.

In India, the Reserve Bank of India (RBI) conducts an inflation expectations survey of households (IESH) quarterly to estimate 3 months ahead and 1-year ahead of inflation expectations. However, Sharma and Bicchal (2018) showed that survey respondents do not build expectations rationally, hinting that the IESH by the Reserve Bank of India (RBI) has a low level of credibility. Das et al. (2019) analysed the dynamics of IESH data and concluded quantification of directional expectations is better than the simple average of the quantitative expectations on the future inflation rate.

The literature on machine learning methods for inflation forecasting for India is scarce, though some recent ones may be worth mentioning. Patrap and Sengupta (2019) estimated CPI inflation with several machine-learning models using univariate data and observed that machine-learning models are in general able to outperform standard econometric models. Pradhan (2011), used ANN models in his study and observed that simple multivariate ANN models forecast better over the other univariate models. Thakur et al. (2016) analysed monthly data of India from January 2000 to December 2012 and built an inflation forecasting model based on a neural network model. Rani et al. (2017) outlined forecasting of monthly inflation using ANN in a multivariate setup.

Though all these studies did not use a data-rich environment and assessed the strength of ML models.

The objective of this article is to answer the question that whether any suitable ML models with large number of explanatory variables can provide higher precision in predicting the inflation rate in the context of India.

Methodology

Benchmark Models: Linear Regression

A regression equation is an equation that expresses the linear relationship between dependent and independent variables, as follows,

$$Y = \beta_0 + \beta_1 X_1 + \cdots + \beta_p X_p + \varepsilon \qquad \ldots(1)$$

where Y is the dependent variable, which is the inflation rate in our study, and X_1, X_2, …, X_p are the K independent variables, ε is the error term. Only the significant variables have been considered after considering the multicollinearity test.

Time Series Models: ARIMA

We obtain ARIMA (Auto-regressive Integrated Moving Average) model by combining the Autoregressive (AR) and Moving Average (MA) model. The model can be written as,

$$y't = c + \phi 1y't - 1 + \ldots + \phi py't - p + \theta 1\varepsilon t - 1 + \ldots + \theta q\varepsilon t - q + \varepsilon t \qquad \ldots(2)$$

where y't is the differenced series. The 'predictors' on the right-hand side include both lagged values of yt and lagged errors. It is known as an ARIMA(p, d, q) model, where p = order of the autoregressive part, d = degree of first differencing involved and q is the order of the moving average part.

Shrinkage Methods

Since least squares estimates typically have low variance and hence perform well on test data, they are more likely to be accurate if n, the number of observations, is significantly greater than p, the number of variables. However, there may be a lot of variability in the least squares fit if n is not significantly bigger than p, which could lead to overfitting and, as a result, subpar predictions on future observations that were not utilised in the model training. In the shrinkage method, a model with all p predictors is fitted. In contrast to the results using least squares, the estimated coefficients have shrunk approaching zero. This shrinking, sometimes referred to as regularisation, reduces variation. Depending on the shrinking method used, some of the coefficients might be precisely zero. As a result, variable selection can be done using shrinkage approaches (G. James et al., 2013).

In this article, we calculate a number of shrinkage estimators for linear models where, $T(x_t) = \beta' x_t$ and

$$\hat{\beta} = \arg\min \left[\sum_{t=1}^{T-h} (y_{t+h} - \beta' x_t)^2 + \lambda \sum_{i=1}^{n} p(\beta_i) \right] \qquad \ldots(3)$$

$p(\beta_i; \omega_i)$ is a penalty function that depends on the penalty parameter, λ. We consider different choices for the penalty functions as described below.

- *Ridge Regression (RR):* The Ridge regression was one of the first methods capable of dealing with a very large set of variables in multiple regression (Hoerl &

Kennard,1970). It uses the quadratic penalty or L_2 norm in the right term of equation (3)

$$\lambda \sum_{i=1}^{n} p(\beta_i) = \lambda \sum_{i=1}^{n} p(\beta_i^2) \quad \text{... (4)}$$

The Ridge Regression has the advantage of having an analytic solution that is easy to compute and also shrinks less relevant variables to zero. However, given the geometric shape of the penalty, the coefficients hardly get to exactly zero for any size of λ.

- *Least Absolute Shrinkage and Selection Operator:* Tibshirani was the one who first proposed the LASSO (1996). It is similar to the Ridge regression, however, it penalises the L_1 norm of the coefficients or the sum of their absolute value.

$$\lambda \sum_{i=1}^{n} p(\beta_i) = \lambda \sum_{i=1}^{n} |\beta_i| \quad \text{... (5)}$$

The LASSO reduces the extraneous variables to zero and exhibits several favourable selection and goodness-of-fit characteristics. The irrepresentable condition (IRC) must be met for the LASSO to have a consistent variable selection (Zhao & Yu 2006). The LASSO still has the variable screening property, which means that it selects the pertinent variables with a high probability but may also select some additional variables, even if the IRC is not satisfied.

- *Elastic Net:* The LASSO and the Ridge are two examples of the Elastic Net's special instances. It combines the L_1 and L_2 norms in a convex manner (Zou & Hastie 2005). The Elastic Net picks the most pertinent variables and performs regularisation as well. Since its penalty is between that of the LASSO and the Ridge, it normally selects more variables than the LASSO, at least for the same value of λ. The ElNet penalty is defined as:

$$\lambda \sum_{i=1}^{n} p(\beta_i) = \alpha \lambda \sum_{i=1}^{n} \beta_i^2 + (1-\alpha) \lambda \sum_{i=1}^{n} |\beta_i| \quad \text{... (6)}$$

Random Forest (RF)

Recursively partitioning the space of the covariates in a regression tree allows it to approximate an unknown nonlinear function with local predictions (Breiman, 1996). Breiman (2001) created the RF model, which is based on the bootstrap aggregation (bagging) of regression trees constructed randomly, to lessen the variance of those trees.

Given a dependent variable π_{t+h}, a set of predictors x_t, and a number of terminal nodes K, the splits are determined to minimizes the sum of squared errors of the following regression model

$$\pi_{t+h} = \sum_{k=1}^{K} C_k l_k(x_t; \theta_k)$$

where $l_k (x_t; q_k)$ is an indicator function such that

$$l_k (x_t; \theta_k) = 1, \text{ if } x_t \, \varepsilon \, R_k (\theta_k) \text{ and } 0, \text{ otherwise,} \quad \text{... (7)}$$

θ_k is the set of parameters that define the kth region, $l_k (x_t; \theta_k)$ is a product of indicator functions, each of which defines one of the splits that yields the kth region.

Artificial Neural Network (ANN) Model

The most generic model type is an artificial neural network. Any multi-layer neural network, however, has a number of parameters that must be estimated using the data. For the sake of simplicity, we will illustrate one single-layer neural network structure as given below:

$$\eta_{t+s} = \beta'_0\zeta_t + \sum_{j=1}^{n_1} \beta_j g\left(\gamma_0 j + \sum_{i=1}^{m} \gamma_{ij}\, \eta_{t-(i-1)d} + u_{jt+h}\right) \quad \ldots (8)$$

where g() is logistic(activation) function.

In this study, we use a multilayer perceptron that minimises the squared error loss. We use three hidden layers and solve for the weight in R in the neuralnet package.

Model Evaluation

We used Root Mean Squared Error (RMSE) and relative RMSE to assess each model's forecasting accuracy. Both trained and test data have been used to evaluate the model. It is more crucial to look at the prediction accuracy in relation to test data because the model was already constructed using trained data.

$$\text{Root Mean Squared Error (RMSE)} = \sqrt{\frac{1}{t}\sum_{i=1}^{t}(y_i - \hat{y}_i)^2} \quad \ldots (9)$$

$$\text{Relative RMSE} = \frac{\text{RMSE of Model } i}{\text{RMSE of Benchmark Models}} \quad \ldots (10)$$

Data Sources

In general, the term 'inflation' refers to a measurement of an increase in the average level of prices for goods and services over time in an economy. The inflation rate, or percentage change in an index of prices over time, is the most widely used indicator of price inflation. India publishes four different price indices: the Consumer Price Index (CPI), the Wholesale Price Index (WPI), the CPI for three different worker types (industrial, urban non-manual, and agricultural/rural sectors), and the Gross Domestic Product (GDP) deflator, published by the Ministry of Statistics and Programme Implementation (MOSPI). With a lag of one month for the provisional index and three months for the final index, the WPI and CPI are both available on a monthly basis. Until 2014, India's official inflation rate was the WPI. It was decided to compute the CPI-based Index for the measurement of inflation since 2014. The CPI, which measures the cost of living, is the primary factor used in most nations to calculate inflation rates.

For calculating the inflation rate, the year-on-year inflation rate is more persistent and meaningful than the monthly inflation rate (Raj and Dhal, 2008). From the view of price stability, a less volatile annual inflation rate has more utility than a highly volatile monthly inflation rate. To calculate the inflation rate, we have used year-on-year inflation in this study. As an example, to calculate inflate rate as of March 2020, we observed the changes in CPI in March 2020 from March 2019.

All data in this study have been collected from the CMIE database. For CPI, the data is available from January 2011 to July 2020. On the other hand, WPI is available from April 1982 to July 2020. In this paper, we have focused on the study of the inflation rate based on CPI, data from April 2012 to March 2020 considering the COVID situation in India after March 2020 and the availability of other predictor variables. It may be mentioned here, official CPI data is being published by MoSPI, Government of India, and we have crosschecked with CMIE data.

A large number of research have been carried out on keying out the determinants of Inflation in different countries. These determinants may be categorised mainly into two factors, vis.-supply-side, and demand-side factors. Supply-side factors drive enhancing the price of production (cost-push inflation). Some important supply-side factors include crude oil imports, rainfall, Bank rate, Net Foreign Direct Investment, etc. On the other hand, demand-side factors contribute to higher inflation by creating more consumption scenarios for goods and services in the country (demand pull information). Some important demand side factors are the currency with public, Government expenditure, average wage rate, etc., considering this, we have observed a vast literature to consider all determinants, and a total of 50 variables have been considered. Justification of undertaking all variables is being skipped here for time being as it would take a lot of additional space. However, metadata has been prepared and a glimpse of all variables along with its data availability and intersecting data points with the inflation rate considering WPI and CPI both in Annexure-A. This analysis of metadata further helped in considering a maximum number of important variables in this study. It may also be mentioned here CMIE compiles the data from different sources of Official Statistics, and we have also cross-examined the data with sources like RBI, MoSPI, etc.

The frequency of data points is another important aspect of this analysis. We have considered the variables only with data availability of 'monthly' frequency for the time being. Another important aspect of the preparation of data is to make it spliced/linking series in terms of base. All relevant data for the different base periods has been corrected to make a single series of data. For example, CPI data has been made a single series data with base 2012 = 100.

To sum up, our data consists of 99 time points/observations for each variable (from January 2012 to March 2020) and consists of 50 variables (including the inflation rate) that describes the Indian Economy and probable predictors for the inflation rate. The data up to March 2020 has only been considered in this study to avoid the negative effect of the Covid-19 pandemic on the Indian Economy since April 2020.

For using ML techniques, we divided our analysis and fixed into two periods, i.e. January 2012 to December 2017(72 observations) as trained data sample on which the models are built and January 2018 to March 2020 (27 observations) as test data, where the models have been tested.

Empirical Results

Table 1 summarises the results. We report the value of RMSE and Relative RMSE concerning the benchmark linear regression Model (with significant variables) for both train and test data.

Table 1 shows, the Artificial Neural Network model outperforms all other forecasting models to predict the inflation rate (relative RMSE for test data = 0.622). It may also be observed that the ARIMA model fits better than even shrinkage models. But the performance of Random Forest is poor even in the benchmark model.

Table 1: RMSE and Relative RMSE for Both Train and Test Data for All Models

Model Name	*RMSE_ Trained*	*RMSE_Test*	*Relative_RMSE Trained*	*Relative RMSE_ Test*
LR (with significant variables)	0.943	2.631	1.000	1.000
Ridge Regression	0.884	2.413	0.938	0.917
LASSO regression	0.886	2.370	0.940	0.901
ElNet regression	0.324	2.390	0.343	0.908
ARIMA	0.593	1.789	0.629	0.680
Random Forest	0.956	2.882	1.013	1.095
Artificial Neural Network	0.543	1.637	0.575	0.622

Source: Authors' calculation

Conclusion

In this paper, we tried to forecast the inflation rate on a large-scale macroeconomic database base on CMIE data containing more than fifty variables. Also, we present a non-exhaustive review of the machine learning models for forecasting macroeconomic indicators.

Two important features have been explored from the dataset. First, Artificial Neural Network (ANN) model outperforms all other models. Second, all machine learning models, vis., Shrinkage models (Lasso Regression, Ridge Regression, and ElNet Regression), Random Forest (RF), and Artificial Neural Network (ANN) model showed good performance in forecasting inflation rate than benchmark linear regression model. ARIMA model also showed very good performance only behind the ANN model, but the RF model couldn't perform well.

The first inference to be drawn from this finding is that even though there aren't many large data samples available for macroeconomic analysis, ML models can still be successfully used to forecast macroeconomic variables. We strive to make the following advancements:

1. Develop results for other nonlinear classification ML techniques like Bagging and Boosting.
2. Develop results for other NN models like BNN (Backpropagation Neural network model) and RNN (Recurrent Neural Network Model).

3. Include features with different frequencies like quarterly, annual, etc. and deploy suitable statistical techniques.
4. Develop feature importance on ML models specifically the NN model.
5. Include forecasting horizons in the analysis.

Finally, we would like to point out that we left many more recently developed machine and deep learning models, like- Long Short-term Memory (LSTM), Transfer model, etc. However, we trust that the conclusion presented in this paper can be of value to anyone interested in applying ML models to macroeconomic forecasting in the Indian context.

References

[1] Binner, J.M., Bissoondeeal, R.K., Elger, T., Gazely, A.M., & Mullineux, A.W. (2005). A comparison of linear forecasting models and neural networks: An application to Euro inflation and Euro Divisia. *Applied Economics, 37*(6), 665–80.

[2] Box, G.E., Jenkins, G.M., Reinsel, G.C., & Ljung, G.M. (2015). *Time series analysis: Forecasting and control.* John Wiley & Sons.

[3] Brouwer, G.D., & Ericsson, N.R. (1998). Modeling inflation in Australia. *Journal of Business & Economic Statistics, 16*(4), 433–49.

[4] Cavallo, A., & Rigobon, R. (2016). The billion prices project: Using online prices for measurement and research. *Journal of Economic Perspectives, 30*(2), 151–78.

[5] Cavallo, A., Cruces, G., & Perez-Truglia, R. (2017). Inflation expectations, learning, and supermarket prices: Evidence from survey experiments. *American Economic Journal: Macroeconomics, 9*(3), 1–35.

[6] Goulet Coulombe, P., Leroux, M., Stevanovic, D., & Surprenant, S. (2022). How is machine learning useful for macroeconomic forecasting? *Journal of Applied Econometrics, 37*(5), 920–64.

[7] D'Amuri, F., & Marcucci, J. (2017). The predictive power of Google searches in forecasting US unemployment. *International Journal of Forecasting, 33*(4), 801–16.

[8] Das, A., Lahiri, K., & Zhao, Y. (2019). Inflation expectations in India: Learning from household tendency surveys. *International Journal of Forecasting, 35*(3), 980–93.

[9] Goyal, A., & Parab, P. (2019). Modeling heterogeneity and rationality of inflation expectations across Indian households. *Indira Gandhi Institute of Development Research, Working Paper.*

[10] Inoue, A., & Kilian, L. (2008). How useful is bagging in forecasting economic time series? A case study of US consumer price inflation. *Journal of the American Statistical Association, 103*(482), 511–22.

[11] James, G., Witten, D., Hastie, T., & Tibshirani, R. (2013). *An introduction to statistical learning* (Vol. 112, p. 18). New York: springer

[12] Medeiros, M.C., Vasconcelos, G.F., Veiga, Á., & Zilberman, E. (2021). Forecasting inflation in a data-rich environment: the benefits of machine learning methods. *Journal of Business & Economic Statistics, 39*(1), 98–119.

[13] Nakamura, E. (2005). Inflation forecasting using a neural network. *Economics Letters, 86*(3), 373–78.

[14] Pratap, B., & Sengupta, S. (2019). Macroeconomic Forecasting in India: Does Machine Learning Hold the Key to Better Forecasts? *Pratap, B., & Sengupta, S.(2019). Macroeconomic Forecasting in India: Does Machine Learning Hold the Key to Better Forecasts?*

[15] Pradhan, R. P. (2011). Forecasting inflation in India: An application of ANN Model. *International Journal of Asian Business and Information Management (IJABIM), 2*(2), 64–73.

[16] Rambaccussing, D., & Kwiatkowski, A. (2020). Forecasting with news sentiment: Evidence with UK newspapers. *International Journal of Forecasting, 36*(4), 1501–516.

[17] Rani, S.J., Haragopal, V.V., & Reddy, M.K. (2017). Forecasting inflation rate of India using neural networks. *International Journal of Computer Applications, 158*(5), 45–48.

[18] Rothman, P. (1998). Forecasting asymmetric unemployment rates. *Review of Economics and Statistics, 80*(1), 164–68.

[19] Sharma, N.K., & Bicchal, M. (2018). The properties of inflation expectations: Evidence for India. *Economia, 19*(1), 74–89.

[20] Stock, J.H., & Watson, M.W. (1998). A comparison of linear and nonlinear univariate models for forecasting macroeconomic time series.

[21] Stock, J.H., & Watson, M.W. (1999). Forecasting inflation. *Journal of Monetary Economics, 44*(2), 293–335.

[22] Stock, J.H., & Watson, M.W. (2002). Macroeconomic forecasting using diffusion indexes. *Journal of Business & Economic Statistics, 20*(2), 147–62.

[23] Stock, J.H., & Watson, M.W. (2007). Why has US inflation become harder to forecast? *Journal of Money, Credit and banking, 39*, 3–33.

[24] Thakur, G.S.M., Bhattacharyya, R., & Mondal, S. S. (2016). Artificial neural network based model for forecasting of inflation in India. *Fuzzy Information and Engineering, 8*(1), 87–100.

[25] Tibshirani, R. (1996). Regression shrinkage and selection via the lasso. *Journal of the Royal Statistical Society: Series B (Methodological), 58*(1), 267–88.

[26] Zhang, G., Patuwo, B. E., & Hu, M. Y. (1998). Forecasting with artificial neural networks:: The state of the art. *International journal of forecasting, 14*(1), 35–62.

[27] Zou, H., & Hastie, T. (2005). Regularization and variable selection via the elastic net. *Journal of the royal statistical society: series B (statistical methodology), 67*(2), 301–20.

[28] Zou, H. (2006). The adaptive lasso and its oracle properties. *Journal of the American statistical association, 101*(476), 1418–429.

Annexure-A

Sl. No.	*Name of Variables*	*Source of Literature*	*Observed Relationship with Inflation*
1	Inflation rate (based on CPI)		
2	Currency with public	Milo, P. (2012). The impact of the budget deficit on the currency and inflation in the transition economies. *Journal of Central Banking Theory and Practice*, 1(1), 25-57.	Positive

Sl. No.	*Name of Variables*	*Source of Literature*	*Observed Relationship with Inflation*
3	M1 growth	Jane M Binner, Rakesh K Bissoondeeal, Thomas Elger, Alicia M Gazely, and Andrew W Mullineux. A comparison of linear forecasting models and neural networks: An application to euro inflation and euro divisia. *Applied economics*, 37(6): 665–680, 2005.	Positive
4	Net bank credit growth	Korkmaz, S. (2015). Impact of bank credits on economic growth and inflation. *Journal of Applied Finance and Banking*, 5(1), 51.	No relation
5	Cash reserve ratio (CRR)	Okotori, T. W. (2019). The Dynamics of monetary policy and inflation in Nigeria. *IOSR Journal of Economics and Finance* (*IOSR-JEF*), 10(2), 37-49.	Positive
6	Statutory liquidity ratio (SLR)	Chaudhary, N. Impact Of Inflation On Monetary Policy Of Indian Economy. *International Journal of Research in Management & Social Science*, 50.	Positive
7	Bank rate		Negative
8	Base rate	Ashima Goyal, Prashant Parab et al. Modeling heterogeneity and rationality of inflation expectations across indian households. Indira Gandhi Institute of Development Research, Working Paper, 2019.	Negative
9	Crude oil imports		Negative
10	Crude oil production		Negative
11	Tax receipt	Poterba, J.M., & Rotemberg, J.J. (1988). Inflation and taxation with optimizing governments.	Both Positive and Negative
12	Central government expenditure	Mehrara, M., & Sujoudi, A. (2015). The relationship between money, government spending and inflation in the Iranian economy. *International Letters of Social and Humanistic Sciences*, 51, 89-94.	No significant effect
13	Revenue deficit	Ezeabasili, V.N., Mojekwu, J.N., & Herbert, W.E. (2012). An empirical analysis of fiscal deficits and inflation in Nigeria. *International Business and Management*, 4(1), 105-120.	Positive
14	Gross fiscal deficit (GFD)		Positive
15	Exports	Sahoo, Malayaranjan, and Narayan Sethi. 'The dynamic relationship between export, import and inflation: Empirical evidence from India.' The Indian Economic Journal 66.3-4 (2018): 294-311.	Positive
16	Imports		Positive
17	Net foreign direct investment	Omankhanlen, A.E. (2011). The effect of exchange rate and inflation on foreign direct investment and its relationship with economic growth in Nigeria.	No effect
18	ECCBs & FCCBs_ total	Misra, P., & Shettigar, J. (2020). Macroeconomic Variables Affecting External Commercial Borrowings: An Investigation. In *Innovation, Technology, and Market Ecosystems* (pp. 241-263). Palgrave Macmillan, Cham.	Positive

Sl. No.	*Name of Variables*	*Source of Literature*	*Observed Relationship with Inflation*
19	Tourist arrivals	Shaari, M.S., Ahmad, T.S.T., & Razali, R. (2018). Tourism led-inflation: A case of Malaysia. In *MATEC Web of Conferences* (Vol. 150, p. 06026). EDP Sciences.	Positive
20	Total foreign exchange reserves	Gour Sundar Mitra Thakur, Rupak Bhattacharyya, and Seema Sarkar Mondal. Artificial neural network based model for forecasting of inflation in india. *Fuzzy Information and Engineering*, 8(1): 87–100, 2016.	Negative
21	Exchange rate		Negative
22	Actual rainfall	Dua, P., & Goel, D. (2021). Determinants of inflation in India. *The Journal of Developing Areas*, 55(2).	Positive
23	Coal imports	Guo, J., Zheng, X., & Chen, Z. M. (2016). How does coal price drive up inflation? Reexamining the relationship between coal price and general price level in China. *Energy Economics*, 57, 265-276.	Negative
24	Coal production	Philippe Goulet Coulombe, Maxime Leroux, Dalibor Stevanovic, and Stephane Surprenant. How is machine learning useful for macroeconomic forecasting? arXiv preprint arXiv:2008.12477, 2020.	Positive
25	Production_ Natural Gas		Positive
26	Production_ Refinery products		Positive
27	Production_ fertilizers		Positive
28	Production_steel		Positive
29	Production_ cement		Positive
30	Production_ electricity		Positive
31	Production of Sugar		Positive
32	Production_Tea		Positive
33	Index of industrial production (IIP)		Positive
34	production_ Passenger cars		Positive
35	Electricity generation (Utiltiies)	Atems, B., & Hotaling, C. (2018). The effect of renewable and nonrenewable electricity generation on economic growth. *Energy Policy*, 112, 111-118.	Positive
36	Railways: freight traffic	Mandal, S., & Chakraborty, S. *International Journal of Business Economics and Management Research.*	Positive
37	Cargo handled at major ports	Cheteni, P. (2013). Transport infrastructure investment and transport sector productivity on economic growth in South Africa (1975-2011). *Mediterranean Journal of Social Sciences*, 4(13), 761.	Positive

Sl. No.	*Name of Variables*	*Source of Literature*	*Observed Relationship with Inflation*
38	Cargo handled at aviation	Alıcı, A., & Akar, A.S. (2020). Macroeconomic determinants of air cargo demand: A panel data analysis. *International Journal of Shipping and Transport Logistics*, 20(48), 11-23.	Negative
39	Capital issues	Olanipekum, B. O., & Akeju, F. K. (2013). Money supply, inflation and capital accumulation in Nigeria. *Journal of economics and sustainable development*, 4(4).	Positive
40	Average wage rates for rural labourers in agricultural and non-agricultural sectors	James H Stock and Mark W Watson. A comparison of linear and nonlinear univariate models for forecasting macroeconomic time series. Technical report, National Bureau of Economic Research, 1998.	Positive
41	Total: Aircraft movements	Aderamo, A.J. (2010). Demand for air transport in Nigeria. *Journal of Economics*, 1(1), 23-31.	Negative
42	Total: Passengers handled		Negative
43	NSE_NIFTY50_ Closing Prices	Atsushi Inoue and Lutz Kilian. How useful is bagging in forecasting economic time series? a case study of us consumer price inflation. *Journal of the American Statistical Association*, 103(482): 511–522, 2008.	Positive
44	Crude oil (petrolium) price		Positive
45	Bank credit to commercial sector and components	Korkmaz, S. (2015). Impact of bank credits on economic growth and inflation. *Journal of Applied Finance and Banking*, 5(1), 51.	No relationship found
46	Stocks of Foodgrains	KU, G., & Pandit, V. (2014). Production, procurement and inflation: A market model for foodgrains. *Margin: The Journal of Applied Economic Research*, 8(4), 431–456.	Positive
47	Reservoir levels: Current live storage	https://www.livemint.com/Opinion/OvuM9z8ErSWAufCqCTXsdN/Rains-reservoirs-and-food-prices.html	Positive
48	Motor Vehicles Registered	https://www.cnbc.com/2022/01/13/why-used-car-prices-are-pushing-inflation-higher.html	Positive
49	Mobile Subscribers	Ehsan, Z.A. (2021). Assessing the nexus between mobile financial service usage and inflation–evidence from Bangladesh.	Positive
50	Teledensity	Adeleye, N., & Eboagu, C. (2019). Evaluation of ICT development and economic growth in Africa. *NETNOMICS: Economic Research and Electronic Networking*, 20(1), 3	Positive

Moderating Effect of Organisational Creativity between Artificial Intelligence Capability and Organisational Performance

Dr Pankaj A. Tiwari[1] and Shweta Rastogi[2]

[1]*Assistant Professor, School of Management, CMR University, Bengaluru, Karnataka, India*

[2]*Ph.D. Scholar, University of Technology, Jaipur, Rajasthan, India*

E-mail: pankaj.a@cmr.edu.in; adatiya.pankaj@gmail.com; ras.shweta@gmail.com

Abstract

In a dynamic and competitive corporate environment, organizational creativity is considered a potential reason for any organisation to remain competitive in the dynamic environment. Creativity is an enabler to improve organisational productivity as it is employed to go beyond innovation, technological advancements, skill sets, and ideas. The dynamic changes in the modern business ecosystem make organisations' creativity more important today than it ever has been. By remaining creative, teams focus on more inimitable and state-of-the-art solutions. Creativity fosters newer ideas and often a fresh approach to challenges. This paper highlights the use of artificial intelligence and organisational creativity in innovative ideas as the AI technologies used within organisations are constantly evolving. To examine the conceptual research framework, data was collected from a sample of 125 senior managers working in IT/ITeS. The research findings based on Ordinal regression analysis establish a significant relationship between capability, organisational creativity, and organisational performance. Furthermore, the present paper determines the AI-specialised resources that mutually generate IT business value. The study outcomes determine that by fostering an AI capability firms can realise long-term benefits from a business value perspective considering the overall business success and organisational performance. Hence, organisations need additional resources to influence AI investments as per the contingent context. Empowering employees with creative insights and implementation at work can positively impact the firm's performance. It would result in utilising the resources proficiently, and effectively to maximise the firm overall performance. However, employees may be hesitant in contributing their ideas or do not take them seriously towards their development. For any successful business and organisation, an appropriate approach is needed to make employees highlight their unique ideas. Consequently, support from organisations is key to enriching organisational creativity. The limitation of this paper is that the outcomes presented cannot be generalised to the wider population from a cross-sectional perspective.

Keywords: *Artificial Intelligence, Performance, Organisational Creativity, Resources, Employees, Enhancement, Value*

Introduction

Progressively, Artificial Intelligence has evolved as the highest priority for all information technology organisations, considering the big data availability and related infrastructure (Davenport, 2018). Based on the recent report from Gartner, organisations that implemented artificial intelligence grew enormously in recent years. Organisations that adopted artificial intelligence to bring significant business value to realise long-term gains are challenged by the dynamic nature of the market (Fountain et al., 2019; Howard et al., 2019). It is also evident that as reported by MIT SMR, artificial intelligence has impacted the overall business value to none. Brynjolfsson et al. (2018) indicated that every organisation faces a productivity paradox and the key reason for the same is the restructuring lag generated by artificial intelligence while implementation. Therefore, organisations should consider complementary resources while investing in artificial intelligence-related initiatives. Hence, it is important to assess how organisations develop AI capabilities (Ransbotham et al., 2019).

Artificial intelligence (AI) is proclaimed in the information system literature as the next source of business value (Gupta et al., 2016). Based on the resource-based perspective and the latest research on AI, this research paper aims to examine the influence of artificial capability and firm creativity on organisational performance. In a dynamic and competitive corporate environment, organisational creativity is seen as a probable source of an organisation's competitiveness. Creativity is an enabler to improve the performance of an organisation as it is employed to go beyond innovation, technological advancements, skill sets, and ideas. The dynamic changes in the modern business ecosystem make organisations' creativity more important today than it ever has been (Kohali et al., 2008; Schryen, 2013). Earlier research work has determined that resource-based is a suitable theoretic lens for uncertain events, especially when resources are cultivated integrally, and focused on idiosyncratic skills around their corresponding reserves (Priem et al., 2001).

Hence the query:

- *How do artificial intelligence and organisational creativity influence the organisation's performance?*

This paper enriches existing research by applying the resource-based theoretical framework and demonstrates that AI capability and increased organisational creativity results in organisational performance. Organisational creativity encompasses tapping into the unknown arena of potentialities be it a new product, an innovative technique, or improved efficiency, delving into a subtler aspect of human skills like motivation-job satisfaction, teamwork-training, and development, or out-of-the-box thinking at all levels. By being creative, individuals in an organisation are expected to develop exceptional and pioneering solutions. Creativity fosters newer ideas and often a fresh approach to challenges (Mikalef et al., 2019). Also, this paper highlights the use of artificial intelligence and organisational creativity in innovative ideas as the AI technologies used within organisations are constantly evolving.

Literature Review

Artificial Intelligence Capability

The available research work on artificial intelligence usage and its applicability in creating business value are limited, a very few studies have found the challenges with respect to the effective implementation of projects with AI features. Several practice-based research draws attention to organisations with respect to the adoption of AI and its implementation, stating technical competency as one of the factors for creating business value through artificial intelligence (Ransbotham, 2019). These findings showcased that organisations with a lack of technical capabilities are unable to understand data-related requirements and infrastructure. Consequently, it is important for organisations to focus on complementary resources that need to be nurtured apart from technological advancement so that any AI-related capabilities cannot be imitated and should be specific to an organisation (Sirmon, 2007).

As per Grant (1991), the resources are grouped tangible, human, and intangible in nature. Tangible resources are data-driven, specific to technology, and basic in nature, while the human part comprises business and technical in nature. Intangible resources consist of coordination between different departments, capacity relating to organisational change, and a tendency towards risk. The tangible resources are physically accessible which does not offer any benefit in the market. Data is one of the key influencers for AI capability. Organisations describe a significant multiplicity of data stemming from several resources and in varied formats though concentrated on structured data conventionally. The combination of big data and Artificial Intelligence is an evolving trend and is determining the way organisations create value from data-specific resources. Not only this but the type of information considered to formulate algorithms in big data is of immense significance. As AI requires enormous preparation in datasets, and its applications successfully pick up from the readily accessible data in a way like the human approach, there is a huge need for a substantial volume of high-quality information. Technological infrastructure is the key area in utilising huge and building complex data sources to develop AI systems (Dwivedi et al., 2021). It calls for profoundly newer, creative, and innovative advancements in technology to work on data in various stages from procurement to awareness creation, and for preparation in AI applications and support. The constraints with respect to the storage of data for AI differ as per the application and data sources. Also, the data requirements differ in various stages for the development and usage of artificial intelligence, which lays the need for the organisation to focus on the investment related to the storage infrastructure that can sustain the huge volume and different formats (Ågerfalk, 2020).

The human skill set is the asset, and capital of an organisation that embraces the skills, experience, knowledge, wisdom, creativity, strong leadership traits, effective exchange of ideas, vision, and problem-resolving capabilities of its human resources. Technical skills refer to the technical knowledge and skill necessary to work on the different AI algorithms by managing data-related infrastructure and ensuring AI applications stick to the expected goal considering the latest research. Business skills are important to adopt and make use of AI-related technologies to overcome the challenges related to when and where to apply AI technologies. Organisations function in a highly competitive and global ecosystem, making creativity vital for change and transformation. It is the source of evolved ideas, challenges one's way of thinking, and unfolds the possibilities to creative potential and opportunities. It opens the organisation to diverse perspectives and fosters the production of high-quality, original, and elegant solutions to problems. Creative employees may come up with innovative solutions to the impediments they are confronted with to solve complex problems (Alonso, 2015; Townsend et al., 2019).

Intangible resources can manage and align project activities and contribute to a common goal considering various departments in an organisation. Its involvement is a key factor in enabling creative and innovative organisations. A perspective of prominent levels of mutual values and objectives, duties, and collaboration across the shared vision of creativity, advancements, and progress. It is essential to note the continuous relationships between divisions or units rather than simple transactions between divisions. The literature reviews done by recent studies bring forth the idea that to understand the importance of AI skills, organisations must nurture and encourage a positive culture to remain creative and focus on teamwork and shared goals. The organisation's capability to continue to focus on the plan execution is the prime success factor when it comes to digital transformation (Conboy et al., 2020). An organisation's capacity related to dynamic changes centers around the prospective challenges that may appear due to failure in adapting to any new process. Building a capability that decreases conflicts and disinterest related to any organisational change are a significant source to create value along with digital transformation capabilities. Capacity related to organisational change involves the capability to establish new processes and practices. Applications based on artificial intelligence introduce substantial shifts in the way organisations execute key processes, either by enhancing existing practices or replacing conventionally executed tasks by humans. To plan and work on such changes in an organisation considering various management levels, used to realise business value from investment in the Artificial intelligence domain. By adopting a risk-oriented methodology, organisations work on AI-related new ventures and gain benefits by remaining competitive. Such strategic orientation of an organisation to work in the dynamic environment has been highlighted by various terms such as risk proclivity, attitude towards proactiveness, and alignment of entrepreneurial activities, etc. to emphasise the approaches adopted by organisations to work aggressively to achieve competitive advantage (Spector et al., 2019).

Organisational Creativity

The three stages of organisational innovation as postulated by Damanpour et al. (2006) are initiation, the decision to adopt, and the implementation of an idea, with the goal of successful innovation adoption. With the absence of any creative ideas, it is challenging for organisations to aim for innovation adoption and decision-making. Therefore, organisational creativity is the key player in the entire process of innovation. With no creative ideas, it is always difficult to differentiate adoption from isomorphism and as a result, the idea implementation may not consider any new idea (Amabile et al., 1996). Rigolizzo and Amabile (2015) indicated the definition of organisational creativity as the formulation of a new idea that is relevant to an organisation. Thus, organisational creativity at the societal level can be distinguished based on the conceptualisation of an idea. As organisational creativity is complex in nature, it is recommended to encourage creativity at the individual level, in the work environment, and in the association between the two. When it comes to the creativity of employees it relates to the novel ideas produced by employees which in turn significantly impacted innovation within an organisation through specific efforts to improve processes, services, and products (Amabile, 2020).

Organisation Performance

In the information system literature, organisational performance is represented as a multifaceted phenomenon. Organisational performance encompasses the actual outcomes achieved by an organisation. The definite outputs can be determined compared to anticipated outcomes, targets, and intentions. The organisational performance includes the financial performance of the organisation considering the ROI and anticipated profits, etc.; returns related to the shareholder such as overall shareholder and economic value added, etc.; and market-related performance concerning the service and product such as annual sales and gained share in the market, etc. (Gavrea, et al., 2011; Kumar & Mishra, 2020).

Theoretical Perspective

The resource-based theory (RBT) is one of the widely used context-based theories applied in the information technology domain supporting organisational resources if controlled appropriately resulting in greater performance (Barney, 2012). The RBT postulates that organisations contend based on resources that offer value-add, are rare, not easy to replicate, and result in profits (Bharadwaj, 2000). As per the strategic management literature and work by Rapheal et al. (1993), a difference was clarified between resources such as specific tradeable resources and represent organisational assets, and non-tradable resources which can be used and deployed within the organisation. Thus, resources and capabilities correspond to the input and output of any process resulting in productivity improvement. Considering the RBT context, it is assumed that organisations can independently develop competencies based on the available resources. As a result, the capabilities of an organisation and its strength is defined based on the resource developed. Therefore, the RBT has been the key context in realising information technology business value and enabling organisations to achieve performance benefits (Sirmon et al., 2011). Hence, the RBT context is more appropriate when considering artificial intelligence resources to generate profits for an organisation (Mikalef et al., 2021).

Hypotheses Development and Conceptual Framework

AI adoption is not motivated by the desire to reduce costs, but instead by the yearning to improve product, service, and quality. These developments are associated with enhanced organisational performance. As AI become increasingly used by firms as the next mechanism of innovation and growth, its effects on firm practices and performance have become a subject of growing importance (Mikalef et al., 2021).

- H1: *Organisational performance is substantially influenced by AI Capability.*

Fostering creativity can help boost organisational performance. Creativity allows entities to develop innovative designs and challenge norms or old-fashioned ways of thinking. These activities can help organisations create products, services, and other offerings that differentiate themselves from the market. Today's businesses often confront changing environments. As a result, professionals need to assess new circumstances quickly and expand on approaches to navigate through (Mikalef et al., 2021). Hence combining the effect of both key frameworks is even more important to gauge the impact of AI and organisational creativity on overall performance. A combination of moderation effect is a thoughtful approach in analysing as stated in the hypothesis below.

- H2: *Organisational Creativity does have a significant influence on organisational performance.*
- H3: *Organisational Creativity does have moderation effects between Artificial Intelligence capability and Organisational performance.*

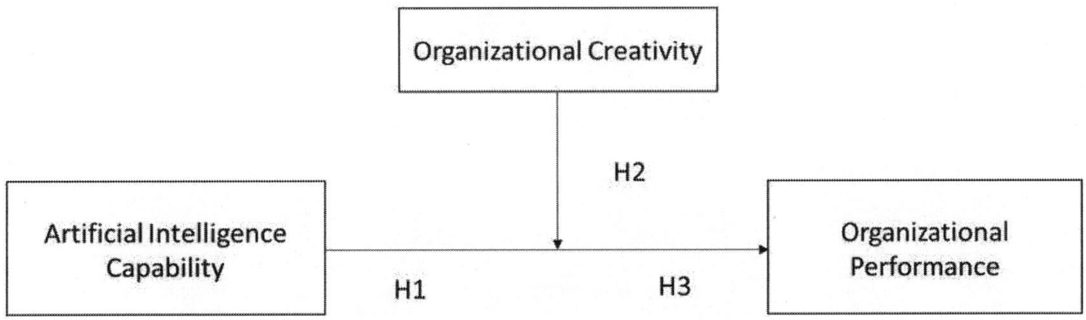

Fig. 1: Conceptual Framework
Source: Author (Mikalef & Gupta, 2021)

Research Design/Methodology

Sampling

For hypotheses analysis, a sample size of 125 data is collected. To examine the effects of Organisational creativity and AI capability on organisational performance, the IT/ITES organisations were chosen for the study. In total, approximately three hundred respondents were emailed to answer a web-based survey questionnaire. All responses were cautiously verified during the data cleaning and analysis considering the participants from the targeted organisations (Hair, 2011). The rate of response or this survey was 26.8 per cent. No significant differences (alpha 5 per cent) between initial and later responses were observed. Respondents at various positions/roles were contacted to reduce the bias risk as per the common-method variance (Podsakoff et al., 2003) to assess the study variables.

Sample and Respondents' Characteristics

Figure 2 shows the sample characteristics. Most of the participants are from a firm size of more than 250 employees and belong to the Senior Manager (IT) role considering 1 to 2 years of overall AI Experience in IT/ITES organisations.

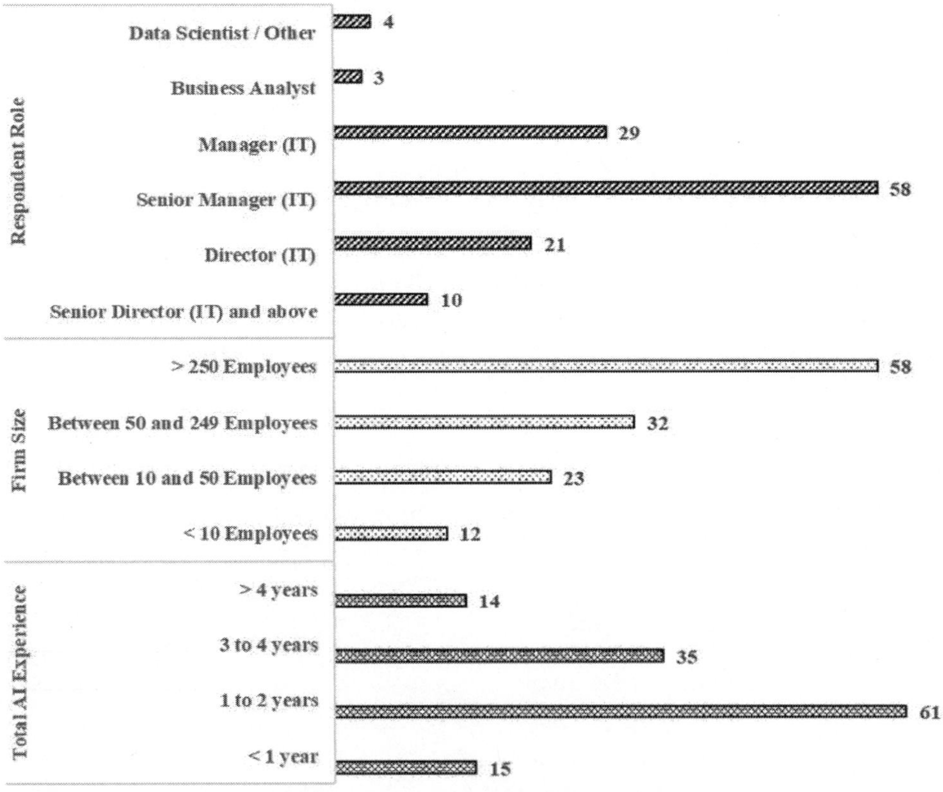

Fig. 2: Sample Characteristics
Source: Author's Compilation

Measures

The study variables were based on multiple-item scales referred from information system literature and the latest studies performed. Some of the scales were re-worded and adapted to fit into the scope of the study. Three domain experts from the sample organisation were asked to evaluate measures based on a five-point Likert scale, and by averaging the items each study variable was made (Hair, 2011), and a pilot test was carried out to validate the appropriate meaning to the respondent (Nunnally, 1978). All item scales' validity was verified by applying PCFA, followed by CFA. The PCFA was accomplished to examine all items loaded in one factor. Cronbach's alpha (α) appropriate values were found to be greater than 0.7 for the scale reliability. A confirmatory factor analysis (CFA) was carried out for measurement model validation. The measurement model is considered satisfactory at CMIN/DF = 2.837, CFI = 0.924, RMSEA = 0.069, and SRMR = 0.031 (Guide & Ketokivi , 2015; Hu & Bentler, 1999).

Study Variables

The independent variable *Artificial Intelligence Capability* is measured using an 8-item scale (α = 0.798) developed by Mikalef and Gupta (2021). The dependent variable *Organisational Performance* is measured using a 5-item scale (α = 0.875) developed by Lee and Choi (2003). The moderating variable of *Organisational Creativity* is measured using five items (α = 0.882), conceptually based on work by Scheibe and Gupta (2017). The control variable used in the study is ***Firm size*** is one of the significant bases of organisational performance and is measured with items adapted as Mikalef and Gupta (2021) and captured by the natural logarithm of the mean value of the number of employees.

Research Findings

This research adds value to practices and information systems literature by examining the moderation effect of organisational creativity on artificial intelligence capability and organisational performance in IT/ITES organisations.

Descriptive Statistics

Table 1 represents the descriptive statistics including the correlation between variables.

Table 1

		Variables	0	1	2
		Mean	3.574	3.152	3.043
		Std. Dev.	1.153	1.318	1.233
		Reliability	0.875	0.798	0.882
Kendall's tan_b	0	Organizational Performance	1		
	1	AI Capability	.663***	1	
	2	Organizational Creativity	.445***	.324***	1
Spearman's rho	0	Organizational Performance	1		
	1	AI Capability	.738***	1	
	2	Organizational Creativity	.577***	.419***	1

*** Correlation is significant at the 0.011 level (2 tailed)

Source: Author's Compilation

Moderation Analysis with the Ordinal Regression Analysis

In the present research paper, the relationship between ordinal outcome variables i.e., organisational performance, artificial intelligence capability, and organisational creativity is being created. The study variables were measured on an ordinal, categorical, and five-point Likert scale. It was not possible to assume the homogeneity of variance and normality for the ordinal categorical outcomes. The ordinal regression method was preferred because it does not assume constant variance and normality but needs the assumption of parallel lines throughout all levels of the categorical outcome (Tiwari et al., 2021; Norusis, 2008). Diagnostic tests were performed before performing the regression analysis to determine any assumption violation. No variables were found with any missing values. Also, the data analysis using ordinal regression was performed using the SPSS tool.

Table 2 depicts the outcomes of the ordinal regression analysis. To measure the direct effects of the independent variable on organisational performance, Model 1 introduced artificial intelligence capability (B = .838, $p < 0.001$) along with the control variable, i.e. firm size (B = .121, $p < 0.001$). Model 1 shows the significant direct impacts of artificial intelligence capability on organisational performance and explained 50.2 per cent of the variation as per the Cox and Snell pseudo-R^2. The moderating variable organisation creativity (B = .312, $p < 0.001$) is included in Model 2 along with the independent variable artificial intelligence capability (B = .568; $p < 0.001$). As per Cox and Snell pseudo-R^2, the variables in Model 2 described 59.7 per cent of the variation of organisational performance. Model 3 introduced the interaction between artificial intelligence (B = .245, $p < 0.001$) and organisational creativity (B = .178, $p < 0.001$).

Table 2: Ordinal Regression Analysis

	Organizational Performance					
Variables	*Model 1*		*Model 2*		*Model 3*	
Control Variable						
Firm Size	0.121***	0.032	0.09***	0.002	0.005***	0.013
Independent Variable						
AI Capability	0.838***	0.016	0.568***	0.017	0.245***	0.089
Moderating Variable						
Organizational Creativity	0.312***	0.034	0.178***	0.076		
Interaction						
AI Capability* Organizational Creativity					0.313***	0.086
-2 log likelihood	447.768		472.771		472.771	
Likelihood ratio (Chi-Square)	87.256***		113.636***		125.283***	
Pesudo R^2 Cox and Snell	0.502		0.597		0.633	

Notes: N = 125; Unstandardized regression coefficients and standard errors are shown; ***Significance at 0.001 level (2-tailed).

Source: Author's Compilation

Model 3 described a 63.3 per cent variation in organisational performance as per Cox and Snell pseudo-R^2. Model 3 showed the variation inflation factor (VIF) as 2.15.

Discussion

This study addresses the research gaps and supports the notion that organizational performance is impacted by organisational creativity and artificial intelligence capability, and it is supported by the study findings. The strong technological capability in terms of artificial intelligence helps in achieving business value and long-term benefits and it is in line with the resource-based theory and offers significant insights into IT business value-related studies. The research outcomes help in understanding the resources that require effective leveraging of advanced technology results in realising overall performance benefits to an organisation. As a result, organisations should cultivate the use of AI-related technologies more operationally. Organisational creativity has become a 'must-have' in any organisation's highly competitive and global environment. Creativity helps to keep work and businesses updated with new concepts and continuous improvements considering the new products or services by modernising organisational efficiency and productiveness. Consequently, organisations need additional resources to leverage AI investments based on a contingent perspective. Hence, H1 and H2 are accepted.

Organisations that continuously focus on developing AI capability help in focusing on organisation-based key performance indicators. In the present study, the extent of organisational creativity and artificial intelligence is assessed in terms of the moderation effect and found to positively influence organisational performance. The research outcomes reveal that IT/ITES organisations are focusing on resources and technological advancement to deliver significant business outcomes. The research findings also indicate that AI capabilities have a positive contribution towards organisational-based creative processes in terms of enhancement of knowledge as well as innovation-based outcomes. It also indicates that the organisations are pursuing ambidextrous strategies to deploy business solutions and help in developing new capabilities. Hence, H3 is accepted.

Conclusion and Implications

This research work combines insights on tangible, intangible, and human skills as a source of strategic organisational performance management and creativity to examine how moderating effect can facilitate creativity and performance by considering the resource-based theory (RBT), thus boosting organisational performance. This paper contributes by delineating the mechanisms through which capabilities influence key organisational performance, thus better refining the creativity and performance relationship. In today's dynamic economic reality, these conclusions can help organisations improve overall organisational performance and hence that of their resources along with tapping into the subtler aspects of intelligence and creativity. A major focus on organisational creativity depicts that it unblocks old patterns of organisational settings, allowing non-linear thinking. Empowering employees with creative insights and implementation at work can positively impact the firm's performance. It would result in utilising the resources proficiently, and effectively to maximise the firm overall performance. However, employees may be hesitant in contributing their ideas or do not take them seriously towards their progress. A suitable system is required by many organisations to let employees express their creativity by having organisational support and enhancing the same. Hence, this study adds value to the present body of information system research by considering the context of AI-related resources resulting in higher business value and related investments.

Limitations and Future Recommendations

The limitation of this paper is that the outcomes presented cannot be generalised to the wider population as the study is conducted on the cross-sectional view of IT/ITES organisations. First, while the study is based on the types of resources used by any organisation in deploying AI-related programmes, it is also expected that a few organisations may consider other factors such as industry-specific, different geographies and types of AI applications and related operations. Thus, future research can assess other contingent factors. Secondly, organisations use different strategic planning processes to deploy AI-related business solutions to invest in long-term gains. In doing so, organisations face various challenges considering the different stakeholders and policies involved. Thus, future studies can perform qualitative research to unfold the issues in achieving IT business value.

References

[1] Ågerfalk, P.J. (2020). Artificial intelligence as digital agency. *European Journal of Information Systems*, *29*(1), 1–8.

[2] Amabile, T.M. (2020). Creativity, artificial intelligence, and a world of surprises. *Academy of Management Discoveries*, *6*(3), 351–54.

[3] Barney, J.B. (2012). Purchasing, supply chain management and sustained competitive advantage: The relevance of resource-based theory. *Journal of Supply Chain Management*, *48*(2), 3–6.

[4] Bharadwaj, A.S. (2000). A resource-based perspective on information technology capability and firm performance: An empirical investigation. *MIS* quarterly, 169–96.

[5] Brynjolfsson, E., Rock, D., Syverson, C. (2018). Artificial intelligence and the modern productivity paradox: a clash of expectations and statistics. *The Economics of Artificial Intelligence: An Agenda*, University of Chicago Press.

[6] Amabile, T.M., Conti, R., Coon, H., Lazenby, J., & Herron, M. (1996). Assessing the work environment for creativity. *Academy of Management Journal*, *39*(5), 1154–184.

[7] Conboy, K., Mikalef, P., Dennehy, D., & Krogstie, J. (2020). Using business analytics to enhance dynamic capabilities in operations research: A case analysis and research agenda. *European Journal of Operational Research*, *281*(3), 656–72.

[8] Davenport, T.H., & Ronanki, R. (2018). Artificial intelligence for the real world. *Harvard Business Review*, *96*(1), 108–16.

[9] Damanpour, F., & Schneider, M. (2006). Phases of the adoption of innovation in organisations: effects of environment, organisation and top managers. *British Journal of Management, 17*(3), 215–36.

[10] Dwivedi, Y.K., Hughes, L., Ismagilova, E., Aarts, G., Coombs, C., Crick, T., ... & Williams, M.D. (2021). Artificial Intelligence (AI): Multidisciplinary perspectives on emerging challenges, opportunities, and agenda for research, practice and policy. *International Journal of Information Management, 57*, 101994.

[11] Fountaine, T., McCarthy, B., & Saleh, T. (2019). Building the AI-powered organisation. *Harvard Business Review*, 97(4), 62–73.

[12] Gavrea, C., Ilies, L., & Stegerean, R. (2011). Determinants of organisational performance: The case of Romania. *Management & Marketing*, *6*(2), 50–57.

[13] Grant, R.M. (1991). The resource-based theory of competitive advantage: Implications for strategy formulation. *California Management Review, 33*(3), 114–35.

[14] Guide, V.D.R., & Ketokivi, M. (2015). Notes from the Editors: Redefining some methodological criteria for the journal. *Journal of Operations Management*, (37), v–viii.

[15] Gupta, M., & George, J.F. (2016). Toward the development of a big data analytics capability. *Information & Management, 53*(8), 1049–064.

[16] Hair, J.F. (2011). Multivariate data analysis: An overview. *International Encyclopedia of Statistical Science*, 904–07.

[17] Hu, L. T., & Bentler, P. M. (1999). Cutoff criteria for fit indexes in covariance structure analysis: Conventional criteria versus new alternatives. *Structural Equation Modeling: Aa Multidisciplinary Journal*, 6(1), 1–55.

[18] Kohli, R., & Grover, V. (2008). Business value of IT: An essay on expanding research directions to keep up with the times. *Journal of the Association for Information Systems, 9*(1), 1.

[19] Kumar, R., & Mishra, R.S. (2020). Linking TQM Critical Success Factors to strategic goal: Impact on Organisational Performance. *IOSR Journal of Mechanical and Civil Engineering, 17*(3), 1–13.

[20] Lee, H., & Choi, B. (2003). Knowledge management enablers, processes, and organisational performance: An integrative view and empirical examination. *Journal of Management Information Systems*, 20(1), 179–228.

[21] Mikalef, P., Fjørtoft, S. O., & Torvatn, H. Y. (2019). Artificial Intelligence in the public sector: a study of challenges and opportunities for Norwegian municipalities. In *Conference on e-Business, e-Services and e-Society*. Springer, Cham. 267–77.

[22] Mikalef, P., & Gupta, M. (2021). Artificial intelligence capability: Conceptualisation, measurement calibration, and empirical study on its impact on organisational creativity and firm performance. *Information & Management*, 58(3), 103434.

[23] Norušis, M.J. (2008). *SPSS statistics 17.0: Statistical Procedures Companion*. Prentice Hall/ Pearson Education.

[24] Nunnally, J.C. (1973). *Research Strategies and Measurement Methods for Investigating Human Development.*

[25] Podsakoff, P.M., MacKenzie, S.B., Lee, J.Y., & Podsakoff, N.P. (2003). Common method biases in behavioural research: a critical review of the literature and recommended remedies. *Journal of Applied Psychology*, 88(5), 879.

[26] Priem, R.L., & Butler, J.E. (2001). Is the resource-based 'view' a useful perspective for strategic management research?. *Academy of Management Review, 26*(1), 22–40.

[27] Ransbotham, S., Khodabandeh, S., Fehling, R., LaFountain, B., & Kiron, D. (2019). Winning with AI. *MIT Sloan Management Review, 61180.*

[28] Raphael, A., & Schoemaker, P.J. (1993). Strategic assets and organisational rent. *Strategic Management Journal,* 14(1), 33.

[29] Rigolizzo, M., & Amabile, T. (2015). Entrepreneurial creativity: The role of learning processes and work environment supports. *The Oxford Handbook of Creativity, Innovation and Entrepreneurship*, 61–78.

[30] Rowell-Jones, A., Howard, C. (2019). *CIO Survey: CIOs Have Awoken to the Importance of AI,* Retrieved in December 2022.

[31] Scheibe, K.P., & Gupta, M. (2017). The effect of socialising via computer-mediated communication on the relationship between organisational culture and organisational creativity. *Communications of the Association for Information Systems,* 40(1), 13.

[32] Schryen, G. (2013). Revisiting IS business value research: What we already know, what we still need to know, and how we can get there. *European Journal of Information Systems, 22*(2), 139–69.

[33] Sirmon, D.G., Hitt, M.A., & Ireland, R.D. (2007). Managing firm resources in dynamic environments to create value: Looking inside the black box. *Academy of Management Review, 32*(1), 273–92.

[34] Sirmon, D.G., Hitt, M.A., Ireland, R.D., & Gilbert, B.A. (2011). Resource orchestration to create competitive advantage: Breadth, depth, and life cycle effects. *Journal of management,* 37(5), 1390–1412.

[35] Spector, J.M., & Ma, S. (2019). Inquiry and critical thinking skills for the next generation: From artificial intelligence back to human intelligence. *Smart Learning Environments,* 6(1), 1–11.

[36] Tiwari, P., & Suresha, B. (2021). Moderating role of project innovativeness on project flexibility, project risk, project performance, and business success in financial services. *Global Journal of Flexible Systems Management,* 22(3), 179–96.

[37] Townsend, D.M., & Hunt, R.A. (2019). Entrepreneurial action, creativity, & judgment in the age of artificial intelligence. *Journal of Business Venturing Insights,* 11, e00126.

A Study of Employee Acceptance of Artificial Intelligence in Real Estate Sector: Empirical Evidence from Delhi-NCR

SEEMA SHARMA

Research Scholar, Faculty of Management Studies, Mohanlal Sukhadia University, Udaipur, (Raj) India
E-mail: seemaashish24@gmail.com

Abstract

Purpose: This paper aims to highlight the concept of artificial intelligence (AI), antecedents and consequences of AI adoption by employees in real estate industry.

Design/Methodology/Approach: This descriptive study adopts quantitative approach to understand the adoption of AI in real estate sector of Delhi-NCR. 50 respondents were reached out where 42 were responded. Primary data was collected through self-reported questionnaire which has 5 sections and 26 items and secondary data was collected using different databases.

Findings: This paper suggests that the field of artificial intelligence holds incredible potential as a tool for employees of real estate. Here age and work experience of employees are significant variables in adoption of AI.

Research Limitation: This research is confined to Delhi-NCR so further research can be done to explore other antecedents & dimensions in different geographical areas.

Implications: This paper lays a foundation in emerging area of AI in real estate and ideas expressed herein can be approached by academicians for further study.

Originality/Value: This study has explored new area of AI adoption in Real estate sector and provided knowledge about antecedents and outcomes to help academicians to understand the concept furthermore.

Keywords: *Artificial Intelligence, Digital Transformation, Covid-19, Real Estate Sector, AI Enabled Services, AI Acceptance*

Introduction

New technologies have wreaked havoc on a variety of businesses, with some seeing a greater influence than others. In the real estate industry, technology has significantly altered the selling-purchase process in India. Artificial intelligence (AI) is currently one of the most revolutionary breakthroughs in the property industry. Artificial intelligence (AI) needs to be exposed in order to expand in all areas of real estate, including commercial, residential and retail. AI is unlikely to completely replace real estate intermediaries such as lawyers, agencies and brokers for the time being. Instead, it will give them a more stable and secure base on which to expand their company activities. They can gain a competitive advantage in the industry by having access to predictive models, strategies, and actionable inputs. Despite this, increasing globalisation and digitisation have accelerated the development of new avenues in which AI will definitely hold an important role in the real estate sector in the coming years (Bawack & Desveaud, 2022). In the opinion of Mijwel, (2015) the significance of the real estate market cannot be overstated. It is a major element of an individual's wealth, and it is a separate asset class for professional investors that may be utilised to better diversify their stakes. It is vital to recognise that real estate assets share some similar qualities in order to appropriately analyse market fluctuations and appraise pricing of various properties accessible. Because housing is one of humanity's most fundamental requirements, real estate has always been in great demand in developing cities. According to Kabaivanov & Markovska, (2021) the real estate industry has always been resistant to change, it has been slow to integrate AI into its domain. Many factors, such as availability of the data, transparency, standardisation, organisation, and legal aspects, act as major impediments to technology adoption. Governments, businesses, and other industry participants have identified the potential of AI in recent years and are focusing on digital transformation. According to the Morgan Stanley (2016) Digitisation Index, the real estate sector is not proactive as it is second least digitised industry. Digitalisation will make accurate and near-term predictions in order to boost AI in a variety of industries. Cloud-based analyses are currently limited to property valuation and prediction (Alkhwaldi et al., 2022). However, artificial intelligence will enable the integration of large pipelines of algorithms with valuable social data and much more to provide a more precise and accurate insight into the property market. These will not only help potential buyers find the right property fit, but it will also help brokerage houses and listing agencies gear up the entire business cycle. The emergence of new technology has reshaped India's real estate sector. Construction processes have become more specialised, and access to facilities has vastly improved. Most importantly, it has changed the way customers, agents, and contractors interact with one another. Meanwhile, the Covid-19 outbreak has hastened the adoption of digital solutions at an unprecedented rate. In the light of above mentioned concerns, this study aims:

- To elaborate the concept of Artificial Intelligence, antecedents & consequences of its applications in different areas of real estate industry.
- To examine the awareness and acceptance levels of employees regarding AI enabled services in real estate industry.
- To analyse the influence of demographic variables on awareness, acceptance & performance of employees in real estate sector.
- To study the benefits and challenges faced by employees to implement the AI enabled practices in real estate in India.

This study contributes to better understanding of why employees are adopting AI in real estate sector. It includes discussion about definition, components and stages of AI. The study highlighted that how employees in global & Indian scenario using AI-enabled services in different operations like lead generation, content marketing, property valuation & management. It provides most important antecedents related to AI technology and employee adoption level. A conceptual framework is also suggested by researcher on the basis of SST (self-serving technology) (Chen et al., 2021) & TAM (Technology acceptance model) theoretical models to support quantitative analysis of relationship between different variables.

What is Artificial Intelligence?

John McCarthy, the man known as father of AI, defined it as 'the science and engineering of building intelligent machines, especially intelligent computer programmes.' According to Vijai, (2019) 'The name Artificial Intelligence refers to the Artificial Intelligence which means making the Machines capable of executing intelligent activities and actions like Humans'. Artificial intelligence always uses intelligence to complete automated tasks. Elliott et al., (2021) stated that Artificial intelligence is created by researching how the human brain and how people make decisions and solve problems while attempting to find solutions, then either using the results of the research as the basis for creating intelligence software and systems.

Components and Stages of AI

AI is a vast technology which has two main key components like Automation & Intelligence that also includes a number of sub-concepts like machine learning, vision, expert system, robotics and natural language processing. These technologies are revolutionising and can transform the way of human interaction with data, machines. Along with this, it can make decisions (Fernandez & Gallardo-Gallardo, 2021). Machine learning, machine intelligence and machine consciousness are different Stages of AI technologies. Machine learning's first stage is all about the algorithms that intelligent systems use to learn from their experiences. Machine intelligence, or stage 2, is the application of sophisticated algorithms by machines to learn from experience. This is an illustration of deep neural networks at this stage. Artificial intelligence technology is now at this point. Stage 3—Machine Consciousness—is all about the ability to learn on its own without the aid of external inputs (Cao et al., 2021).

AI in Real Estate Industry

Since the advent of the industrial revolution, the world has seen talents alter in ways that have resulted in continually changing occupations and novel abilities required to keep pace with expanding technology. AI technologies and automation are transforming how people work, particularly in the real estate, finance, and banking industries. Numerous advances have been taken on to help property experts make their positions more effective. Machine learning, Artificial intelligence, robotics, the Internet of Things (IoT), and more are the new technologies that are constantly changing scenario of the real estate industry (Kabaivanov & Markovska, 2021). This section deals with usage of AI in different operations of Real estate sector in the world and in India.

Global Scenario

The use of AI in decision-making by the majority of high-end realtors is having an impact on the global real estate market and the findings are telling. Information management is the main use of AI in the real estate sector. A neural network-based model is used by online real estate marketplaces like Zillow to glean insights from a vast data set and direct feeds from hundreds of multiple listing agencies and brokerages. A mathematical model is used by RENTestimate, an automated valuation tool, and Airbnb's pricing recommendations to predict how likely it is that a guest will book a certain listing, at a range of alternative rates, on a given set of dates. Indian scenario: Artificial intelligence is being used by the Indian real estate sector to address issues with property building and safety. As its predictive RF model serves as a safety signal to highlight problematic construction sites, an Indian environmental conservation organisation called 'Tradecost' uses artificial intelligence for environmental health and safety (Bhardwaj et al., 2020). The safety performance of a project is reported on a monthly basis by the machine learning model. The Indian government established a system in 2008 known as the 'Digital India Land Records Modernization Programme', which ensures irrefutable titles to immovable assets. This programme uses AI and IoT to speed up the procedure. NestAway rental platform uses predictive analysis and AI for recommending properties to customers. In reality 'NObroker' utilises ML algorithms to match tenants and landlords and every transaction makes its self-learning algorithm more powerful. This system has higher accuracy level to predict the rent of a property. More importantly, top 5 Indian real estate companies—NBCC, Prestige Estate, Roustomjee developers, Suntech realty & Oberoi Realty Ltd—are making most of AI applications in their day-to-day working operations. Indeed, AI applications practically have affected every aspect of real estate sector in recent years. Here are few instances that offer a clear picture of how AI is changing face of real estate.

- *Lead Generation:* Real estate agents struggle to generate potential leads for their various listings. They frequently wind up spending several hours on meetings with non-convertible prospects. Based on data collected from website visits, landing pages, and digital advertising, artificial intelligence is used to determine the greatest possible leads.
- *Content Marketing – Virtual Assistant:* AI-powered consumer applications and chatbots are already benefiting e-commerce enterprises. Real estate firms are also making progress in this approach by employing the same technology to provide personalised material directly to prospects. AI-powered chatbots can react to common client inquiries without the need of forceful sales messaging or frantic efforts to get a prospect's contact information. PropertySimple' is an excellent example of a real estate company that employs AI for content marketing. This property social media advertising tool creates eye-catching property adverts for use on various social media sites. The advertising is then shown to the appropriate

prospects using AI technology. It also delivers real-time performance statistics on clicks, views, and demographics as feedback (Pillai & Sivathanu, 2020).

- *Virtual Tour of Property:* Movement was restricted by the COVID-19 pandemic, and the real estate sector was severely impacted. As a result, it had no choice but to use AI technology to continue operating. A recent technical advancement in the real estate sector is virtual tours. Clients can enjoy 3D views of homes without ever visiting them thanks to AI-powered technologies. It has features including a zoom-in tool, spoken notes, and a panoramic view. This is useful, especially for houses that are still under construction or those that are located overseas. Regular meetings between landlords and tenants are also possible without face-to-face encounters.
- *Property Valuation and Recommendation*: Conducting an existing property appraisal and estimating its future market worth is a difficult task. The price is affected by several variables and might vary at any time. As a result, a realtor may be unable to keep track of all the minor details. This is where AI in real estate comes in handy. The greater the amount of information that real estate brokers can provide to potential clients, the more likely it is that agreements will be closed. AI technologies can assist real estate agencies in giving a client accurate, comprehensive information about a home. AI in real estate can help businesses determine the ideal moment to buy or sell a property as well as project future sale or rental pricing. In order to determine a reasonable pricing range, it can also use a regression technique that takes into account property characteristics like size, age, the number of rooms, and house furnishings. By focusing their search on a smaller set of essential criteria, AI in real estate can assist clients in making the right decisions.
- *Property Management:* It takes a lot of work to manage rental properties. There are many steps in the process, including creating lease agreements, dealing with rental applications and transactions, and producing disclosure statements. AI technologies have the potential to streamline property management in a variety of ways. One of them allows realtors to focus on other tasks by automatically creating documents. AI may also analyse real estate documents for mistakes like missing signatures, blank fields, etc. Chatbots and AI assistants can help property managers, landlords, and tenants communicate better. The chatbots can accurately respond to frequently asked queries from tenants and can automatically deliver alarms and utility bills. The accounting work can be handled by AI. It allows for the tracking of rental transactions as well as payables and receivables. It can also be used to amend tax payments.

AI-enabled Services in Real Estate

AI technology plays different roles in service encounter like supporter, augmenter and task performer. In **AI-Supporter** role, technology assists the front line employee by providing required information related to task and decision making (Malali & Gopalakrishnan, 2020). AI works behind the scene while frontline employees directly interact with customers. For example 'InnerEye' an AI system to help oncologists recognise tumours vs. healthy tissues. Second category is **AI as augmenter**, where AI works directly with both frontline employees and end users at a time. Robot-assisted surgery and real time language translation are few examples of this kind of service encounter. The third service encounter includes **AI-performed** task where artificial intelligence directly work with end customer. In these cases AI substitutes completely the front line employees and performs brand new services that frontline employees were never ever capable of performing like autonomous cars, etc.

Employee Acceptance of AI Technology in the Real Estate Sector

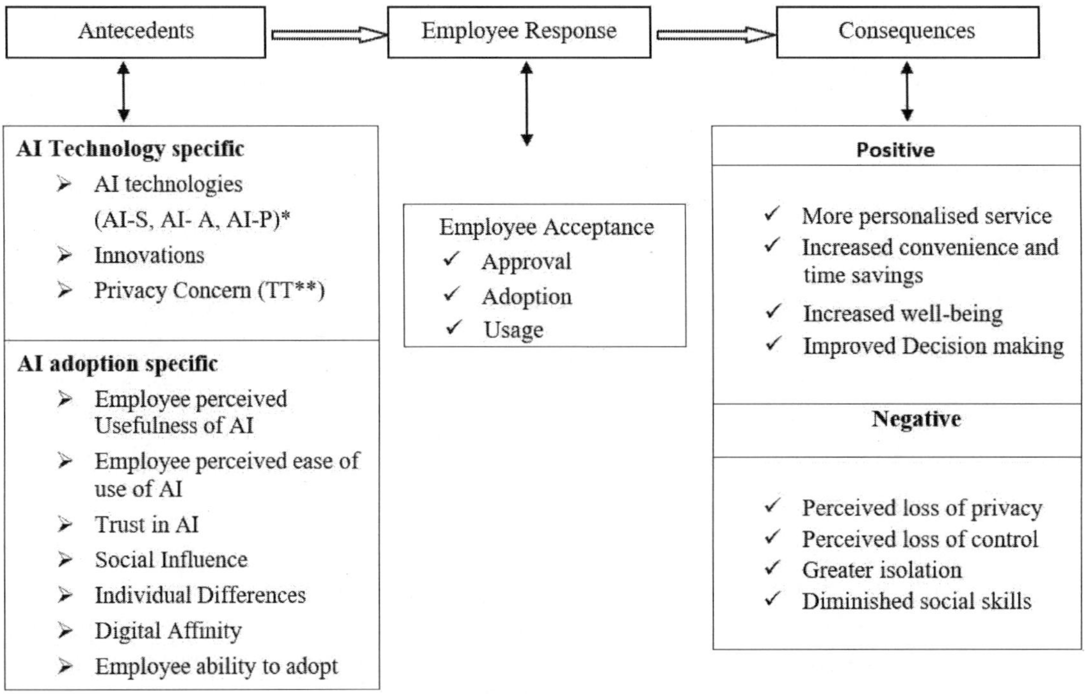

Fig. 1: AI Acceptance in Real Estate
Source: Researcher's own creation.
Note: *AI-S = AI-Supporter, AI-A = AI-Augmenter, AI-P = AI-Performer;
**TT = Technology Threats like privacy concerns

In this study, the main focus of the researcher is on exploring, understanding and explaining employee acceptance of artificial intelligence in real States sector. To fullfil this objective the researchers identified the antecedents, employee responses and consequences of adopting artificial intelligence technology. These antecedents, employee responses and consequences are shown is the Figure 1. The brief overview of framework is also given by researcher here. On the left side of figure 1, the proposed theoretical antecedents of AI acceptance are shown. Previous studies have empirically investigated the antecedents of self serving Technology adoption (Meuter et al. 2005), and researcher included the key variables from this theoretical framework in her model in this study. Meuter et al. demonstrated that employee adoption of artificial intelligence is influenced by motivation, role clarity, and employee's ability to use the technology. As shown in the Figure 1, the adoption of artificial intelligence in real estate sector is influenced by AI Technology specific antecedents and human specific antecedents which include a number of variables. In the Figure 1, researcher also highlighted the potential consequences of adopting this technology like increased convenience and time savings, improved decision making, etc. A detailed discussion on antecedents and consequences is given in the next section below.

Antecedents and Consequences of AI Adoption in Real Estate Sector

This section deals with detailed description of each antecedent related to AI Technology and its adoption by employees. AI Technology specific antecedents are AI enable services, innovations and threats of new technology. In previous section AI-enabled services have described in detail so in this section, we will discuss only remaining antecedents, i.e. innovation, privacy concerns and employee related variables.

AI Technology Specific Antecedents

- *Innovation:* In terms of relative advantage, complexity, perceived risk, and compatibility, the employees evaluate the innovation features of technology that influence the decision to try and embrace new technology (Gillani et al., 2020). Employees evaluate if new technology aligns with their lifestyle and values. If the technology improves their way of life and is in line with their ideals, they could be inclined to adopt it. Juma (2016) and several research have demonstrated that when new technologies are viewed as a danger to or a replacement for people, they are more likely to be rejected.
- *Privacy Concern:* Perceived risk is another characteristic which places an important role in employee acceptance of new technology. Employees will evaluate the potential risk to benefit ratio of using in AI-based technology and if the technology is having more privacy concerns, it will increase perceived risk and create a potential barrier to its adoption.

Adoption/Employee Specific Antecedents

- *Perceived Usefulness:* Perceived usefulness is the degree to which employees believe using a particular technology or system will improve their performance of a specific task. This antecedent is explained by Technology acceptance model (TAM).
- *Perceived Ease of Use:* It means simplicity of operations or it's a degree to which employees believe that using a particular system is easy. The functioning of system is easy to understand & complexity level is very low for the same.
- *Trust:* This antecedent is explained in UTAUT (Universal theory of technology acceptance & usefulness) modal where it defined as psychological state of accepting

to be vulnerable to the other entity. In simple words trust is an extent to which employees believe that new technology or AI is reliable and credible and it will not affect vulnerability negatively.

- *Social Influence:* In previous studies social influence is mostly explained using UTAUT model where it directly affects the adoption of AI by group of employees in the organisations.
- *Individual Differences:* Meuter et al. (200) suggested in their framework that personal characteristics of employees like, need for interaction, technology anxiety, inertia & prior experience with self serving technology and other demographic characteristics influence the adaptation of AI in service sector.
- *Digital Affinity:* Peter et al. (2021) defined the digital affinity as the degree to which human has pleasure, interest, attraction in learning & using digital technologies.
- *Employee Ability to Adopt:* Within the SST framework, ability referred to potential of employee to perform the steps involved in the interaction with AI technology. It also depends on technological factors like convenience, efficiency, speed of service to get motivation to adopt AI.

Consequences

It is universally true that every technology has both positive and negative outcomes. The extent and scale of outcomes depends on decisions regarding rules and regulation related to AI adoption in organisation. In the following paragraph, potential outcomes both positive and negative are being discussed resulting from adoption of AI by employees in real estate sector.

- *Positive outcomes*
  - *More personalised service:* One of the key positive outcomes of AI enabled services adoption by employees in real estate is providing more specialised services to customers. Through AI enabled services employees can analyse the customer's preferences, pattern for property search and accordingly can provide property recommendations to them.
  - *Increased convenience and time savings:* AI-enabled services in real estate like voice assistant, virtual tour of property, lead generation, property valuation and recommendations are the tasks which employee can do with more ease and quickness. AI is proving itself a great help by increasing convenience & saving time to employees as it is performing all these tedious jobs in less time with more ease.
  - *Increased well-being:* The above mentioned positive outcomes contribute to increase the wellbeing of employees because AI applications are providing more personalised service and increased convenience and saving the time for employee. These positive outcomes lead to improved performance, more efficiency & satisfaction to employees which ultimately increasing wellbeing of employee.

   - *Improved Decision making:* With the help of plenty of data, trend analysis and valuable insights by AI applications to employees, their decision making is improving every day. In real estate, now employees are having data on property inventory, information about customer preferences and buying pattern, data related to industry trends at a time which make them well informed and better decision makers.
- *Negative Consequences*
   - *Perceived loss of control:* Along with many positive outcomes AI technology applications in real estate sector also has some negative consequences like employees are developing perception about loss of control. AI can handle big data, can analyse customer preference and trends and can give recommendations accordingly. In this way employees are developing perceived loss of control (Saßmannshausen et al., 2021).
   - *Diminished social skills:* Increasing use of technology resulting in diminishing the social kills of people which is a great cause of concern nowadays. In real estate employees and customers are interacting through technology, spending more time with technology than personal face to face interaction with each other. Covid-19 has faster the process of diminishing the social interaction.
   - *Greater isolation:* AI voice assistant and other applications are performing many day to day tasks in our lives nowadays. AI assistant is helping in searching property and also proving recommendations which leads to greater isolation at customer's part because customer is not needed to ask other for their suggestions & guidance. At employees part it is also increasing isolation in terms of less interaction with colleagues & with customers as well as.

Conceptual Framework and Hypothesis Development

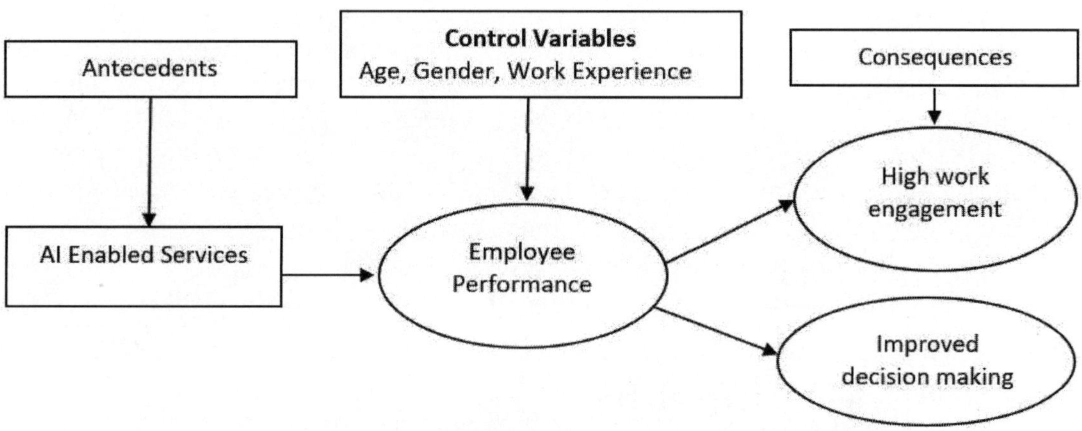

Fig. 2: Conceptual Framework of AI Adoption in Real Estate

To achieve the research goals, a conceptual model was developed by researcher which includes potential antecedents of AI enabled services adoption by real estate employees and its consequences. The framework includes control variables and effect of these variables on employee performance. As the technology is in initial phase of technology life cycles as real estate sector is just started using it in its operations so positive consequences highlighted more prominently in results.

Hypothesis

To identify the effect of gender on awareness, acceptance and performance following assumptions were made:

- H1a: There is a significance association between gender & acceptance level.
- H1b: There is a significance association between gender & employee performance.
- To analyse the association of age and work experience with awareness, acceptance & performance level of employees following assumptions were made-
- H2a: There is a significance association between age & acceptance level
- H2b: There is a significance association between age & performance of employee.
- H3a : There is a significance association between work experience & acceptance level
- H3b : There is a significance association between work experience & performance

Following assumptions were developed to analyse the association between acceptance level of employees and their performance level:

- H4: There is a significance association between acceptance and performance.

Methodology

In this descriptive study, quantitative approach is being used to achieve the research goals. Area of study was Delhi-NCR & employees working in real estate sector were study population. Purposive quota sampling method is used for selecting the sample. 50 employees were approached and 42 were responded. For primary data collection self reported questionnaire was used which has 5 sections and 26 items related to AI acceptance by employee and effect on their performance. Secondary data was collected through different database like Google Scholar, Research gate, ProQuest, EBSCO, Web of Science, JSTOR, Science Direct (Elsevier), Springer Link, Wiley Online Library, Taylor & Francis Online. Mendeley, MS Excel, IBM SPSS v26.0 software were used for data analysis and reference management. Different statistical techniques were used for data analysis like reliability analysis was done using Cronbach's alpha test, Normality test, Descriptive analysis using frequency and mean, Inferential statistic analysis was done using nonparametric tests-Mann Whitney U test and Kruskal-Wallis 1-way ANOVA.

Data Analysis and Interpretation

To analyse the data, preliminary, descriptive and inferential analysis was done. For preliminary analysis reliability, normality, Skewness, kurtosis & homoscedasticity were analysed. The composite reliability Cronbach's Alpha value is .893 which is greater than

.60 threshold value set by Cronbach & Sapiro 1982. This means constructs have a good reliability.

Table 1: Individual Reliability of Study Contracts

S. No.	*Constructs*	*No. of Items*	*Reliability (α)*
1	AI enabled services	3	.762
2	Perceived Awareness level of employees regarding AI enabled services in real estate	7	.784
3	Perceived acceptance level of employees regarding AI enabled services in real estate	8	.922
4	Outcome of AI enabled services on performance of employees in real estate (work engagement and decision making)	8	.867

For testing normality of data, Shapiro-Wilk test values are used which were (.008, .000, .001) for awareness, acceptance and performance that denotes data is not normally distributed. Mean & Standard deviation measures were calculated for descriptive analysis & values revealed that data is not normally distributed.

Table 2: Demographics of Respondents

Demographics	*Characteristics*	*Frequency*	*Percentage %*
Age	21–30 years	16	38.1
	31–40 years	26	61.9
	41–50 years	0	0
	Above 50 years	0	0
Gender	Male	38	90.5
	Female	4	9.5
Work Experience	> 5 years	0	0
	5–10 years	8	52.4
	10–15 years	8	19.0
	15–20 years	22	18. 6

For inferential analysis, as the data was not normally distributed, SPSS automatically used Mann-Whitney U test & the Kruskal-Wallis 1-way ANOVA nonparametric tests to test the hypotheses. Hypothesis testing results are shown in Table 3.

Table 3: Hypothesis Testing

S. No.	*Hypothesis Statement*	*Test*	*Sig*	*Result*	*Decision*
	There is a significance association between gender & acceptance level	Independent samples Mann-Whitney U test	.249	Retain the null hypothesis	No significance association
2	There is a significance association between gender & performance	Independent samples Mann-Whitney U test	.075	Retain the null hypothesis	No significance association

S. No.	*Hypothesis Statement*	*Test*	*Sig*	*Result*	*Decision*
3	There is a significance association between age & acceptance level	MW Utest	.012	Reject the null hypothesis	Significant association
4.	There is a significance association between age & performance	MW U test	.645	Retain the null hypothesis	No significance association
5	There is a significance association between work experience & acceptance level	Independent samples Kruskal Wallis test	.019	Reject the null hypothesis	Significant association
6	There is a significance association between work experience & performance	KW test	.000	Reject the null hypothesis	Significant association
7	There is a significance association between acceptance & performance	KW test	.001	Reject the null hypothesis	Significance association

As depicted in Table 3, some associations were showing significant P values which mean the variables were significantly associated with each other. For instance age is significantly associated with acceptance levels of employees. Likewise, work experience is having positive effect on acceptance level of employees for AI-enabled services. Work experience and their acceptance level have significant association with performance of employees.

Findings, Suggestions and Limitations

The key findings are gender is not having any effect on study constructs but Age is significantly associated with acceptance level of employees regarding AI enabled services in real estate sector. Work experience of employees is significantly associated with all three constructs, i.e. awareness, acceptance and performance of employees in real estate. Awareness about AI applications is significantly associated to acceptance level & performance of employees in real Estate organisations. Acceptance level is significantly associated to performance of employees with special regard to decision making and work engagement in real estate sector.

After the data analysis and interpretation it is suggested that the field of artificial intelligence holds incredible potential as a tool for employees of real estate to imagine and create a new industry. Managers must work towards eliminating the barriers which make AI focused practices less effective. As the study shown that most of the employees are facing technical challenges to adopt the technology in day-to-day work life so management should impart the training for proper use of AI. Study also revealed that most of the employees are using basic AI applications to limited extent so management should facilitate implementations of advance AI applications in more operations.

Limitations and Implications

This study is confined to Delhi-NCR geographical area. In this study the initial analysis is done about the associations between demographical variables and study constructs. Thus further study can be done to find out degree of association among different variables using correlation, regression analysis, and moderation and mediation analysis. This paper lays a foundation in emerging area of AI in real estate and ideas expressed herein can be approached by academicians for further study. The conceptual framework given by researcher can be use as basis for applying recent theoretical models like TOE, TOP, TTF for extended analysis.

Conclusion and Future Prospects

On the basis of discussion thus far, it is clear that Real estate organisations in Delhi-NCR are significantly adopting AI-enabled services in Lead Generation, Content marketing-Virtual assistant, Virtual Tour of Property, Property Valuation & Recommendation, and Property Management. Efficient adoption of these relevant technologies will provide competitive advantages to them. As increasing globalisation and digitalisation have accelerated the development of new avenues, so AI will definitely perform an important role in the real estate sector in the coming years. And managers should formulate & develop strategy for better digital inclusion in coming future.

References

[1] Alkhwaldi, A. F., Alobidyeen, B., Abdulmuhsin, A. A., & Al-Okaily, M. (2022). Investigating the antecedents of HRIS adoption in public sector organisations: integration of UTAUT and TTF. *International Journal of Organisational Analysis, September*. https://doi.org/10.1108/IJOA-04-2022-3228

[2] AlSheibani, S., Cheung, Y., & Messom, C. (2020). Re-thinking the competitive landscape of artificial intelligence. *Proceedings of the Annual Hawaii International Conference on System Sciences, 2020-January*, 5861–5870. https://doi.org/10.24251/hicss.2020.718

[3] Bawack, R., & Desveaud, K. (2022). Consumer Adoption of Artificial Intelligence: A Review of Theories and Antecedents. *Proceedings of the 55th Hawaii International Conference on System Sciences, 7*, 4306–4315. https://doi.org/10.24251/hicss.2022.526

[4] Bhardwaj, G., Singh, S.V., & Kumar, V. (2020). An Empirical Study Of Artificial Intelligence and its Impact on Human Resource Functions. *2020 International Conference on Computation, Automation and Knowledge Management (ICCAKM), April*, 47–51. https://doi.org/10.1109/ICCAKM46823.2020.9051544

[5] Cao, G., Duan, Y., Edwards, J.S., & Dwivedi, Y.K. (2021). Understanding managers' attitudes and behavioral intentions towards using artificial intelligence for organisational decision-making. *Technovation, 106*. https://doi.org/10.1016/j.technovation.2021.102312

[6] Chen, H., Li, L., & Chen, Y. (2021). Explore success factors that impact artificial intelligence adoption on telecom industry in China. *Journal of Management Analytics, 8*(1), 36–68. https://doi.org/10.1080/23270012.2020.1852895

[7] Chaphalkar, N.B., & Sandbhor, S. (2013). Use of artificial intelligence in real property valuation. *International Journal of Engineering and Technology*, *5*(3), 2334–337.

[8] Chiu, T.K.F. (2021). A Holistic Approach to the Design of Artificial Intelligence (AI) Education for K-12 Schools. In *TechTrends* (Issue July). https://doi.org/10.1007/s11528-021-00637-1

[9] Elliott, K., Price, R., Shaw, P., Spiliotopoulos, T., Ng, M., Coopamootoo, K., & van Moorsel, A. (2021). Towards an Equitable Digital Society: Artificial Intelligence (AI) and Corporate Digital Responsibility (CDR). *Society*, *58*(3), 179–188. https://doi.org/10.1007/s12115-021-00594-8

[10] Fernandez, V., & Gallardo-Gallardo, E. (2021). Tackling the HR digitalisation challenge: key factors and barriers to HR analytics adoption. *Competitiveness Review*, *31*(1), 162–187. https://doi.org/10.1108/CR-12-2019-0163

[11] Gillani, F., Chatha, K.A., Sadiq Jajja, M.S., & Farooq, S. (2020). Implementation of digital manufacturing technologies: Antecedents and consequences. *International Journal of Production Economics*, *229*, 107748. https://doi.org/10.1016/j.ijpe.2020.107748

[12] Kabaivanov, S., & Markovska, V. (2021). Artificial intelligence in real estate market analysis. *AIP Conference Proceedings*, *2333*(March). https://doi.org/10.1063/5.0041806

[13] Malali, A.B., & Gopalakrishnan, S. (2020). Application of Artificial Intelligence and Its Powered Technologies in the Indian Banking and Financial Industry Application of Artificial Intelligence and Its Powered Technologies in the Indian Banking and Financial Industry: An Overview. *IOSR Journal of Humanities and Social Science (IOSR-JHSS)*, *25*(6), 55–60. https://doi.org/10.9790/0837-2504065560

[14] Mijwel, M.M. (2015). History of Artificial Intelligence Yapay Zekânın T arihi. *Computer Science*, *April 2015*, 3–4. https://doi.org/10.13140/RG.2.2.16418.15046

[15] Meuter, M.L., Bitner, M.J., Ostrom, A.L., & Brown, S.W. (2005). Choosing among alternative service delivery modes: An investigation of customer trial of self-service technologies. *Journal of Marketing*, *69*(2), 61–83.

[16] Meuter, M. L., Ostrom, A. L., Roundtree, R. I., & Bitner, M. J. (2000). Self-service technologies: Understanding customer satisfaction with technology-based service encounters. *Journal of Marketing*, *64*(3), 50—64.

[17] Pillai, R., & Sivathanu, B. (2020). Adoption of artificial intelligence (AI) for talent acquisition in IT/ITeS organisations. *Benchmarking*, *27*(9), 2599–2629. https://doi.org/10.1108/BIJ-04-2020-0186

[18] Saßmannshausen, T., Burggräf, P., Wagner, J., Hassenzahl, M., Heupel, T., & Steinberg, F. (2021). Trust in artificial intelligence within production management – An exploration of antecedents. *Ergonomics*, *64*(10), 1333–350. https://doi.org/10.1080/00140139.2021.1909755

[19] Vijai, C. (2019). Artificial Intelligence in Indian Banking Sector: Challenges and Opportunities. *International Journal of Advanced Research*, *7*(4), 1581–1587. https://doi.org/10.21474/ijar01/8987

Web Links

[20] https://analyticsindiamag.com/how-ai-is-changing-the-real-estate-landscape/

[21] https://www.techugo.com/blog/artificial-intelligence-technology/

[22] https://www.financialexpress.com/money/is-indian-real-estate-standing-at-the-edge-of-an-ai-revolution/2324793/

[23] https://www.gopalanenterprises.com/impact-of-AI-on-the-real-estate-market-in-the-coming-years.html

[24] https://www.analyticsinsight.net/top-5-real-estate-companies-using-ai-and-ml-to-attract-more-buyers/

[25] https://cio.economictimes.indiatimes.com/news/next-gen-technologies/ai-based-solutions-can-help-indias-real-estate-sector/79771627

SECTION IV

Reinventing Management through Sustainability, Innovation and Analytics: Business Policy, Strategy and Entrepreneurship

Assessing the Readiness of Academic Staff in Adopting Learning Analytics in Higher Education

Dr Riyaz A. Sheikh and Dr Syed Md. Faisal Ali Khan

College of Business Administration, Jazan University, Jazan, Saudi Arabia
E-mail: rasheikh@jazanu.edu.sa; smfaisal@jazanu.edu.sa

Abstract

Purpose: The main goals of LA are to boost student performance and give students more tools for success, with more support. However, it may show a disconnect between what institutions believe customers should receive and what customers actually want. Prior to deploying LA, addressing these issues and comprehending academic staff's expectations are essential for improving end-user buy-in and improved resource planning.

Methodology: This study contains a thorough literature analysis that concentrates on the significance, current models, and difficulties with LA implementation. A survey based on SHIELA framework was carried out based on the identified gap to examine teaching staffs' views, usage, and difficulties with LA adoption. The data is tested for reliability and validity using factor loading, construct validity and discriminant validity by using SmartPLS 4.

Findings: The findings of our study demonstrated that the teaching staff believed that the best use of LA was to facilitate early intervention. The academic staff believed that one of LA's potentials was to assist students in making decisions and offer feedback on their learning progress. They argue that although establishments and students should share the responsibility, it is the institutions' moral and legal responsibility to act, i.e., to also include, encourage, and empower students must take the essential precautions to reduce risks.

Originality/ Value: The study gives educational leaders the tools they need to design better strategies to achieve success in teaching and learning, and it gives students new information to aid in making the right learning choices. We believe that the implementation of this paradigm and the higher education industry's ongoing effective interest in learning, analytics will improve outcomes for students, universities, and a larger part of society. On the basis of the current findings, the research also suggests a number of methodologies and research topics for ongoing investigations.

Keywords: *Data Mining, Learning Analytics, Strategic Value, Predictive Analytics, Higher Education*
Paper Type: *Research Paper*

Introduction

Learning analytics uses formal analysis technologies, like machine learning and statistical tools, to provide information that improves decision-making in higher education (El Alfy et al., 2019). This programme was developed with the goal of utilising digital technology to gather and examine user data traces in order to comprehend their continuing to learn behaviours and actions(Han et al., 2020; Siemens et al., 2013). They are being adopted in higher education all around the world, which is evidenced by both their explosive expansion and the abundance of literature produced by ongoing research in this field (Başaran & Daganni, 2020; El Alfy et al., 2019; Ngqulu, 2018). They have gained popularity because of their potential benefits for active learning, better teaching and learning strategies, the use of early interventions to assist student learning, increased student throughput, and greater student retention (El Alfy et al., 2019; Fan et al., 2020). The emphasis on learning is changing in higher education institutions (HEIs) of the twenty-first century from teacher-centric to student-centric (Kivunja, 2014). According to El Alfy et al. (2019), this technology is helping students, academics, and educational leaders prepare pupils for the twenty-first century while addressing the obstacles and issues they face. There are still issues with LA adoption and acceptance among academics at HEIs, despite the fact that LA developments have not been a recent phenomenon in higher education (West et al., 2018). Uncertainty over LA's goals (Mor et al., 2015; R.A. Sheikh et al., 2021), disparities in academics' data literacy (Corrin L.K., 2016), a shortage of data that can be used to make decisions (Bennett et al., 2021), and ethical and privacy concerns are all problems that could potentially impede the advancement of LA (Ifenthaler & Tracey, 2016). Even while the need for early stakeholder participation has been emphasised, particularly for LA (Ferguson et al., 2014; Kollom et al., 2021), there are few cases where this is really occurring (Y.S. Tsai et al., 2017).

Without stakeholder participation, it is possible that the institutional managers' expectations and opinions will dominate the many LA policies that are currently available (Sclater, 2020). Even though the main reasons for adopting LA in those circumstances are to improve learning performance (Y. S. Tsai et al., 2018) and offer supplementary assistance to students (Siemens & Gasevic, 2012), those reasons are still shaped by the managers' preconceived notions and aren't always representative of what other stakeholders (such as students and teaching staff) would expect. Services may therefore show a mismatch between what organisations believe customers should receive and what they actually want (Ng & Forbes, 2009). Prior to deploying LA, addressing these issues and comprehending academic expectations are essential for improving end-user buy-in and improved resource planning.

Even though the widespread use of LA in developed nations, there is little knowledge of how it is used in developing countries, and the people who benefit from its adoption and implementation and the attitudes that result (Hommel et al., 2019; Parrish & Richman, 2020). The literature review undertaken in this study corroborated El Alfy et al. (2019) and Mahmoud et al. (2021) assertion that there is little research in particular regions, such as North Africa and the Middle East. In the current study, we have made an effort to fill this gap by exploring the expectations of teaching staff for the adoption of LA services in the Gulf region specifically in Saudi Arabia. Accessibility and comprehension of the items from the viewpoint of the teaching staff were always taken into consideration during the formulation of this study. There is a thorough analysis of the relevant studies that results in the creation of a conceptual model for investigating the expectations of the teaching staff towards the adoption of LA. The survey data is used to test and validate the model using structural equation modeling, which identifies the key factors influencing learning analytics. By doing this, the HEIs can pinpoint certain areas for their LA implementation that will be the emphasis of their teaching staff's direct engagement tactics.

Literature Review

Learning analytics' quick development is constantly defining the important topics of higher education (El Alfy et al., 2019; Gasevic et al., 2019). The adoption rate has significantly increased and utilisation of online learning for a variety of reasons, including COVID-19 contact limits and stronger faith in the benefits of online learning (Gibson & de Freitas, 2016). Learning analytics and the application of data analytics in higher education have produced a number of advantages, including the ability to identify at-risk students, monitor students' progress, anticipate each student's unique learning requirements, and identify potential factors influencing academic achievement (Clark et al., 2020; El Alfy et al., 2019). Learning management systems (LMS) like Moodle, Canvas, and Blackboard are where learning analytics get their data from (R. Sheikh & Goje, 2021; Xin & Singh, 2021).

One of LA's potentials is the ability to give students feedback on their academic tasks, performance and progress; prompt, accurate, and on-task feedback (Banihashem et al., 2022; Schumacher & Ifenthaler, 2018). Giving students constructive criticism can be viewed as any method or piece of information that could improve their ability to control their own learning (Cavalcanti, 2020). However, teachers must devote a lot of resources to providing effective feedback to encourage students to manage their own learning (Jin et al., 2022; Pinheiro Cavalcanti et al., 2019). It can be challenging for academic staffs to evaluate the learning progresses and give feedback to their students on their own when learning environments become more scattered, moving away from the teacher and onto formal as well as informal online platforms. However, by giving teachers information about their students' performance, The teaching team can receive help from LA in encouraging pupils' ability to learn independently(Lodge et al., 2019). Cazan (2013) advised teachers to help their pupils build activity in metacognition, abilities for adjusting self-monitoring tactics, the ability to use feedback strategically, metacognitive awareness of academia, and task-specific methodologies.

Although the teaching staff has the capacity to help students' feedback processes, develop their metacognitive skills, and, in turn, improve their own instructional practices, there is still a gap in LA adoption that needs to be closed (Durall & Gros, 2014). Increasing interest in LA's potential has been noted; nevertheless, Ferguson et al. (2016) have noted that LA adoption by organisations is not as systematic as one might anticipate. Only 6 per cent of the 252 papers included in a recent evaluation of the literature on the state of LA in HE by Viberg et al. (2018) met the criterion of 'LA are taken up and used widely, including deployment at scale.' Multiple causes contribute to this, however one of the most important is the fact that LA's end users' needs and preferences are taken into consideration during the planning and development of the service. The failure to incorporate student and teacher feedback into LA solution development has the potential to impede its widespread adoption in educational institutions and classrooms. (Alvarez et al., 2020). According to Shum et al. (2019), integrating emerging technology into real-world settings presents both technical and human (cognitive, social, organisational, and political) challenges. The same issue is also raised by Tsai et al. (2017), who claim that one of the factors contributing to the level of use of LA services in HE is the insufficient participation of pertinent stakeholders and the resulting lack of a shared understanding. As effective adoption of LA demands highly qualified instructors and solutions that take into account their needs (Siemens et al., 2013), this could be detrimental to the effectiveness of LA. Dollinger et al. (2019) contend that a technology's value lies less in its technical prowess and functions and more in its significance to its users. It is difficult to create LA services that meet the needs of users for whom the tools are intended and are appropriate for teachers' educational goals.

Teachers ought to be included in that process because they can analyse the facts and know how to apply it to enhance the instructional design (Alhadad et al., 2018). In order to incorporate key stakeholders, many strategies have been proposed (Prieto et al., 2018; West et al., 2018); other research have looked at academic staff intentions of and outcomes with LA solutions as well as involvement of employees in LA procedures. To overcome the disconnect between LA solutions & academic personnel needs and to promote LA adoption in HEIs, Dollinger & Lodge (2018) suggested co-creating LA with educators. Similar to this, Chatti & Muslim (2019) proposed the concept of user-centred LA as a solution that highlights the user components in LA and the imperative to meet user needs. In order to effectively meet the demands of multiple users, it is essential to involve users in the planning, design, implementation and evaluation of LA. Alvarez et al. (2020) suggested a card-based co-design tool to assist with inter-stakeholder design of LA improvements. Early evaluations of this tool's ability to give many stakeholders a voice in the development of technologies that are expected to be utilised by learners, instructors, and other non-technical users are encouraging. In a survey conducted by West et al. (2018), academic staff members from Australia and Malaysia were asked about their needs and experiences with regard to LA, with a focus on their participation in LA projects. The study's findings demonstrated that academics preferred to employ LA to enhance their instruction over student retention. The study carried out by Howell et al. (2018) and Wong & Li (2018) are another noteworthy instance of examining teaching staff opinions of LA. Their research revealed that teaching staff members not only foresaw advantages for student learning but also suggestions that would simplify teaching and learning. The teaching staff also wants to be able to intervene early with underachievers by understanding how LA services could impact their duties. Given these findings, it is clear that in order to successfully incorporate LA into teaching methods, HEIs must involve the teaching staff in LA processes from the beginning phase (Demetriosssampsonn et al., 2022).

This study aims to advance knowledge of academic staff expectations for LA services. By examining four distinct specialisations, we hope to determine what academic staff members in HEIs in the Gulf Region anticipate from LA services. We examine teaching staff expectations on two levels: first, we asked them about their general expectations, and second, we asked them to clearly differentiate between what they would prefer to happen (i.e. their desired ideal) and what they anticipate will actually occur (i.e. predicted reality).

Therefore, we have proposed following four hypotheses to assess the readiness of teaching staff in adopting LA in HEIs:

- H1: Teaching staffs' awareness related to the goals of LA significantly affects HEIs readiness for it
- H2: Teaching staffs' perception related to their need of LA services significantly affects HEIs readiness for it
- H3: Teaching Staffs' view about students' need to LA services significantly affects HEIs readiness for it
- H4: Teaching staffs' awareness related to the implementation challenges of LA services significantly affect HEIs readiness

Research Methodology

Research Design

The purpose of this study is to better understand faculty members' anticipations regarding the use of LA in HEIs. The research purpose was achieved through the use of a survey approach. To confirm the necessary components for the adoption of LA & to evaluate the proposed model, a survey was deemed appropriate for this research. Data was collected from four higher education institutions teaching staffs (Arts, Business, Computer Sciences, & Medicine) from Saudi Arabia to better understand the critical factors influencing their acceptance and use of LA for supporting student learning outcome.

Instrument

The questionnaire was created employing the theoretical foundation as that of the 'Student Expectations of Learning Analytics Questionnaire (SELAQ)', that featured two scores evaluating ideal and predicted expectations (i.e., what a person hopes to receive versus what a person actually expects to receive) (Whitelock-Wainwright et al., 2019). The 16 items in the questionnaire measuring teaching staff expectations of LA services can be found in Appendix A. These components are grouped into four constructs based on Y.-S. Tsai et al. (2018) 's SHEILA framework: F1-goals of LA (2 items), F2-teaching staffs' need for LA services (4 items), F3-teaching staffs' assessment of students' need for LA services (5 items), and F4-implementation problems (5 items). A theoretical framework of the model is developed using SmartPLS 4 as shown in Figure 1:

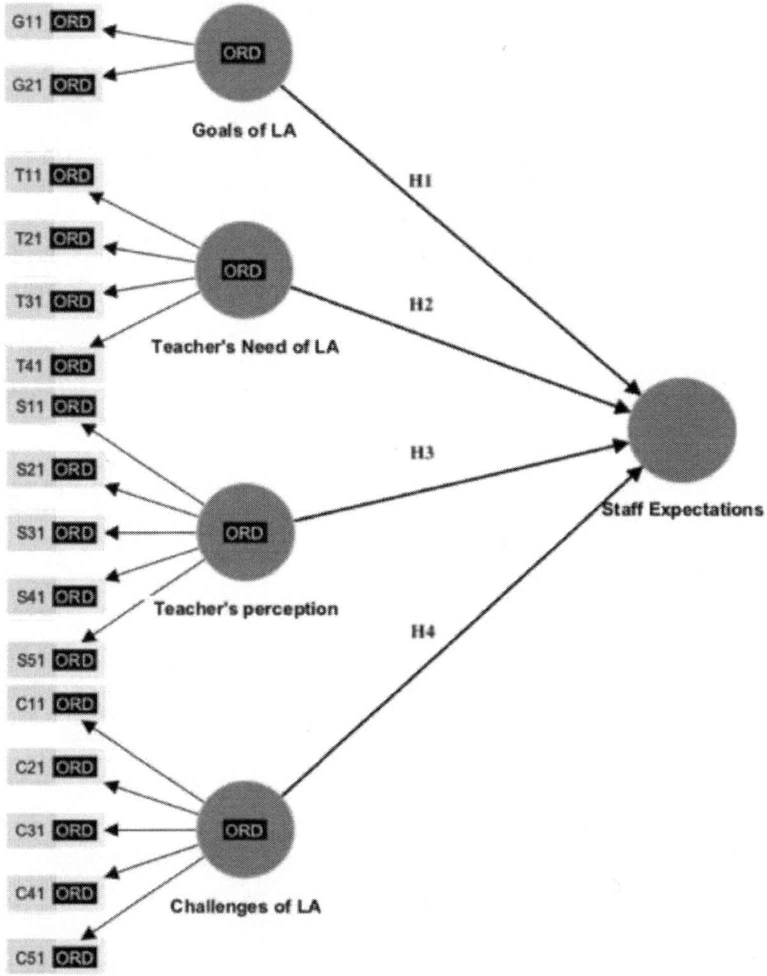

Figure 1: Theoretical Framework for Staff Expectations from LA
Source: Theoretical model using SmartPLS 4

In order to increase the concepts' linguistic and cultural validity, a small number of groups took part in pilot study to map ideas to the cultural context by substituting specific concepts to foster better understanding in the local context. Responses were scored using two 'seven-point Likert scales (1 = Strongly Disagree, 7 = Strongly Agree)', which were matched to the teaching staff's idealised and practical expectations for a LA service (predicted expectations). Email was used to distribute the participation invitations. The ideal and projected expectations for LA services for the four components were compared using SmartPLS 4 to compare the mean averages of the ideal and expected ratings for each item in each example, and the discrepancies between the two were assessed using paired t-tests.

Results

Construct Reliability and Validity

For the purpose of determining the validity and reliability of the constructs, the measurement model was evaluated. Table 1 presents the reliability and validity results for the entire sample, including the Ideal (I) and Predicted (P) expectations, as well as the factor loading for the satisfied items. First, all model components' factor loading values are higher than the minimal acceptable value of .50 (Hair et al., 2010). Although factor loading greater than 0.7 is preferred (Vinzi et al., 2010), social science studies usually provide weaker outer loading (below 0.7). Cronbach's Alpha, rho_a, and composite reliability (CR) statistics were used to evaluate dependability; both were higher than the suggested value of .700 (Wasko & Faraj, 2005).The rho a value was between the Cronbach's Alpha and the composite reliability (Hair et al., 2017). Convergent validity is supported by the fact that the Average Variance Extracted (AVE) and CRs were all above or very near to 0.500 and 0.700, respectively. According to Fornell & Larcker (1981), discriminant validity was evaluated by comparing the correlation between the latent variables with the square root of AVE (see Table 2). Therefore, discriminant validity is also confirmed.

Table 1: Reliability and Validity of the Constructs

		Outer Loadings		*Cronbach's Alpha*		*Composite Reliability (rho_a)*		*Average Variance Extracted (AVE)*	
		I	*P*	*I*	*P*	*I*	*P*	*I*	*P*
Challenges of LA	C1 ← Challenges	0.938	0.852	0.896	0.911	0.911	0.915	0.767	0.74
	C2 ← Challenges	0.865	0.861						
	C3 ← Challenges	0.743	0.769						
	C4 ← Challenges	0.942	0.883						
	C5 ← Challenges		0.928						
Goals of LA	G11 ← Goals	0.961	0.943	0.918	0.884	0.918	0.887	0.924	0.896
	G21 ← Goals	0.961	0.95						
Teacher's Perception about students' Need	S11 ← Perception	0.931	0.892	0.917	0.873	0.919	0.876	0.8	0.725
	S21 ← Perception	0.911	0.895						
	S31 ← Perception	0.942	0.892						
	S41 ← Perception	0.885	0.835						
	S51 ← Perception	0.938	0.895						
Teacher's Need of LA	T11 ← Need of LA	0.884	0.845	0.956	0.929	0.957	0.929	0.85	0.779
	T21 ← Need of LA	0.881	0.877						
	T31 ← Need of LA	0.899	0.874						
	T41 ← Need of LA	0.913	0.807						

Source: Author's compilation using SmartPLS 4.

Table 2: Discriminant Validity: Fornell-Larcker Criterion (Ideal Scenario)

Ideal Scenario	*Challenges of LA*	*Goals of LA*	*Teacher's Need of LA*	*Teacher's Perception*
Fornell-Larcker Criterion (Ideal Scenario)				
Challenges of LA	0.88			
Goals of LA	0.945	0.961		
Teacher's Need of LA	0.944	0.929	0.894	
Teacher's perception	0.948	0.956	0.928	0.922
Fornell-Larcker Criterion (Predicted Scenario)				
Challenges of LA	0.86			
Goals of LA	0.877	0.947		
Teacher's Need of LA	0.939	0.862	0.851	
Teacher's perception	0.902	0.846	0.897	0.882

Source: Author's compilation using SmartPLS 4.

Descriptive Statistics

The teaching staff's expectations were measured by finding the difference between the two responses (ideal and predicted) using SmartPLS 4. Out of a possible 178 teaching staffs, 75 teaching staff responders (females = 28; men = 47 years) from four disciplines at the Jazan University completed the 16-item survey (Appendix A), which was delivered via email and direct handouts. In all, 75 responses were received, with 37 per cent of female respondents and 63 per cent of male respondents (arts = 12, business = 34, computers = 18, medicine = 8). This represents a 42 per cent response rate. This was a self-selected sample of academic staff members from all four disciplines who willingly consented to be contacted for research. To make sure that the sample was representative of the teaching staff as a whole, this sample was then compared to gender, teaching experience, speciality, and other demographic data (see Table 3).

Table 3: Sociodemographic Characteristics of the Respondent

Domain	*Characteristic*	*N*	*% of the Sample*
Gender	Male	47	63%
	Female	28	37%
Teaching experience	0-5 years	22	29%
	6-10 years	20	27%
	11-15 years	19	25%
	> 15 years	14	19%
Specialisation	Business	34	45%
	Computer Science	18	24%
	Arts	12	16%
	Medicine	8	11%
	Others	3	4%

Domain	*Characteristic*	*N*	*% of the Sample*
Academic Position	'Professor	8	11%
	Associate Professor	15	20%
	Assistant Professor	21	28%
	Lecturer'	31	41%
Administrative Position	HOD	7	9%
	Head of any Committee	43	57%
	Others	25	33%

Source: Author's compilation using SmartPLS 4.

The descriptive statistics give a broad understanding of what the teaching staff anticipates from LA services (Table 4). As expected, a ceiling effect was seen in the responses to the ideal expectations scale. Responses are probably too optimistic because this scale reflects what teaching staffs would aspire for in a service. However, the responses fell short of the ideal expected responses when compared to the teaching staffs' predicted expectations. The measure's validity is increased by this distinction between ideal and anticipated expectation responses since the results are compatible with two degrees of belief (see Figure 2).

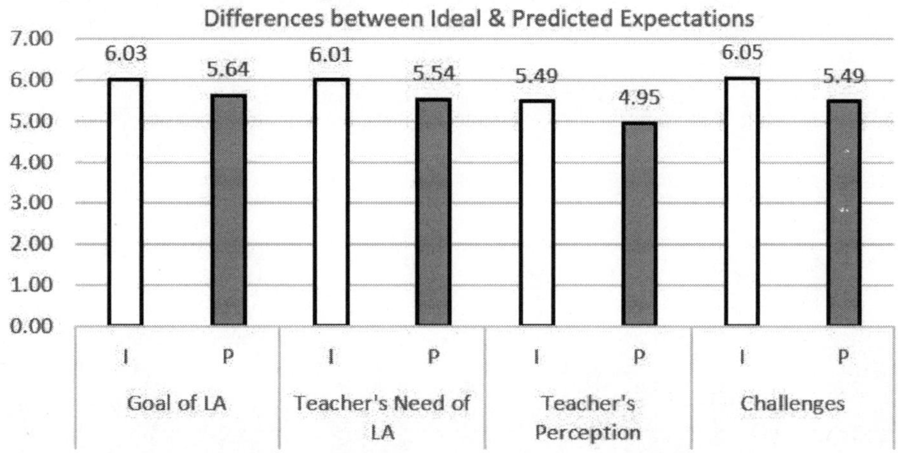

Fig. 2: Ideal and Predicted Expectations Across Four Factors of LA
Source: Author's Compilation

When comparing the four LA constructs, it is seen that construct F4 is the most significant. This is based on the distribution of common answers across ideal and predicted expectation (see Figure 2). F1 is the second-most significant element, followed by F2 and F3. Item 4 ('I will be able to obtain data on my students' development in a course that I am teaching/tutoring'; Appendix A) had the highest mean answer across both the ideal (M = 6.24, SD = 1.54; Table 4) and predicted (M = 5.60, SD = 1.57; Table 4) expectations for factor F4. Item 5 (I will have access to data about all students enrolled in a programme; M = 5.68, SD = 1.54; has the highest average predicted expectation; M = 5.68, SD = 1.54; Table 4).

Descriptive analysis for each item are also supplied, along with the mean for each factor by gender and other demographics (see Figure 3, Figure 4, Table 5). The average relevance for both the ideal and predicted expectation across four factors for LA is clearly larger for the male respondents, as shown in Figure 2, than it is for the female respondents. The Saudi culture may be to account for this, as females are more prone to disclose information. The additional responses depending on experience, speciality, academic rank, and administrative experience were displayed in Figure 3.

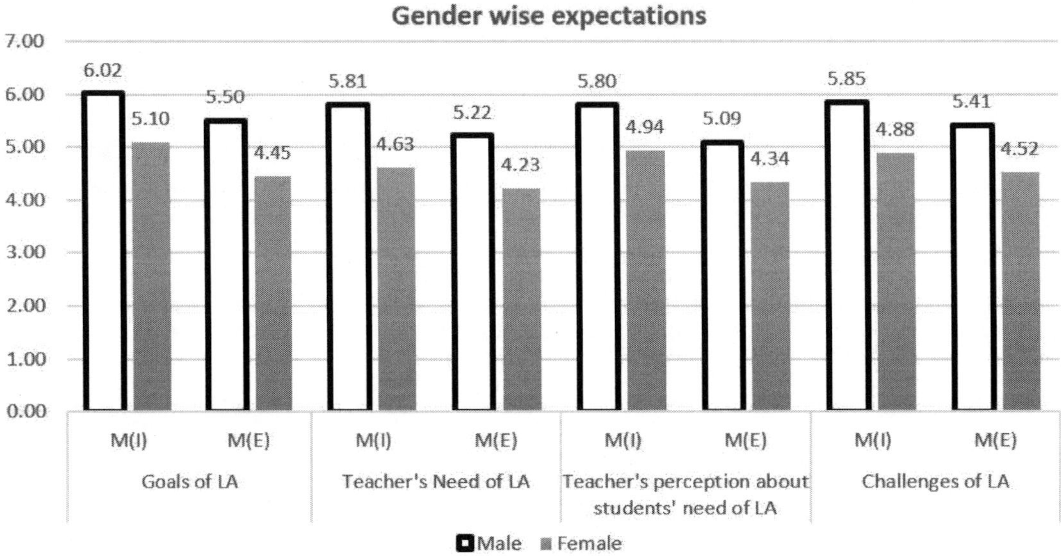

Fig. 3: Gender-wise Teaching Staff Expectations for LA
Source: Author's Compilation

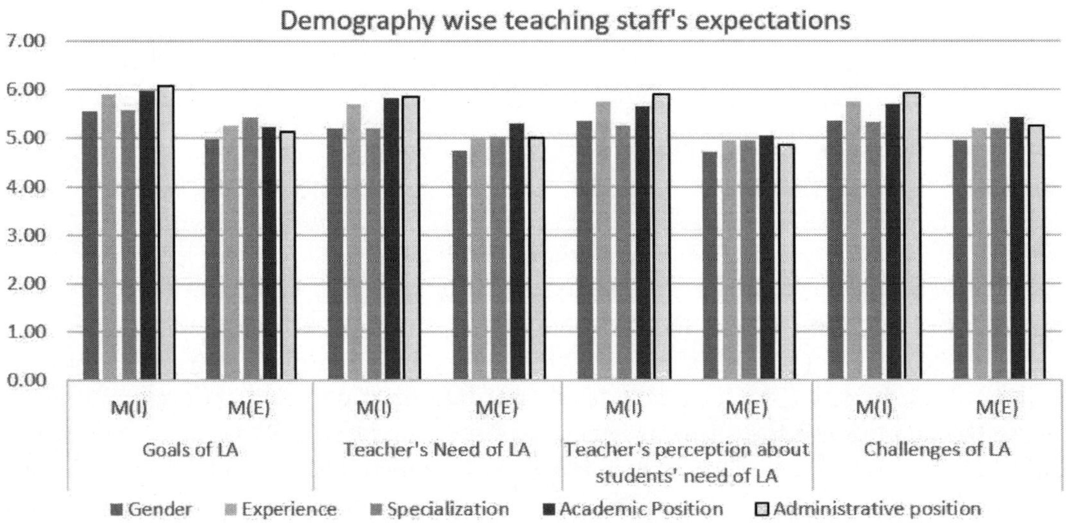

Fig. 4: Demography-wise Teaching Staffs' Expectation (ideal vs predicted)
Source: Author's Compilation

Table 4: Descriptive Statistics for Teaching Staffs' Expectation (ideal vs predicted)

Item	*Key*	*Ideal Expectation*		*Predicted Expectation*	
		M	*SD*	*M*	*SD*
1	G1	6.21	1.45	5.64	1.46
2	G2	5.85	1.47	5.65	1.50
3	C1	6.15	1.52	5.66	1.54
4	C2	6.24	1.54	5.60	1.57
5	C3	5.98	1.59	5.68	1.54
6	C4	6.01	1.57	5.62	1.58
7	C5	5.89	1.58	5.54	1.61
8	T1	5.97	1.65	5.55	1.68
9	T2	6.11	1.69	5.45	1.73
10	T3	6.06	1.68	5.56	1.72
11	T4	5.89	1.77	5.63	1.78
12	S1	6.20	1.84	5.57	1.87
13	S2	6.17	1.94	5.67	1.76
14	S3	6.09	1.65	5.40	1.87
15	S4	5.89	1.23	5.13	1.56
16	S5	5.92	1.75	5.67	1.93

Source: Author's Compilation using SmartPLS 4.

Structural Model Analysis

The next stage is to handle the evaluation of the structural model results once it has been established that the constructs are being measured in a valid and reliable manner (see Table 1, Table 2). We have checked the structural model for any possible collinearity problems in this stage. This is because the structural model bases its estimation of the path coefficient on OLS regressions between each endogenous construct and its related predictor construct. If there is significant collinearity among the predictor constructs throughout the estimate process, the path coefficient may be skewed. The 5,000 samples used in this study also produce 95 per cent confidence intervals. A confidence interval that differs from zero denotes a significant relationship. Results of the testing of hypotheses are summarised in Table 6.

1. H1 evaluates whether teaching staffs' awareness related to the goals of LA significantly affects HEIs readiness. The result revealed that it has a significant impact on hypothesised variable. Hence H1 was supported.
2. Furthermore, H2 evaluates whether Teaching staffs' perception related to their need of LA services significantly affects HEIs readiness for it. The result revealed that it has a significant impact on hypothesised variable. Hence H2 was supported.

3. And H3 evaluates whether Teaching Staffs' view about students' need to LA services significantly affects HEIs readiness for it. The result revealed that it has a significant impact on hypothesised variable. Hence H2 was supported.
4. And H4 evaluates Teaching staffs' awareness related to the implementation challenges of LA services significantly affect HEIs readiness. The result revealed that it has a significant impact on hypothesised variable. Hence H2 was supported

When comparing the means of the ideal and predicted observations for each the items, a further significant observation in support of the hypotheses was made using the paired-t test (see Table 7). From the perspective of the teaching staff, the results indicate positive differences for all four criteria, leading one to believe that they are crucial for implementing LA in HEIs.

Table 5: Differences between Ideal and Predicted Expectations Based on Demographics (as appendix)

	Goals of LA		*Teacher's Need of LA*		*Teacher's Perception about Students' Need of LA*		*Challenges of LA*	
	M(I)	*M(E)*	*M(I)*	*M(E)*	*M(I)*	*M(E)*	*M(I)*	*M(E)*
Gender	5.56	4.98	5.22	4.72	5.37	4.71	5.37	4.97
Male	6.02	5.50	5.81	5.22	5.80	5.09	5.85	5.41
Female	5.10	4.45	4.63	4.23	4.94	4.34	4.88	4.52
Experience	5.91	5.25	5.70	5.01	5.76	4.96	5.76	5.20
0-5 years	6.63	5.38	6.81	5.31	6.70	5.30	6.60	5.30
6-10 years	5.91	4.68	5.66	4.41	5.71	4.33	5.75	4.53
11-15 years	5.60	5.60	5.28	5.23	5.54	5.26	5.66	5.68
above 15 years	5.50	5.33	5.06	5.10	5.08	4.95	5.05	5.30
Specialisation	5.58	5.44	5.22	5.03	5.25	4.97	5.33	5.22
Arts	5.10	5.60	4.70	5.45	4.44	5.08	4.76	5.56
Business	5.93	4.74	5.80	4.67	5.88	4.60	5.86	4.87
Computer Science	5.64	6.07	5.04	5.50	5.34	5.60	5.37	5.77
Medicine	5.67	5.33	5.33	4.50	5.33	4.60	5.33	4.67
Academic Position	5.97	5.23	5.83	5.31	5.67	5.05	5.72	5.43
'Professor	6.00	5.00	5.50	5.25	5.20	5.30	5.60	5.70
Associate Professor	6.50	5.50	7.00	6.25	6.40	5.20	6.20	5.80
Assistant Professor	5.69	5.08	5.52	4.69	5.58	4.80	5.58	4.91
Lecturer'	5.70	5.35	5.31	5.05	5.48	4.91	5.49	5.30
Administrative position	6.07	5.14	5.85	5.02	5.90	4.87	5.94	5.27
HOD	6.83	5.00	6.75	5.25	6.73	4.87	6.80	5.60
Head of other committees	5.77	5.08	5.50	4.83	5.58	4.77	5.66	4.95
Other	5.62	5.33	5.30	4.99	5.39	4.96	5.37	5.25

Source: Author's Compilation

Table 6: Hypotheses Testing

Hypotheses		*Original Sample (O)*		*Standard Deviation (STDEV)*		*T Statistics (|O/STDEV|)*		*P Values*	
		Ideal	*Expected*	*Ideal*	*Expected*	*Ideal*	*Expected*	*Ideal*	*Expected*
H4	Challenges of LA → Staff Expectations	0.275	0.271	0.02	0.023	13.892	11.812	0.0000	0.0000
H1	Goals of LA → Staff Expectations	0.232	0.24	0.026	0.017	9.042	14.268	0.0000	0.0000
H2	Teacher's Need of LA → Staff Expectations	0.272	0.279	0.026	0.02	10.296	13.697	0.0000	0.0000
H3	Teacher's perception → Staff Expectations	0.243	0.254	0.025	0.022	9.662	11.514	0.0000	0.0000

Source: Author's Compilation using SmartPLS 4.

Table 7: Paired t-Test for Items Describing Teaching Staff's Expectations (ideal vs predicted)

		Mean	*STD*	*Paired Differences*				
				Md	*STD*	*t*	*df*	*Sig. (2-tailed)*
Goal of LA	Ideal	6.03	1.46	.394	1.235	2.729	36	.010
	Predicted	5.64	1.48					
Teacher's Need of LA	Ideal	6.01	1.70	.462	1.422	1.781	36	.083
	Predicted	5.54	1.73					
Teacher's Perception	Ideal	5.49	1.436	.578	1.456	2.231	36	.032
	Predicted	4.95	1.323					
Challenges	Ideal	6.05	1.68	.441	1.405	2.948	36	.006
	Predicted	5.49	1.80					

Source: Author's Compilation using SmartPLS 4.

Discussion and Conclusion

Four constructs were identified after a study of the LA literature (Whitelock-Wainwright et al., 2019), including the goals of LA, the need for LA among teachers, the need for LA among students, and difficulties encountered during LA implementation in HEIs. The expectations of the teaching staff for LA services were based on these four elements, and 16 items were identified(Y.-S. Tsai et al., 2018). These items were developed within the theoretical framework of expectancies, primarily using the work of David et al. (2004) and Dowling & Rickwood (2016) to provide a more complex understanding of the stakeholder's view. Based on the aforementioned framework, a 16-item questionnaire was created and validated in order to gain a general grasp of the ideal and predicted expectations of academic staffs related to LA tools. Our study's results showed that staff members thought the ideal way to use LA was to encourage prompt early intervention if a review of a student's academic records suggested that they might be having any problems or issues. The teaching staff also believed that one of LA's potentials was to assist students in making decisions and to give feedback on their progress in learning, both of which have been noted in other studies (Pinheiro Cavalcanti et al., 2019). The academic staff learned that it was essential to have open discussions about the subject while adding LA into their lesson plans. This suggests that effective communication is essential for the adoption of LA.(Colvin et al., 2016).

Of the hypothesis regarding what the teaching staff expected from LA, we discovered that while they recognised LA's significant potential to help learning and teaching, academic staff members were less certain that all of their ideal expectations would be met. Ideal and predicted expectations for teaching staffs from various backgrounds differed significantly. Another intriguing finding from the survey information in all circumstances was the usually consistently low expectation and willingness for teaching staff to be required to act in response to information indicating students are threat of not succeeding or doing adequately below expectations. Similar to this, a study by Prinsloo & Slade (2017) found that although LA helps various stakeholders learn more about kids, it does not always lead to action. They argue that while institutions and students should share responsibility, institutions also have a moral and legal obligation to act, i.e., to include students and provide them with the knowledge and tools they need to take the necessary safety precautions. This would imply that, although being aware of the value and benefits of LA for both the students and their own practices, the academic staff did not view it as a substantial part of their instructional strategies.

We are aware that our survey does not fairly represent the opinions of the entire country. Additionally, the low number of 'skeptics' indicates that teachers who found the topic of our study to be challenging or irrelevant did not respond to the poll. Our findings therefore most likely just represent the viewpoints of the teaching staff members who were curious about LA. But these results are significant for HEIs since they show what the academic staff expects from LA tools. We may envision a number of future directions for our study's research. We discovered that academic personnel ought to be involved in diverse ways even within the same organisation depending on their experiences and expectations, which supports our study's finding that LA cannot be controlled with a one-size-fits-all strategy (Y.S. Tsai et al., 2018). For the future, we recommend the following ideas. First, we found statistically significant disparities in the teaching staff's ideal and predicted expectations for the LA services. While most employees seem to be aware of the potential, some are unsure of what can actually be accomplished. We advise further research into these reservations to determine whether they are related to past experiences with LA applications, instructor expertise, philosophical viewpoints, etc. It is crucial to highlight that we did not specifically take academic staff members' prior LA experience into account, but we will do so in the future. This may offer a chance to assess whether desired and anticipated expectations are due to recently gained experience or a knowledge deficit of the potential of LA innovations, and to tailor the interventions accordingly.

Without a doubt, the involvement of stakeholders is a crucial requirement for the successful adoption of LA since it ensures that LA services are widely accepted inside the institution. This study outlined the expectations of the teaching staff in order to better understand their requirements. As a result, it can serve as a roadmap for higher educational institutions and LA system developers to provide standardised tools that are simple for users to adopt.

References

[1] Alhadad, S.S.J., Thompson, K., Knight, S., Lewis, M., & Lodge, J.M. (2018). Analytics-Enabled teaching as design: Reconceptualisation and call for research. *ACM International Conference Proceeding Series*. https://doi.org/10.1145/3170358.3170390

[2] Alvarez, C.P., Martinez-Maldonado, R., & Shum, S.B. (2020). LA-DECK: A card-based learning analytics co-design tool. *ACM International Conference Proceeding Series*. https://doi.org/10.1145/3375462.3375476

[3] Banihashem, S.K., Noroozi, O., van Ginkel, S., P. Macfadyen, L., & Biemans, H.J.A. (2022). A systematic review of the role of learning analytics in enhancing feedback practices in higher education. *Educational Research Review*, *37*(October), 100489. https://doi.org/10.1016/j.edurev.2022.100489

[4] Başaran, S., & Daganni, A.M. (2020). Learning analytics tool adoption by university students. *International Journal of Advanced Computer Science and Applications*, *11*(7). https://doi.org/10.14569/IJACSA.2020.0110740

[5] Bennett, A.A., Lo, K. D., Pervez, A., Nelson, T. A., Mullane, K., Farrell, M., Wilson, S., Decker, M., & Tarr, E.K. (2021). The International Journal of Management Education Exploring business doctoral students attitudes , training , and use of classroom experiential learning activities. *The International Journal of Management Education*, *19*(2), 100493. https://doi.org/10.1016/j.ijme.2021.100493

[6] Cazan, A.-M. (2013). Teaching Self Regulated Learning Strategies for Psychology Students. *Procedia - Social and Behavioral Sciences*, *78*. https://doi.org/10.1016/j.sbspro.2013.04.387

[7] Chatti, M.A., & Muslim, A. (2019). The PERLA framework: Blending personalization and learning analytics. *International Review of Research in Open and Distance Learning*, *20*(1), 244–261. https://doi.org/10.19173/irrodl.v20i1.3936

[8] Clark, J.A., Liu, Y., & Isaias, P. (2020). Critical success factors for implementing learning analytics in higher education: A mixed-method inquiry. *Australasian Journal of Educational Technology*, *36*(6). https://doi.org/10.14742/AJET.6164

[9] Colvin, C., Rogers, T., Shane, A.W., Dragan, D., Simon, G., Shum, B., Nelson, K., Alexander, S., Lockyer, L., Kennedy, G., Corrin, L., & Fisher, J. (2016). Student retention and learning analytics: A snapshot of Australian practices and a framework for advancement. In *Research.Ed.Ac.Uk* (Issue April 2017).

[10] David, D., Montgomery, G.H., Stan, R., DiLorenzo, T., & Erblich, J. (2004). Discrimination between hopes and expectancies for nonvolitional outcomes: Psychological phenomenon or artifact? *Personality and Individual Differences*, *36*(8). https://doi.org/10.1016/j.paid.2003.08.013

[11] Demetriosssampsonn, S.D., Papamitsiouu, Z., & Dirkkifenthaler, M. (2022). *Advances in Analytics for Learning and Teaching Educational Data Analytics forrTeachers and School Leaders.*

[12] Dollinger, M., Liu, D., Arthars, N., & Lodge, J.M. (2019). Working together in learning analytics towards the co-creation of value. *Journal of Learning Analytics, 6*(2). https://doi.org/10.18608/jla.2019.62.2

[13] Dollinger, M., & Lodge, J.M. (2018). Co-Creation strategies for learning analytics. *ACM International Conference Proceeding Series.* https://doi.org/10.1145/3170358.3170372

[14] Dowling, M., & Rickwood, D. (2016). Exploring hope and expectations in the youth mental health online counselling environment. *Computers in Human Behavior, 55.* https://doi.org/10.1016/j.chb.2015.08.009

[15] Durall, E., & Gros, B. (2014). Learning analytics as a metacognitive tool. *CSEDU 2014 - Proceedings of the 6th International Conference on Computer Supported Education, 1,* 380–384. https://doi.org/10.5220/0004933203800384

[16] El Alfy, S., Marx Gómez, J., & Dani, A. (2019). Exploring the benefits and challenges of learning analytics in higher education institutions: a systematic literature review. *Information Discovery and Delivery, 47*(1), 25–34. https://doi.org/10.1108/IDD-06-2018-0018

[17] Fan, Z., Lu, M., & Li, X. (2020). Peer Assessment Based on the User Preference Matrix. *Proceedings - 2020 International Conference on Artificial Intelligence and Education, ICAIE 2020,* 7–10. https://doi.org/10.1109/ICAIE50891.2020.00009

[18] Ferguson, R., Brasher, A., Clow, D., Cooper, A., Hillaire, G., Mittelmeier, J., Rienties, B., Ullmann, T., & Vuorikari, R. (2016). Research Evidence on the Use of Learning Analytics – Implications for Education Policy. In *A European Framework for Action on Learning Analytics* (Issue 2016).

[19] Ferguson, R., Clow, D., Macfadyen, L., Essa, A., Dawson, S., & Alexander, S. (2014). Setting learning analytics in context: Overcoming the barriers to large-scale adoption. *ACM International Conference Proceeding Series, 1,* 251–253. https://doi.org/10.1145/2567574.2567592

[20] Fornell, C. and Larcker, D.F. (1981), 'Evaluating structural equation models with unobservable variables and.pdf. *Journal of Marketing Research, XVIII* (February).

[21] Gasevic, D., Tsai, Y.S., Dawson, S., & Pardo, A. (2019). How do we start? An approach to learning analytics adoption in higher education. *International Journal of Information and Learning Technology, 36*(4), 342–353. https://doi.org/10.1108/IJILT-02-2019-0024

[22] Gibson, D., & de Freitas, S. (2016). Exploratory Analysis in Learning Analytics. *Technology, Knowledge and Learning, 21*(1). https://doi.org/10.1007/s10758-015-9249-5

[23] Hair, J.F., Black, W.C., Babin, B.J., & Anderson, R.E. (2010). Multivariate Data Analysis. In *Vectors.* https://doi.org/10.1016/j.ijpharm.2011.02.019

[24] Hair, J.F., Hult, G.T., Ringle, C., & Sarstedt, M. (2017). A Primer on Partial Least Squares Structural Equation Modeling (PLS-SEM) - Joseph F. Hair, Jr., G. Tomas M. Hult, Christian Ringle, Marko Sarstedt. In *Sage.*

[25] Han, J., Kim, K.H., Rhee, W., & Cho, Y.H. (2020). Learning Analytics Dashboards for Adaptive Support in Face-to-Face Collaborative Argumentation. *Computers & Education,* 104041. https://doi.org/10.1016/j.compedu.2020.104041

[26] Hommel, M., Egetenmeier, A., & Maier, U. (2019). Supporting stakeholders with learning analytics to increase study success: A case study. In *Utilizing learning analytics to support study success*. https://doi.org/10.1007/978-3-319-64792-0_3

[27] Howell, J.A., Roberts, L.D., Seaman, K., & Gibson, D.C. (2018). Are We on Our Way to Becoming a 'Helicopter University'? Academics' Views on Learning Analytics. *Technology, Knowledge and Learning, 23*(1). https://doi.org/10.1007/s10758-017-9329-9

[28] Ifenthaler, D., & Tracey, M.W. (2016). Exploring the relationship of ethics and privacy in learning analytics and design: implications for the field of educational technology. *Educational Technology Research and Development, 64*(5). https://doi.org/10.1007/s11423-016-9480-3

[29] Jin, H., Martinez-maldonado, R., Li, T., Wing, P., Chan, K., & Tsai, Y. (2022). *Towards Supporting Dialogic Feedback Processes Using Learning Analytics : the Educators' Views on Effective Feedback*. 1–10.

[30] Kivunja, C. (2014). Teaching Students to Learn and to Work Well with 21st Century Skills: Unpacking the Career and Life Skills Domain of the New Learning Paradigm. *International Journal of Higher Education, 4*(1). https://doi.org/10.5430/ijhe.v4n1p1

[31] Kollom, K., Tammets, K., Scheffel, M., Tsai, Y.S., Jivet, I., Muñoz-Merino, P.J., Moreno-Marcos, P.M., Whitelock-Wainwright, A., Calleja, A.R., Gasevic, D., Kloos, C.D., Drachsler, H., & Ley, T. (2021). A four-country cross-case analysis of academic staff expectations about learning analytics in higher education. *Internet and Higher Education, 49*(October 2021). https://doi.org/10.1016/j.iheduc.2020.100788

[32] Lodge, J.M., Panadero, E., Broadbent, J., & de Barba, P.G. (2019). Supporting self-regulated learning with learning analytics. In *Learning Analytics in the Classroom*. https://doi.org/10.4324/9781351113038-4

[33] Mahmoud, M., Dafoulas, G., Abd ElAziz, R., & Saleeb, N. (2021). Learning analytics stakeholders' expectations in higher education institutions: a literature review. *International Journal of Information and Learning Technology, 38*(1), 33–48. https://doi.org/10.1108/IJILT-05-2020-0081

[34] Mor, Y., Ferguson, R., & Wasson, B. (2015). Editorial: Learning design, teacher inquiry into student learning and learning analytics: A call for action. *British Journal of Educational Technology, 46*(2). https://doi.org/10.1111/bjet.12273

[35] Ng, I.C.L., & Forbes, J. (2009). Education as service: The understanding of university experience through the service logic. *Journal of Marketing for Higher Education, 19*(1). https://doi.org/10.1080/08841240902904703

[36] Ngqulu, N. (2018). Investigating the adoption and the application of learning analytics in South African Higher Education Institutions (Heis). *Proceedings of the International Conference on E-Learning, ICEL, 2018-July*.

[37] Parrish, A.H., & Richman, L.J. (2020). Dual perspectives on learning analytics in higher education. *Journal of Applied Research in Higher Education, 12*(1). https://doi.org/10.1108/JARHE-12-2018-0254

[38] Pinheiro Cavalcanti, A., Ferreira Leite De Mello, R., Rolim, V., André, M., Freitas, F., & Gasevic, D. (2019). An analysis of the use of good feedback practices in online learning courses. *Proceedings - IEEE 19th International Conference on Advanced Learning Technologies, ICALT 2019*. https://doi.org/10.1109/ICALT.2019.00061

[39] Prieto, L.P., Jesús Rodríguez-Triana, M., Martínez-Maldonado, R., & Gašević, D. (2018). *Preprint submitted for review Orchestrating Learning Analytics (OrLA): supporting the adoption of learning analytics at the practitioner level.*

[40] Prinsloo, P., & Slade, S. (2017). An elephant in the learning analytics room - The obligation to act. *ACM International Conference Proceeding Series*. https://doi.org/10.1145/3027385.3027406

[41] Schumacher, C., & Ifenthaler, D. (2018). Features students really expect from learning analytics. *Computers in Human Behavior, 78*. https://doi.org/10.1016/j.chb.2017.06.030

[42] Sclater, N. (2020). *Senior managers' guide to learning analytics*. 21.

[43] Sheikh, R.A., Bhatia, S., Metre, S.G., & Faqihi, A.Y.A. (2021). Strategic value realization framework from learning analytics: a practical approach. *Journal of Applied Research in Higher Education, ahead-of-p*(ahead-of-print). https://doi.org/10.1108/JARHE-10-2020-0379

[44] Sheikh, R., & Goje, N. (2021). Role of Big Data Analytics in Business Transformation. In *Internet of Things in Business Transformation*. Wiley Online Library.

[45] Shum, S.B., Ferguson, R., & Martinez-Maldonado, R. (2019). Human-centred learning analytics. *Journal of Learning Analytics, 6*(2). https://doi.org/10.18608/jla.2019.62.1

[46] Siemens, G., Dawson, S., & Lynch, G. (2013). Improving the Quality and Productivity of the Higher Education Sector. Policy and Strategy for Systems-Level Deployment of Learning Analytics. *Solar, December*.

[47] Siemens, G., & Gasevic, D. (2012). Guest editorial - learning and knowledge analytics. In *Educational Technology and Society* (Vol. 15, Issue 3).

[48] Tsai, Y.-S., Moreno-Marcos, P.M., Jivet, I., Scheffel, M., Tammets, K., Kollom, K., & Gašević, D. (2018). The SHEILA Framework: Informing Institutional Strategies and Policy Processes of Learning Analytics. *Journal of Learning Analytics, 5*(3). https://doi.org/10.18608/jla.2018.53.2

[49] Tsai, Y.S., Gasevic, D., Muñoz-Merino, P.J., & Dawson, S. (2017). La policy: Developing an institutional policy for learning analytics using the RAPID outcome mapping approach. *ACM International Conference Proceeding Series*, 494–495. https://doi.org/10.1145/3027385.3029424

[50] Tsai, Y.S., Moreno-Marcos, P.M., Tammets, K., Kollom, K., & Gašević, D. (2018). SHEILA policy framework: Informing institutional strategies and policy processes of learning analytics. *ACM International Conference Proceeding Series*, 320–329. https://doi.org/10.1145/3170358.3170367

[51] Viberg, O., Hatakka, M., Bälter, O., & Mavroudi, A. (2018). The current landscape of learning analytics in higher education. In *Computers in Human Behavior* (Vol. 89). https://doi.org/10.1016/j.chb.2018.07.027

[52] Vinzi, V.E., Trinchera, L., & Amato, S. (2010). PLS Path Modeling: From Foundations to Recent Developments and Open Issues for Model Assessment and Improvement. In *Handbook of Partial Least Squares*. https://doi.org/10.1007/978-3-540-32827-8_3

[53] Wasko, M.M.L., & Faraj, S. (2005). Why should I share? Examining social capital and knowledge contribution in electronic networks of practice. *MIS Quarterly: Management Information Systems, 29*(1). https://doi.org/10.2307/25148667

[54] West, D., Tasir, Z., Luzeckyj, A., Kew, S.N., Toohey, D., Abdullah, Z., Searle, B., Jumaat, N.F., & Price, R. (2018). Learning analytics experience among academics in Australia and Malaysia: A comparison. *Australasian Journal of Educational Technology, 34*(3). https://doi.org/10.14742/ajet.3836

[55] Whitelock-Wainwright, A., Gašević, D., Tejeiro, R., Tsai, Y.S., & Bennett, K. (2019). The Student Expectations of Learning Analytics Questionnaire. *Journal of Computer Assisted Learning, 35*(5), 633–666. https://doi.org/10.1111/jcal.12366

[56] Wong, B.T.M., & Li, K.C. (2018). Learning Analytics Intervention: A Review of Case Studies. *Proceedings – 2018 International Symposium on Educational Technology, ISET 2018, 2*, 178–182. https://doi.org/10.1109/ISET.2018.00047

[57] Xin, O.K., & Singh, D. (2021). Development of Learning Analytics Dashboard based on Moodle Learning Management System. *International Journal of Advanced Computer Science and Applications, 12*(7). https://doi.org/10.14569/IJACSA.2021.0120793

Appendix A: Teaching Staffs' Expectation Questionnaire

Responses to each question are scored on two seven-point Likert scales (1 = Strongly Disagree, 7 = Strongly Agree), which represent the ideal expectations of the teaching staff and the predicted expectations of the teaching staff for the service (predicted expectations). The following topics were used to organise the items for our analysis: the goals of learning analytics (15, 16), teaching staffs' needs for LA services (2, 3, 13, 14), teaching staffs' perceptions of students' needs for LA services (6, 7, 8, 10, 12), and challenges in implementing LA services at HEIs (1, 4, 5, 9, 11).

1. The university will provide me with guidance on how to access learning analytics about my students.
2. The University will provide staff with opportunities for professional development in using learning analytics for teaching.
3. The university will facilitate open discussions to share experience of learning analytics services.
4. I will be able to access data about my students' progress in a course that I am teaching/tutoring.
5. I will be able to access data about any students within a programme.
6. The learning analytics service will allow students to make their own decisions based on the data they receive.
7. The university will provide support (e.g., advice from personal tutors) as soon as possible if the analysis of a student's educational data suggests they may be having some difficulty or problem (e.g., underperforming or at-risk of failing).
8. The university will regularly update students about their learning progress based on the analysis of their educational data.
9. The learning analytics service will collect and present data that is accurate (i.e., free from inaccuracies such as incorrect grades).
10. The learning analytics service will show how a student's learning progress compares to their learning goals/ the course objectives.
11. The feedback from the learning analytics service will be presented in a format that is both understandable and easy to read.

12. The learning analytics service will present students with a complete profile of their learning across every course (e.g., number of accesses to online material, learning outcomes, and attendance).
13. The teaching staff will be competent in incorporating analytics into the feedback and support they provide to students.
14. The teaching staff will have an obligation to act (i.e., support students) if the analytics show that a student is at-risk of failing, underperforming, or that they could improve their learning.
15. The feedback from the learning analytics service will be used to promote students' academic and professional skill development (e.g., essay writing and referencing) for their future employability.
16. The use of learning analytics will allow me to better understand my students' learning performance.

Assessment of Environmental, Social and Governance (ESG) Disclosure Practices among Varied Industrial Sectors

SWETA BANIA[1] AND JHUMOOR BISWAS[2]

[1]*Research Scholar, Department of Business Management,*
University of Calcutta, Kolkata, West Bengal, India
[2]*Professor, Indian Institute of Social Welfare and Business Management (IISWBM),*
Kolkata, West Bengal, India
E-mail: baniasweta08@gmail.com; jhumoor@iiswbm.edu

Abstract

Purpose: The goal is to assess the significance of integrating environmental, social and corporate governance disclosure procedures across representative of several industrial sectors.

Design/Methodology/Approach: Non-parametric tests have been performed not only for analysing the differences in the yearly ESG disclosure scores of the companies but also year-to- year variations in this disclosure for each company.

Findings: The empirical analysis reveals that there is significant disparity in the disclosure of ESG information among sample companies. Furthermore, ITC Ltd. shows the most increasing trend of ESG disclosures over the years followed by UltraTech Cement Ltd. and Infosys Ltd.

Research limitations: The study only uses one sample from each of the three industrial sectors. Hence, the results cannot be generalised to these sectors and the spectrum of other industrial sectors.

Social implications: The social criterion, a part of ESG, looks at a company's capabilities and shortcomings in relation to labour and social trends. Concentrating on these issues can enhance the industrial sectors' corporate responsibility functions while benefitting a wide range of stakeholders.

Originality/Value: By evaluating the level of ESG disclosure procedures among the representative of the most important industries in the global financial markets, this study contributes to the area of research.

Keywords: *Sustainability, Environmental, Social, Governance, Reporting, Disclosure*

Introduction

Organisational global sustainability has received a great deal of focus from academics during the last few decades., notably in the wake of the global economic crises of 2007–2009 brought on by unethical behaviors, political issues, and environmental catastrophes linked to subpar risk management system. (Ali, Alsayegh, Ahmad, Mahmood, & Iqbal, 2018). Incorporating non-financial content in business reports was considered, up until the mid-1960s, as an act of a company's social responsibility. This type of information mostly covered a company's commitment to offering high-quality products and its involvement in the community, as well as its human resources and employee relations policies. However, environmental tragedies like the Bhopal tragedy and the BHP Billiton accident have elevated the significance of ESG disclosures in the public discourse (Lokuwaduge & Heenetigala, 2016). In response to the growing desire of accountable investors to consider performance of the company on the ESG factors when considering their business decisions, companies have started to develop stakeholder-oriented strategies and enhance value in society. Additionally, the authors have offered proof that businesses that actively manage ESG sustainability benefit from stronger shared value for both the organisation and society (Taliento, Favino, & Netti, 2019). As a result of growing public awareness and corporate recognition, more organisations are utilising sustainability initiatives and actively reporting their relevant ESG data on a worldwide scale (Xie, Fujii, Nozawa, & Yagi, 2018).The mounting pressure on organisations to provide information on the effects of social, political, and environmental related matters. Given the huge repercussions, businesses must be aware of such ESG concerns. Additionally, the relevance of many of these issues for society appears to support the necessity for mandatory reporting. Therefore, it is clear that ESG effects and dependencies are becoming more important as a part of the core business activities that increase an organisation's value. It is challenging to assess or compare such data due to inconsistencies and a lack of standardised reporting procedures or disclosure standards. Investors expect a company's external reports to contain high-quality, reliable, timely, and trustworthy ESG material that is relevant to and presented in a consistent manner with any changes to the methodology used for data collection, assessment and information dissemination. According to KPMG (2008), there are two key reasons why sustainability reporting is necessary. They find that, first, sustainability-related concerns have an impact on the long-term financial success of the company and, second, that the corporate world must respond correctly to sustainability-related issues. As a result, sustainability reporting is becoming more popular among those businesses as a tool for communication, which also improves the interaction with internal and external stakeholders. International organisations have recently offered suggestions to improve ESG reporting procedures all around the world.

About Selected Companies

- **UltraTech Cement Limited (Sector: Cement)** – The flagship cement business of the Aditya Birla Group is UltraTech Cement Limited. With a market worth of USD 7.1 billion, UltraTech is India's biggest producer of white cement, ready mix concrete (RMC), and grey cement. This Group has established a sustainability strategy that specifies three strategic pillars in order for the Group's businesses to achieve a common sustainability goal. These three strategy pillars are Future Proofing, Stakeholder Engagement, and Responsible Stewardship. Through its operations,

UltraTech is dedicated to advancing sustainability along the whole value chain. The company focuses on lowering its consumption of energy, carbon emissions, water, waste, and while also managing its resources, relationships with the community, occupational health and safety, human rights, employee well-being, and product innovation. Innovation and the evolution of technology are major forces behind our work in these sectors. Its R&D Center pioneers the development of sustainable business solutions and offers complete technical and analytical support to the industry in order to achieve this goal. Through the Global Cement and Concrete Association, UltraTech compares its sustainability standards with those of other major firms worldwide (GCCA).

- **ITC Limited (Sector: FMCG)** – One of India's top private sector companies is ITC. It is a diverse organisation with businesses in agribusiness, hotels, fast-moving consumer goods, and information technology etc. ITC is the best FMCG marketer in the nation, the undisputed market leader in the paperboard and packaging industry in India, and a well-known hotel chain that popularised 'Responsible Luxury' there and a global leader in farmer empowerment with its large Agri Business. ITC's desire to set an example for sustainability initiatives may be shown in the fact that it is the only industry of its diversity and size in the world to be carbon, water, and solid waste recycling positive. Additionally, more than 6 million people—the majority of whom are among the poorest in rural India—are provided with sustainable means of subsistence by ITC's businesses and value chains. ITC's Well-being Out of Waste programme (WOW), which offers an end-to-end scalable and sustainable solution to the problem of solid garbage management, has had an impact on over 1.8 crore people in the country. ITC is investing in India's future and boosting its competitiveness globally by building top-notch production facilities for consumer goods and recognisable hospitality facilities.
- **Infosys Limited (Sector: IT)** – The multinational technology services company Infosys Ltd. defines, designs, and provides clients with information technology (IT)-enabled business services and corporate solutions. The company offers its customers complete business solutions that make use of technology, such as infrastructure business solutions, package-enabled consultancy and implementation, as well as tech support, design implementation, design, development, and professional services. Infosys and The Economist Group recently established a strategic partnership in order to enable and enhance ecological solutions, make an impact through a business-to-business perspective, and foster long-term support assistance across international Infosys has collaborated with a number of global hyper-scalers in order to provide its smart buildings and spaces solutions and govern the longevity of systems, such as monitoring and guest management. Infosys has the ability to install and manage IoT devices, beacons, sensors, and way finding systems that enable the physical workplace to become digital. Employee-centric solutions include things like smart workplace platforms/return to the workspace, employee experiences,

and hands free experiences. From the perspective of sustainability, it's crucial to have skills in managing water, carbon control and monitoring solid waste, energy analysis and consultation, and Greenfield building consultation.

Literature Review

The empirical study (Singh & Joshi, 2009) looked at the environmental management and disclosure procedures used by 100 of the largest companies registered on the Bombay Stock Exchange. The extent to which businesses have disclosed their environmental policies under consideration varied greatly. Using content analysis, the scope and type of environmental disclosure in 22 growing industrial Indian firms from the cement, steel, mining and minerals, and oil and chemical products industries was evaluated. According to the study, the level of environmental reporting varies between the four sectors and the corporations included in the study (Sen, Mukherjee, & Pattanayak, 2011). According to a survey, the majority of Nigerian businesses publish their social and environmental disclosure actions. The most prevalent type of disclosure was found to be regarding employees, but despite large-scale businesses, the environmental category tends to be low (Odera, Scott, & Gow, 2016). A case study technique was used to examine the most presently popular reporting patterns of social and environmental consequences and challenges in the global mining industry. The case study approach was undertaken on the 10 largest mining corporations worldwide, as measured by market capitalisation. The analysis discovered differences between the corporations in reporting procedures and the extent of social and environmental disclosures. In addition, the survey discovered that the corporations' disclosure standards were not universal, and that only four out of the top ten participated in the Global Report Initiatives (GRI)(Jenkins & Yakovleva, 2006). In this study, the level of social and environmental disclosures was investigated using 95 textile companies that were placed on the Bombay Stock Exchange during the period from 2010 to 2012. The variation in social and environmental disclosures is statistically justified by company size, established brand, audit committee independence, CEO diversity, profitability, global recognition gained, and year of reporting according to the Ordinary Least Square (OLS) analysis (Nurhayat, Taylor, & Tower, 2015). A study looked at a relationship between CEO pay and the effectiveness of a company's corporate governance practices and argued that companies with weaker governance structures would perform worse in the future. The study discovered a strong correlation between the ownership structure and board of director characteristics and CEO remuneration levels (Core, Holthausen, & Larcker, 1997). A study provides compelling evidence that strengthening corporate sustainability performance among Asian enterprises involves both implementing and publicly reporting a solid framework combining the three pillars (ESG). Giving stakeholders access to transparent and high-quality firm ESG data improves prospects for building stakeholder confidence, which boosts firm performance (Alsayegh, Rahman, & Homayoun, 2020). The majority of shareholders, according to the survey, use ESG information for fiscal rather than ethical consideration on ESG data is vital to investment success, according to the vast majority of respondents. The information that is pertinent, however, probably varies consistently across countries (for instance, a country where water contamination is a severe problem versus a nation where corruption is a severe problem), industries (for instance, a sector that is remarkably influenced by climate change versus a sector that is influenced by violations of human rights in the supply network), and sometimes even firm approaches (e.g. companies that emphasise distinctiveness as opposed to a low pricing approach) (Amel-Zadeh & Serafeim, 2017). The majority of businesses are concentrating on CSR initiatives relating to education, such as offering educational resources to poor schools, encouraging girls' education, providing vocational training for employment, etc. Healthcare and environmental protection are the other key emphasis areas on which the businesses have focused their attention. Environmental protection involves a wide range of tasks, such as planting trees, recycling waste, properly disposing of industrial waste, etc. (Kadam, 2021). The study looks at how Australian businesses improved their ESG performance between 2007 and 2017. The study's findings demonstrate a significant improvement in corporate ESG performance over the chosen time period and offer guidance to corporate managers on how to prioritise allocating resources to ESG-related activities that might have a different effect on financial performance depending on the industry sector. Resource and budget apportionment to ESG activities that significantly affect financial operation in the various industry sectors should be given wise priority by managers (Gholami, Sands, & Shams, 2022).

Objectives

- To assess the importance of incorporating ESG information across the representative of important industrial sectors.
- To assess the inter comparison of changes in individual ESG disclosure scores across the representative of important industrial sectors.
- To assess the difference between ESG parameters for five years (2017-18 to 2021-22) across the representative of important industrial sectors.

Methodology

Three companies from each of the different sectors (Cement, FMCG & IT) represented in the NIFTY 50 are used as a sample for this research paper. For the years 2017–18 to 2021–22, this research draws on secondary data from annual and sustainability reports following prior studies (Tilt, 1994) that believed that company annual reports were the most extensively read and trustworthy type of documents that regularly provide significant ESG information. A dichotomous procedure is used to score the companies. Non-parametric tests have been used to analyse the data of the present study, since the data is qualitative in nature. Kruskal-Wallis and Mann-Whitney tests have been used not only for analysing the differences in the yearly ESG disclosure scores of the companies, but also year-to-year variations in this disclosure in each company. To evaluate if there are statistically significant variations between two or more categories of explanatory variables and an ordinal or continuous response variable, apply the Kruskal-Wallis test. When the outcome variable is random or ordinal although not identically distributed, the test that is employed to compare contrasts between two categories is Mann-Whitney test.

Analysis and Findings

Representation of Total ESG Disclosure Scores

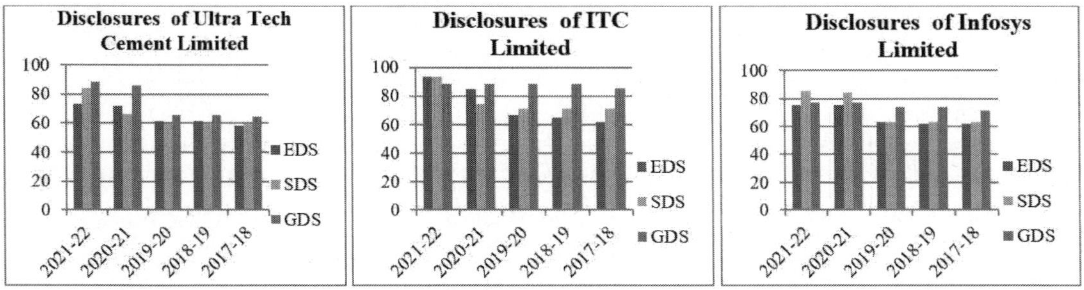

Fig. 1: ESG Disclosure Scores of Companies for the Period from 2017-18 to 2021-22

Interpretation: ESG disclosure scores of three companies across five years from 2017-18 to 2021-22 have been shown in Figure 1. Here, UltraTech Cement Ltd. is the representative of cement sector, ITC Ltd. is the representative of FMCG sector and Infosys Ltd. is the representative of IT sector. The column charts shows that the ESG disclosure scores in the current year, i.e. 2021-22 has recorded maximum disclosures compared to the past years which shows a positive and increasing trend for all the industries. But the rate of increase in ESG disclosures is more across the years for ITC Ltd. and Ultra Tech Cement Ltd. in comparison with Infosys Ltd. To determine whether or whether these differences are significant, additional analysis has been done using statistical tests such the Kruskal-Wallis and Mann-Whitney tests.

Non-parametric Test Across Five Years (2017–18 to 2021–22)

Table 1: Kruskal-Wallis Test

Null Hypothesis	*Alternate Hypothesis*	*P-Value*	*Decision*
The distribution of ESGDS is similar across five years for Ultra Tech Cement Ltd.	The distribution of ESGDS is not similar across five years for Ultra Tech Cement Ltd.	0.005	Reject the null hypothesis.
The distribution of ESGDS is similar across five years for ITC Ltd.	The distribution of ESGDS is not similar across five years for ITC Ltd.	0.000	Reject the null hypothesis.
The distribution of ESGDS is similar across five years for Infosys Ltd.	The distribution of ESGDS is not similar across five years for Infosys Ltd.	0.001	Reject the null hypothesis.

Interpretation: For the purpose of determining if there is a substantial difference in the environmental, social & corporate governance disclosure scores (ESGDS) across five years (2017-18 to 2021-22) in each of the three companies, the Kruskal-Wallis test has been used. Table 1 displays the outcomes of the Kruskal-Wallis test. Results indicate that the p-value for all the three companies is less than .05. Hence, the null hypothesis for all the companies is rejected. Hence, there are notable differences in the environmental, social and corporate governance disclosure scores (ESGDS) across five years (2017–18 to 2021–22) in each of the three companies.

Table 2: Mann-Whitney Test

Null Hypothesis	Alternate Hypothesis	P-Value	Decision
The distribution of ESGDS is similar across categories of Ultra Tech Cement Ltd. for the year 2017–18 & 2021–22.	The distribution of ESGDS is not similar across categories of Ultra ech Cement Ltd. for the year 2017–18 & 2021–22.	0.001	Reject the null hypothesis.
The distribution of ESGDS is similar across categories of ITC Ltd. for the year 2017–18 & 2021–22.	The distribution of ESGDS is not similar across categories of ITC Ltd. for the year 2017–18 & 2021–22.	0.000	Reject the null hypothesis.
The distribution of ESGDS is similar across categories of Infosys Ltd. for the year 2017–18 & 2021–22.	The distribution of ESGDS is not similar across categories of Infosys Ltd. for the year 2017–18 & 2021–22.	0.002	Reject the null hypothesis.

Interpretation: To determine whether there is a significant disparity in the level of ESG disclosure score for the period 2017–18 & 2021–22 in each of the three companies, the Mann–Whitney test has been used. Table 2 presents the outcomes. The p-value for each of the three companies, according to the findings, is less than.05.Hence, the null hypothesis for all the companies is rejected. Hence, the level of ESG disclosure score for 2017–18 and 2021–22 in each of the three corporations varies significantly. So it can be concluded that there is much satisfactory improvement in the disclosure of ESG information in case of all companies in recent years.

Non-parametric Test of Hypothesis Across Industries

Table 3: Mann-Whitney Test

Null Hypothesis	*Alternate Hypothesis*	*P-Value*	*Decision*
The distribution of ESGDS is similar across categories of Ultra Tech Cement Ltd. & ITC Ltd. for the year 2021-22.	The distribution of ESGDS is not similar across categories of Ultra Tech Cement Ltd. & ITC Ltd. for the year 2021-22.	0.003	Reject the null hypothesis.
The distribution of ESGDS is similar across categories of Ultra Tech Cement Ltd. & Infosys Ltd. for the year 2021-22.	The distribution of ESGDS is not similar across categories of Ultra Tech Cement Ltd. & Infosys Ltd. for the year 2021-22.	0.887	Accept the null hypothesis.

Null Hypothesis	*Alternate Hypothesis*	*P-Value*	*Decision*
The distribution of ESGDS is similar across categories of ITC Ltd. & Infosys Ltd. for the year 2021-22.	The distribution of ESGDS is not similar across categories of ITC Ltd. & Infosys Ltd. for the year 2021-22.	0.002	Reject the null hypothesis.

Interpretation: To determine whether there are any notable differences in the degree of ESG disclosure score for 2021–22 among the companies, the non-parametric Mann–Whitney test has been applied. Table 3 presents the outcome. Results revealed that the p-value is below .05 in case while comparing the level of ESG disclosure scores for 2021–22 between Ultra Tech Cement Ltd. & ITC Ltd. and also between ITC Ltd. & Infosys Ltd. Therefore, in both scenarios, the null hypothesis is denied. The p-value exceeds .05. in case while comparing the level of ESG disclosure scores for 2021-22 between Ultra Tech Cement Ltd. & Infosys Ltd. Hence, in this case null hypothesis is accepted. So it can be concluded that ITC Ltd. has the highest disclosure, followed by Ultra Tech Cement Ltd. & Infosys Ltd.

Table 4: Mann-Whitney Test

Null Hypothesis	*Alternate Hypothesis*	*Ultra Tech Cement Ltd.*		*ITC Ltd.*		*Infosys Ltd.*	
		P-Value	*Decision*	*P-Value*	*Decision*	*P-Value*	*Decision*
The distribution of EDS & SDS is similar for the year 2017-18	The distribution of EDS & SDS is not similar for the year 2017-18	0.881	Accept the null hypothesis.	0.279	Accept the null hypothesis.	0.961	Accept the null hypothesis.
The distribution of EDS & GDS is similar for the year 2017-18	The distribution of EDS & GDS is not similar for the year 2017-18	0.014	Reject the null hypothesis.	0.014	Reject the null hypothesis.	0.423	Accept the null hypothesis.
The distribution of SDS & GDS is similar for the year 2017-18	The distribution of SDS & GDS is not similar for the year 2017-18	0.019	Reject the null hypothesis.	0.103	Accept the null hypothesis.	0.397	Accept the null hypothesis.
The distribution of EDS & SDS is similar for the year 2018-19	The distribution of EDS & SDS is not similar for the year 2018-19	0.823	Accept the null hypothesis.	0.482	Accept the null hypothesis.	0.961	Accept the null hypothesis.
The distribution of EDS & GDS is similar for the year 2018-19	The distribution of EDS & GDS is not similar for the year 2018-19	0.031	Reject the null hypothesis.	0.012	Reject the null hypothesis.	0.275	Accept the null hypothesis.
The distribution of SDS & GDS is similar for the year 2018-19	The distribution of SDS & GDS is not similar for the year 2018-19	0.019	Reject the null hypothesis.	0.048	Reject the null hypothesis.	0.255	Accept the null hypothesis.

Null Hypothesis	*Alternate Hypothesis*	*Ultra Tech Cement Ltd.*		*ITC Ltd.*		*Infosys Ltd.*	
		P-Value	*Decision*	*P-Value*	*Decision*	*P-Value*	*Decision*
The distribution of EDS & SDS is similar for the year 2019-20	The distribution of EDS & SDS is not similar for the year 2019-20	0.823	Accept the null hypothesis.	0.610	Accept the null hypothesis.	0.810	Accept the null hypothesis.
The distribution of EDS & GDS is similar for the year 2019-20	The distribution of EDS & GDS is not similar for the year 2019-20	0.031	Reject the null hypothesis.	0.018	Reject the null hypothesis.	0.350	Accept the null hypothesis.
The distribution of SDS & GDS is the same similar year 2019-20	The distribution of SDS & GDS is not similar for the year 2019-20	0.019	Reject the null hypothesis.	0.048	Reject the null hypothesis.	0.255	Accept the null hypothesis.
The distribution of EDS & SDS is similar for the year 2020-21	The distribution of EDS & SDS is not similar for the year 2020-21	0.511	Accept the null hypothesis.	0.141	Accept the null hypothesis.	0.319	Accept the null hypothesis.
The distribution of EDS & GDS is similar for the year 2020-21	The distribution of EDS & GDS is not similar for the year 2020-21	0.119	Accept the null hypothesis.	0.627	Accept the null hypothesis.	0.958	Accept the null hypothesis.
The distribution of SDS & GDS is similar for the year 2020-21	The distribution of SDS & GDS is not similar for the year 2020-21	0.037	Reject the null hypothesis.	0.094	Accept the null hypothesis.	0.415	Accept the null hypothesis.
The distribution of EDS & SDS is similar for the year 2021-22	The distribution of EDS & SDS is not similar for the year 2021-22	0.157	Accept the null hypothesis.	0.962	Accept the null hypothesis.	0.215	Accept the null hypothesis.
The distribution of EDS & GDS is similar for the year 2021-22	The distribution of EDS & GDS is not similar for the year 2021-22	0.080	Accept the null hypothesis.	0.423	Accept the null hypothesis.	0.958	Accept the null hypothesis.
The distribution of SDS & GDS is similar for the year 2021-22	The distribution of SDS & GDS is not similar for the year 2021-22	0.529	Accept the null hypothesis.	0.395	Accept the null hypothesis.	0.302	Accept the null hypothesis.

Interpretation: Any variations between environmental disclosure scores (EDS) and social disclosure scores (SDS), between environmental disclosure scores (EDS) and corporate governance disclosure scores (GDS), and between social disclosure scores (SDS) and corporate governance disclosure scores (GDS), across each of the representative of industrial sectors for the entire five-year period (2017-2018 to 2021-22) were evaluated for statistical significance using the Mann-Whitney U test. The results are shown in Table 4. In the year 2017-18 for UltraTech Cement Ltd and ITC Ltd. null hypothesis is rejected (p-value $< .05$) in case of difference between EDS and GDS and null hypothesis is retained for the same in case of Infosys Ltd. In the same year for UltraTech Cement Ltd., alternative hypothesis is retained in case of difference between SDS and GDS and null hypothesis is accepted in case of difference between EDS and SDS. In the above year, for ITC Ltd. & Infosys Ltd. the alternative hypothesis is rejected in case of difference between EDS and SDS as well as between SDS and GDS. In the year 2018–19 and 2019–20 for UltraTech Cement Ltd and ITC Ltd. null hypothesis is denied in case of difference between EDS and GDS as well as between SDS and GDS and null hypothesis is retained in case of difference between EDS and SDS and null hypothesis is accepted in all the cases for Infosys Ltd. In the year 2020-21, for UltraTech Cement Ltd, null hypothesis is denied in case of difference between SDS and GDS and null hypothesis is accepted for difference between EDS and SDS as well as between EDS and GDS. In the same year, for ITC Ltd. and Infosys Ltd. null hypothesis is retained in all the three cases. Lastly, in the year 2021–22, for all the three companies from different sector, alternative hypothesis is accepted as there are no significant variations between EDS and SDS, between EDS and GDS as well as between SDS and GDS. So we can conclude that there is a significant improvement in ESG performance over the years.

Conclusion

The study examines ESG disclosure scores for five years (2017–18 to 2021–22) across the three industrial sectors. According to the study's findings, ESG performance has significantly improved over time. The ESG performance improvement is strong and consistent with the earlier study (Gholami, Sands, & Shams, 2022), which found that the ESG performance significantly improved from 2007 to 2017. This study reveals that ITC shows the highest increasing trend on ESG disclosures over the years, followed by UltraTech Cement Ltd. and Infosys Ltd. Industries are placing more emphasis on governance since corporate governance is crucial in establishing relationship between company and its stakeholders and, thus it is an important factor for measuring performance of every company. However, in recent years it is seen that environmental disclosure are also gaining in priority for all the three organisations in comparison to previous years which augur well for a company's sustainable growth. The rate of increase in ESG disclosures is more across the years for ITC Ltd. and UltraTech Cement Ltd. in comparison with Infosys Ltd. For long term success, business and investors are expected to step up their efforts in sustainability and embrace quantifiable ESG practices. Companies and markets can respond and so create sustainable value by comprehending risks and possibilities related to ESG through measuring tools and clear, consistent and thorough disclosures.

Bibliography

[1] Ali, W., Alsayegh, M. F., Ahmad, Z., Mahmood, Z., & Iqbal, J. (2018). The Relationship between Social Visibility and CSR Disclosure. *Sustainability* , *10* (3).

[2] Alsayegh, M., Rahman, R. A., & Homayoun, S. (2020). Corporate Economic, Environmental, and Social Sustainability Performance Transformation through ESG Disclosure. *Sustainability, 12* (9).

[3] Amel-Zadeh, A., & Serafeim, G. (2017). Why and How Investors Use ESG Information: Evidence from a Global Survey. *SSRN Electronic Journal , 74* (3).

[4] Core, J., Holthausen, R. W., & Larcker, D. F. (1997). Corporate Governance, CEO Compensation, and Firm Performance. *Journal of Financial Economics , 51*, 371–406.

[5] Gholami, A., Sands, J., & Shams, S. (2022). The Impact of Corporate ESG Performance Disclosure Across Australian Industries. *Australasian Accounting Business and Finance Journal , 16* (4).

[6] Jenkins, H., & Yakovleva, N. (2006). Corporate social responsibility in the Mining Industry: Exploring Trends in Social and Environmental Disclosure. *Journal of Cleaner Production , 14*, 271–84.

[7] Kadam, V. R. (2021). Corporate Social Responsibiity Practices: A Study of Large Scale Companies. *International Journal of Multidisciplinary Educational Research*, 10 (1(6)).

[8] Lokuwaduge, C.S., & Heenetigala, K. (2016). Integrating Environmental, Social and Governance (ESG) Disclosure for a Sustainable Development: An Australian Study. *Business Strategy and he Environment*, 26(4), 438–50.

[9] Nurhayat, R., Taylor, G., & Tower, G. (2015). Investigating social and environmental disclosure practices by listed Indian textile firms. *The Journal of Developing Areas , 49* (6), 361–72.

[10] Odera, O., Scott, A. H., & Gow, J. (2016). An examination of the quality of social and environmental disclosures by Nigerian oil companies. *Corporate Governance International Journal of Business in Society*, 16 (2), 400–19.

[11] Sen, M., Mukherjee, K., & Pattanayak, J. (2011). Corporate environmental disclosure practices in India. *Journal of Applied Accounting Research*, 12 (2), 139–56.

[12] Singh, G., & Joshi, M. (2009). Environment management and disclosure practices of Indian companies. *International Journal of Business Research*, 9 (2), 116–28.

[13] Taliento, M., Favino, C., & Netti, A. (2019). Impact of Environmental, Social, and Governance Information on Economic Performance: Evidence of a Corporate 'Sustainability Advantage' from Europe. *Sustainability*, 11 (6).

[14] Tilt, C. A. (1994). The Influence of External Pressure Groups on Corporate Social Reporting. *Accounting, Auditing & Accountability Journal*, 7 (4), 47–72.

[15] Xie, J., Fujii, H., Nozawa, W., & Yagi, M. (2018). Do Environmental, Social and Governance Activities Improve Corporate Financial Performance? *Business Srategy and the Environment, 28* (2), 286–300.

[16] https://www.ultratechcement.com/about-us/overview (Last accessed on 07.11.2022)

[17] https://www.ultratechcement.com/about-us/sustainability/sustainability#:~:text=Committed%20to%20double%20the%20energy,Water%20Positive%20company%20by%202024. (Last accessed on 06.11.2022)

[18] https://www.itcportal.com/about-itc/profile/index.aspx (Last accessed on 07.11.2022)

[19] https://www.itcportal.com/about-itc/index.aspx (Last accessed on 08.11.2022)

[20] https://www.business-standard.com/company/infosys-2806/information/company-history (Last accessed on 08.11.2022)

[21] https://research.nelson-hall.com/blogs/?avpage- (Last accessed on 09.11.2022)

[22] views=blog&type=post&post_id=1098#:~:text=Infosys%20became%20carbon%20neutral%20in,20%25%20improvement%20in%20operational%20efficiencies (Last accessed on 09.11.2022)

Intellectuals in Action Mode: World Wide Cooperation Web

DR AMIT M. BHATTACHARYA

Director, Research Innovation & Development Associates [RIDA], Kolkata
E-mail: amitmbhattacharya@gmail.com; rida18660@gmail.com

Abstract

Visibly disturbed, frustrated and deeply agonised, H.E. Antonio Guterres, the Secretary General of the United Nations 'in his opening remarks on Tuesday [20.09.2022] said that the world was in peril, and geopolitical divides were undermining international law, trust in democratic institutions and all forms of international cooperation.'[1] His angst denotes that the world leaders and policy makers are more concerned for high/higher growth rate and precariously inclined to protect respective national interest and precipitating on tech-centric and profit-centric economies totally ignoring the socio-psycho-economic environment of their countries. Under the circumstances, the intellectuals have to be action oriented in promoting the business directly with their innovative thoughts and knowledge.

Keywords: *International Law, Democratic Institutions, International Cooperation, Socio-psycho-economic Environment, Tech-centric, Profit centric, Self-interest*

'Why society does not change – poor have no guts, middle-class has no time and rich people don't need it.'

– Sampat Saral (*political satirist & poet*)

Background

The central theme of the Conference 'Reinventing Management through Sustainability, Innovation and Analytics' holds paramount importance. This theme is all encompassing because the contemporary political thoughts and actions are the prime determinant of it. Politics is the sole decisive factor that continuously shapes and reshapes the socio-psycho-economic environment thereby deciding the present and future of any nation as such. Sustainability can never be ensured, till the political leaders and policy makers worldwide do not *Audit* and *Edit* themselves. However, the management gurus, intellectuals, social scientists, philanthropists and like-minded volunteers with their good intentions can change the miserable face of the world entirely only by promoting collaboration, compassion and cooperation through whatsoever tiny steps they take towards re-establishing changed business models in this VUCA age. The need of the hour is to delve into action research with lesser number of intellectual exercises.

The author, an economist and entrepreneur by nature, always thinks, understands, writes and performs, considering the climate of political-economics as the prime factor.

This working paper, too, is framed in the same line. The author has followed descriptive, analytical and practical approach method in putting forth the business models for survival and development of teeming millions in the unorganised sector. Basic needs of human being is very limited but dangerous elements like 'greed', 'competition' and 'perception of power' are rapidly replacing the basic values of 'welfare' and 'satisfaction' thereby making things unnecessarily complex and frustrating.

Purpose of the Paper

Global economic growth system can no more afford to be conflictive and competitive to grow in seclusion. Mutual cooperation has become imperative from local to global levels of business system not only for socio-economic development but also for its sustainability. Prerequisite for such economic/business model is to bring paradigm shift in perception and practice promptly. Now, it is no more a matter of intellectual luxury to discuss the pros and cons of the problems only but they are required to involve themselves directly at all levels of business with their finer intellectual caliber and understanding for creating decisive impact in the lives and living of the teeming millions.

The author has been directly involved in perceiving, establishing, promoting and sustaining the tiny sector units continuously and looking into its striking success; intends to share the experience with the participants of the conference.

Methodology

The researcher has adopted empirical, descriptive and analytical case-study method for justifying the purpose of the study.

Research Limitations/Implications

Following the near absent ecosystem for business development, the study is limited to the tiny sector cash-cow units however; the impact is far greater than the expected ones.

Originality/Value

So far as the scholar has adopted the empirical method of the study, it ought to be original and its value is enormous because such business model fundamentally helps the marginalised people for their growth and long term sustainability

Findings

It has been observed by the author that ideation, motivation, little financial support and continuous monitoring of the tiny sector units by a mentor with better understanding, brings considerable impact in the local ecosystem and on the forward and backward linkages of the surrounding areas. This in turn, motivates other marginalised people to initiate their business and through high turnover, earn better profits and upgrade their standard of living continuously.

Reality Bites

H.E. Antonio Guterres had further asserted 'We cannot go on like this.We have a duty to act. And yet we are gridlocked in colossal global dysfunction.' Addressing the gathering of heads of the states and the concerned officials, Mr Guterres accused the fossil fuel industry of 'feasting on hundreds of billions of dollars in subsidies and windfall profits' and alerted that the leaders of the affluent countries advising 'Today I am calling on all developed economies to tax the windfall profits of fossil fuel companies' for helping the weaker countries which were suffering from irreparable damage due harsher climate change.[2]

More than 200 executives of volunteer organisations raised the shuddering issue, during the 77th General Assembly Meeting of the UN on Tuesday, that in every four seconds a person was dying of starvation worldwide following income/ joblessness and climate change. In an open letter, the executives of 238 volunteer organisations from 35 countries had given a SOS call to all the member countries to address the crisis together.

According to the report submitted by such organisations, at least 350 million people were suffering from acute food crisis and further 50 million were cliff-hanging in another 55 countries on date. Though at the onset of twenty-first century, the world-leaders had promised that 'starvation' would be mitigated completely, the things were appearing just the reverse. Mr. Mohana Ahmed Ali Eljabali, the chief of organisation of Yemen said 'this is not a crisis of a single country. Famine/Starvation does not happen due to a single reason. 'Gross injustice to Humanity' caused by the privileged people is the real reason of it. While a small group of affluent people are submerged in abundance, a huge number of people are struggling for living in acute dearth of food.' He further pointed out that millions of people in Somalia, Ethiopia, Nigeria, and Yemen were dying daily due to severe absence of food, water, shelter, sanitation and nutrition.

The above account denotes that there is something very wrong at the perception and perspective level worldwide that has led to extreme concentration of wealth and power in fewer hands and forced the major portion of people to survive as 'cliff-hangers' or in destitution. The 'trickle down theory' that tried to justify 'distributive justice' derived

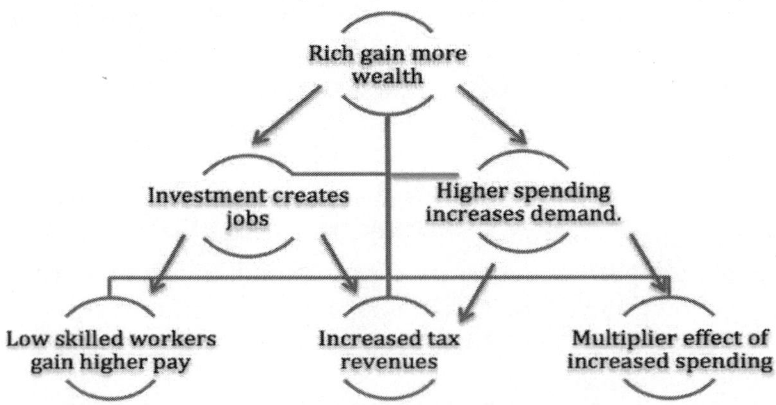

Fig. 1: Trickle Down Effect

from Laffer Curve, proved to be a mere politically motivated economic proposition that never acted in reality and the yawning gaps inequity and inequality between affluent and deprived class kept on progressively increased with every effort for aggregate developmental and welfare policies.

Had the simple model of trickledown effect acted effectively and in reality, there would be no alarming and spine-chilling Oxfam reports challenged the validity of economic policies drawn out by best of the brains of western economists and the number of socio-economically deprived persons would not have gone up exponentially.

Referring to the world famous novel *The Tale of Two Cities* by Charles Dickens (1812–70), columnist Tanveer Malik assessing the impact of the policy of 'liberalisation, privatisation, globalisation', comments 'It was the best of times, it was the worst of times; it was the age of wisdom, it was the age of foolishness; it was the epoch of belief, it was the epoch of incredulity; we had everything before us, we had nothing before us.' At present, we can also say about the tale of two Indias: We have the best of times; we have the worst of times. There is sparkling prosperity, there is stinking poverty. We have dazzling five star hotels side by side with darkened ill-starred hovels. We have everything by globalisation, we have nothing by globalisation. He further cites, 'IN his Making Globalization Work, Nobel laureate Stiglitz wrote: Trade liberalization opening up markets to the free flow of goods and services was supposed to lead to growth. The evidence is at best mixed. Part of the reason that international trade agreements have been so unsuccessful in promoting growth in poor countries is that they were often unbalanced. The advanced industrial countries were allowed to levy tariffs on goods produced by developing countries that were, on average, four times higher that those on goods produced by other advanced industrial countries.'[3]

The following photos depict there is dangerous flaws in economic modeling and MANAGEMENT of economy that never followed the integrity and inclusivity and virtually worked for only ten per cent of population of the country.

Fig. 2: Destitute in India: Utterly Starved Children in India – Common sights anywhere

India's ever-increasing dependence on China, Russia, Germany, the USA, and other middle-east countries has resulted in deep trade-imbalance and yawning fiscal gap whatsoever narrative for 'Atmanirbhata' or 'Vocal for Local' is created. When India is largely dependent on China for even raw materials for making medicines to microchips

Fig. 3: Oppulent India: Overpacked Food Zones in the Indian Malls – Common sights anywhere

to even idols of Luxmi-Ganesh and LED lights used for decorating majority of population during Deepawali celebration; India's 'Atmanirbharta' may be well adjudged.

Justifying his assertions, Tanveer Malik further cited 'Measured in the 2000 purchasing power parity (PPP) terms, *the gap between the incomes of the poorest 20 per cent of the world's population* and the $ 1 a day poverty line amounts to about $ 300 billion. That figure appears large, but it *is less than two per cent of the income of the world's wealthiest 10 per cent*.'[4] Is this the real developmental design, the national and world leaders had thought to achieve through 'open economy'. India, which is largely populated by illiterate, inefficient, ignorant and very poor people; should the country adopt LPG three decades' back and still boasting of it's 'world's most rapidly growing economy' as such? Is it not the proper time to stop the wrong concept of growth and efforts immediately and establish a business management policy that fits the Indian ecosystem with its inherent contradictions?

The eminent economists have pointed out that the Covid19 pandemic alone has caused skyrocketing Sensex as well as astronomical jump in the assets of the wealthiest people while food crisis has gained the momentum worldwide at the same time. The mystery of such economic contradictions could not be explained even by the Nobel Laureate economist Prof. Abhijit Vinayak Bandopadhyaya during a press conference in Kolkata last year. Or, knowingly he avoided the question due its geopolitical implications! He also did not answer as to why the 'trickle down' theory did not work for India and for other vulnerable societies in the world elsewhere! The first wave of Covid19 witnessed 114000000 people lost their jobs and livelihood (ILO) permanently and the second wave witnessed much more chaotic situation. Very few philanthropists and states threw sporadic 'alms' to the distressed ones to save the people from committing suicide out of frustrations, depression and following sudden loss of financial and social dignity. Collaboration, cooperation and compassion, as everyone knows, can be initiated by the capable learned and wealthy people having 'Empathy' for the less-privileged ones only.

'The progressive use of AI, Virtual Reality, Internet of Things, MR and all such mind-boggling jargon-based complex reality has now become order of the day. On date, the human civilisation is witnessing Industrial Revolution 4.0 where electronic powers, in combination with human innovative faculties, have not only gobbled up majority of menial jobs forever but also, it has brought fundamental change in the human perception and behavior awfully. Tech-driven insecurities and uncertainties are continuously reshaping the human being's individual behavior and collective conduct and its age-old and time-tried beliefs and perceptions. The world is now divided digitally consequent upon which endless confusions, conflicts and blame-games are taking place regularly thereby causing rapid erosion in human values and ethics. The human society which had evolved on the basis of cohesion, resilience and welfare-centric; it is metamorphing into 'tech-centric', 'money-centric' and 'profit centric' conspicuously.'[5]

Technology is continuously empowering the already privileged small section of population who may easily afford to stoically exclude the majority of people in protecting their 'self-interest' at the costs of the latter. The Tech-driven deprivation is not only augmenting the inequity but also pushing back the sustainable development goals beyond horizon.

Part I

India: A 'Functioning Anarchy'

While focusing on framing this write up; the author tried to analyse the factors in the backdrop of *Diversity, Inclusion and Social equity* of Indian system and culture, the author realised that though India held utmost demographic diversity in the world; the religions, social customs and traditions and economic practices remained extremely non-inclusive and carefully promoted and maintained social inequity since the ages immemorial. Witnessing such mind-boggling socio-economic-politico complexities, the then American ambassador to India and world-renowned economist and Statesman, Prof. J.K. Galbraith (1963) had said 'India functions because of its people and not its government or its institutions. India is a "functioning anarchy"'. However, the people of India have progressively lost their 'strength' and 'trust' in the last seven and half decades within the restructured political power equations and has literally converted into powerless onlookers losing their status of change-agents.

Even few years back, the world was deeply concerned with endangered sustainability and repeatedly trumpeted for enhancing 'cooperation and collaboration' but the terminology 'compassion' (showing kindness) was not in the intellectual horizon as the social perception of the Indians about 'compassion' is 'Alms' and 'Pittance' to the poorest section of members of the society since the ages.

The descriptions in the epics like Ramayana and Mahabharata, post-Vedic scriptures and Manu-Samhita hold plethora of incidents of gross social injustice like Birthocracy (social supremacy by birth and not by worth/skill), social apartheid (untouchability), racial discrimination (upper-castes, lower-castes), mass exclusion (under Brahminical arrangements), social immobility, social exclusion (of females), structural violence and Triple oppressions.

Situations are not much different either in the twenty-first century 'New India' though, technological advancement and professional compulsions have bound people to some extent, the undercurrent of deeply trenched bigotry and xenophobia flow freely and it appears that no radical change has taken place in the social texture for the last five thousand years. It is difficult to imagine the ideas of equity and inclusivity in a caste-ridden, gender-bias unsustainable society to achieve economic and managerial sustainability in any way.

Even today, the scheduled caste people are not only restrained but also punished in many parts of the country if the grooms are riding decorated mares during their marriages, sit on a chair or on an elevated platform in front of higher caste person, wearing shoes or maintain moustaches. The recent incidents of killing (April '22) of a innocent thirsty Muslim boy (12) who dared to drink water from a Hindu temple tap or the students (aged 12 and 13) succumbed to their injuries inflicted upon by their upper-caste teachers for touching the pitcher kept in the classroom and for making a single spelling mistake in a class-test (July & September, 2022), in their respective schools. Inclusivity and compassion in Indian society – you see!!

Economic Anarchy in India

Diversity, like rainbow hues, makes a society rich in spirit of harmony and ensures 'peaceful co-existence' and also augments 'collective empathy' thereby strengthening cohesive culture. It obviously lead to 'inclusion' abhorring the tendency of 'self-centeredness' at large. Making harsh comment on Indian system, the Oxfam Report (17 January 2022) 'projects that the economic transaction that directly or indirectly determine the social equality and justice have completely divorced the morality, trust, empathy, and humane values long ago in Indian context.'[6] The report reflects that 'when 84 per cent of households in the country suffered a decline in their income in a year marked by tremendous loss of life and livelihoods, the number of Indian billionaires grew from 102 to 142' – Oxfam India's latest briefing 'Inequality Kills' has revealed. The briefing was published ahead of the World Economic Forum's Davos Agenda. The briefing indicates that the collective wealth of India's 100 richest people hit a record high of INR 57.3 lakh crore (USD 775 billion) in 2021'.[5] Oxfam CEO, Mr Amitabh Behar, said, 'In India, during the pandemic (since March 2020, through to November 2021) the wealth of billionaires increased from INR 23.14 lakh crore (USD 313 billion) to INR 53.16 lakh crore (USD 719 billion). More than 4.6 crore Indians meanwhile are estimated to have fallen into extreme poverty in 2020 (nearly half of the global new poor according to the United Nations.) The stark wealth inequality in India is a result of an economic system rigged in favour of the super-rich over the poor and marginalised.' He further says, 'our economic system is and how it fuels not only inequality but poverty as well. We urge the Government of India to commit to an economic system which creates a more equal and sustainable nation. India can show the world that democratic systems are capable for wealth redistribution and inclusive growth where no one is left behind. India's fight against inequality and poverty must be supported by the billionaires who made record profits in the country during the pandemic.'[7]

There was a time when Emperor Harshavardhana (606 to 647) ruled over India and whose 'rule was renowned for peace, stability and prosperity, and attracted many artists and scholars from far and wide'. A famous Chinese traveler, Xuanzang, described Harshavardhana as a messiah for his generosity and administrative skills. Having deep empathy and compassion for his subject, the emperor used to empty his entire exchequer and distribute every farthing among his subject gathered at Kumbha Mela (at the confluence of Ganga and Yamuna at Prayagraj) every sixth year so that their socio-economic sustainability could be ensured. Xuanzang further described 'there was no slavery in his empire and people were free to lead their life according to their wish. His empire also took good care of the poor by building rest houses that provided all the amenities required. In many texts, Harshavardhana has been described as a noble emperor who made sure all his subjects stayed happy. He did not impose heavy taxes on his people and the economy was somewhat self-sufficient.'[8] In one word, he was the epitome of 'hand-holding' and 'compassion' together as such.

After 1,400 years of civilisation's journey since, can any super-rich person/s or any political ruler even dream of such act that are ever busy in amassing wealth by sucking up the last farthing from the pockets of the commoners. Policymakers are ever-busy in defining the 'Below Poverty Line' (BPL); however, would they ever think in defining 'Above Affluence Line'(AAL) where a logical and legitimate distributive pattern for hugely concentrated wealth be found!

The awestruck world found that a person having owned a 'Bitcoin' having a face value of Rs 7.50 in 2010 has registered the asset value at Rs 37.33 lacs per Bitcoin in December 2021. Such uncontrolled e-currency generated from unknown source has further disrupted the socio-economic texture suddenly and silently thereby destroying the element of 'trust' and 'commitment' of those who preferred to keep clean and doing away with gambling and unethical practices. On date, the market is flooded with innumerous 'Cryptocurrency Start-Ups' who are alluring the common people to indulge into the abyss of greed and uncertainty. On 12 October, the *Times of India* reported that there are 'Over 10 crore Indians own cryptocurrency'*9 gaining the top position in the world. While the USA and Russia are showing only 6 and 7 millions investors in Cryptocurrencies; India has already crossed 100 million marks with over USD $10 billion and that is counting every day. Now a day the Indians at large perceive 'He who works for money, is an idiot – the money should work for the owner and one should not work for money.' However, the shadow of naked gains earned from such virtual currencies the citizens of B and C class cities in India are showing off with 'Lamborghini' (Rs. 5.5 crore) cars and the like for which neither the road qualities nor the infrastructure is created yet. Most of such opulent people prefer to donate (Gupt Daan) in the coffers of the temples than donating it for the better causes like free-meals and clothing for the have-nots.[9]

Part II

Practical Approach

Finding that any number of intellectual exercises, seminars, conferences or for that matter, best of advices from the spiritual leaders to the people are becoming futile in ensuring sustainability; the author stepped ahead to connect people, motivating them to be cooperative, collaborated with capable individuals and social organisations and to establish a network of economic activities the forward and backward linkages of which are considerably large and which might ensure livelihoods of those young people with low mental and technical skills and who lost their jobs pre and post Covid-19 periods in Kolkata.

The concerted efforts of the author and some well-wishers came-up with exemplary success though, at the atomic level. All the workers and the stake holders were enthused to dream big and put their heart and soul into their respective tiny enterprises. The experiment was initiated under the banner of Research, Innovation & Development Associates (RIDA) since October 2014, even through the harsher second wave of COVID-19 that struck in the year 2020 and 2021. While the author remained successful in mobilising groups of poor ladies to sustain their livelihoods by running road-side small tea-stalls to vegetable vending shops providing them seed money and management tips.

Case I

A poor lady, Mrs Deepa Bera (35), whose husband lost his job as a guard in a local company, was motivated to run a tea and snacks shop near Howrah railway station

Fig. 4: Deepa Bera: Selling Tea and Snacks in her Stall. Author in the backdrop

in October 2020. She was given with a seed capital of Rs 15,000/- and some informal training in running the stall. Till date, she toils for 10 hours a day. She is capable of earning on an average Rs 1,000/- a day and has successfully mobilised Rs 25,000/- in her bank account. She is motivating other poor ladies to run small units akin to their domestic skills for earning livelihoods gracefully.

Case II

Being enthused with the tremendous success of a numerous tiny projects, the author mobilised few well-off people and motivated them to run food-trucks that may employ low-skilled people for earning their livelihoods. With their collaboration, three food-trucks were created thereby employing 20 people directly and 50 people indirectly.

The project was initiated on 15 August and its initial success has energised all the stake holders to establish a brand name of 'Snack Track Pure Veg'. in the coming days. Regular deployment of the 'Snack Track' food-trucks at different locations are fetching good revenues from the very first day and to date, the economics of the project showing early hitting of 'break-even' ensuring substantial cash-flow.

Fig. 5: The Author (second from left) with Other Stakeholders on 15 August 2022

Case III

The author chalked out a plan to provide opportunities of earning livelihoods to few jobless youths who were having cooking, catering and general managerial skills sans capital to start any project. He invited a Muslim boy, a Punjabi boy and few rootless girls to create a group and to start a small eatery with western food items and Indian beverages. The author infused an initial capital Rs 20,000/- and hired a food-stall, keeping the festive season in view, within a local housing complex. All the participants were enthusiastic to find a platform of their liking and joined hands with a vow to make it's branding in due course. The cliff-hanging youths soon collaborated with the local food-stalls and pushed up their sales and profits with concerted efforts.

The first day sale of Rs1,060/- was a moderate start but soon picked up and reached to Rs 4000+ per day thereby covering up their operational costs as well with a sound cash flow to grow up without infusing more capital into it. However, the stakeholders promptly agreed to highlight the words 'Collaboration, Cooperation and Compassion' in its banner which is conspicuous in the banner.

Fig. 6: The 'Desi Hollywood' Running Successfully since 20th September '22

It might be a tiny start but the youths were dreaming of creating a chain of eateries (branding) under the same banner.

The author has been successful in establishing more than 150 such tiny units with various activities since 2004 and except three, all are running well thereby giving more than adequate livelihoods opportunities gracefully. The most creditworthy aspect is that the majority of such units are being run by marginalised ladies in West Bengal and Uttar Pradesh alike. This is the perfect example of diversity, inclusion and social equity for which the author is advocating for initiatives to be taken by the intellectuals.

Conclusion

Blind imitations of the western model of doing business, their management style and techniques by India have caused irreparable damage to the economy as such. India is already on fire due to inequality, inequity, injustice, hunger, greed, and violence. People around the author often ask 'Is India sitting on a economic time-bomb and waiting helplessly for its explosion?' Should ***India*** afford such iconic socio-economic injustice anymore as the photograph reveals.

Fig. 7: Photojournalist Kevin Carter's 'The Struggling Girl'

Viewing the photograph above; an orphaned Kolkata girl Ms Alka Rajput (18) who is an entrepreneur and an upcoming journalist, commented with fathomless depression, 'We are not ugly; we are born and growing up in an ***ugly age***', leaving the author dumbfounded with awe and agony.

There is no alternative but to join hands together at the earliest to douse such spreading fire because the fire does not discriminate with anyone and stoically and equally ruin the rich and poor alike elsewhere!

It is always useful to dissent, debate and discuss the burning issues to find out the concrete solutions at every possible platform from global to local levels but it would be of apex importance to create a physical **World Wide Cooperation Web** to counter the adversaries by basic human efforts based on inclusivity shunning all sorts of inhibitions and discriminatory feelings, countering strong resistance from the people with vested interests who want to clip the naturally rich developing countries' wings from its efforts to fly freely as per their ecosystem. Of course, continuously developing communication technology can make the formation of such global cooperation web happen even at a faster pace.

References

[1] *The Telegraph Calcutta*, Wednesday, 21 September, 2022.

[2] Ibid., p 3.

[3] https://www.fibre2fashion.com/industry-article/2993/impact-of-globalisation-on-indian-economy-an-overview

[4] Ibid.

[5] 'Microchip Versus Ethics and Values' Paper submitted by Dr. Amit M. Bhattacharya, in the international conference held by Manav Rachana University in February, 2022.

[6] https://www.oxfamindia.org/press-release/inequality-kills-india-supplement-2022?page=3

[7] http://timesofindia.indiatimes.com/articleshow/86962167.cms?utm_source=contentofinterest&utm_medium=text&utm_campaign=cppst

[8] https://www.culturalindia.net/indian-history/ancient-india/harshavardhan.html

[9] 'Microchip Versus Ethics and Values' paper submitted by Dr. Amit M. Bhattacharya, in the International Conference held by Manav Rachana University in February, 2022.

The Study Related to Identification of Challenges and Practices of Sustainability in Indian Clothing and Textile Industries

TANYA GAUTAM[1] AND DR. MEENU SHANT PRIYA[2]

[1]*Research Scholar, School of Business, Galgotias University, Uttar Pradesh*
[2]*Professor, Galgotias University, Uttar Pradesh*
Email: tanya.20gsob3010015@galgotiasuniversity.edu.in; meenu.priya@galgotiasuniversity.edu.in

Abstract

Purpose: This paper aims to identify the challenges and practices of sustainability in the Indian clothing and textile industries.

Methodology: This study used screening to identify related author literature. Three screenings were done. First, 191 publications from Google Scholar, Science Direct, Research Gate, etc., were screened. Thereafter, 57 articles were selected based on keywords, abstracts, titles, related material, and contributions. Next, 33 papers were discovered and studied for this study based on relativity, impact factor, citation, and review procedure.

Findings: The study outlined the obstacles to the sustainability of the Indian apparel and textile sectors, including insufficient infrastructure, poor raw material quality, waste management in the textile sector, etc., as well as strategies like reuse, recycling, and using less energy during manufacturing.

Implications: Given that the textile and apparel sector in India is one of the most polluting, this study's findings on the sector's sustainability concerns and practices would be useful in shaping regulations to curb pollution.

Originality: The paper's originality is supported by a survey of related literature on sustainability challenges and approaches in the Indian clothing and textile sectors.

Keywords: *Sustainability, Indian Clothing, Textile Industry, Environment, Challenges, Fashion*

Introduction

The use of textiles is crucial to the functioning of human society (Desore & Narula 2018). After food, textiles are among the most fundamental needs of humankind. Every person on Earth is a user of it. Culture, social status, economic status, political beliefs, and religious values are all represented via a person's textiles. A variety of byproducts and effluents were produced and discarded at each stage of the textile production process. As of late, the textile industry has been recognised as one of the most harmful polluters worldwide. Environmental, social, economic, and governmental problems are all intertwined in the textiles and apparel industry. Producers and merchants have been making strides to lessen the environmental and social implications of textiles over their entire life cycles. These strides include better working conditions, social norms, pay, and safety precautions, as well as a prohibition on child and forced labor (Muthu, 2017).

One of the most important industrial sectors, the 'textiles and apparel (T&A)' industry, makes a significant contribution to the national economy, job creation, and exports in developing nations (Karthik and Gopalakrishnan, 2014). Clothing and textiles from India are the results of a culture that is used to making do with very little, thanks to a blend of ingenuity, philosophy, artisanal ability, and communal dedication. The practice of reusing and repurposing textiles is deeply ingrained in Indian culture and has contributed to the country's success in lowering its contribution to global warming.

Sustainability in the fashion industry is working to improve local ecosystems and social conditions. One way to do this is to find ways to extend the shelf life of materials, increase the value of timeless clothing, decrease the quantity of trash produced, and lessen the environmental damage caused by manufacturing and use. The promotion of the 'green customer', or someone who makes ecologically conscious purchasing decisions, can be considered as another of its goals. The term 'sustainable textiles' refers to products made from renewable resources such as organic cotton and recycled plastic bottles. For a long time, natural fibers were almost synonymous with the concept of eco-friendly fabrics. Cotton, wool, silk, and bamboo are all examples of natural fibers that are more eco-friendly than synthetic fibers like nylon, acrylic, and polyester.

Indian Clothing and Textile Industries

India is a major player in the global textile and clothing industry. Textile production in India dates back centuries and is a major economic sector. The textile industry is exceptionally diverse, including hand-woven, hand-spun, and several mills. Because of the exceptional quality of the fabric and the low price, consumers all over the world import textiles from India.

India's textile industry dates back four thousand years. Textile production in India suffered greatly under colonial rule, but it began to flourish again in the early nineteenth century. Although Calcutta was home to the first mill of its kind, the major action took place 36 years later in Bombay with the opening of the world's first cotton textile factory. Historically, the textile industry in India has been the only industry to provide substantial employment for both skilled and unskilled workers, second only to agriculture. Even now, the textile industry is responsible for a significant number of jobs in India. Approximately 35 million people in the country are directly employed as a result. In the fiscal year 2022, India's textile and garment exports were worth US$ 44.4 billion, making it the world's second-largest exporter in this sector (IBEF.org).

India's rich textile heritage and the plethora of natural resources make the country a prime location for textile design and manufacturing. The innovative and traditional design principles employed in production and the connection with agriculture set India apart from its worldwide rivals. The design is made all the more vibrant by the myriad guidelines that emerge from the region's varied customs and points of view. This ensures that Indian textiles are competitive in both the domestic and global textile markets.

The textile sector in India is as diverse and complicated as the nation itself, and it mixes this enormous diversity into a coherent whole with the same kind of serenity as it does with its other strengths. Having the oldest looms in the world, the second oldest spindles after China, a strong base of multi-fiber raw materials, a vast pool of skilled workers, flexible production systems, dynamic entrepreneurs, and vibrant design creativity have all contributed to the creation of a thriving textile industry in India, which has been the primary driver of the country's economy for a very long time. The textile and apparel industry in India is a mammoth, intricate beast. There are upstream and downstream weavers, artisans, and farmers, as well as an organised and disorganised industry. Handmade, semi-mechanical, mechanical, and extremely advanced information-based and microprocessor-based technologies all coexist across a wide technological range (Devaraja, 2011).

The liberalisation of trade and economic policies instituted by the Government in the 1990s has been largely responsible for the explosive development pattern of the Indian textile sector during the past decade. Growth and development in the textile sector have also been significantly impacted by the industry's unique tax and regulation framework. Fiscal policies have long seen the textile industry as one in which 'little is beautiful', and this has led to structural oddities, such as the concentration of downstream components of the business in the decentralised sector and the devastation of the organised sector. In addition to natural fibers like cotton, jute, silk, and wool, the textile industry also relies heavily on the manufacture of synthetic fibers like polyester, viscose, nylon, and acrylic, which together form the industry's backbone.

Sustainability

A large-scale goal of society, sustainability is to ensure that people can continue to coexist in a secure environment on Earth for an extended period of time. It is difficult to get a consensus on precise definitions of sustainability; as a result, there is a great deal of variation in the relevant literature and across the course of history. The idea of sustainability can serve as a compass to direct decision-making on all scales, including the global, national, and personal levels. Environmental, economic, and social sustainability are the three facets that are typically discussed when discussing sustainability. These aspects are also referred to as pillars (Purvis et al., 2019).

Social Sustainability

Social sustainability requires taking into account the fact that healthy communities are led by leaders who are fair to all members of the community, treat everyone on an equal footing, and make certain that workers' rights, cultural rights, and personal rights are respected. Individuals are shielded from being discriminated against. Everyone has access to universal human rights as well as fundamental requirements.

Economic Sustainability

This pillar ensures that economic systems are stable and that activities such as having access to reliable sources of income are available to people in every country on the planet. People are able to keep their independence and have access to the resources that are necessary for them to meet their day-to-day requirements, so this is another benefit.

Environmental Sustainability

Environmental sustainability refers to the idea that people use the Earth's natural resources at a rate at which they can be replaced. The environmental component is frequently highlighted. Carbon footprints, packaging waste, water consumption, and other environmental impacts are all areas of attention for the manufacturing industry and consumer-facing firms. Many businesses have found that their bottom lines benefit from these environmentally friendly initiatives. For instance, lowering packaging material consumption typically results in less money spent on packaging materials.

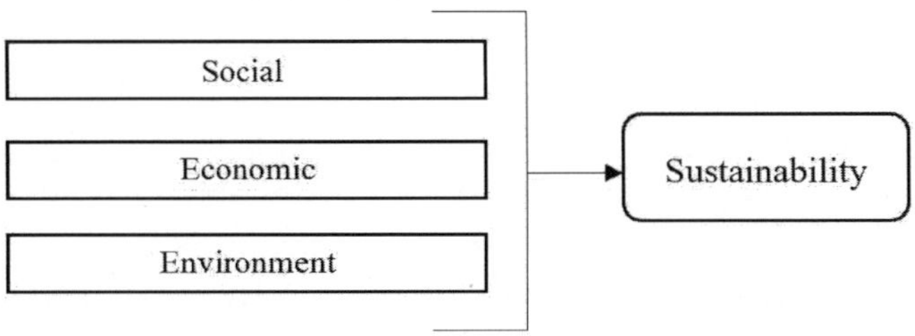

Fig. 1: Sustainability
Source: https://en.wikipedia.org/wiki/Sustainability

The term 'triple bottom line' refers to the goals of sustainability, which are the peaceful coexistence of people, the planet, and profit, as well as equal development of all three (Geissdoerfer et al., 2017).

Sustaining anything is giving it the power to keep going, keeping it afloat, or keeping it from sinking. Every person has a unique set of priorities and ideals when it comes to how they want to spend their time in this world. Still, no one's ease should come at the expense of another's pain. Sustainable development is predicated on preserving the Earth's natural resources for the benefit of future generations. In order to live in peace now and in the future, people must take steps to ensure the survival of nature, the planet, biodiversity, and ecosystems.

Practices of Sustainability in Indian Clothing and Textile Industries

The textile industry is one of the fastest-growing sectors of the economy and workforce in the twenty-first century, with far-reaching consequences for these spheres of life. Furthermore, textile production uses vast quantities of water, a resource that is steadily declining in availability. Since the textile sector has been named one of the most polluting, eco-friendly manufacturing processes are essential if people are to protect the planet.

In order to be considered sustainable, textiles must use only renewable or recycled resources for their inputs, processes, and final products at every stage of the product's life cycle. It can also imply that materials can be safely cycled back into either natural or industrial systems and that all parts of the product's lifecycle can contribute to improved societal well-being. Better textile recycling and the use of more environmentally friendly raw materials are two key components of a truly sustainable textile supply chain. What one means by 'sustainability' in the textile industry is production without depleting natural resources.

Standards are essential for the current trend of adapting or replacing business processes in pursuit of sustainability. Among the many sustainable practices implemented by the textile industry are the reduction or elimination of the use of water, harmful chemicals, pesticides, and fertilisers; the adoption of environmentally friendly production processes; the conservation of energy; and the promotion of the three R's: reduction, reuse, and recycling. The demand for eco-friendly goods reflects a growing consciousness about the environment among consumers. Consumer, producer, societal, and environmental welfare are all primary concerns for sustainability standards and related certifications (Amutha, 2017).

The use of organic ingredients and energy-saving techniques is just the beginning of what constitutes sustainable textile production. Extreme amounts of water and energy are used in the textile industry, and a number of chemicals and potentially dangerous compounds are also employed during the production process. The majority of textile factories release a substantial quantity of toxic waste, which endangers ecosystems. Modern, eco-friendly production techniques and the wise use of scarce natural resources are essential to the continued success of not only the textile industry but also the entire ecosystem.

Ecological concerns have come to the fore in recent years, particularly in the traditionally unfriendly textile and garment sector. Every piece of clothing produces hazardous compounds that harm the environment. There is an urgent requirement for green textiles due to the traditional textile industry's excessive use of natural resources and pollution of the environment during manufacture and processing, both of which require Chemical Intensive Applications. Toxic effects in manufacturing processes must be eliminated, making pollution control just as important. However, the introduction of more eco-friendly materials like organic cotton, hemp, and bamboo fibers has mitigated the negative effects of rayon's use in the fashion industry on the environment. Products made from petroleum have negative effects on the ecosystem.

To prevent these harmful impacts, people require an all-encompassing strategy for reducing pollution. Eco-friendly fabrics can replace non-sustainable materials. The term 'green textiles' is used to describe articles of clothing and other textile products that are made with fewer harmful chemicals, less wasteful packaging, and less energy. In order to help the environment, it is important to utilise items with less of an influence on the environment or to reduce the environmental impact that textiles have over their whole life cycle. Water usage, energy use, pollution, and the consumption of nonrenewable resources are four important environmental essential aspects in the textile industry (Curteza, 2011).

Challenges of Sustainability in Indian Clothing and Textile Industries

Some firms in the apparel and textile industries have been adopting eco-friendly policies and procedures in recent years. Sustainable design and manufacturing practices in the garment industry were developed by corporations that placed a premium on ethical and environmental decision-making. And in recent years, with the use of renewable materials and natural energy, these methods have become more widespread. Such alterations are not simple to implement and have their own unique difficulties. As understanding has grown over the years, many businesses have fought to implement the necessary adjustments and overcome the barrier.

Fast-paced Changes in the Fashion Industry

To be profitable in the fast fashion industry, several companies have turned to exploit low-wage labor and non-sustainable materials to save prices. These conventional methods of production are diametrically opposed to the views held by those who promote environmental responsibility. The genesis of this problem is the general public's obliviousness to environmental issues (Bhardwaj & Fairhurst, 2010). Since clothing is readily available at low prices, consumers often buy more than they need to keep up with the latest trends. This results in consumers discarding clothing before the end of its useful lifespan. The issue of clothes waste and disposal was therefore brought to light (Gupta et al., 2018).

Inadequate Infrastructure

Inadequate facilities are a key issue. Most small and medium-sized enterprises (SMEs) in developing nations lack entry to cutting-edge technologies that would improve their capacity for environmentally friendly manufacturing. As an illustration, consider the facilities required to manage dangerous chemical waste or support the development of renewable energy sources. The textile and clothing sector in India is severely underdeveloped in terms of mechanisation. The majority of textile mills still employ antiquated methods of garment production. Power outages also occur often. These issues need to be resolved in order to maintain international competitiveness. In addition to more money and research, this issue needs more attention (Umarji, 2015). The collapse of buildings and industrial fires can be directly attributed to the state of the infrastructure today.

Poor Quality of Raw Materials

The quality of cotton must be increased. Low output is directly related to raw material quality. The raw material quality might be enhanced by using cutting-edge new technologies. In order to produce higher-grade raw materials, high-quality seeds or hybrid seeds are necessary. The process of ginning and pressing helps to purify cotton and boost its quality (You et al., 2009). The high price of raw materials is a significant barrier for the textile industry, particularly in countries that must import these materials. Sustainable practices are out of reach due to high costs and issues like inflation. There is also a price premium associated with using organic or renewable materials instead of traditional textiles.

Lack of Skilled Labour for Sustainable Processes

Many textile businesses are hesitant to embrace sustainable practices due to a shortage of competent labor available to implement new technology. Workers in this sector are not required to undergo any formal training. Training employees is not a priority for most companies. Because of a lack of qualified workers, production has slowed down, and product quality has suffered. There has to be a comprehensive training program and workshops for all employees to solve this issue (Aboagyewaa-Ntiri et al., 2016). In addition, poor pay contributes to the widespread usage of child labor. It's not only illegal and unethical, but it also leads to lower-quality work.

Waste Management in the Textile Industry

Many companies, in an effort to cater to shoppers' preferences, manufacture low-quality, low-priced garments that wear out quickly. The amount of deadstock fabric that ends up in landfills is comparable to the number of worn clothing items. Garments that are thrown away take a long time to degrade, which wastes money and resources. The textile and garment industry contributes significantly to environmental degradation. It contaminates the environment on all levels (air, soil, and water). Due to insufficient regulation and education, many businesses are careless about the environment and release their wastewater into nearby bodies of water. Industries often release toxic chemicals into the water supply, endangering both aquatic life and human health (Raichurkar & Ramachandran, 2015).

Lack of Sufficient Governmental Policies

Good government policy is necessary for the effective regulation of this industry, which can make up for its deficiency in ways that trained labor in this industry cannot match. Moreover, government policy needs to consider the following concerns: protecting the environment, minimising trash, recycling, and garbage disposal are all difficult tasks (Albloushy & Hiller Connell, 2019).

Review of Literature

Sustainability in the Indian Textile Manufacturing Sector

Hiremath R.B. et al. (2012) focused on the city of Solapur in the Indian state of Maharashtra to examine the environmental impacts of the state's large-scale but poorly managed textile industry. Impacts on the environment (climate, health, agriculture, biodiversity, water, air, and soil) were factored into the technique, along with quantitative data. By reviewing several articles, the authors were able to conduct a thorough investigation. In order to cope with the effects of climate change, a sustainable networking model was proposed as a potential answer.

Raj D. et al. (2017) remarked that there had been a dramatic rise in the recent several decades in both the understanding of the environmental effect and the use of production management methods like 'lean production (LP)' in response to global environmental challenges and general business competitiveness. The study looked at the impediments to the adoption of LP and environmental sustainability (ES) techniques in the Indian clothing manufacturing sector, as well as the prevalence and effects of cost-of-production and waste management measures. The findings suggested that the Indian clothing manufacturing industry may benefit from greater adoption of LP and ES techniques if the obstacles highlighted in the study were removed.

Sharma, A., & Narula, S.A. (2020) revealed the characteristics that encourage and discourage textile companies in India from pursuing sustainability and the effect this has on the rate at which these companies implement sustainable business practices. The initial cost of compliance is the main hurdle in implementing sustainable practices, whereas regulatory, market, and economic reasons are more crucial in persuading enterprises to embrace them.

Gbolarumi F.T. et al. (2021) introduced a broad idea and provided a high-level summary of the textile industry's sustainability evaluation. According to the analysed studies, most sustainability assessments in the textile and apparel industry were undertaken at the sector, product, and process/ work cell levels.

Environmental Impact of Textile Processes

Yacout, D.M., & Hassouna, M.S. (2016) examined two strategies for handling hazardous solid waste from acrylic fiber production (landfill and incineration). Statistical analysis showed that burning waste in an incinerator was the more environmentally benign option. Ecotoxicity and carcinogenic potential were most strongly impacted by both methods due to the release of metals from pigment wastes.

Gita S. et al. (2017) observed that one of the most significant sources of pollution is wastewater from textile dyeing. It is acknowledged as one of the main factors contributing to environmental contamination. There is presently no universal standard for emissions, despite the fact that many nations have passed rigorous emission regulations. Waste reduction is crucial for lowering manufacturing costs and pollution levels.

Sandin, G., & Peters, G.M. (2018) examined studies on the effects of recycling and reusing textiles. The reviewed publications offered solid evidence to back up claims that reuse is better than recycling, and that recycling and incineration of textiles have a greater negative impact on the environment than landfilling and reuse. The studies did, however, highlight circumstances in which recycling and reuse are not advantageous for specific environmental effects.

Khattab T.A. et al. (2020) claimed that color has a significant role in attracting attention to a cloth, regardless of how well constructed it may be. As a result, the manufacturing and application of synthetic dyestuffs for textiles have grown into a multibillion-dollar market. Bio colours, natural mordants, and waterless dyeing with the help of supercritical carbon dioxide are only some of the ecosystems that have been investigated. The study investigated the ecological impacts of the textile dyeing business, including but not limited to water use, pollution, and treatment.

Solutions Regarding Sustainability in Indian Clothing and Textile Industries

Moon K.K.L. et al. (2015) investigated ways to increase the number of sustainable clothing options available to consumers. The study added to the knowledge of how customers feel about the tension between fashion and sustainability and of the obstacles to the widespread adoption of sustainable clothing.

Nimkar, U. (2018) observed that there has been tremendous growth in chemical output as a result of the world's rising population and advances in chemistry over the previous century. The survey concluded that the industry had taken great steps to solve this concern. Long-term, sustainable chemistry is the answer, and innovation is the way to get there.

Pandey R. et al. (2020) found that the manufacturing, use, and disposal phases of the life cycle of sustainable fashion result in less environmental damage. Eco-innovation, eco-selection, effluent treatment, eco-labelling, exploitation of textile wastes, reuse, and popular recycling procedures are all included in the study, along with other green alternatives for the fashion and textile industries.

de Abreu, M.C.S., et al. (2020) looked at the collaborative decision-making process behind sustainable textile and garment sector solutions. The study used a focal net viewpoint to analyse how businesses work together to create sustainable goods. Conditions for achieving sustainable company performance were highlighted in the study, and they include things like a corporate policy that takes on and expresses responsibility for social interest, key business stakeholders, and regulatory mandates.

Method of Review

Table 1: Review Method

Screening No.	*Screening Method*	*No. of Articles/Case Laws Studied*
1st screening	Google Scholar, science direct, research gate, and related sites were chosen to find the articles.	191 articles were identified after 1st search.
2nd screening	The articles were selected based on keywords, abstract, title, relevant content, and contributions.	57 articles were selected after 2nd screening.
Final screening	The articles were identified and analysed based on relativity, impact factor, citation, and review process.	33 articles were chosen for investigation after the final screening.

Discussion

This study reviewed the various types of material written by different writers to examine the identification of sustainability problems and practices in India's textile and apparel sectors. The study used a screening process to find the relevant literature for the investigation. There were apparently three stages of screening. The initial step of the study was to select 191 publications from different sources, including Google Scholar, Science Direct, Research Gate, etc., for further review. After the second round of screening, 57 articles made the cut because they satisfied the criteria for relevance, originality, and accessibility. After using criteria like relevance, impact factor, citation, and review procedure, a total of 33 articles were selected for further investigation. Some authors are noted below for their discussion of the issues, difficulties, and solutions related to textile sustainability:

Using a survey of textile companies in India, Sharma, A., & Narula, S.A. (2020) determined the characteristics that encouraged and discouraged participation in sustainability initiatives and the effect this had on company adoption of sustainable business practices. Gbolarumi F.T. et al. (2021) provided a high-level explanation of the idea behind assessing the textile industry's sustainability and an overview of the field as a whole. According to the examined literature, most textile and apparel industry sustainability evaluations were performed at the sector, product, and process/work cell levels. Sandin, G., & Peters, G.M. (2018) evaluated the literature on the effects of recycling and reusing textiles on the environment and identified instances in which recycling and reuse are not recommended for particular environmental consequences and benefits. Khattab T.A. et al. (2020) studied the ecosystems involved in the textile dyeing business, including the various dyeing processes, water usage, pollution, and treatment options. Pandey R. et al. (2020) discovered that there is less environmental damage caused by the production, use, and disposal phases of the life cycle of sustainable fashion. de Abreu, M.C.S., et al. (2020) investigated how business-to-business collaboration contributes to the development of environmentally friendly practices in the textile and clothing industry.

Conclusion

The clothing and textile industries are one of India's most significant manufacturing industries. The study concluded that sustainability initiatives assist companies prevent greenwashing, decrease investment risks in green innovations, and accelerate the transition to a sustainable future. To be sustainable, the textile sector must overcome several obstacles, including the production of substantial amounts of harmful waste. Findings from the study emphasised the importance of industrial firms realising that becoming green is about more than simply doing the right thing from an ethical standpoint; it's also about making money. When energy- and water-efficient goods and methods are used, expenses are decreased, and profits are raised. In addition to the obvious financial benefits, a company's bottom line can also benefit from adopting environmentally friendly policies. The study uncovered the difficulties that may potentially stand in the way of attaining sustainability, and it presented the sustainable business methods that are now being used in the Indian apparel and textile sectors. This study also offered some suggestions for environmentally responsible behaviors. These behaviors contribute to and promote environmental sustainability. The use of the life cycle assessment approach, eco-labeling of the garment, environmentally friendly procedures, environmentally friendly textile fibers, and recycled clothing are some of the methods that are covered in this category. All of these methods offer a variety of benefits, including the protection of the environment, the raising of consumer awareness, etc.

References

[1] 'A brief history of Textile Industry in India, January, 2010' (PDF). Archived from the original (PDF) on 22 May 2012.

[2] Aboagyewaa-Ntiri, J., Mintah, K., & Aboagyewaa, J. (2016). Challenges and opportunities for the textile industry in Ghana: a study of the Adinkra textile sub-sector. *International Business Research*, 9(2), 127–136.

[3] Albloushy, H., & Hiller Connell, K.Y. (2019). Purchasing environmentally sustainable apparel: The attitudes and intentions of female Kuwaiti consumers. *International Journal of Consumer Studies*, 43(4), 390–401.

[4] Amutha, K. (2017). Sustainable practices in textile industry: Standards and certificates. In *Sustainability in the Textile Industry* (pp. 79–107). Springer, Singapore.

[5] Bhardwaj, V., & Fairhurst, A. (2010). Fast fashion: Response to changes in the fashion industry. *The international review of retail, distribution and consumer research*, 20(1), 165–73.

[6] Curteza, A. (2011). Sustainable textiles. In *Radar* (Vol. 2, No. 1, pp. 19–21).

[7] de Abreu, M.C.S., Ferreira, F.N.H., Proença, J.F., & Ceglia, D. (2020). Collaboration in achieving sustainable solutions in the textile industry. *Journal of Business & Industrial Marketing*.

[8] Desore, A., & Narula, S. A. (2018). An overview on corporate response towards sustainability issues in textile industry. *Environment, Development and Sustainability*, 20(4), 1439–459.

[9] Devaraja, T.S. (2011). Indian textile and garment industry – An overview. Department of Commerce Post Graduate Centre University of Mysore Hassan: India.

[10] Gbolarumi, F.T., Wong, K.Y., & Olohunde, S.T. (2021, February). Sustainability assessment in the textile and apparel industry: A review of recent studies. In *IOP Conference Series: Materials Science and Engineering* (Vol. 1051, No. 1, p. 012099). IOP Publishing.

[11] Geissdoerfer, M., Savaget, P., Bocken, N.M., & Hultink, E.J. (2017). The Circular Economy – A new sustainability paradigm?, *Journal of Cleaner Production*.

[12] Gita, S., Hussan, A., & Choudhury, T.G. (2017). Impact of textile dyes waste on aquatic environments and its treatment. *Environ*.

[13] Gupta, S., Dangayach, G.S., Singh, A.K., Meena, M.L., & Rao, P.N. (2018). Adoption of sustainable supply operation quality practices and their impact on stakeholder's performance and sustainable performance for sustainable competitiveness in Indian manufacturing companies. *International Journal of Intelligent Enterprise*, 5(1-2), 108–24.

[14] Hiremath, R.B., Kattumuri, R., Kumar, B., Khatri, V.N., & Patil, S.S. (2012). An integrated networking approach for a sustainable textile sector in Solapur, India. *Urbani izziv*, 23(2), 140–51.

[15] https://curiositysavestheplanet.com/sustainable-textile-and-clothing-practices-from-traditional-indian-culture/

[16] https://textilelearner.net/an-overview-of-indian-textile-industry/

[17] https://www.apexmills.com/media_post/sustainable-fabrics/

[18] https://www.ibef.org/industry/textiles

[19] https://www.sutlejtextiles.com/blogs/blog-post.php?id=C1

[20] Karthik, T., & Gopalakrishnan, D. (2014). Environmental analysis of textile value chain: an overview. *Roadmap to sustainable textiles and clothing*, 153–88.

[21] Khattab, T.A., Abdelrahman, M. S., & Rehan, M. (2020). Textile dyeing industry: environmental impacts and remediation. *Environmental Science and Pollution Research*, 27(4), 3803–818.

[22] Moon, K.K.L., Lai, C.S.Y., Lam, E.Y.N., & Chang, J.M. (2015). Popularization of sustainable fashion: barriers and solutions. *The Journal of the Textile Institute*, 106(9), 939–52.

[23] Muthu, S. S. (Ed.). (2017). Sustainability in the textile industry. Singapore: Springer.

[24] Nimkar, U. (2018). Sustainable chemistry: a solution to the textile industry in a developing world. *Current Opinion in Green and Sustainable Chemistry*, 9, 13–17.

[25] Pandey, R., Pandit, P., Pandey, S., & Mishra, S. (2020). Solutions for sustainable fashion and textile industry. *Recycling from Waste in Fashion and Textiles: A Sustainable and Circular Economic Approach*, 33–72.

[26] Purvis, B., Mao, Y., & Robinson, D. (2019). Three pillars of sustainability: in search of conceptual origins. *Sustain Sci* 14 (3): 681–95.

[27] Raichurkar, P., & Ramachandran, M. (2015). Recent trends and developments in textile industry in India. *International Journal on Textile Engineering & Processes*, 1(4), 47–50.

[28] Raj, D., Ma, Y.J., Gam, H.J., & Banning, J. (2017). Implementation of lean production and environmental sustainability in the Indian apparel manufacturing industry: a way to reach the triple bottom line. *International Journal of Fashion Design, Technology and Education*, 10(3), 254–64.

[29] Sandin, G., & Peters, G.M. (2018). Environmental impact of textile reuse and recycling–A review. *Journal of cleaner production*, 184, 353–65.

[30] Sharma, A., & Narula, S. A. (2020). What motivates and inhibits Indian textile firms to embrace sustainability?. *Asian Journal of Sustainability and Social Responsibility*, 5(1), 1–23.

[31] Umarji, V. (2015). Dumping, lack of ftas, incentives hurting textile industry. *Business Standard*, http://www.businessstandard.com/article/economypolicy/dumping-lackof-ftas-incentives-hurting-textile-industry-115090900877_1. html.

[32] Yacout, D.M., & Hassouna, M.S. (2016). Identifying potential environmental impacts of waste handling strategies in textile industry. *Environmental monitoring and assessment*, 188(8), 1–13.

[33] You, S., Cheng, S., & Yan, H. (2009). The impact of textile industry on China's environment. *International Journal of Fashion Design, Technology and Education*, 2(1), 33–43.

A Systematic Study on Interoperability of Eco-Friendly Cars by Virtue of Sustainable Development in Automobile Industry

CHIRANJIB MITRA AND S. ROYCHOWDHURY

Indian Institute of Social welfare and Business Management, University of Calcutta, Kolkata, India
E-mail: chiranjibmitra9@gmail.com; srcdb@rediffmail.com

Abstract

With global warming and health concerns on the rise because of the substances the vehicles produce, it is important to adopt the right vehicles that are eco-friendly. The holistic transition from conventional fuel cars to electric cars is crucial for implementing the concept of sustainable development. Under the present circumstances, automobile companies have adopted an innovative way of working in cohesion with organisational goals and environmental protection. Now the eco-friendly cars are a lot more affordable than they were in the past, and their use is a way to protect the environment and health of people. Hybrids and battery-operated cars are considered to be eco-friendly cars. Electric cars do not burn any fuel. Hybrid cars are somewhat divergent from any other fuel cars or electric vehicles. This study seeks to understand the elements that have an impact on the adoption of sustainable measures in the automobile industry through the use of eco-friendly cars through the exploratory factor analysis, and also the interrelationship among the factors and extent of dependability on each other.

Keywords: Conventional Fuel Cars, Exploratory Factor Analysis, Hybrid Cars, Multiple Regression, Sustainable Development

Introduction

Sustainable development is a concept that entails the use of resources in the most appropriate way so that the demand of the present can be satisfied without affecting the resources that can be stored for the next generation. Sustainability altogether has different branches to cater and to address, starting from global issues, discriminations, gender inequality, poverty, natural resources degradation, etc.

Modern notion of sustainable development has shifted from conservation and preservation of ecological and natural assets towards social and economic development. It is one of the pre-dominant concepts of the present time which is widely accepted as the need of the day. Sustainability refers to that comprehensive and extensive approach that posses' terrestrial processes which will lead to human-nature equilibrium.

Contemporary theories are striving to reunite the two oxymoronic concepts, economic development and natural resources conservation. There should be an integrated model that is to be executed throughout the organisation in the form of elevated awareness towards degradation of natural resources. So far, there are dynamic and vigorous steps and initiatives taken by the organisation in the form of green human resources management, green marketing, green supply chain management, etc., which reflect the unambiguity among the mindset of the society towards sustainable development.

When it comes to the Indian automobile market, most of the market segments are pre-dominated with factors like energy efficiency, optimised consumption of fuel, more safety factors, etc. Automobile makers are much more aware and consider these factors not only seriously but with utmost sincerity. That is why most of the companies have launched four wheelers in a most affordable pricing segment.

An integrated model withstanding the conglomeration of two different concepts sustainability and an economic car to be ruling in the Indian market, it takes lot of research and non-primitive dynamic strategy which not only satisfy the demand and the requirement of the customersbut will also safeguard environmental interests, making the entire scenario more cardinal and crucial. Conventional vehicles being one of the major reasons for the depletion of the ecology, still a dearth of reasons is associated with the choice of electric vehicles over the conventional one.

Literature Review and Research Gap

In the present times, major problems regarding environmental issues come from the transportation sector. In a recent study, it has been revealed that the transportation sector is responsible for the maximum emission of hazardous gases in the environment as stated by Balon (2012). Hence, as per the sustainable development goals, authorities are likely to implement all the necessary strategies for effective and optimum utilisation of resources in correlation with safeguarding the environment. It is the responsibility of the auto companies to implement and operate with synergy between organisational goals and environmental goals. It is quite imperative that it will take some time to re-establish the organisational norms in a more synchronised way that will serve both the society and its environment (Bhalla, 2018).

According to modern research, sustainable development is getting world-wide attention because of the catastrophic outcomes of negligence of mankind towards its surroundings. It results in unimaginable natural calamities (Gayathri, 2016). It is very essential for mankind to understand the gravity of the situation and act accordingly. The government should play a lead role in making people not only aware but also making them understand the importance of the situation by providing adequate knowledge.

Hundal (2015): In the last few years the concern towards ecological aspects and its degradation has been insulated more than ever. In spite of the fact that there are multiple differences in opinion, still, when it comes to safeguarding natural resources, they have illuminated harmonical uniformity of opinion.

As environmental issues have been major concerns for almost all the sectors in the economy, organisations and employees must work together with collaboration in order to achieve the sustainability spectrum within the organisation (Searcy, 2009).

There are more pertinent branches of management, however, among all other; operations stand out especially when it comes to technical front (Seuring, 2008).

Sukati (2012): Operations management is the structured centralised process of inflow of goods, services, information that is transformed from raw materials to finished goods and then distributed to end customer.

Verma (2006): In the present difficult circumstances and market saturation, the structure of logistics has become more composite in nature, and along with that understanding and controlling, monitoring with this situation has become more difficult.

Sustainable development in the field of automobile industry is absolutely a new theory, especially when it comes to the complex technological breakthrough invention. Most of the research concentrated on operations emphasised on the sustainability aspects in terms of the synergy between technology and environmental aspects. There is very limited literatures available on these aspects in context of eco-friendly cars and acceptability in the market.

Objective of the Study and Research Hypotheses

Main objective of the present study is to identify the factors affecting the implementation of electric vehicles in automobile industry. It is important to determine the characteristics of the variables in automobile industry with respect to eco-friendly cars. The main research hypotheses considered in this study are as follows:

- H1: Cross-departmental collaboration has an impact on the environmental auditing of the organisation.
- H2: Cooperation with supplier has a role in reusing and recycling of materials that are used.
- H3: Green packaging has a significant relation with awareness of manufacturing of green product.
- H4: Reduced consumption of hazardous and toxic material has a significant impact on the decreased cost of energy consumption.

Research Methodology

This study includes analyses using a combination of exploratory and descriptive research designs with a major focus on making use of inferential statistical procedures. Primary data was collected from eighty employees from various organisations of Kolkata with different job positions and responsibility, and secondary data was collected from websites, journals, magazines, etc. Exploratory factor analysis (EFA), chi-square tests for independence of categorical variables, step-wise regression model, have been used to analyse the data with the help of the statistical software SPSS v.25.

A structured set of questionnaires were used for collecting the primary data, which consisted of questions for understanding the importance level towards implementing sustainability, the perception level towards eco-friendly cars, measured with the questions collected on a 4-point scale, where '1' represents lowest perception level, '4' indicates the highest.

First the relationship between main characteristics of sustainability and its perception has been examined using Pearsonian chi-square (χ^2) test, a nonparametric test.

Next, an exploratory factor analysis (EFA) has been done to identify the factors that mainly influence the organisation to sustainable production system for eco-friendly cars. For the purpose of scale reliability, Cronbach alpha has been also obtained. KMO measure and Bartlett's test have been used, respectively, for assessing sampling adequacy and testing sphericity. Finally, a step-wise regression model has been used to establish a relationship between importance level towards sustainability and the major factors, extracted by the method of factor analysis, which may influence the implementation decision, from which it will also be evident that which of the extracted factors have more effect on importance level of the organisation to implement such system for production of eco-friendly cars.

Analysis and Interpretations

This section explains the results of (i) hypothesis testing on association among different variables of sustainability, (ii) factor analysis, which identifies major factors that affect the sustainability, and (iii) step-wise regression analysis, from which how the sustainability depends on various identified factors can be obtained.

Testing the Association among Different Variables of Sustainability

Pearsonian chi-square tests have been conducted to tests the hypotheses. The tests have been performed to examine if there exists a significant impact of (a) cross-departmental collaboration on the environmental auditing of the organisation, (b) cooperation with supplier in reusing and recycling of materials that are used, (c) green packaging

Table 1: Results of Pearsonian Chi-square Tests

Categorical Variables Involved	*Observed Value of Test Statistic*	*df*	*Asymptotic Significance*
(a) Cross-departmental collaboration and environmental auditing	100.143	16	.000
(b) Cooperation with supplier and reusing and recycling of materials used	76.508	12	.000
(c) Green packaging and awareness towards manufacturing green products	36.360	12	.000
(d) Reduced consumption of toxic material and decreased cost of energy.	77.725	9	.000

Source: Author's Compilation

towards the awareness of manufacturing of green product and (d) reduced consumption of hazardous and toxic material on the decreased cost of energy consumption. The findings of the tests are presented together in Table 1, which include the observed value of Pearsonian test statistic, degrees of freedom and the p-value for the tests.

(a) For research hypothesis H1, it has been found that the p-value (=0.000) is less than 0.05. Hence the alternate hypothesis that there is a significant relationship between the two categorical variables is accepted, suggesting that there does exist a significant effect of cross-departmental collaboration on the environmental auditing of the organisation.
(b) For research hypothesis H2, the p-value is found to be 0.000, which less than 0.05, indicating that the effect of cooperation with supplier on the reusing and recycling of materials that are used, is significant.
(c) For research hypothesis H3, p-value < 0.05, suggesting a significant effect of awareness towards manufacturing green products on the green packaging.
(d) For research hypothesis H4, again p-value < 0.05, which suggests that there is a significant effect of reduced consumption toxic and hazardous materials on the decreased cost of energy.

In the above cases, all the associations have been found to be significant.

Exploratory Factor Analysis

Study reveals that there are twelve essential parameters that are used for understanding the factors that influence the implementation of sustainable development in automobile industries. Every industry has their unique method of operation, though it may differ from industry to industry. In order to understand the consistency of the data collected, Cronbach alpha has been computed as a measure to assess the reliability, which ranges from 0 and 1.

Table 2: Reliability Statistics

Cronbach Alpha	*Cronbach Alpha Based on Standardised Items*	*Number of Items*
0.812	0.788	12

Source: Author's Compilation

Table 2 shows the value of Cronbach alpha as 0.812, which is a high value from which it can be inferred that there is a presence of internal consistency of the items in the scale. It does not mean that the scale is one-dimensional. The scales used for measuring sustainability in supply chain management in automobile industry are reliable enough to understand and interpret. Here twelve parameters have been considered with Likert scale, which gives a reliable scaling measure through Cronbach alpha value. The crucial parameters found are as follows:

1. Reduction in cost of energy consumption
2. Reduction in cost of waste management
3. Reduction in cost of purchase material

4. Eco-labelling of products
5. Green products
6. Green packaging and billing
7. Cooperation with supplier
8. Reuse and recycle of material
9. Reduced energy consumption
10. Environmental auditing
11. Commitment from senior manager
12. Cross departmental collaboration

Table 3: KMO and Bartlett's Test Result

Kaiser-Meyer-Olkin measure of sampling adequacy	0.720
Pearsonian chi-square test-statistic (for Bartlett's test of sphericity)	375.400
Degrees of freedom (df)	66
p-value (for statistical significance)	.000

Source: Author's Compilation

Table 3 shows that the p-value in Bartlett's test is less than 0.05, as a result of which it can be concluded that the statements are significant at level 0.05 (two-tailed test).

In this research, EFA has been used to explore the various dimensions of sustainability towards implementation in automobile industry. Principle component analysis has been used with varimax rotation depending on the assumption that any extracted factor

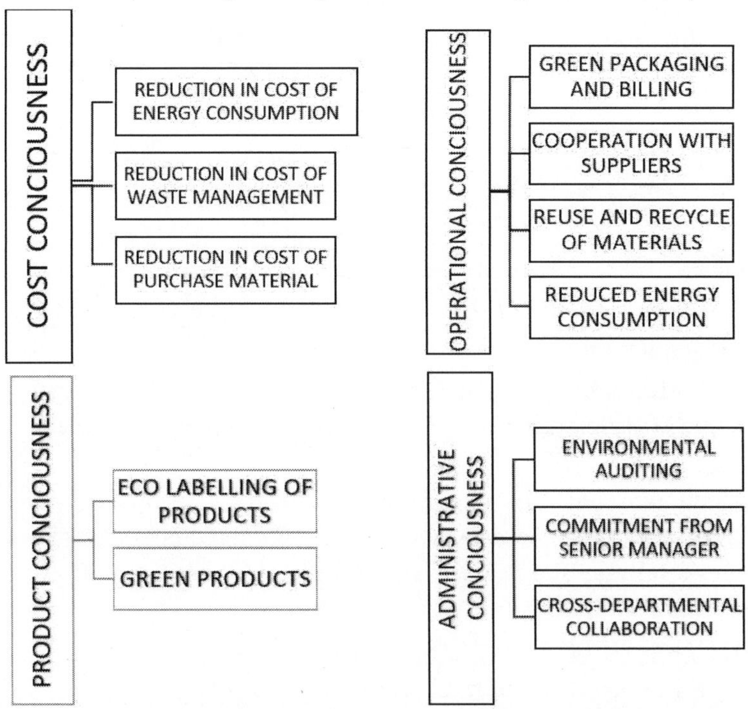

Fig. 1: Factors Affect the Automobile Industry towards Sustainability

important to attributes of the electric vehicles should be inter-related. Eigen value of 1 has been used as cut-off value for extraction. Four-factor structure with the extracted factors explaining 70.8 per cent of the total variance has been identified. The KMO measure yields a value of 0.72, indicating that the data were suitable for factor analysis.

Figure 1 displays the four factors extracted from the twelve through EFA. For all of these four factors, the eigen values are more than 1. The grouping is based on the rotated component matrix. These four factors can be named as convenience, attributes, environmental consciousness and cost consciousness, operational consciousness, product consciousness, administrative consciousness. All of these factors are associated with sustainability and ecological aspects of the organisation which can be achieved with effective and systemised implementation of eco-friendly practices within the organisation.

Step-wise Regression Model

A step-wise regression has been done with all four factors to measure the sustainability of the organisation. This stepwise regression model also shows how these four independent variables, vis., cost consciousness, operational consciousness, product consciousness and administrative consciousness, are impacting the dependent variable, Y, the sustainability.

Initially it started with the correlation analysis with every independent variable with the dependent variable that has been shown in Table 4.

Table 4: Pearson Correlation Value

Variables	*Sustainability (Pearson correlation)*
Administrative consciousness	0.785
Product consciousness	0.762
Operational consciousness	0.712
Cost consciousness	0.305

Source: Author's Compilation

It can be seen that the highest correlation value with the importance level towards sustainability is with administrative consciousness with 0.785 followed by product consciousness with 0.762 then operational consciousness with 0.712 and lastly cost consciousness with 0.305. Now step-wise regression can be done to understand the final independent variables that can be selected for the final multiple regression model.

The process will start from regression analysis with importance level towards sustainability considering it to be dependent variable (Y) and administrative consciousness (x) and then all the variables as per their correlation values they will be added sequentially. After adding each of the independent variables, the R^2 values will be measured to witness if there is any significant change or not.

From Table 5, it can be understood that when administrative consciousness variable is added with product consciousness variable, the change in the R^2 value is

Table 5: R^2 Values

Variable Names	R^2 *Values*
Administrative consciousness	0.616
Administrative consciousness and product consciousness	0.703
Administrative consciousness, product consciousness, and operational consciousness	0.728
Administrative consciousness, product consciousness, operational consciousness, and cost consciousness	0.825

Source: Author's Compilation

quite significant similarly. When both of these variables are added with operational consciousness variable, the value has also increased and in the same manner when cost consciousness has been added, it has increased to 0.825. Hence it can be concluded that all the variables can be included while running multiple regression model. Hence the final regression equation is as follows:

$$Y = 0.057 + 0.158X_1 + 0.350X_2 + 0.187X_3 + 0.301X_4$$

Here

X_1 = Administrative consciousness

X_2 = Product consciousness

X_3 = Operational consciousness

X_4 = Cost consciousness

Conclusion

In recent years, the elements of sustainability in an organisation have changed drastically. There has been a conglomeration and inclusion of several multidimensional aspects, which has given the understanding of optimum utilisation of sustainability aspects in an organisation a new direction. With technological advancements, corporates have realised the importance of sustainability and its implications. Sustainable development has been one of the most technically driven branches among other management branches. From the above research, it can be concluded that most of the organisations are aware of the growing concern of global warming and the importance of sustainability, and there have been certain factors that are considered for implementing sustainability aspects in the organisation. The automobile industries are now very much being motivated and driven by technology to maintain certain protocol so that environmental goals can be achieved. They have also understood the need of being socially aware and the need for their contribution to society. Sustainable developmental practices are now being treated as one of the cataclysmic social responsibilities of organisations which are now adopting and implementing viable and sustainable practices in almost all the areas of a company, not only to survive in the competitive age but also to stimulate the growing concern of environmental aspects in society.

References

[1] Balon, V. (2012). Assessment of Barriers in Green Supply Chain Management Using ISM: A Case Study of the Automobile Industry in India. *Global Business Review*, 17(1), 1–20.

[2] Bhalla, P. (2018). A Study of Consumer Perception and Purchase Intention of Electric Vehicles. *European Journal of Scientific Research*, 149(4), 262–68.

[3] Gayathri (2016). ENVIRONMENTALLY FRIENDLY CARS THE ECO CARS. *Imperial International Journal of Eco-friendly Technologies*, 1(1), 115–12.

[4] Hundal, B.S. (2015). Consumer Perception towards Green Products: A Factor Analytic Approach. *Pacific Business Review International*, 7(10), 111–32.

[5] Searcy (2009). Designing corporate sustainable development indicators: reflections on a process. *Environmental Quality Management*, 19, 31–42.

[6] Seuring (2008). Assessing the rigor of case study research in supply chain management. *Supply Chain Management: An International Journal*, 13, 128–37.

[7] Sukati, I. (2012). The Study of Supply Chain Management Strategy and Practices on Supply Chain Performance. *Procedia-Social and Behavioral Sciences*, 225–33.

[8] Touboulic (2015). Theories in sustainable supply chain management: a structured literature review. *International Journal of Physical Distribution and Logistics Management*, 45, 16–42.

[9] Tupe, O. (2020). Consumer perception of electric vehicles in India. *European Journal of Molecular and Clinical Medicine*, 7(8), 108–19.

[10] Upadhyaya, A. (2019). Consumer awareness and perception towards hybrid cars. *The Journal of Indian Management and Strategy*, 24(3), 46–53.

[11. Utami, M.W. (2020). Consumer perception analysis of electric car vehicle in Indonesia. *AIP Conference Proceedings*, 2217(1), 88–110.

[12] Varma (2006). Implementing supply chain management in a firm: issues and remedies. *Asia Pacific Journal of Marketing and Logistics*, 223–43.

Relation Between Emission, Economic Structure, and Energy Structure in India: ARDL Analysis

SATRAJIT DUTTA[1] AND SOUMYANANDA DINDA[2]

[1]*Assistant Professor, Department of Economics, Gorubathan Government College, Fagu, Kalimpong, West Bengal, India*
[2]*Professor, Department of Economics, University of Burdwan, Burdwan, West Bengal, India*
E-mail: jit2458@gmail.com; sdinda@eco.buruniv.ac.in

Abstract

Purpose – The article examines the effect of economic composition, energy structure and technology on CO_2 emission empirically in India during 1990–2020.

Design/Methodology/Approach – Representative variables like percentage share of industry in Gross Domestic Product (GDP) for economic composition, percentage share of non-fossil fuel use in non-electricity sector for energy structure, percentage share of research and development (R&D) expenditure in GDP for technology have been used. Cointegrating relationship among the study variables was tested by applying Auto Regressive Distributed Lag (ARDL) Model.

Findings – Use of non-fossil fuel in non-electricity sector has significant effect on total CO_2 emission reduction. R&D expenditure is positively increasing emission. Industry's share in GDP has positive effect on emission.

Practical Implications – More R&D in non-fossil energy sector and for reduction of energy intensity in high energy consuming sectors are needed. Direct use of non-fossil fuel in sectors like industry, transport can improve emission scenario.

Originality/Value – This paper used updated data sets for the study variables and focussed exclusively on effect of composition change in economy and energy sector and technological improvement on emission.

Keywords: *Environmental Kuznets Curve, CO_2 Emissions, Energy Consumption, Economic Growth, Auto Regressive Distributed Lag Model*
Paper type: *Research Paper*

Introduction

Global warming and climate change has been confronting policymakers around the world. Renewable energy and energy efficiency are considered vital for making a balance between development of the economy and environmental quality improvement to resolve this problem. The present article is based on theoretical concepts of the Environmental Kuznets Curve (EKC) hypothesis composed of scale, composition and technological effect, I = PAT theory decomposing environmental impact into three factors – population (P), Affluence (usually measured by GDP growth rate) and Technology (T). and extended Kaya identity which focuses on energy sector and decomposes the emission into population, per capita GDP, energy intensity, carbon intensity, energy composition.

Use of ARDL model has been done to find out short and long run relationship of the four selected variables: total CO_2 emission from fossil fuel burning, percentage share of industry in GDP, percentage share of non-fossil fuel in non-electricity consumption, percentage share of research and development expenditure in GDP.

Theoretical Background

EKC Hypothesis

Dynamic interplay among the three effects—scale, composition and technical—determines relationship between economic growth and environmental deterioration (AlKhars et al., 2022). During initial period of economic growth, there is scale effect on environment and increase in consumption (both direct and indirect) of natural resources for supporting economic growth but causes industrial waste generation with negative environmental effect (AlKhars et al., 2022). In the second phase, environmental quality gets more importance and manufacturing and industrial sectors see shift towards adoption of cleaner technologies, which increase energy efficiency (AlKhars et al., 2022).

With adoption of clean and modern technologies, 3rd stage arrives when economic growth has the technical effect on the quality of environment. Service sector prospers and gradual shift is from capital-intensive phase to knowledge-intensive phase with increase research and development investment and experienced simultaneous increase in both economic growth and quality of environment (AlKhars et al., 2022).

The resultant bell shape or an inverted U-shape curve graphically depicting transitional dynamics of growth of the economy and environment quality and it is known as the EKC Hypothesis (AlKhars et al., 2022), which is in contrast to the Limits to Growth theory (Ekins, 1997).

Structural Transformation

In contrast to the neoclassical one-sector growth model, the Structural transformation (ST) implies inter-sector and intra-sector reallocation of economic activity towards higher productivity activities which has been neglected in developing countries (Behera & Tiwari, n.d.). In neoclassical model, growth is driven by savings incentives, accumulation of physical and human capital and innovation. But ST implies that change in structure itself is an important driver of growth because of productivity difference between and even within sectors. (Behera & Tiwari, n.d.)

IPAT/STIRPAT

Ehrlich and Holdren has mentioned that there is negative impact on environment from human beings and society's total negative effect on environment is expressed as:

$$I = P \times F \qquad \text{... (1)}$$

where, P = population, F = function measuring per capita impact which increases with consumption per capita with constant technology, but there is possibility of its reduction in the event of introduction of more benign technologies (Ehrlich & Holdren, 1971). The IPAT model is criticised due to its identity relationship between environmental impact, population, economic affluence and technological improvement and therefore, it is not possible to make any hypothetical analysis (Dietz & Rosa, 1994).

The IPAT model was reformulated by Dietz and Rosa (Dietz & Rosa, 1994) in stochastic form – STIRPAT, i.e. Stochastic Impacts by Regression on Population, Affluence and Technology) – an important improvement from the accounting model of the IPAT where one term is derived from the values of other three variables:

$$I = aP^{b}A^{c}T^{d}e \qquad \ldots (2)$$

where I = Impact on environmental, P = size of population, A = economic activity per capita and T = technological impact; b, c, d are elasticity coefficients, e = a residual term.

Empirical Literature Survey

1. Khoshnevis Yazdi and Dariani examined 18 Asian countries for the period of 1980 – 2014 and concluded two-way causality between urbanisation and emissions of CO_2 and bi-directional causality between GDP and CO_2 emissions in the panel (Khoshnevis Yazdi & Dariani, 2019).
2. P. Zhang et al., found energy related carbon emissions is affected by population, GDP per capita, rate of urbanisation, energy intensity positively in Henan Province, China, but proportion of tertiary sector negatively influences emission (P. Zhang et al., 2017).
3. Kanjilal and Ghosh showed that long term relationship among carbon emission, use of energy, economic activity and trade openness and found 2 structural breaks. The article validates existence of EKC hypothesis (Kanjilal & Ghosh, 2013).
4. Jihuan Zhang used ARDL method on per capita energy consumption, trade openness, urbanisation, per capita real GDP, CO_2 emissions per capita and confirmed long run EKC Hypothesis for China (J. Zhang, 2021).
6. David I. Stern showed that in USA during 1948-1994, energy Granger causes GDP either unidirectionally or bidirectionally (Stern, 2000).
7. Ozturk et al., found long run Granger causality from production in industrial sector and consumption of coal to CO_2 emissions in China during 1971-2011 and similar long run causal relationship was found in India (Ozturk et al., 2013).
8. Kentaka Aruga found that both panel regression and cointegration models showed existence of Energy-Environment Kuznets Curve (EEKC) hypothesis in 19 Asia-Pacific countries during 1984–2014 (Aruga, 2019).
9. Chai et al., 2021 showed evidence of EKC model between GDP per capita and direct carbon emissions of households (DCEH), though the inflection point is yet to be reached (Chai et al., 2021).

10. Bouznit & Pablo-Romero showed that energy use positively affects per capita CO_2 emissions implying higher industrialisation causing higher emissions and export coefficients are found to be negative and import coefficients are positive (Bouznit & Pablo-Romero, 2016).
11. Saidi & Hammami found financial development has positive effect on energy consumption for a global panel (Saidi & Hammami, 2015).
12. Khan et al., used long run ARDL during 1965–2015 for Pakistan and showed that energy consumption affects emissions of CO_2 positively and economic growth affects positively CO_2 emissions in short and long run as well (Khan et al., 2020).
13. al Sayed and Sek confirmed inverted U-shape relation in developing countries in 1960–2011 (al Sayed & Sek, 2013).
14. Balogh & Jámbor used (Balogh & Jámbor, 2017) the Generalised Method of Moments (GMM) on 168 countries during 1990–2013 and confirmed EKC hypotheses. International tourism and trade can increase and financial development can reduce air pollution, respectively (Balogh & Jámbor, 2017).
15. Dong et al., used the STIRPAT Model, OLS method, Ridge Regression Analysis in Xinjiang, China during 1989–2012 and showed that diesel consumption in transportation and population increase for domestic migration causes emission (Dong et al., 2017).
16. Shahbaz et al., used ARDL cointegration and Gregory-Hansen structural break cointegration test in Pakistan for 1971–2009 and found evidence of EKC hypothesis and one-way causal relationship from income to emission of CO_2 (Shahbaz et al., 2011). Emission of CO_2 increases due to consumption of energy in short and long run as well. In the long run, emissions of CO_2 is reduced by Trade Openness (Shahbaz et al., 2011).
17. Demissew Beyene and Kotosz used Pooled Mean Group approach for 12 countries of East Africa during 1990–2013 and confirmed bell-shape like relationship between income per capita and CO_2 emissions (Demissew Beyene & Kotosz, 2020).
18. Geyikci et al., found relationships among economic growth, use of energy and emissions of CO_2. Financial development causes acceleration of environmental pollution in 13 developing countries during 1993–2018 (Geyikci et al., 2022).
19. Abumunshar et al., using McNown ARDL bootstrapping and Granger causality (GC) analysis for Turkey during 1985–2015 and found Granger unidirectional causality from oil price to consumption of renewable and non-renewable energy (Abumunshar et al., 2020). Carbon emissions has been influenced by GDP and oil price during short and long runs.
20. C.S. Saba found evidence of EKC hypothesis, long-run equilibrium relationship between emissions of CO_2, consumption of energy, economic growth and militarisation (Saba, 2022). One-way causality running from energy consumption to economic growth and from CO_2 emissions to growth of the economy were found. in South Africa during 1960–2019 (Saba, 2022).

21. Sultana et al., confirmed both short and long run EKC hypothesis in the STIRPAT framework and one-way causality from GDP to ecological footprint, from urbanisation to ecological footprint and from trade openness to ecological footprint, while bidirectional causality between GDP and urbanisation are found (Sultana et al., 2022).
22. Dogan and Ozturk used Gregory-Hansen cointegration test; ARDL model on USA for 1980–2014 and found that EKC hypothesis is not valid (Dogan & Ozturk, 2017).
23. Ziyuan et al., under the STIRPAT model used ridge regression method; GA-BP neural network for Xinjiang, China (2000–2019) and found that number of vehicles, urbanisation, GDP per capita, mutton consumption per capita and education level in promoting carbon emissions (Ziyuan et al., 2022).
24. Karimi et al., used non-linear ARDL model during 1975–2017 and found short-term relationship between CO_2 emissions and growth of the economy (Karimi et al., 2021). Neutral causal relation between renewable energy and long run economic growth was found implying very less effect of renewable energy (RE) on GDP (Karimi et al., 2021).
25. Jiang et al., employed non-linear ARDL (NARDL) under the STIRPAT-Kaya-EKC framework and found asymmetric impact of renewable energy on environmental quality – negative shocks to use of renewable energy causes more damage for environment (Jiang et al., 2022). Population has resulted in short run environmental degradation with no long run effect and technology have improved environmental quality (Jiang et al., 2022).

Research Gap, Aim and Objective

Research Gap

The surveyed articles mostly showed the relationship between emission and its determining factors like GDP, trade, foreign direct investment (FDI) and other relevant factors. Some articles found direction of causality among these variables. Some articles also tested the existence of EKC. But there is lack of research work which is particularly related to the effect on environmental degradation on account of composition of economy and energy and technological improvement embodying theoretical concepts of EKC, IPAT/STIRPAT and Kaya Identity.

Research Aim

The article aims to find out the effect of structural change in the economy and energy use and technology on emissions.

Research Objective

The article has been written with the objective of checking cointegration relationship among proxy variables for the economic structure (share of industry in GDP) and energy structure (share of non-fossil fuel in non-electricity use) and technological development (share of research and development expenditure in GDP).

Research Methodology

Model Formulation with Theoretical Logic

Environmental Kuznets Curve (EKC) hypothesis is composed of the scale, composition, technology effects:

$$d(ED)/dt = (dY/dt) + \Sigma ei\ (dT/dt) + \Sigma ei\ (dSi/dt) \quad \text{... (3)}$$

where, ED = environmental degradation, percentage change in output (Y) = scale effect; the second term within summation incorporates rate of technical change (%) = the technique effect; and the third term incorporates rate of change of different sectors of economy (%); S_i = economic development's composition effect on environment, e_i = share of environmental effect in sectors (Ekins, 1997).

I = PAT theory decomposes the environmental impact into three factors like Population (P), Affluence (A) (usually measured by GDP growth rate) and Technology (T).

Taking logarithm of equation (2), the transformed equation is as follows:

$$\ln I = a + b \ln P + c \ln A + d \ln T + e \quad \text{... (4)}$$

The Kaya Identity is a variation of the I = PAT theory and it is given by the Japanese professor Yoichi Kaya (1989), with various factors like economic, energy, demographic and environmental factors to estimate global CO_2 emissions of human activities (Tavakoli, 2017).

$$\text{Carbon Emission (C)} = \text{Population} \times (\text{GDP/Population}) \times (\text{Energy / GDP}) \times (\text{C / Energy}) \quad \text{...(5)}$$

Equation (5), can be extended by including the energy structure into it :

$$\text{Carbon Emission (C)} = \text{Population} \times (\text{GDP/Population}) \times (\text{Energy / GDP}) \times (\text{Fossil energy / Energy}) \times (\text{C / Fossil Energy}) \quad \text{... (6)}$$

The Kaya Identity equation (5) or (6) can be viewed as a derivative of the STIRPAT identity equation (2) as in both these equations Population, Affluence and Technology are present – 'Technology' in the Kaya Identity is found in decomposed form as the product of carbon intensity and primary energy intensity (Timma et al., 2014).

The equation (6) can be written as

$$C_T = P_T \times (Y_t/P_T) \times (E_t/Y_t) \times (FE_t / E_t) \times (C_T / FE_t) \quad \text{... (7)}$$

where, C_T = carbon emission, E_t = energy use, FE_t = fossil energy use

The proposed model under consideration for analysis in functional form is derived in following way –

The functional form of equation (1): $ED_t = f(Y_t, T_t, S_t)$ ... (8)

The functional form of equation (3): $I_t = f(P_t, A_t, T_t)$ ... (9)

The functional form of equation (4): $C_t = f(P_t, A_t, ES_t, T_t)$ ... (10)

where $A_t = (Y_t/P_T)$, T_t represents (E_t/Y_t) and (C_T / FE_t), $ES_t = (FE_t / E_t)$

It can be there are similarities and dissimilarities as evident from these three functions which in fact decomposes the environmental degradation into multiple factors so this research work takes the elements of these three functional forms and forms the following functional form –

$C_t = f(S_t, ES_t, T_t)$ ... (11)

where, S_t = structure of the economy proxied by share of industry sector of GDP $(\text{IndustryGDP})_t$ in India (%).

ES_t = energy structure proxied by share of non-fossil fuel use in non-electricity sector $(\text{NFFEC})_t$ (%).

T_t = technology proxied by RD_t, where RD_t = share of research and development expenditure in GDP (%) as it causes technological development which has positive spill over effect in the economy which helps in carbon emission reduction.

Data Description

The selected variables chosen for ARDL are:

- **Dependent Variable:** $\ln CO_{2t}$; ln (total CO_2 emission from fossil fuel burning)
- **Independent Variable:** $\ln NFFNEC_f$: ln(percentage share of total non-fossil fuel used in total non-electricity fuel consumption)$_t$

  $\ln IndustryGDP_t$: ln(percentage share of Service sector in GDP)$_r$

  $\ln RD_t$: ln(percentage share of research and development expenditure in GDP)$_t$

So the details of the final variables selected in this model along with their relationship are shown in Table 1.

Table 1: Details of Variables Used in this Article and Source

Original Variables	*Variables Used*	*Definition*	*Unit of Original Variable*	*Notations Used*	*Purpose*	*Source of Original Variables*	*Relation with Theories*
CO_2 emissions	Natural logarithm of CO2 emissions	Total CO_2 emissions from fuel combustion, i.e., Total = coal + oil + natural gas + other	Metric tons of carbon dioxide emissions	$\ln CO_2t$	Indicator for environmental degradation	IEA data base (Https://Www.Iea. Org/Data-and-Statistics, n.d.)	EKC, IPAT, Kaya Idenitity
Share (%) of industry sector in GDP	Natural logarithm of Share (%) of Industry sector in GDP	Manufacturing, mining, construction, electricity, water & gas	Percentage	lnIndustry GDPt	Indicator for structural shift in the economy	World Bank data base. (Https:// Data.Worldbank. Org/, n.d.)	EKC
Share (%) of non-fossil fuel in non-electricity consumption	Natural logarithm of Share of non-fossil fuel in non-electricity consumption	Share of non-fossil fuels – wind, solar, etc., biofuels & waste	Percentage	lnNFFNECt	Indicator of energy structure in non-electricity generation sector	Authors' calculation from IEA data base	Kaya Idenitity

Original Variables	*Variables Used*	*Definition*	*Unit of Original Variable*	*Notations Used*	*Purpose*	*Source of Original Variables*	*Relation with Theories*
Share (%) of research & development (R&D) in GDP	Natural log of share of research & development in GDP	Capital & current expenditures in sectors, e.g. Businesses, higher education, Government, & private non-profit segments	Percentage	lnRDt	Indicator of technological improvement	World Bank data base (Https:// Data.Worldbank. Org/, n.d.)	EKC, IPAT

Period of Research

Study period of the research: 1990 to 2020.

Research Method

The ARDL cointegration method is used to check whether the variables ($\ln C_t$, $\ln NFFNEC_t$, $\ln IndustryGDP_t$, $\ln RD_t$) are cointegrated or not.

Econometric Model Specification

The ARDL unrestricted error correction model (UECM). Model –

$$\Delta \ln CO_{2t} = \alpha + \beta_1 \ln CO_{2t-1} + \beta_2 \ln IndustryGDP_{t-1} + \beta_3 \ln NFFNEC_{t-1}$$

$$+ \sum_{i=1}^{p_1} \delta_1 \Delta \ln CO_{2t-1} + \sum_{i=0}^{p_2} \delta_2 \Delta \ln IndustryGDP_{t-i}$$

$$+ \sum_{i=0}^{p_3} \delta_3 \Delta \ln NFFNEC_{t-i} + \sum_{i=0}^{p_4} \delta_4 \Delta \ln RD_{t-1} + \varepsilon_t \quad ...(12)$$

where, Δ = the first-order differential operator, ε_t = white noise, α = drift, $p_1, \ldots, p_4$ = the optimal no. of lags as determined by Akaike Information Criterion (AIC).

The model chosen here is: Unrestricted intercept and no trend. The terms within summation in equation (12) denotes dynamics of error correction model (ECM) dynamics and coefficients – $\beta_{1,} \beta_{2,} \beta_3, \beta_4$ denote long-run relationship and $\delta_1, \delta_2, \delta_3, \delta_4$ are short-run coefficients.

Steps of ARDL Method

The ARDL cointegration model has the following steps to be followed:

1. Determination of stationarity of all variables, whether [I(0)] or [I(1)] by applying Unit Root Test methods
2. AIC is used as lag length criteria for selecting optimum lag lengths of the selected variables for performing ARDL.
3. Perform Bounds Test to determine any cointegration relationship among the variables, i.e. whether there is existence of long-term relationship among the selected variables. In order to check the long-term equilibrium relation among $\ln C_t$, $\ln IndustryGDP_t$, $\ln NFFNEC_t$, $\ln RD_t$. ARDL Bound Test is done using F-tests – Hypothesis Testing:

On the basis of equation (12),

- the Null Hypothesis: H_0: $\beta_1 = \beta_2 = \beta_3 = \beta_4 = 0$, i.e., variables are not cointegrated.
- the Alternative Hypothesis: H_1: $\beta_1 \neq \beta_2 \neq \beta_3 \neq \beta_4$, i.e., variables are cointegrated.

The Null Hypothesis (H_0) is tested by the joint significance of F-statistics and is compared with 2 sets of critical values at each significance level (1%, 2.5%, 5%, 10%) as given by Pesaran, et. al. (Pesaran et al., 2001). The first level (Lower Level) of each set of a particular significance level is calculated assuming all variables are I(0) and the second level (Upper Level) is calculated assuming that all variables are I(1). If calculated F-statistics value > Upper Bound (Upper Level), then H_0 (No Cointegration) is rejected and the existence of long run relationship among the variables is confirmed. On the other hand, if calculated F-statistics value is found to be less than Lower Bound (Lower Level), then the test fails to reject H_0. But if the F-value is within the two values of Upper and Lower Bounds, then the decision remains inconclusive.

1. If the series of variables are found to be cointegrated, i.e. there is long term relationship within the variables then the Vector Error Correction (VECM) Model is to be conducted for investigating long run dynamic relationship and also short run ARDL for testing short run dynamics among the variables.
2. If the series of variables are not found to be integrated then only short run ARDL is to be done.
3. Diagnostics are to be run for checking the serial correlation, heteroskedasticity, model stability.

Results and Discussion

Primary Discussion

Coal has been the most polluting fuel because of its high global warming potential in comparison to oil or natural gas. If a comparison is made among the BRICS-U [BRICS (Brazil, Russian Federation, India, China, South Africa) and USA] countries then, it is found that total CO_2 emission has increased from 1990 to 2020 in most of the countries except Russia (Fig. 1). China and India are the highest emitting nations in 2020 and China has seen the biggest jump in emission over the years mainly because of it coal-based energy structure and high manufacturing sector in GDP. In 2020, the share of electricity production from coal has decreased since 1990 in all countries – but it is still very high in both China and India. For China it decreased from 73 per cent to 67 per cent but in case of India it increased from 65 per cent to 72 per cent during that period (Fig. 2). In the developed countries like USA, the share of electricity generation from coal has come down to 17 per cent (2020) while that of Natural Gas which is considered less polluting has increased to 40 per cent (Fig. 2). In case of Russia, electricity generation from Natural Gas has been consistently holding more than 50 per cent share, because of its availability. Among the BRICS-U countries, the share of electricity from non-fossil fuels is highest in Brazil (96 per cent) in 2020 because of its high dependence on hydropower (92 per cent), while both India and China have their shares of around 27 per cent (2020). Share of electricity from fossil fuel is highest in South Africa (88 per cent in 2020) due to high coal dependence. In all these countries use of coal has been reduced in non-electricity sector (e.g., industry, transport, agriculture), which can be explained by high energy efficiency and gradual shift of economic activity from high to low energy-intensive sectors like service sector (Fig. 3).

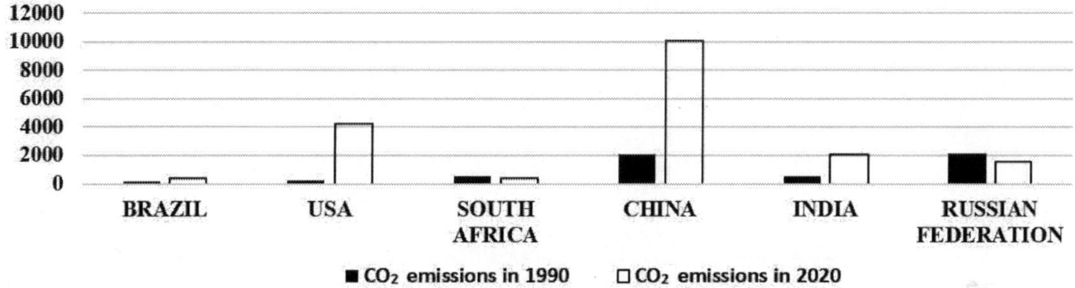

Fig. 1: Total CO_2 emission ($MtCO_2$)
Source: Authors' calculation from IEA database

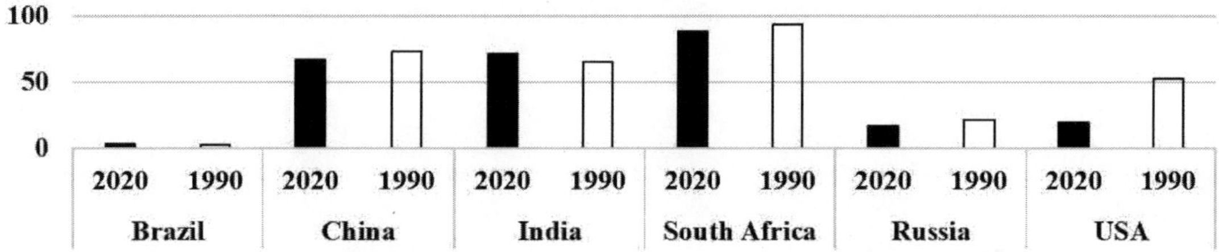

Fig. 2: Electricity Produced from Coal (%)
Source: Authors' calculation from IEA database

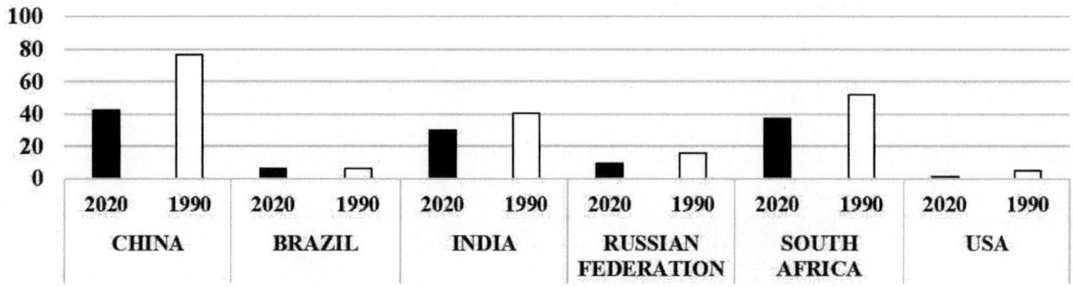

Fig. 3: Coal in Fossil Fuel (%) in Non-electrcity Consumption
Source: Authors' calculation from IEA database

In order to combat emission related issue, Govt. of India has taken plethora of measures in various sectors in the economy. India has made international commitments under Paris Agreement, UNFCCC for 45 per cent reduction of Emissions Intensity by 2030 and to attain about 50 per cent installed capacity of electricity (cumulative) generated from non-fossil fuel-based energy resources by the same time (*India's*

Updated First Nationally Determined Contribution Under Paris Agreement (2021-2030), Submission to UNFCCC, 2022).

India became a member of the International Solar Alliance (ISA) for higher deployment of solar energy technologies for low-carbon growth. Initiatives have been taken like National Solar Mission (NSM) for installing 100 GW solar power, National Smart Grid Mission (NSGM) (2015) to make grid amenable to renewable energy inputs through distributed generation, Faster Adoption and Manufacturing of (Hybrid &) Electric Vehicles in India (FAME India) for growth of Electric Vehicle (EV) industry, Implementation of Bharat Stage VI (BS-VI) emission norm for vehicles, etc.

Results & Discussion of the Empirical Study

Table 2: Summary Statistics of the Variables

Variables	*Mean*	*Median*	*Std. Dev.*	*Min*	*Max*	*Skewness*	*Kurtosis*
$lnCO_2$	7.054675	6.980076	0.4791676	6.272877	7.745003	0.0373038	1.650585
lnIndustryGDP	3.329533	3.318837	0.0641022	3.19994	3.438388	0.1461689	2.50329
lnNFFNEC	3.719929	3.775727	0.1722538	3.475537	3.951035	-0.1973126	1.436634
lnRD	-0.4054745	-0.3512752	0.2102884	-1.040692	- 0.1522658	-1.533925	4.88085
Observations	31	31	31	31	31	31	31

Source: Authors' calculations (using STATA-IC-15)

From Table 2, it can be seen that the standard deviation of the logarithmic variables are not high (< 1) and normality is apparent as the means are closer to median of the variables.

Step 1

Unit Root Tests are done on all the variables by employing Dicky-Fuller (DF) Unit Root Test, Augmented Dicky-Fuller (ADF) Unit Root Test, Phillips-Perron (PP) unit Root Test. Here, the variables are considered Stationary when the test statistic satisfies 1 per cent or 5 per cent significance level at the base [I(0)] or 1st difference level [I(1)]. I(2) variables can not be considered in ARDL model to prevent spurious results. All the variables were found to be either I(0) or I(1) at 1 per cent or 5 per cent level of significance. The detailed results of Unit Root Test are shown in Table 3:

Table 3: Results of Unit Root Tests

Variable	*DF*		*ADF*		*PP*	
	With Trend	*With Drift*	*With Trend*	*With Drift*	*With Trend*	*Without Trend*
$lnENFF_t$	-5.156 (0.0001)[a2]	-2.589 (0.0076)[a1]		-2.482 (0.0099)[a1]	-5.166 (0.0001)[b1]	-4.637 (0.0001)[b1]
$lnCO_{2t}$	-4.311 (0.0030) [b2]	-4.286 (0.0001)[b1]	-4.311 (0.0030)[b2]	-4.286 (0.0001)[b1]	-4.451 (0.0018)[b1]	-4.419 (0.0003)[b1]
$lnRD_t$	-3.690 (0.0230)[b2]	-2.648 (0.0067)[b2]	NS	-2.036 (0.0280)[b2]	-3.614 (0.0287)[b2]	NS

Variable	*DF*		*ADF*		*PP*	
	With Trend	*With Drift*	*With Trend*	*With Drift*	*With Trend*	*Without Trend*
lnNFFNEC	NS	-3.926 (0.0003)^{b1}	NS	NS	-4.094 (0.0010)^{b1}	-4.024 (0.0081)^{b5}
lnIndustryGDP	-5.970 (0.0000)^{b1}	-5.102 (0.0000)^{b1}	NS	NS	-5.901 (0.0000)^{b1}	-5.239 (0.0000)^{b1}

* The figures within parenthesis indicate p-values.
1 = 1 per cent level of significance, 2 = 5 per cent level of significance, 3 = 10 per cent level of significance; a = I(0), b= I(1); NS = Non-stationary data series after 1st difference
Source: Authors' calculations (using STATA-IC-15)

Step 2: Bound Test

- **Lag Selection** – The normal ARDL regression is done for selecting optimals of the variables as per the AIC criteria. The lags of the variables in equation (12) are found to be as follows:

Table 3: Lag Selection of Variables using AIC

lnC_t	$lnIndustryGDP_t$	$lnNFFNEC_t$	$lnRD_t$
4	0	2	3

Source: Authors' calculations (using STATA-IC-15)

- **Bound Testing** – ARDL Bound Test is conducted with the optimum lag structure in ARDL equation (12) with intercept and without trend. The Pesaran et al. (2001) Critical Values (from 10 per cent level of significance to 1 per cent level of significance) of F-statistic is shown in Table 4. The calculated F-value is F = 5.996.

Table 4: Critical Values of ARDL Bound Test (Pesaran et al., 2001)

10% Level of Significance		*5% Level of Significance*		*2.5% Level of Significance*		*1% Level of Significance*	
I(0) (LB)	I(1) (UB)	I(0) (LB)	I(1) (UB)	I(0) (LB)	I(1) (UB)	I(0) (LB)	I(1) (UB)
2.72	3.77	3.23	4.35	3.69	4.89	4.29	5.61

LB = Lower Bound, UB = Upper Bound
Source: Authors' calculations (using STATA-IC-15)

The Hypothesis Testing is:

- Accept H_0: if calculated F < Lower Bound [I(0)] critical value
- Reject H_1: if calculated F > Upper Bound [I(1)] critical value

As here, calculated F-value > Upper Bound [I(1)] critical value, H_0 is rejected, i.e. long run relationship exist among the variables. The Error Correction Model (ECM) is also applied.

So the long and short run coefficient of ARDL equation (12) and adjustment coefficient is shown in Table 5.

Table 5: Coefficients of ARDL Result

Variable		*Long Run Coefficients*	*t-value*	*p-value*
lnIndustryGDP$_t$		0.6119518	1.41	0.181
lnNFFNEC$_t$		–2.864646	–21.41	0.000
lnRD$_t$		0.411994	3.08	0.008
Variable		*Short Run Coefficients*	*t-value*	*p-value*
lnCO2	LD	–0.3988859	–2.22	0.044
	L2D.	–0.3549428	–1.72	0.108
	L3D.	–0.337951	–1.67	0.117
lnNFFNEC	D1	0.7744776	1.79	0.096
	LD	0.4602487	1.30	0.214
lnRD	D1	0.1661818	1.21	0.246
	LD	–0.0429108	–0.33	0.746
	L2D	0.2786089	2.14	0.051
Cons		6.83352	2.60	0.021
Variable		*Adjustment Coefficient*	*t-value*	*p-value*
lnCO$_2$	L1	–0.4257261	–3.04	0.009

Source: Authors' calculations (using STATA-IC-15)

ARDL Post-Estimation Diagnostic Tests Results

Table 6: Correlation Matrix

	lnCO$_2$	*lnIndustryGDP*	*lnNFFNEC*	*lnRD*
lnCO$_2$	1.0000			
lnIndustryGDP	–0.0158	1.0000		
lnNFFNEC	–0.9915	0.0131	1.0000	
lnRD	0.5254	0.4966	–0.4502	1.0000

Source: Authors' calculations (using STATA-IC-15)

As all the corelation coefficient between any two exogeneous variables is less than 0.50 so it can be concluded that no significant multicollinearity among the exogeneous variables.

The other diagnostic results are shown below (Table 7).

Table 7: Results of Diagnostic Tests

Test Methods	*Test Statistic*	*Value*	*p-value*	*Result*
Breusch-Pagan test for Heteroskedasticity	Chi-square	1.77	0.1834	No Heteroskedasticity
Breusch-Godfrey LM test for autocorrelation	Chi-square	1.939	0.1637	No Autocorrelation

Test Methods	*Test Statistic*	*Value*	*p-value*	*Result*
Ramsey RESET	F-statistic (3, 23)	0.38	0.7703	No Misspecification
J-B Normality	Chi-square	0.9356		Normality
Skewness of residuals			0.6866	Normality
Kurtosis of residuals			0.4906	Normality
R-Square (R^2)		0.7927		
Adjusted R-Square (Adj-R^2)		0.6151		

Source: Authors' calculations (using STATA-IC-15)

CUSUM and CUSUM Square Test Results

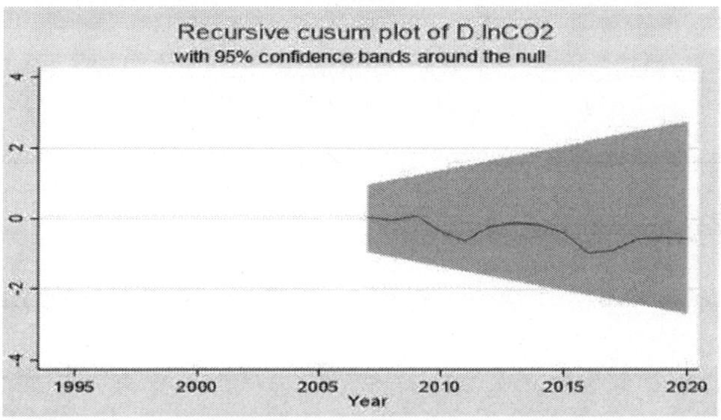

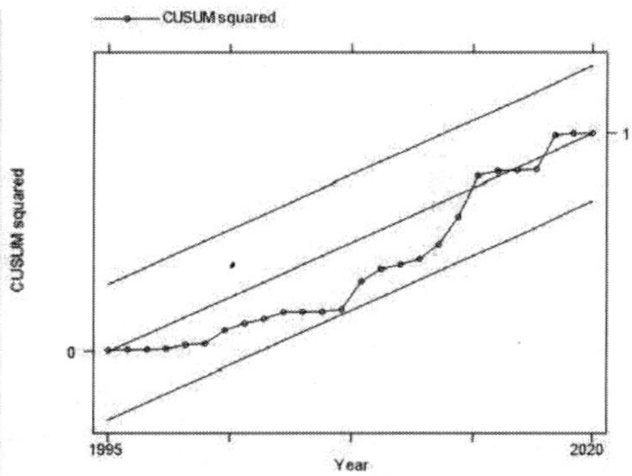

Fig. 4: CUSUM Test **Fig. 5:** CUSUMsq Test

Source: Fig. 4 and Fig. 5, Authors' calculation (using STATA-IC-15)

Both cumulative sum of recursive residuals (CUSUM) (Fig. 4) and cumulative sum of the square of recursive residuals (CUSUMsq) (Fig. 5) are within the bounds so it indicates the stability of the residual variance and thus implies absence of any instability of ARDL error correction model coefficients.

Analysis and Conclusion

It shows that both the $lnNFFNEC_t$, $lnRD_t$ variables are significant. The negative coefficient of $lnNFFNEC_t$ implies that the non-fossil fuel use in non-electricity sector has the potential to reduce emissions. R&D as they are positively contributing to the emission, implies that such expenditure requires shift from energy-intensive sectors to renewable or clean energy sector and more R&D is required in low energy intensive sectors. The negative adjustment coefficient is found to be significant and shows that lnC_t adjusts its long-run equilibrium in case of any disequilibrium at a speed of 42.5 per cent. It is to be noted that in India, despite having a large share in service sector, the emission is rising and it has become the one of the top emitting nations in the world. So far the focus of the Govt. is more on secondary energy (i.e., electricity generation) from renewable energy but along with this the direct use of renewable energy in transport and industrial sector is needed. Reduction of energy intensity in energy consuming sectors are required through R&D.

References

[1] Abumunshar, M., Aga, M., & Samour, A. (2020). Oil price, energy consumption, and CO2emissions in Turkey. New evidence from a bootstrap ARDL test. *Energies, 13*(21). https://doi.org/10.3390/en13215588

[2] al Sayed, A.R.M., & Sek, S.K. (2013). Environmental kuznets curve: Evidences from developed and developing economies. *Applied Mathematical Sciences, 7*(21–24). https://doi.org/10.12988/ams.2013.13098

[3] AlKhars, M.A., Alwahaishi, S., Fallatah, M.R., & Kayal, A. (2022). A literature review of the Environmental Kuznets Curve in GCC for 2010–2020. In *Environmental and Sustainability Indicators* (Vol. 14). https://doi.org/10.1016/j.indic.2022.100181

[4] Aruga, K. (2019). Investigating the energy-environmental Kuznets curve hypothesis for the Asia-Pacific region. *Sustainability (Switzerland), 11*(8). https://doi.org/10.3390/su11082395

[5] Balogh, J.M., & Jámbor, A. (2017). Determinants of CO_2 emission: A global evidence. *International Journal of Energy Economics and Policy, 7*(5). http://zbw.eu/econis-archiv/bitstream/11159/1311/1/1005319871.pdf

[6] Behera, D.K., & Tiwari, M. (n.d.). *Structural Transformation in India: An Econometric Investigation*. Retrieved December 12, 2022, from https://www.siecon.org/sites/siecon.org/files/oldfiles/uploads/2014/10/Behera-Tiwari-56.pdf

[7] Bouznit, M., & Pablo-Romero, M. del P. (2016). CO2 emission and economic growth in Algeria. *Energy Policy, 96*. https://doi.org/10.1016/j.enpol.2016.05.036

[8] Chai, Z., Simayi, Z., Yang, Z., & Yang, S. (2021). Examining the driving factors of the direct carbon emissions of households in the ebinur lake basin using the extended STIRPAT model. *Sustainability (Switzerland), 13*(3). https://doi.org/10.3390/su13031339

[9] Demissew Beyene, S., & Kotosz, B. (2020). Testing the environmental Kuznets curve hypothesis: an empirical study for East African countries. *International Journal of Environmental Studies, 77*(4). https://doi.org/10.1080/00207233.2019.1695445

[10] Dietz, T., & Rosa, E.A. (1994). Rethinking the Environmental Impacts of Population, Affluence and Technology '. *Human Ecology Review, 1*(Weeh 1986). https://doi.org/10.2307/24706840

[11] Dogan, E., & Ozturk, I. (2017). The influence of renewable and non-renewable energy consumption and real income on CO2 emissions in the USA: evidence from structural break tests. *Environmental Science and Pollution Research, 24*(11). https://doi.org/10.1007/s11356-017-8786-y

[12] Dong, J., Deng, C., Li, R., & Huang, J. (2017). Moving low-carbon transportation in Xinjiang: Evidence from STIRPAT and rigid regression models. *Sustainability (Switzerland), 9*(1). https://doi.org/10.3390/su9010024

[13] Ehrlich, P.R., & Holdren, J.P. (1971). Impact of population growth: complacency concerning this component of man's predicament is unjustified and counterproductive. *Science, 171*(3977).

[14] Ekins, P. (1997). The Kuznets curve for the environment and economic growth: Examining the evidence. *Environment and Planning A, 29*(5), 805–30. https://doi.org/10.1068/a290805

[15] Geyikci, U.B., Çınar, S., & Sancak, F.M. (2022). Analysis of the Relationships among Financial Development, Economic Growth, Energy Use, and Carbon Emissions by Co-Integration with Multiple Structural Breaks. *Sustainability, 14*(10).

[16] https://data.worldbank.org/. (n.d.).

[17] https://www.iea.org/data-and-statistics. (n.d.).

[18] *India's Updated First Nationally Determined Contribution Under Paris Agreement (2021-2030), Submission to UNFCCC.* (2022). https://unfccc.int/sites/default/files/NDC/2022-08/India%20Updated%20First%20Nationally%20Determined%20Contrib.pdf

[19] Jiang, Y., Batool, Z., Raza, S.M.F., Haseeb, M., Ali, S., & Zain Ul Abidin, S. (2022). Analyzing the Asymmetric Effect of Renewable Energy Consumption on Environment in STIRPAT-Kaya-EKC Framework: A NARDL Approach for China. *International Journal of Environmental Research and Public Health, 19*(12). https://doi.org/10.3390/ijerph19127100

[20] Kanjilal, K., & Ghosh, S. (2013). Environmental Kuznet's curve for India: Evidence from tests for cointegration with unknown structuralbreaks. *Energy Policy, 56*, 509–515. https://doi.org/https://doi.org/10.1016/j.enpol.2013.01.015

[21] Karimi, M.S., Ahmad, S., Karamelikli, H., Dinç, D.T., Khan, Y.A., Sabzehei, M.T., & Abbas, S.Z. (2021). Dynamic linkages between renewable energy, carbon emissions and economic growth through nonlinear ARDL approach: Evidence from Iran. *PLoS ONE, 16*(7 July). https://doi.org/10.1371/journal.pone.0253464

[22] Khan, M.K., Khan, M.I., & Rehan, M. (2020). The relationship between energy consumption, economic growth and carbon dioxide emissions in Pakistan. *Financial Innovation, 6*(1). https://doi.org/10.1186/s40854-019-0162-0

[23] Khoshnevis Yazdi, S., & Dariani, A.G. (2019). CO_2 emissions, urbanisation and economic growth: evidence from Asian countries. *Economic Research-Ekonomska Istrazivanja , 32*(1). https://doi.org/10.1080/1331677X.2018.1556107

[24] Ozturk, I., Shahbaz, M., & Farhani, S. (2013). Coal Consumption, Industrial Production and CO_2 Emissions in China and India Coal Consumption, Industrial Production and CO_2 Emissions in China and India. *Munich Personal RePEc Archive.*

[25] Pesaran, M.H., Shin, Y., & Smith, R.J. (2001). Bounds testing approaches to the analysis of level relationships. *Journal of Applied Econometrics, 16*(3). https://doi.org/10.1002/jae.616

[26] Saba, C.S. (2022). CO2 emissions-energy consumption-militarisation-growth nexus in South Africa: Evidence from novel dynamic ARDL simulations. *Environmental Science and Pollution Research.* https://doi.org/10.1007/s11356-022-23069-7

[27] Saidi, K., & Hammami, S. (2015). The impact of CO_2 emissions and economic growth on energy consumption in 58 countries. *Energy Reports, 1.* https://doi.org/10.1016/j.egyr.2015.01.003

[28] Shahbaz, M., Lean, H.H., & Shabbir, M. (2011). Environmental Kuznets Curve and the Role of Energy Consumption in Pakistan. *MPRA Paper No. 34929.*

[29] Stern, D.I. (2000). A multivariate cointegration analysis of the role of energy in the US macroeconomy. *Energy Economics, 22*(2). https://doi.org/10.1016/S0140-9883(99)00028-6

[30] Sultana, N., Rahman, M.M., & Khanam, R. (2022). Environmental kuznets curve and causal links between environmental degradation and selected socioeconomic indicators in Bangladesh. *Environment, Development and Sustainability, 24*(4). https://doi.org/10.1007/s10668-021-01665-w

[31] Tavakoli, A. (2017). How Precisely 'Kaya Identity' can Estimate GHG Emissions: A Global Review. *Jordan Journal of Earth and Environmental Sciences, 8*(2).

[32] Timma, L., Vilgerts, J., Vanaga, R., Kļavenieks, K., & Blumberga, D. (2014). Decomposition analysis based on IPAT and Kaya identity for assessment of hazardous waste flow within enterprise. *Proceedings of the 27th International Conference on Efficiency, Cost, Optimization, Simulation and Environmental Impact of Energy Systems, ECOS 2014.*

[33] Zhang, J. (2021). Environmental Kuznets Curve Hypothesis on CO_2 Emissions: Evidence for China. *Journal of Risk and Financial Management, 14*(3). https://doi.org/10.3390/jrfm14030093

[34] Zhang, P., He, J., Hong, X., Zhang, W., Qin, C., Pang, B., Li, Y., & Liu, Y. (2017). Regional-level carbon emissions modelling and scenario analysis: A STIRPAT case study in Henan province, China. *Sustainability (Switzerland), 9*(12). https://doi.org/10.3390/su9122342

[35] Ziyuan, C., Yibo, Y., Simayi, Z., Shengtian, Y., Abulimiti, M., & Yuqing, W. (2022). Carbon emissions index decomposition and carbon emissions prediction in Xinjiang from the perspective of population-related factors, based on the combination of STIRPAT model and neural network. *Environmental Science and Pollution Research, 29*(21). https://doi.org/10.1007/s11356-021-17976-4

Sustainable Development Goals Compass (SDG Compass) Strategic Tool for Integrating Sustainability in Business Schools

Dr Neeraj Singhal

Assistant Professor (Strategy), Management Development Institute, Murshidabad, India
E-mail: neeraj.singhal@mdim.ac.in

Abstract

The imbalances between social, economic and environmental actions enhanced the concerns of relevant stakeholders over a period of time since conceptualisation of Sustainable Development (SD) term by Brundtland Commission in 1987 (Brundtland, G., 1987). Sustainable Development Goals (SDGs) were conceptualise in the Rio+20 United Nations Summit in 2012 to address the SD concerns and ensure well-planned action and roadmap by all stakeholders. In 2015, the 2030 agenda for Sustainable Development rolled out with declaration of 17 SDGs along with monitoring and review measures. The Sustainable Development Goals Compass (SDG Compass) is one of the monitoring and measurement tools suggested for the action on the part of industries. This paper tries to explore the SDG compass as a strategic tool for addressing the sustainability concerns of business schools and suggesting the framework for the integration of the same.

Keywords: *SDG, SDG Compass, Sustainability*

Introduction

Education has always been the central theme of the United Nations (UN) initiatives since the formation of UNESCO (United Nations Educational, Scientific and Cultural Organisation) in 1945. The core focus of UNESCO was to contribute for peace, elimination of poverty, sustainable development, science, communication, information, and intercultural connect. The Brundtland Commission in 1987 (Brundtland, G., 1987), redefine the focus of Sustainable Development without compromising the needs of future generations. Over a period of time, many academic institutions started to incorporate the SD initiatives as the part of various academic functions and activities such as policy documents, academic curriculum, infrastructure, etc. The Association of University Leaders for Sustainable Futures (ULSF) was a widely accepted initiative started during 1992.

United Nations as the part of UN Global Compact programme introduced Principles for Responsible Management Education (PRME) in the year 2007 to address the SD concerns. The six principles of PRME are inspired by international values and concerns towards SD. Many international accreditation and ranking organisations across the globe incorporated PRME and SD agenda as the part of evaluation and measurement criteria. During Rio+20 United Nations Summit in 2012, the Sustainable Development Goals (SDGs) were conceptualise to further streamline the SD initiatives. The SDGs monitoring, evaluation and implementation further streamlined this as part of the 2030 agenda in 2015.

The Sustainable Development Goals Compass (SDG Compass) was introduced in 2015 as one of the tools for mapping industry initiatives towards SDGs. This paper is an effort in the same direction—to use SDG Compass for mapping business school initiatives and suggesting a framework for the same.

Sustainable Development Goals Compass (SDG Compass)

The Sustainable Development Goals (SDGs) supersede the Millennium Development Goals (MDGs) in 2015, with the motive of an effective implementation and monitoring of SD. The Sustainable Development Goals Compass (SDG Compass) emerged as an effective strategic tool which can help the companies to map, measure and implement the SDG contribution. The five blocks of the SDG compass include: SDG understanding, defining priorities, setting goals, integration, reporting and communication.

The integration of SDGs in business school activities is a strategic process; the SDG compass can be used to map and stream line the process. Lozano et al. (2013) suggest the seven elements for integrating sustainability in higher education institutions: institutional framework, campus operations, education, research, outreach and collaborations, SD and campus experience, assessment and reporting.

Framework for Integrating SDG Compass in Business Schools

Gupta, H., & Singhal, N. (2017) suggest the framework for integrating sustainability in business school based on the input, process and output activities of the institutions. The input mapped regulatory pressure, peer pressure and corporate pressure. The process mapped institutional framework, course curriculum, research and development, campus operations, outreach and collaboration, on campus experience, assessment and reporting. The output is based on the social, environmental and economic impact.

The proposed framework is the integration of a model proposed by Gupta, H., & Singhal, N. (2017) and SDG compass a strategic tool suggested by UN for mapping, measuring and implementing the SDGs across business school value chain.

The first step of the proposed model is to identify the input, process and output activities of the business school as shown in Figure 1 of the proposed model in each of the three heads. The second step is mapping the 17 SDGs: 'No poverty, zero hunger, good health and wellbeing, quality education, gender quality, clean water and sanitation, affordable and clean energy, decent work and economic growth, industry innovation and infrastructure, reduced inequalities, sustainable cities and communities, responsible consumption and production, climate action, life below water, life on land, peace justice and strong institutions, partnership for the goals.'Third step of the process is to define the priorities and set goals with respect to relevant SDGs for making significant

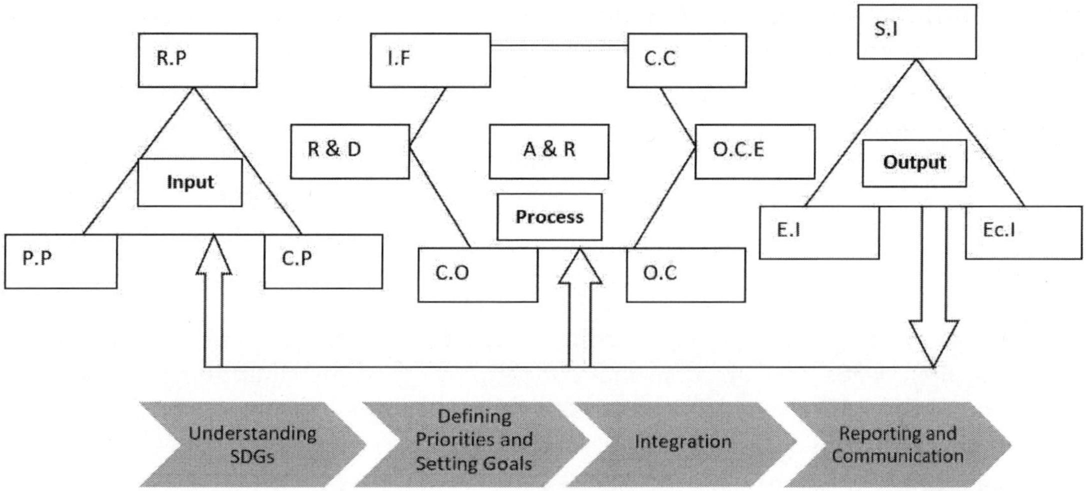

Input
- R.P: Regulatory Pressure
- P.P: Peer Pressure
- C.P: Corporate Pressure

Process
- I.F: Institutional Framework
- C.C: Course Curriculum
- R&D: Research & Development (Faculty participation)
- C.O: Campus Operations
- O.C: Outreach and Collaboration
- O.C.E: On Campus Experience
- A&R: Assessment & Reporting

Output
- S.I: Social Impact
- E.I: Envi. Impact
- Ec.I: Econ. Impact

Fig. 1: Proposed Framework
Source: Adaptation and Modification Gupta, H., & Singhal, N. (2017)

contribution. The fourth step is the integration of SDGs in the institution processes such as institutional framework, course curriculum, research and development, campus operations, outreach and collaborations, on campus experience, assessment and reporting.

The fifth and final step of the proposed framework is reporting and communication in context of larger social, environment and economic impact and also introducing the appropriate feedback mechanism at every stage to ensure the implementation and desired outcome.

Discussions and Way Forward

In 2015, 193 member states of the United Nations adopted SDGs plan for a better tomorrow. All major stakeholders including governments, businesses, civil society, higher education institutions and citizen showed their commitment for the same. Business schools are also one of the major connecting links between governments, businesses, civil society and citizens to implement the task. The different authors pointed out certain challenges and obstacles in the mapping, measurement and implementation of SDGs across different industries.

Kumi et al. (2014), discussed about SDGs and its implications from social, economic and development perspective in the coming fifteen years. Person et al. (2016) draw the attention towards implementation and responsibility part of SDGs. Reed et al. (2016) pointed out integration and implementation challenges across actors and sectors. Van Vuuren et al. (2016), identified that there is a huge gap between long term goals and current short term policies of organisations.

Mboumboue and Njomo (2016) discussed about corruption and red tape the as main hurdle in the adaptation of renewable energy and constraint for SD. Jasovsky et al. (2016) mentioned that international collaboration and distribution are the key for implementation of SDGs, wider involvement of international agencies and UN can help a lot in the achievement of the desired results.

Shan and Khan (2016) have reached the conclusion that sustainability evaluation is the most difficult task due to complex interrelations between the evaluation parameters. Urmee and Md (2016) draw the attention towards attitude and energetic needs and involvement of the community towards achievement of SDGs.

Business schools are also facing similar challenges as identified by the different authors in various studies, such as identification and mapping of appropriate SDGs with current practices, and prioritisation with respect to short and long term goals in alignment with current practices. Integration across the academic value chain activities such as institutional framework, research and development, campus operations, outreach and collaboration, on campus experience are the most challenging task. Developing the assessment and reporting parameters is another equally challenging task for business schools.

References

[1] Brundtland, G. (1987). Report of the World Commission on Environment and Development: Our Common Future. United Nations General Assembly document A/42/427.

[2] Gupta, H., & Singhal, N. (2017). Framework for embedding sustainability in business schools: A review. *Vision*, 21(2), 195–203.

[3] Jasovský, D., Littmann, J., Zorzet, A., Cars, O., 2016. Antimicrobial resistance—A threat to the world's sustainable development. *Ups. J. Med. Sci.* 121, 159–64. doi:10.1080/03009734.2016.1195900

[4] Kumi, E., Arhin, A.A., Yeboah, T., 2014. Can post-2015 sustainable development goals survive neoliberalism? A critical examination of the sustainable development – Neoliberalism nexus in developing countries. *Env. Dev Sustain* 16, 539–554. doi:10.1007/s10668-013-9492-7

[5] Lozano, R., Young, W., 2013. Assessing sustainability in university curricula: exploring the influence of student numbers and course credits. *Journal of Cleaner Production*, 49, 134-141. http://dx.doi.org/10.1016/j.jclepro.2012.07.032

[6] Mboumboue, E., Njomo, D., 2016. Potential contribution of renewables to the improvement of living conditions of poor rural households in developing countries: Cameroon's case study. *Renew. Sustain. Energy Rev.* 61, 266–79. doi:10.1016/j.rser.2016.04.003

[7] Persson, Å., Weitz, N., Nilsson, M., 2016. Follow-up and Review of the Sustainable Development Goals: Alignment vs. Internalization. *Rev. Eur. Comp. Int. Environ. Law* 25, 59–68. doi:10.1111/reel.12150

[8] Reed, J., Van Vianen, J., Deakin, E.L., Barlow, J., Sunderland, T., 2016. Integrated landscape approaches to managing social and environmental issues in the tropics: Learning from the past to guide the future. *Glob. Chang. Biol.* n/a–n/a. doi:10.1111/gcb.13284

[9] Shan, J., Khan, M., 2016. Implications of Reverse Innovation for Socio-Economic Sustainability: A Case Study of Philips China. *Sustainability* 8, 530. doi:10.3390/su8060530

[10] Urmee, T., Md, A., 2016. Social, cultural and political dimensions of off-grid renewable energy programs in developing countries. *Renew. Energy* 93, 159–67. doi:10.1016/j.renene.2016.02.040

[11] Van Vuuren, D.P., Kok, M., Lucas, P.L., Prins, A.G., Alkemade, R., van den Berg, M., Bouwman, L., van der Esch, S., Jeuken, M., Kram, T., Stehfest, E., 2014. Pathways to achieve a set of ambitious global sustainability objectives by 2050: Explorations using the IMAGE integrated assessment model. *Technol. Forecast. Soc. Change 98*, 303–23. doi:10.1016/j.techfore.2015.03.005

Author Index